D0679502

Moral Communities

Studies on the History of Society and Culture
Victoria E. Bonnell and Lynn Hunt, Editors

Moral Communities

*The Culture of Class Relations
in the Russian Printing Industry
1867–1907*

Mark D. Steinberg

UNIVERSITY OF CALIFORNIA PRESS
Berkeley • Los Angeles • Oxford

University of California Press
Berkeley and Los Angeles, California

University of California Press, Ltd.
Oxford, England

© 1992 by
The Regents of the University of California

Library of Congress Cataloging-in-Publication Data

Steinberg, Mark.
    Moral communities: the culture of class relations in the Russian
printing industry, 1867–1907 / Mark D. Steinberg.
        p.   cm.—(Studies on the history of society and culture;
    14)
    Includes bibliographical references and index.
    ISBN 0-520-07572-2 (alk. paper)
    1. Printing industry—Social aspects—Soviet Union—History—19th
century.   2. Printing industry—Social aspects—Soviet Union—
History—20th century.   3. Industrial relations—Soviet Union—
History—19th century.   4. Industrial relations—Soviet Union—
History—20th century.   5. Social classes—Soviet Union—
History—19th century.   6. Social classes—Soviet Union—
History—20th century.   7. Soviet Union—Social
conditions—1801–1917.   8. Soviet Union—Moral conditions.
I. Title.   II. Series.
    Z244.6.S65S84   1992
    381'.45002'0947—dc20   91-39493

Printed in the United States of America
9   8   7   6   5   4   3   2   1

The paper used in this publication meets the minimum requirements of
American National Standard for Information Sciences—Permanence of Paper
for Printed Library Materials, ANSI Z39.48-1984. ⊚

DISCARDED
WIDENER UNIVERSITY

WOLFGRAM
LIBRARY

CHESTER, PA

To my parents, Dina and Norman

Contents

Acknowledgments

One of the most pleasurable rituals of academia is the opportunity to thank publicly, and with the permanence of print, the many people who have contributed to a scholarly work. I trust that Victoria Bonnell and Reginald Zelnik already know my appreciation of their encouragement, astute criticism, and friendship over the years. They continually challenged me to think with all my senses about human history. Their generosity as teachers and colleagues, especially their critical encouragement of others, serves as a model of how an intellectual community can work.

The valuable advice and criticism given by many other people who have read all or part of this manuscript further demonstrates that scholarship is best not a solitary act. I wish to thank Abraham Ascher, Laura Engelstein, Jane Hedges, Diane Koenker, Thomas Owen, Alfred Rieber, William Rosenberg, William Sewell, Jr., Steve Smith, and Ronald Suny. Valuable comments and suggestions have also been made by participants in David Montgomery's comparative labor history colloquium at Yale University, in the Russian and Soviet studies seminar at Columbia University, and in discussions at both the Kennan Institute for Advanced Russian Studies and the Russian Research Center of Harvard University. Ellen Stein contributed to this project her fine craft skills as manuscript editor. Sheila Levine and her colleagues at the University of California Press did much to help turn a manuscript into a book.

I also recognize the importance of the environment in which this study first took shape: the unusual atmosphere of friendship and intellectual community among students and faculty of the department of history at the University of California at Berkeley. I would especially like to acknowledge teachers who in many different ways helped to shape my intellectual growth: John Ackerman, Gregory Freidin, Lynn Hunt, Peter Kenez, Thomas Laqueur, Martin Malia, and Nicholas Riasanovsky, who has my particular respect and gratitude. I would also mention my fellow workers, as well as managers and employers, at E. N. Operators taxi company on 135th Street and Shaw Press on Van Dam Street in New York City, whose lessons about everyday values, solidarities, and conflicts still inform this study.

Assistance in the preparation of this study was given by the staffs of a number of libraries and research institutions: the state historical archives in Moscow and Leningrad (now St. Petersburg); the Lenin Library in Moscow; the Library of the Academy of Sciences and the Public Library in Leningrad; the Library of Congress; the New York Public Library; the Hoover Institution on War, Revolution, and Peace; and the libraries at the University of California at Berkeley, and of Stanford, Columbia, Harvard, and Yale universities. I would especially thank Edward Kasinec and Elena Balashova for their assistance in obtaining from the Soviet Union copies of invaluable sources.

Many institutions generously provided essential financial support for this project: the Kennan Institute for Advanced Russian Studies of the Smithsonian Institution's Woodrow Wilson Center; the Joint Committee on Soviet Studies of the Social Science Research Council and the American Council of Learned Societies; the International Research and Exchanges Board; Fulbright-Hayes dissertation research–abroad program; the Mable McLeod Lewis Foundation; and the Institute for International Studies at the University of California at Berkeley.

Finally, to Sasha, who thinks I ought to spend more time playing, and to Jane, who knows he is right, I am more than grateful.

Introduction

Printers are a compelling subject for the close study of social relationships and values during the years of deepening change and crisis in Russia from the 1860s to the aftermath of the 1905 revolution. Class relations among printers underwent a dramatic transformation as the industry evolved from a small handicraft producing mainly for the state and the church to a large and technologically developed capitalist industry. Occupational involvement in the spread of knowledge and ideas—and contact with official efforts to control these—made printers more than usually sensitive to the country's contentious civic life. Printers' efforts to preserve social unity in the face of increasingly hierarchical relationships of wealth and power, their participation in strikes and class organizations, and their demands for political change illustrate the evolution and increasing fragility of Russia's social and political order.

For the historian, printers are generous subjects for study. Relatively high levels of literacy and familiarity with print encouraged employers, supervisors, and workers to leave an exceptionally rich record of their lives in trade papers, letters, poems, and memoirs. I have used these materials to investigate closely the social life in the industry as it evolved during this lengthy and vital period, examining all of the groups involved—owners, managers, foremen, and workers—and especially the relations between and among them. Most important, I explore printers' experiences and relationships

1

amidst the perceptions, moral judgments, and ideas with which they were intertwined.[1]

The complex and variable ways that people have given meaning, especially ethical meaning, to their economic and social lives is a central theme in this study. Historians of class relations in Western Europe and North America have shown the importance of moral reasoning and judgment in the lives of workers and employers, especially in times of social change. Entrepreneurs, particularly when the authority and legitimacy of capitalism was still insecure, defended their honor and status by asserting a new ethic of work and individual success, but also by adapting customary notions of paternalistic authority and filial loyalty.[2] Workers, especially artisans, confronted the new marketplace ethos of individual liberty, competition, and acquisitiveness—and on occasion social subordination itself—with a moral arsenal stocked variously with customary notions of economic fairness and social responsibility, ideals of a corporative economic community, older manners of work and sociability, and newer conceptions of individual dignity, civic inclusion, and justice.[3]

In Russia, too, workers and employers responded to a changing society with the aid of both familiar and newly found values and standards. Recent studies of Russian entrepreneurs and merchants have revealed much about their business practices, their efforts to build corporative unity and to assert their needs before the state, as well as their deep and

1. The existing literature on social relations within the printing industry is small. Although a number of Russian and Soviet scholars, and more recently some Western historians, have examined Russian book publishing and journalism, there has been little attention paid to printing as an industry or to the social relationships within it. The only detailed economic study is B. P. Orlov's 1953 monograph on prerevolutionary printing in Moscow, *Poligraficheskaia promyshlennost' Moskvy*. Three historical accounts of social relations in printing exist, written by union activists, and focusing on the emergence of trade unionism: V. V. Sher's 1911 study of Moscow printers, *Istoriia professional'nogo dvizheniia rabochikh pechatnogo dela v Moskve*; the 1925 study of the history of Petersburg printers through 1907 written by a collective of union members who had been active in those years, *Istoriia leningradskogo soiuza rabochikh poligraficheskogo proizvodstva*; and the 1925 collection of historical sketches of printers' unions, *Materialy po istorii professional'nogo dvizheniia rabochikh poligraficheskogo proizvodstva (pechatnogo dela) v Rossii*.
2. Bendix, *Work and Authority in Industry*, ch. 2; Newby, "Paternalism and Capitalism."
3. See esp. E. P. Thompson, *The Making of the English Working Class*; Joyce, *Work, Society and Politics*; Jones, *Languages of Class*; Moore, *Injustice*; Sewell, *Work and Revolution in France*; Rancière, *The Nights of Labor*; Gutman, "Work, Culture, and Society in Industrializing America, 1815–1819"; Dawley, *Class and Community*; Wilentz, *Chants Democratic*; and Katznelson and Zolberg, *Working-Class Formation*.

lasting fragmentation and isolation.[4] We also know from these studies that many merchants and manufacturers, especially the most successful, tried to distance themselves from the image of the capitalist pursuing self-interest by representing themselves as patrons of culture, philanthropists, and benefactors of the poor. But we still have only a fragmentary picture of employers' relations with their own workers, and especially of the values that influenced managerial practice. These are the central concerns in my own study of employers in the printing industry.

Historians of Russian labor have recognized the need to better understand workers' cultural, intellectual, and moral life as a guide to interpreting workers' behavior and demands. During the 1960s a number of Soviet historians sought to broaden the Marxist concept of consciousness (*soznatel'nost'*) to include the notion of workers' *oblik,* or mentality, and suggested including under this rubric social psychology, cultural ideals, spiritual life, and moral norms, in addition to political attitudes and class consciousness.[5] But with the partial exception of studies by Mark Persits of workers' atheism and by Vitalii Shishkin of "proletarian revolutionary morality,"[6] very little empirical work appeared.

Western historians have contributed much to the understanding of workers' attitudes by focusing on the formation of social identities. Urban experience, literacy, occupation, gender, skill, ethnicity, and age have in different combinations been seen as influencing workers' class identification and political radicalization.[7] Historians have also gradually begun to look beyond the experiences that made workers more or less class conscious and revolutionary to the complex and varying meanings that notions such as class, democracy, justice, and socialism actually had for workers.[8] That moral outrage, for instance, influenced workers' perceptions of injustice may be seen in the demand, often

4. Owen, *Capitalism and Politics;* Rieber, *Merchants and Entrepreneurs;* Boiko, "K voprosu o sotsial'noi psikhologii krupnoi rossiiskoi burzhuazii"; Guroff and Carstensen, *Entrepreneurship;* Ruckman, *The Moscow Business Elite.* See also the memoir by the merchant Buryshkin, *Moskva kupecheskaia.*
5. Ivanov, *Rossiiskii proletariat,* particularly the introduction and the essay by Iurii Kir'ianov, "Ob oblike rabochego klassa Rossii."
6. Persits, *Ateizm russkogo rabochego;* Shishkin, *Tak skladyvalas' revoliutsionnaia moral'.*
7. See esp. Haimson, "The Problem of Social Stability in Urban Russia"; Johnson, *Peasant and Proletariat;* Koenker, *Moscow Workers;* Engelstein, *Moscow, 1905;* Bonnell, *Roots of Rebellion;* Smith, *Red Petrograd;* Glickman, *Russian Factory Women;* Reichman, *Railwaymen and Revolution;* Surh, *1905 in St. Petersburg.*
8. As examples of such work, much of which is still unpublished, I would mention the papers on prerevolutionary labor presented by S. A. Smith, Reginald Zelnik, and myself at a conference on "The Making of the Soviet Working Class" in East Lansing, Mich., in November 1990. See also McDaniel, *Autocracy, Capitalism, and Revolution,*

described in accounts of labor protest, for polite address and generally for respect for workers' dignity.[9] Reginald Zelnik's probing essays on workers in the late 1800s, based mainly on the interpretation of workers' autobiographies, are especially valuable for their portrayals of individual workers grappling with personal and social experiences and with ideas about self, society, and God.[10] In this book, the norms, judgments, and ideas that workers applied in making sense of their lives are key themes.

In all such inquiries into the mental world of social groups we face the problem of defining the relationship between structured experiences such as poverty, economic dependence, and subordination and people's understanding of these conditions. Much recent social theory has focused on the same question. The most persuasive arguments, to my mind, avoid both the determinism that views human behavior as merely reflecting social and material structures and the relativism that interprets social reality as entirely constituted by language, belief, and symbol. Neither the material nor the evaluative can simply be reduced to the other in the construction of human experience.[11]

The most telling illustrations of the intertwining of structure and meaning, and the most pertinent to this study, are the different ways that social groups have understood and appropriated common cultural materials, such that shared vocabularies, symbols, and beliefs may disguise self-interest and domination as well as subtle forms of resistance and defiance.[12] Evidence of such reworking of ideas and expressions

---

chs. 7–8; and essays on the revolution and early Soviet years by William Rosenberg in Kaiser, *The Workers' Revolution in Russia,* chs. 5–6.

9. Placing particular emphasis on the importance in workers' protests of offended feelings of "humiliation and insult" (*unizhenie i oskorblenie*) are McDaniel, *Autocracy, Capitalism, and Revolution,* pp. 161, 169–74; and Haimson, "The Problem of Social Identities in Early Twentieth Century Russia," pp. 2–8.

10. Zelnik, "Russian Bebels"; idem, "Passivity and Protest in Germany and Russia"; idem, *A Radical Worker in Tsarist Russia,* pp. xiv–xxx; idem, "To the Unaccustomed Eye."

11. See esp. Geertz, *The Interpretation of Cultures;* Bourdieu, *Outline of a Theory of Practice;* E. P. Thompson, *The Poverty of Theory;* Giddens, *Central Problems in Social Theory;* Certeau, *The Practice of Everyday Life;* Wuthnow, Hunter, Bergesen, and Kurzweil, *Cultural Analysis;* Sider, *Culture and Class in Anthropology and History;* Rabinow and Sullivan, "The Interpretive Turn"; Chartier, *Cultural History;* Hunt, *The New Cultural History,* pp. 1–22. Pierre Bourdieu has written, in intentionally circular language, of the "dialectic of the internalization of externality and the externalization of internality." Bourdieu, *Outline of a Theory of Practice,* p. 72.

12. Bendix, *Work and Authority in Industry;* James C. Scott, *Weapons of the Weak,* esp. pp. 38–44, 304–50; idem, *Domination and the Arts of Resistance.* See also Certeau, *The Practice of Everyday Life;* Chartier, *Cultural History,* pp. 95–110, esp. p. 102; Giddens, *Central Problems in Social Theory,* esp. pp. 6, 148, 188, 193–95, 207–08.

was also to be found among Russian printers. Even before the coming of strikes, lockouts, and class organizations, employers understood and made use of ideals of moral community—of employers and workers united by bonds of sentiment and common interest—to strengthen authority, discipline, and productivity, while workers interpreted and used these same values to contest their own poverty and powerlessness. This is not to say that class domination and struggle were simply translated into the language of moral culture. Alongside the self-interested reworking of norms and muted dissent we see conformity and real community, even after open class struggle had erupted. Employers could promote their own power and position and, at the same time, seek to realize ideals of commonweal and social responsibility. Workers could fight for greater social autonomy and collective power and pursue integration into a community that transcended class.[13] Like most people, printing workers, supervisors, and employers often thought and desired contradictory things, creating a tension that would resist easy resolution even in the heat of revolution.[14] In this sense, though the polarization of Russian society is a part of my story, so is the ambiguity of that conflict.

I treat here both words and behavior—and the relationship between what people said and what they did (and what they said they did)—as necessary evidence of attitudes and values. Printers left records of the words they used in their everyday relations with others, in describing their lives publicly, in demanding improvements, and in envisioning changes in their lives. This language often plainly expressed speakers' intentions, but it also contained more subtly meaningful symbols and metaphors and revealed the intellectual and cultural influences on printers' views of the world. Printers also initiated and participated in a variety of actions as individuals and groups—festivals and rituals, dancing and drinking, reading and writing, attending meetings, joining strikes, and committing violence. In interpreting these behaviors, too, I have looked for both direct intentions and the implied meanings, often more complex and ambiguous, that such actions expressed within their own cultural and social frames of reference. A worker's starched shirt

13. Victoria Bonnell has similarly described a "dualism" and "ambiguity" in the claims of Russian workers, who simultaneously sought social acceptance and challenged the authority of those who denied it to them. Bonnell, *Roots of Rebellion*, esp. pp. 452, 455.

14. For some theoretical discussion of the notion of ambiguity, see Bourdieu, *Outline of a Theory of Practice*, pp. 109–13, 140–43; Rabinow and Sullivan, "The Interpretive Turn," pp. 5–6, 9; Sider, *Culture and Class*, pp. 3–11; Rancière, "The Myth of the Artisan," p. 14.

on Sundays, an employer's gift of a Christmas party for his workers' children, a bout of drunkenness, and a fight over higher wages each expressed ideas, rarely simple, about self, society, and morality.

Printers' words and actions also reveal the social fractures among them. As in the surrounding society, printing employers, supervisors, and workers represented significantly distinct social groups, but important differences of experience and interest also separated immigrant from native employers, owners of large factories from the proprietors of small shops, book publishers from job printers, compositors from pressmen, and men from women. Equally important were the more subtle distinctions, the rare rather than the typical experiences and perceptions, that led minorities of employers, supervisors, and workers to stand forward and speak out. Both the influence and the individuality of these activists need to be considered, especially since they produced much of the written evidence we examine. As leaders, they affected how others thought and acted, and they frequently initiated and led collective actions. But they also remained apart, often in the company of other outspoken and active men and women who shared the belief that it was their right to represent and guide others. This ambiguous relationship to their fellow employers, supervisors, or workers may also have encouraged their ambiguous vision of collective purpose as advancing both morality and material interest, as seeking both greater class benefit and justice for all.

CHAPTER ONE

Capitalist Development

The management of most printing firms is in the hands of
non-specialists, of complete outsiders with absolutely no
understanding of the printing trade. . . . Of course, it is not
possible to forbid a capitalist to open a printing firm.

> Letter to *Survey of the Graphic Arts* (*Obzor
> graficheskikh iskusstv*), February 1882

In the second half of the nineteenth century, the Russian printing industry was transformed from a small artisanal craft closely tied to the state
into a relatively large-scale, diversified, and technologically developed
industry run by capitalist entrepreneurs and professional managers.
How workers or employers perceived these changes is not my concern
here; that is the subject, at least indirectly, of much of the rest of this
book. My focus for the moment is on the more tangible surfaces of that
experience: growth in output, the establishment of new forms of enterprise, career paths of entrepreneurs and managers, changes in the social
composition and structure of the labor force, transformations in the
work process, and the physical environment of the workshop. These
were the economic and social structures in which printing employers,
managers, and workers spent their working lives, and in relation to
which they in large measure defined themselves.

GROWTH AND TECHNICAL CHANGE

Private commercial printing in Russia, legalized only in the late eighteenth century, grew at an exceptional pace in the second half of the
nineteenth century. This growth reflected an increasingly dynamic social and cultural environment: an expanding economy, a rich literary
and intellectual life among educated elites, the spread of reading among
the lower classes, and the softening of official censorship laws and

practices.[1] These conditions generated unprecedented demand for books, journals, and newspapers. From 1855 to 1901, the number of books published annually increased from little more than a thousand titles to over ten thousand, and the number of periodicals increased from slightly more than a hundred to over a thousand (including an increase in daily newspapers from only three to more than a hundred).[2] Circulations and pressruns also grew dramatically.[3] In the view of the writer and bibliographer Nikolai Rubakin, Russia in the late nineteenth century was engulfed by an "irresistible torrent" of books and periodicals.[4] This flood was further intensified by growing demand for the printed paraphernalia of business: labels, letterheads, preprinted business forms, advertisements, bills, and placards.

The structure of the printing industry was permanently altered as it responded to this increasing demand. The most noticeable change was the sheer growth in the number of people involved. From the late 1850s until the economic recession of the 1880s, and again in the 1890s, new printing enterprises proliferated in St. Petersburg and Moscow (see table 1). Almost all of the major private printing firms of the early twentieth century were founded between 1852 and 1882, most in the 1860s and 1870s. The industry's labor force grew at an even more rapid rate, especially in the last decades of the century when fewer new enterprises opened. From 1881 to 1900, the number of typographic and lithographic workers in St. Petersburg and Moscow more or less doubled (see table 2).

As such data suggest, the creation of new enterprises gave way toward the end of the century to the expansion of existing plants. Small-scale production was by no means eliminated. Even after the turn of the century, the majority of printing shops employed fewer than sixteen workers (see table 3). But production and labor were concentrated in-

1. The most important of the censorship reforms was the new code of 1864, which replaced prepublication censorship of most books and periodicals (periodicals that requested exemption, original books of at least ten printed signatures, and translated books of at least twenty signatures) with a system of legal and administrative penalties. *Polnoe sobranie zakonov Rossiiskoi Imperii,* ser. 2, vol. 40, part 1, no. 41988 (April 6, 1865), p. 396; no. 41990 (6 April 1865), pp. 397–406. For a discussion of the law and its initial implementation, see Ruud, *Fighting Words,* pp. 147–80; Balmuth, *Censorship in Russia,* pp. 19–58.

2. *Knizhnyi vestnik,* 1866, no. 9–10 (May 31), p. 231; *Zhurnal Ministerstva Narodnogo Prosveshcheniia,* 1862, vol. 114, pp. 250–55; Kufaev, *Istoriia russkoi knigi v XIX veke,* pp. 173, 217–18; Rubakin, "Knizhnyi potok"; Lisovskii, "Periodicheskaia pechat' v Rossii," pp. 21–26; *Ocherki po istorii russkoi zhurnalistiki i kritiki,* vol. 2, pp. 30–31, 449.

3. Esin, "Russkaia legal'naia pressa," pp. 7–8.

4. Rubakin, "Knizhnyi potok," p. 1.

TABLE ONE NUMBER OF PRINTING
ENTERPRISES, 1833–1900

St. Petersburg

	1833	1864	1875	1887	1900
Official	26	26	18	15	16
Private	22	101	149	179	263
TOTAL	48	127	167	194	279

Moscow

	1833	1865	1876	1887	1900
Official	7	16	19	20	26
Private	12	92	153	161	165
TOTAL	19	108	172	181	191

SOURCES Orlov, *Poligraficheskaia promyshlennost' Moskvy*, pp. 142, 181, 303–04; *Pamiatnaia knizhka S.-Peterburgskoi gubernii na 1864 gg.*, p. 282; *Spisok zavedenii pechati* (1875, 1887, 1900); *Obzor graficheskikh iskusstv* 1879, no. 14–15 (July 15), p. 93; Ginlein, *Adresnaia kniga*, pp. 80–91.
NOTE Table excludes small print shops located in factories, as well as binderies and typefoundries that were independent of printing establishments.

TABLE TWO NUMBER OF TYPOGRAPHIC AND
LITHOGRAPHIC WORKERS, 1881–1902

	1881–82	1897	1902
St. Petersburg	4,990	8,160	11,884
Moscow	4,006	5,990	7,302

SOURCES *S.-Peterburg po perepisi 1881 goda*, vol. 1, part 2, p. 307; *Chislennost' i sostav*, vol. 2, part 2, pp. 22–33; *S.-Peterburg po perepisi 1900 goda*, vypusk 2, pp. 50–51, 66–67; *Perepis' Moskvy 1882 goda*, vypusk 2, tables, pp. 271–78; *Chislennost' i sostav*, vol. 2, pt. 1, pp. 178–79; *Perepis' Moskvy 1902 goda*, pt. 1, vypusk 2, pp. 128–29, 134–35, 150–51, 156–57. To the extent possible, I have made adjustments to correct classificational inconsistencies.

creasingly in the larger enterprises. Before the 1880s, only a few government-owned printing plants employed more than one hundred workers. By 1903, there were forty-six such firms, most of them private enterprises, employing three-fifths or more of printing workers in St. Petersburg and Moscow (table 3).[5] To be sure, compared to Russian metalworking or textile firms—which sometimes employed several

5. For similar data, see Sher, *Istoriia*, pp. 11–15, and Orlov, *Poligraficheskaia promyshlennost' Moskvy*, pp. 191–93.

TABLE THREE   DISTRIBUTION OF LABOR BY SCALE OF ENTERPRISE, C. 1900–1903

Workers per Firm

	0–15	16–50	51–100	101–300	301–600	601+	TOTAL
St. Petersburg							
Enterprises	199	34	18	22	4	2	279
Workers	1,067	1,095	1,371	3,522	1,685	2,317	11,057
% of Workers	9.6	9.9	12.4	31.9	15.2	21.0	100%
Moscow							
Enterprises	110	53	18	13	5	0	199
Workers	329	1,506	1,319	2,441	2,339	0	7,934
% of Workers	4.1	19.0	16.6	30.8	29.5	0	100%

SOURCES Pogozhev, *Adresnaia kniga*, pp. 104–08, 113–15; Orlov, *Poligraficheskaia promyshlennost' Moskvy*, p. 216; Enterprise Card File (compiled from references in trade periodicals, plant publications, and government strike reports).

NOTE Because Pogozhev excluded many small enterprises and a number of state-owned firms, I have added these according to the following calculations. I added government enterprises and their workers from my own Enterprise Card File (but counted only workers in the printing departments of the Office for the Manufacture of Government Paper). To determine the number of firms employing fewer than 16 workers, I calculated the difference between the total number of enterprises calculated by Orlov for Moscow in 1902 and for St. Petersburg in Table 1 above and the number of printing firms listed in Pogozhev plus the added state firms. To estimate the number of workers employed in these small shops I multiplied the estimated number of such firms by the mean size of enterprises excluded from Pogozhev's list (that is, firms employing from 0–11 workers in St. Petersburg and 0–4 in Moscow).

thousand workers—printing firms were not especially large; the largest typically employed only five or six hundred workers, and only one, the printing department of the Office for the Manufacture of Government Paper (Ekspeditsiia zagotovleniia gosudarstvennykh bumag), employed more than a thousand. Still, compared to printing enterprises in other countries, Russian printing was exceptionally concentrated in large plants.[6]

The expansion of Russian printing also altered the structure and organization of production. Until the 1860s, more for economic than for technological reasons, most printing work in Russia was hand work. Mechanized printing presses were available, and European and American producers tried to market them in Russia. The first mechanized press used in Russia was imported in 1818 by a British printer who managed the printshop of the Russian Bible Society in St. Petersburg. Soon after, the Office for the Manufacture of Government Paper began importing printing machines, seeking to improve the quality of paper money, and some private employers soon followed, especially after the cost of this equipment was reduced when domestic manufacture of printing machinery began in the late 1820s.[7] However, for most Russian printing shops before the 1860s, there was little reason to invest in a *skoropechatnaia mashina,* or "fast-printing machine," since relatively low demand made the output of the old hand press quite adequate. As a result, until the 1860s hand presses continued to outnumber mechanized presses,[8] and even those mechanized presses that were in use were usually powered not by steam engines but by "crankmen" (*vertel'-shchiki*), who turned the heavy flywheels by hand.[9] In the 1860s, the process of technical modernization began to accelerate dramatically. In 1871, the Moscow inspector of printing firms reported a "yearly increase in the number of newly opened printing firms, in the number of printing machines, and in the replacement of hand power by steam."[10] In the 1880s and 1890s, the number, size, and productivity of printing machines increased further.[11]

6. Sher, *Istoriia,* p. 15.
7. Zakharov, "Svedeniia o nekotorykh peterburgskikh tipografiiakh," pp. 65, 72–73; *400 let,* vol. 1, pp. 268–69; *Severnaia pchela* July 26, 1829, p. 4.
8. Orlov, *Poligraficheskaia promyshlennost' Moskvy,* p. 150.
9. Zakharov, "Svedeniia o nekotorykh peterburgskikh tipografiiakh," p. 79; Shchelgunov, *Iskusstvo knigopechataniia,* p. 138; *Severnaia pchela,* July 26, 1829, p. 4.
10. Quoted in Sher, *Istoriia,* p. 5.
11. For a detailed account of the mechanization of printing in Moscow, see Orlov, *Poligraficheskaia promyshlennost' Moskvy,* pp. 148–53, 186–90; *400 let,* pp. 367–68; Savinov, *Ukazatel' goroda Moskvy,* p. 267; *Knizhnik* 1865, no. 10–11 (October–November), pp. 621–36.

By the turn of the century, most printing firms had at least one "fast-printing machine."[12] But the impact of mechanization on the industry was far from even. Some techniques were especially difficult to mechanize, notably lithographic printing and bookbinding, whose technologies remained largely traditional.[13] Type composition was even more resistant to mechanization, but for different reasons. Although effective mechanized typesetting became available in the late 1870s and its potential advantages were periodically discussed in the professional press, no typesetting machines were purchased until 1903, and even these were rarities before 1906, when the higher wages that resulted from workers' strikes made them begin to appear a more economical investment.[14] Mechanization also affected different firms differently. The smaller shops usually bought only the simplest of flat-bed presses or one or two of the small and inexpensive platen presses, known as *amerikanki*, which first appeared in the 1860s. The larger firms were able to purchase much more productive machinery, including steam-powered multi-cylindered presses and even continuous-feeding rotary web presses.[15]

ENTREPRENEURSHIP

Although the role of official printing remained strong into the early 1900s, especially in St. Petersburg, where a third of the city's printing workers were employed in the nine largest governmental printing

12. Judging by Moscow data in Orlov, *Poligraficheskaia promyshlennost' Moskvy,* pp. 152, 188–89.

13. Sher, *Istoriia,* p. 35; Bakhtiarov, *Slugi pechati,* p. 42; *Istoriia leningradskogo soiuza,* p. 45; Orlov, *Poligraficheskaia promyshlennost' Moskvy,* pp. 150, 168–69, 186–90; E[izen], *Ocherk istorii perepletnogo dela.*

14. *Knizhnyi vestnik* 1864, no. 23 (July 31), p. 281; *Tipografskii zhurnal* 2:21–22 (May 15, 1869), pp. 80–81; *Obzor graficheskikh iskusstv* 1879, no. 5 (March 1), p. 38; 1882, no. 8 (April 15), p. 48; *Knizhnyi vestnik* 1885, no. 10 (May 15), p. 354; 1885, no. 13–14 (July 15), p. 472; 1890, no. 12 (December), p. 495; *Obzor pervoi vserossiiskoi vystavki* 32 (June 8, 1895), p. 8; *Graficheskie iskusstva i bumazhnaia promyshlennost'* 1:1 (September 1, 1895), pp. 3–4; 3:9 (September 1898), pp. 129–31; 4:9 (February 1900), p. 146; Orlov, *Poligraficheskaia promyshlennost' Moskvy,* p. 228; *Istoriia leningradskogo soiuza,* p. 66; *400 let,* p. 371; *Leninskii zakaz,* p. 20.

15. In a platen press, the type and paper both sit on flat surfaces and are simply pressed against one another. Flatbed cylinder presses, which long predominated in the production of books, move the type on a flat bed beneath a rotating impression cylinder, which carries the paper. The more complex flatbed presses use multiple cylinders to print in two colors and on both sides of the sheet in a single pass through the press. Rotary presses print from curved plates—in Russia, at that time, mainly metal stereotype molds of composed type—attached to a cylinder. This is the most efficient style of press for fast and long-run presswork and can print in multiple colors and on both sides of the paper. Rotary web presses print on rolls of paper called "webs" that are cut into sheets and often folded automatically.

firms,[16] most of the expansion and modernization of production in the
late nineteenth century was the work of private commercial entrepreneurs. Many of these capitalist printers were non-Russians, often immigrants or their children, who brought to printing the "capital, knowledge, and the spirit of enterprise" that Finance Minister Sergei Witte
had hoped foreigners would provide Russian industry.[17] The technical
needs of printing created a particular demand for foreign-trained printers, reflected in their large role. In 1875 in St. Petersburg nearly one-
quarter (23 percent) of the owners of printing firms were foreign na-
tionals, mostly Germans. There were also "immigrants" from lands
that had been annexed as the Russian empire expanded—Germans and
others from the Baltic provinces (9 percent in 1875) and Jews from the
Pale of Settlement (12 percent in 1881).[18] In Moscow as well, non-
Russians played a disproportionate role as entrepreneurs, though less
so than in cosmopolitan St. Petersburg. In 1885, 14 percent of the owners of printing firms were foreign subjects, mostly Germans, with an
additional 4 percent born in the Baltic provinces and 2 percent identified as Jews. By contrast, ethnic non-Russians constituted only 5 percent of the general population in Moscow.[19]

Rudolf Schneider was in many respects typical of these printers of
foreign origin. Born in the then-Prussian city of Danzig (Gdansk) in
1834, he was forced by his family's poverty to quit school at the age of
fourteen and take a position as an apprentice compositor. After completing his apprenticeship, he set out on his traditional *Wanderjahre*.
Working his way around printing houses in Austria, the Rheinland,
France, and Hungary, he arrived in 1858 in St. Petersburg, where he

16. Calculated from sources as in table 3.
17. Von Laue, "A Secret Memorandum of Sergei Witte," esp. pp. 68–69. For a general discussion of foreign investment and entrepreneurship in Russia, see McKay, *Pioneers for Profit*; essays by Fred Carstensen, William Blackwell, and Thomas C. Owen, in
Guroff and Carstensen, *Entrepreneurship in Imperial Russia*, pp. 17–18, 59–60, 140–58;
Rieber, *Merchants and Entrepreneurs*, pp. 247–49, 266–67; Gindin, "Russkaia
burzhuaziia v period kapitalizma," part 1, pp. 63–71.
18. *Spisok zavedenii pechati v S.-Peterburge* (1875); *S.-Peterburg po perepisi 1881
goda*, vol. 1, part 2, pp. 311–12. The 1875 *spisok* does not identify foreign-born individuals who adopted Russian citizenship or Baltic-born individuals who legally registered as
residents of Moscow or St. Petersburg, though a few of these have been identified from
other sources. For comparison, it may be noted that in the general population of the city,
individuals identified as other than Orthodox native Russian-speakers comprised only
17% of the total. *S.-Peterburg po perepisi 1881 goda*, vol. 1, part 1, pp. 242–43.
19. *Torgovo-promyshlennye zavedeniia goroda Moskvy v 1885–1890 gg.*, pp. 62–
65; *Perepis' Moskvy 1882 goda*, vypusk 2, tables, pp. 93–98, 393–94; *Pravitel'stvennyi
vestnik*, August 17 (29), 1883. Again, the percentage of foreign subjects does not include
naturalized foreign-born.

found work first as a compositor and then as a production manager and soon managed to purchase his own small printing shop.[20]

Second-generation immigrants were typically even more successful. For example, Roman Golike's father came to St. Petersburg from the Estonian city of Dorpat (Tartu) in 1837 as a twenty-year-old compositor and worked his way up through the ranks to become manager of the press owned by another immigrant, a shop he was able to buy on credit in 1851. Roman attended the Realschule of the Reformed church in St. Petersburg, a central institution in Petersburg's foreign community,[21] and completed a part-time apprenticeship in his father's shop; in 1869 he was sent to London and Paris to earn his own living as a compositor. On returning to Russia in 1871, he built up his father's firm into one of the most respected quality-printing houses in the capital.[22]

Although most immigrant printing entrepreneurs followed this general pattern of upward mobility from skilled worker to shop owner, some established or purchased printing firms as extensions of successful careers in related fields, especially publishing and bookselling. For example, Adolf Marx, the son of a Stettin clock-factory owner, trained as a bookseller in Schwerin and Berlin before coming in 1859 to St. Petersburg, where he built a successful bookselling and publishing business and on this basis founded a large printing house.[23]

The rapid expansion of printing in the late nineteenth century also created opportunities for skilled workmen to become entrepreneurs. In the 1890s, a foreman complained that in former times only "educated people with means" owned printing shops, whereas now "many are former compositors."[24] Unfortunately, we know little about most of these workers-turned-entrepreneurs because they tended to own inconspicuous shops and were not usually active in professional organizations. However, the career of one, Ivan Frolov, may suggest both the

20. *Obzor graficheskikh iskusstv* 1882, no. 1–2 (January 1 and 15), pp. 2–3; 1884, no. 12 (June 15), p. 91; *Tipografskii zhurnal* 1:2 (July 15, 1867), p. 6; Galaktionov, *Zhurnaly pechatnogo dela*, pp. 3–9.

21. *Entsiklopedicheskii slovar'*, vol. 26, p. 633.

22. *Pechatnia R. R. Golike*, pp. 1–8; *Pechatnoe iskusstvo* 1:4 (January 1902), pp. 125–28.

23. *Knigovedenie: Entsiklopedicheskii slovar'*, p. 334; *400 let*, p. 380; *Obzor graficheskikh iskusstv* 1883, no. 11 (January 1), p. 98.

24. A. A. Filippov in *Novoe vremia*, March 22/April 3, 1895, p. 3; also in *Vestnik graficheskogo dela* 1 (March 14, 1897), p. 3. The early Soviet historians of Petersburg printing agreed:"Before 1905 . . . the owners of typographic, lithographic, binding, and zincographic enterprises for the most part came from among the workers." *Istoriia leningradskogo soiuza*, p. 34. See also Orlov, *Poligraficheskaia promyshlennost' Moskvy*, p. 122; *Piatidesiatiletnii iubilei tipografii Ivana Grigor'evicha Chuksina*, p. 4.

typical upward climb through the ranks and the distinctive personal attributes needed for such mobility. Born in the central Russian city of Riazan in 1851, Frolov finished a local primary school and began attending a gymnasium, but his family's poverty after his father's death forced him to leave school to seek work. Evidently wishing to practice a craft and perhaps to make use of his literacy, he sacrificed immediate earnings in order to accept an apprenticeship as a compositor. In 1878, he moved his family north to St. Petersburg, where for thirteen years he worked in the same shop, first as a compositor, then as a foreman, production manager, and finally director. Three years before his death at the age of forty-four, he purchased his own small press.[25] Although native former workers such as Frolov may have operated many printing firms, they owned none of the major enterprises in the industry. Almost all of these were in the hands of non-Russians (generally immigrants or their children), individuals from privileged social ranks, or the state.

Two partial exceptions to this generalization are worth noting. Ivan Sytin, the owner of Russia's largest private printing company at the turn of the century, was the son of a provincial copy clerk (*pisar'*) and was educated for only three years in a one-room schoolhouse before he started full-time work as an apprentice to a Moscow merchant specializing in the sale of cheap popular prints (*lubki*) and brochures. Ten years later, with the help of this employer, who initially joined him as a partner, and a four-thousand-ruble dowry from his recent marriage, Sytin established a small lithographic printing shop with a half-dozen workers and a single press. Concentrating his initial efforts on meeting the growing demand for simple popular prints and publications for peasants and workers, and profiting especially during the Russo-Turkish War by selling vivid maps of the campaign, Sytin was able to expand his operations quickly, adding a bookstore, a typographic shop, and a bindery during the course of the 1880s.

Sytin was from the first convinced that profit depended on modern techniques as well as good marketing. His first lithographic press was mechanized, and when he organized his typographic shop in 1884, steam power was installed from the outset. Sytin also favored modern financial arrangements to sustain expansion. Soon after his business was established, he raised 75,000 rubles by forming a limited partnership (*tovarishchestvo na vere*), and in 1893 he raised another

25. *Graficheskie iskusstva i bumazhnaia promyshlennost'* 1:10 (June 1896), p. 157.

350,000 rubles by establishing a limited-liability stock corporation (*tovarishchestvo na paiakh*). By the turn of the century, his was the largest printing plant in Moscow, and his business included a plant in St. Petersburg and a network of bookstores throughout the country. His shareholders enjoyed a regular dividend of 10 percent on their investment. In later years he would be praised for his business abilities as a "Russian American."[26]

Another successful printer whose background was neither privileged nor foreign was Petr Soikin, the son of a manumitted serf. While working as an accountant in St. Petersburg in the mid-1880s, he borrowed 800 rubles to purchase a small, unprofitable printing shop. Initially employing six workers on five hand presses, he raised the money for expansion by continuing to work as an accountant—in the daytime for the Baltic railroad and at night for the State Bank. Within a few years, he employed thirty men, many on mechanized presses, and began publishing his own journal, the popular science magazine *Priroda i liudi* (Nature and People). By 1895, Soikin employed 320 workers in a very profitable business. In 1903 he began construction of a new six-story building with its own electric power station.[27]

Unlike Sytin and Soikin, most of the founders of large private printing firms came from relatively privileged backgrounds. Many were members of merchant guilds, such as the Glazunovs, who had been booksellers in St. Petersburg since the 1780s.[28] Many—13 percent at the end of the century—were from the gentry, or had at least earned ranks of nobility through state or other public service.[29] Members of the nobility had in fact been among the first private printers in Russia after Catherine II relinquished the government's monopoly over printing in the late eighteenth century. Their motivations, how-

26. *Ocherk izdatel'skoi deiatel'nosti t-va I. D. Sytina v Moskve;* Miretskii, *Pervaia Obraztsovaia tipografiia,* pp. 18–22; Dinershtein, *I. D. Sytin,* pp. 6–26; Ruud, *Russian Entrepreneur;* 400 let, pp. 417–18; *Aktsionernoe delo v Rossii,* vol. 2, vypusk 5, pp. 1207–08; Dmitriev-Mamonov, *Ukazatel' deistvuiushchikh v Imperii aktsionernykh predpriiatii,* vol. 1, pp. 570–71; *Knizhnyi vestnik* 1903, no. 16 (May 4), pp. 559–61.

27. *Kratkii ocherk razvitiia i deiatel'nosti tipografii P. P. Soikina,* pp. 3–11; *Dvadtsatipiatiletie tipografsko-izdatel'skoi deiatel'nosti P. P. Soikina,* pp. 3–10; *Knizhnyi mir* 1910, no. 51 (December 19), pp. 1–2.

28. Lisovskii, *Kratkii ocherk,* pp. 7–89; *Knigovedenie,* pp. 143–44.

29. *Spisok zavedenii pechati v S.-Peterburge* (1875 and 1900); *Pravitel'stvennyi vestnik,* August 14 (26), 1883, and August 17 (29), 1883; *Perepis' Moskvy 1882,* tables, pp. 38–39; *Torgovo-promyshlennye zavedeniia goroda Moskvy v 1885–1890 gg.,* pp. 62–65; *S.-Peterburg po perepisi 1900 goda,* vypusk 2, pp. 44–45; *Spisok fabrik i zavodov,* pp. 150–55, 162–67; Pogozhev, *Adresnaia kniga,* pp. 104–08, 113–15.

ever, were not mainly commercial. In the tradition of Western European "scholar-printers,"[30] individuals such as Nikolai Novikov, Ivan Krylov, and Ivan Rakhmaninov established publishing and printing firms as extensions of their work as publicists. This tradition was continued into the early twentieth century by gentry printers such as Mikhail Stasiulevich, a professor of history whose publishing and printing firm in St. Petersburg was well known for its contributions to literature and liberal politics.[31] The appeal of printing for nobles, who typically viewed an industrial occupation, according to the gentry industrialist Vasilii Poletika, as "something rather suspicious,"[32] was its perception as the most artistic and intellectual of the trades.[33]

In practice, however, for most noble printers the distinction between intellectual and commercial motives was necessarily blurred. Often having no other source of income, noble entrepreneurs could not disregard the imperatives of profit.[34] Many in fact effectively combined the roles of *Kulturträger* and capitalist. Aleksei Suvorin, for example, left government service in the 1850s to pursue an intellectual career, initially as a journalist. In the 1870s, he decided to begin publishing a newspaper, to be called *Novoe vremia* (New Times). Finding no facilities equipped for the scale and speed of production he had in mind, he established his own plant and imported equipment from Western Europe, including the first web-fed rotary press to be used in Russia. By the time of his death in 1912, Suvorin was the owner of one of the largest and most profitable printing enterprises in the country (as well as an extensive publishing and bookselling business), employing nearly five hundred workers.[35] But in the tradition of the scholar-printer,

30. *Knigovedenie*, pp. 294, 375–76, 436; Marker, *Publishing, Printing, and the Origins of Intellectual Life in Russia, 1700–1800*, pp. 111–14, 120–34; Marker describes this group as "literati" or "intellectual publishers." On "scholar-printers" in Western Europe, see Eisenstein, *The Printing Press as an Agent of Change*, p. 239; idem, "The Early Printer as 'Renaissance Man,'" pp. 6–16; Lowry, *The World of Aldus Manutius*, esp. p. 66.

31. *Knigovedenie*, p. 517.

32. Quoted by Berlin, *Russkaia burzhuaziia*, pp. 217–18. Poletika himself later embarked on an unsuccessful publishing venture. Bakhtiarov, *Slugi pechati*, p. 184.

33. Gary Hamburg identifies book publishing among the perceived "worthy occupations" open to nobles in the late nineteenth century. Hamburg, *Politics of the Russian Nobility*, pp. 14–15.

34. Korelin, *Dvorianstvo v poreformennoi Rossii*, ch. 2; Hamburg, *Politics of the Russian Nobility*, ch. 1.

35. *Kratkii ocherk izdatel'skoi deiatel'nosti A. S. Suvorina*, p. 8; *Fabrichno-zavodskie predpriiatiia rossiiskoi imperii* (Petrograd, 1914), entry 2307; Ambler, *Russian Journalism and Politics*.

Suvorin thought of himself, "despite his business success, as primarily a man of letters."[36]

One of Moscow's largest printing enterprises was also established by a gentry entrepreneur, Ivan Kushnerev, the son of a somewhat penurious serf-owner. One year after the emancipation of the serfs in 1861, at the age of thirty-five, Kushnerev decided to sell his small estate, leave government service, and set himself up as a publisher in St. Petersburg. After several years without success, he moved to Moscow and redirected his efforts to printing rather than publishing. Borrowing money from a fellow member of the English Club, a traditional gathering place for Moscow's nobility, Kushnerev opened in 1869 a small printing shop in rented rooms with a dozen workers, one hand press, and a single printing machine, and immediately began reinvesting his profits for expansion. In 1876, in need of additional capital for expansion, Kushnerev reorganized his firm into a limited partnership with four partners. Twelve years later, he again restructured the company as a limited-liability corporation. When Kushnerev died in 1896, his company included a large-scale, mechanized printing factory housed in a specially constructed four-story building, with branches in Kiev and St. Petersburg and an annual profit of over 90,000 rubles, relatively high for the printing industry at that time.[37] Typically for a gentry entrepreneur, however, Kushnerev aspired to be more than a successful capitalist. He remained active, if less than successful, as a publisher and even printed several volumes of his own rather uninspired publicistic writings.[38]

As the industry became increasingly concentrated and commercialized, ownership began taking new forms. Although some entrepreneurs retained sole or family ownership of their companies, beginning in the 1890s many of the largest firms, seeking capital to expand, invited outside investors to purchase stock. By 1894, three large printing firms in St. Petersburg and five in Moscow had reorganized as limited-liability stock corporations (*tovarishchestva na paiakh* or *aktsionernye obshchestva*), and all of the larger firms established in the 1880s or after were founded as corporations—notably, the enterprises of Iablon-

36. Ambler, *Russian Journalism and Politics*, p. 179.
37. *Dvadtsatipiatiletie tipografii t-va Kushnerev*, pp. 3–18; *Leninskii zakaz*, pp. 11–19; *Kratkii ocherk razvitiia masterskikh* . . . *Tovarishchestva I. N. Kushnerev; Fabrika knigi "Krasnyi proletarii,"* pp. 1–13; *Otchet pravleniia I. N. Kushnerev i Ko. v Moskve za 1896* (Moscow, 1897), in TsGIAgM, f. 2316, op. 1, d. 1; *400 let*, pp. 412–14; *Knigovedenie*, pp. 301–02.
38. Kushnerev, *Zemliakam* and *Sochineniia*.

skii in St. Petersburg and Chicherin, Iakovlev, Vasil'ev, and the Russian Printing and Publishing Company (Russkoe tovarishchestvo pechatnogo i izdatel'skogo dela) in Moscow. By 1902, many of the largest private printing firms in St. Petersburg and virtually every major private enterprise in Moscow had been organized as limited-liability stock corporations. With a few hundred to a thousand available shares—the greater diffusion of shares being characteristic of *aktsionernye obshchestva* and as in other industries more characteristic of St. Petersburg—and totaling from a quarter of a million to over a million rubles of share capital in each firm, the formation of corporations in the 1880s and 1890s infused considerable capital into the industry and further strengthened the largest and most commercially oriented private firms.[39]

As private entrepreneurship became the dominant form of enterprise in Russian printing in the late nineteenth century, even state printing was affected by the process of commercialization. A few official printing houses were leased to individuals to run as private firms, such as the press of the Ministry of Finance. But even when official firms remained fully in state hands, they were increasingly managed as commercial enterprises, taking in private as well as official orders (as private firms increasingly took in government business), mechanizing production to be more cost-effective, and attending to profits. Although almost all of the directors of state printing firms were hereditary nobles and had usually entered the printing business after many years of state service in other areas, many proved themselves to be effective commercial managers. For example, Prince Boris Borisovich Golitsyn, a member of one of Russia's oldest and most influential aristocratic families and a well-known intellectual, was appointed in 1899 to head the Office for the Manufacture of Government Paper. When he took over, this giant papermaking and printing enterprise, after a forty-year history of expansion and modernization, was facing a financial crisis, and the quality of its work

39. *Aktsionernoe delo v Rossii*, vol. 2, vypusk 5, pp. 1192–1211; Dmitriev-Mamonov, *Ukazatel' deistvuiushchikh v Imperii aktsionernykh predpriiatii*, vol. 1, pp. xxiii–xxiv and passim; Orlov, *Poligraficheskaia promyshlennost' Moskvy*, pp. 196–97. On the different patterns of corporate structure in Russian industry generally, specifically the Petersburg industrialists' tendency to sell a relatively large number of less expensive shares while the more traditional Moscow owners preferred to keep closer control of their companies, see Owen, "Entrepreneurship and the Structure of Enterprise," pp. 67–71. I am grateful to Thomas Owen for demonstrating statistically the applicability of his argument to the printing industry on the basis of his *RUSCORP: A Database of Corporations in the Russian Empire, 1700–1914*.

was declining. Golitsyn effectively improved both its finances and its technique.[40]

The history of entrepreneurship in Russian printing in the late nineteenth century included hardship and failure as well as business achievements. In an increasingly competitive marketplace, business failures had become commonplace. One successful employer, perhaps gloating a bit, recalled that in the 1860s it had become "fashionable" to operate a printing firm, leading to an excessively competitive environment in which many enterprises collapsed.[41] Such failures were especially frequent during periods of economic slowdown, as in the 1880s and again after the turn of the century. Of the 149 private printing firms under the supervision of the Petersburg press inspector in 1875, only 97 still existed in 1883, and only 33 were left by 1900.[42]

Competition led also to harsh practices to survive, especially by smaller, more economically marginal firms. Owners cut prices to attract orders, used cheaper materials, and, most relevant to the concerns of this study, squeezed workers to produce more for less pay. To sustain lower prices, profit margins were sometimes reduced even to the point of accepting work below cost solely to ruin the competition.[43] In the view of many contemporaries, competition had produced a "desperate struggle between printing shop owners,"[44] which, it was feared, was "undermining public confidence and leading to the decay of the printing trade."[45] The capitalist transformation of the industry was not viewed as progress by many ordinary business owners.

40. Voznesenskii, *Sto let Ekspeditsii zagotovleniia gosudarstvennykh bumag*, pp. 23–40; *Entsiklopedicheskii slovar'*, vol. 9, p. 53; Mikhailovskii, *Ekspeditsiia zagotovleniia gosudarstvennykh bumag*, pp. 33–35; *Novyi entsiklopedicheskii slovar'*, vol. 13, p. 917. For other examples, see discussions about A. V. Gavrilov of the Synod press in TsGIA, f. 800, op. 1, dd. 92, 176, 338, 457, and in Gavrilov, *Ocherk istorii Sankt-Peterburgskoi sinodal'noi tipografii;* A. I. Iakovlev of the State press in *Pechatnoe iskusstvo* 1:6 (March 1902), p. 186; and S. I. Nedel'kovich of the Naval Ministry press in *Graficheskie iskusstva i bumazhnaia promyshlennost'* 4:11 (June 1900), p. 179.

41. *Pechatnia R. R. Golike*, p. 3.

42. *Spisok zavedenii pechati v S.-Peterburge* (1875); *Pravitel'stvennyi vestnik*, August 14 (26), 1883, p. 3; *Spisok zavedenii pechati v S.-Peterburge* (1900); Pogozhev, *Adresnaia kniga*, pp. 113–15.

43. Orlov, *Poligraficheskaia promyshlennost' Moskvy*, pp. 145–47, 185–88, 195; *400 let*, p. 367; *Obzor graficheskikh iskusstv* 1878, no. 7 (April 15), p. 50; 1881, no. 1 (January 1), p. 1; *Russkii kur'er*, September 14, 1883, p. 2; *Graficheskie iskusstva i bumazhnaia promyshlennost'* 2:5 (May 1897), p. 66; *Naborshchik* 1:1 (October 20, 1902), p. 19; 1:50 (October 12, 1903), p. 749; Russkoe obshchestvo deiatelei pechatnogo dela, Moskovskoe otdelenie [henceforth, RODPD-MO], *Kratkii otchet o deiatel'nosti za 1902–3*, p. 4; Bakhtiarov, *Slugi pechati*, p. 47.

44. *Vestnik graficheskogo dela* 1 (March 14, 1897), p. 3.

45. *Trudy pervogo s"ezda*, pp. 44–45.

LABOR

Central to these perceptions of decline was the image of degraded labor. Many press owners, publishers, booksellers, journalists, and others concerned with the printing industry viewed commercialization and market competition as causing a "terrible decline in wages" and generally having a "ruinous effect" on labor.[46] In fact, this decline was more complex than it was sometimes portrayed by contemporaries, whose harsh judgments of their surroundings, as shall be seen, often reflected images of what ought to be more than of what once was. There was indeed a ruinous decline in the condition of labor in printing, but it was manifested much more as a structural transformation of work than as degradation in the lives of individual workers.

The traditional world of skilled labor in printing broke apart during the mid-nineteenth century under the pressures of industrial expansion, mechanization, and the pursuit of profit in an increasingly competitive marketplace. Before the nineteenth century, most printing workers were either immigrant European craftsmen or the children—recruited as apprentices—of urban artisans (including printers), merchants, or government employees.[47] Almost all were skilled hand workers, trained in a craft that had changed little since the seventeenth century. The work process and division of labor remained in 1818 much the same as it had been in 1618: compositors (*naborshchiki*) hand-set the type; pressmen (*teredorshchiki*) locked the type into place and operated the hand press, and inkers (*batyrshchiki*) inked the form and assisted the pressmen.[48] This traditional order was quickly eroded by innovations that began in the mid-1800s.

Machine work facilitated the creation of new, relatively unskilled crafts in the pressroom.[49] The typical flat-bed cylinder press was worked by three or four men. In charge of the work of the press was a

46. *Russkii kur'er*, September 14, 1883, p. 2; *Trudy pervogo s"ezda*, pp. 44–45. See also *Vestnik graficheskogo dela* 1 (March 14, 1897), p. 3; 2 (March 21, 1897), pp. 12–13; *Graficheskie iskusstva i bumazhnaia promyshlennost'* 2:5 (May 1897), p. 66; *Naborshchik* 1:22 (March 30, 1903), p. 365; 1:50 (October 12, 1903), p. 749; Orlov, *Poligraficheskaia promyshlennost' Moskvy*, pp. 185–86.

47. Orlov, *Poligraficheskaia promyshlennost' Moskvy*, pp. 59–61, 79–83, 108; *Tipografiia Lenizdata*, p. 9; Zakharov, "Svedeniia o nekotorykh peterburgskikh tipografiiakh," p. 75; Iuferovyi and Sokolovskii, *Akademicheskaia tipografiia*, pp. 48–49.

48. Orlov, *Poligraficheskaia promyshlennost' Moskvy*, pp. 53–59, 85.

49. Good descriptions of the work process in the pressroom can be found in Bakhtiarov, *Slugi pechati*, pp. 38–42; Kolomnin, *Kratkie svedeniia po tipografskomu delu*, pp. 554–60; Trotskii, "Ekonomicheskie i sanitarnye usloviia," part 1, pp. 73–76; *400 let*, p. 367.

skilled master printer (known as *pechatnyi master*, or, reflecting the mechanization of the process, *mashinyi master* or simply *mashinist*). He acted in the role of both foreman and worker. As worker, he "made ready" the press much as a hand pressman would: securing the type form, packing the impression cylinder to assure even pressure against the type, examining a first proof, and then adjusting the type, cylinder packing, and inking mechanism to assure a clear and clean impression. As foreman, he supervised the work of other press workers, trained new recruits, and in some cases hired and paid workers himself. Depending on the size of a firm and on the involvement of the owner or manager in the operations of the pressroom, the master printer's authority might extend to several presses, leaving assistant masters to do much of the direct press work.

The master printer supervised less skilled press workers: "press feeders" or "layers-on" (*nakladchiki*), who placed individual sheets of paper into position as the grippers on the cylinder approached to seize the paper and press it against the type for printing, and "takers-off" (*priemshchiki*), who removed the printed sheets and placed them on a pile.[50] When the job was finished, these press helpers would clean the machine and periodically oil it. In addition, on presses not powered by motors, a laborer (the *vertel'shchik*) would turn the heavy flywheel that moved the cylinder. For some traditionalists, accustomed to the old identity of the printer as a skilled worker, these semi-skilled and unskilled workers could not be considered true printers at all. An editorial in the journal of the printing profession stated bluntly in 1878 that "our inkers, press feeders, takers-off, and crankmen cannot properly speaking be called typographic workers."[51]

The decay of apprenticeship, which accompanied these changes in work organization, reinforced this separation of common press workers from the craft traditions of the skilled printer. By the late nineteenth century, uneducated peasant boys of twelve or thirteen—often younger before the child labor legislation of 1882—were typically hired as takers-off, performing work that required little or no skill. Some became press feeders, which required greater dexterity and accuracy, es-

50. Whenever the contemporary English or American equivalents of Russian printing terminology, as here, closely match the meanings of the Russian, I use these terms. When they do not, as in the case of *machine masters*—who were known in England as *machine overseers* or *machine minders*, depending on their degree of authority—I have chosen a more literal translation. I use the term *compositor* rather than the more familiar *typesetter*, as *compositor* was the term in common use in American English prior to the mechanization of typesetting.

51. *Obzor graficheskikh iskusstv* 1878, no. 13 (July 15), p. 95.

pecially when printing multiple colors or on both sides of a sheet. As a press feeder, a young worker might receive something like a true apprenticeship, learning the process of "make-ready" and other skills that, given sufficient ability and good fortune, might lead to his becoming a master printer. But many press feeders received no more training than was necessary to perform their assigned task. In addition, in order to bypass the restrictions imposed by the labor legislation of 1882, employers often preferred to hire older youths, aged seventeen or eighteen, with no intention of training them to become masters. Even on hand presses, peasant boys were often hired ostensibly as "apprentices" but received no instruction beyond the simplest tasks of an inker. Press workers themselves also abused apprenticeship. Given the high demand for labor, many young press feeders found that they could quit their apprenticeships after a year or two and find better-paying jobs in shops willing to hire half-trained workmen in order to lower production costs.[52]

In type composition too, as early as the 1860s, observers began to speak of a "decline" in the "art" and to point to the supplanting of real craftsmen by "undisciplined, drunken, and insolent" workers "of only average skill, producing bad work."[53] Mechanization, however, was not a direct factor, since type composition remained a hand craft until after the turn of the century. But even without typesetting machines, the pressures of increasing demand, the shortage of skilled labor, and the competition to keep prices down conspired against the skill standards of compositors.

The erosion of skill in type composition began at its source in apprenticeship. Notwithstanding proposals that new apprentices be accepted only after an examination to ensure sufficient education and that employers not be allowed to hire a journeyman without proper attestation of completed apprenticeship (as had once been the case),[54] both

52. Ibid. 1880, no. 17 (August 30), p. 127; *Trudy pervogo s"ezda*, pp. 37–38; *Naborshchik* 1:15 (February 9, 1903), p. 255; *Istoriia leningradskogo soiuza*, p. 43; Svavitskii and Sher, *Ocherk polozheniia*, pp. 10–11, 43–44; Sher, *Istoriia*, p. 57; Orlov, *Poligraficheskaia promyshlennost' Moskvy*, pp. 268–71.

53. *Tipografskii zhurnal* 2:1 (July 1, 1868), p. 2; *Vestnik graficheskogo dela* 17–18 (September 25, 1897), p. 176; *Tipografskii zhurnal* 2:3 (August 1, 1868), p. 10. See also *Tipografskii zhurnal* 1:12 (December 15, 1867), p. 52, and 2:2 (July 15, 1868), p. 6; *Obzor graficheskikh iskusstv* 1878, no. 6 (April 1), p. 41; 1882, no. 10 (May 15), p. 64; *Pervaia russkaia shkola, 1884–1894*, p. 6; *Peterburgskaia gazeta*, April 24, 1894, p. 3 (interview with R. Golike).

54. For example, *Obzor graficheskikh iskusstv* 1878, no. 6 (April 1), p. 41; *Trudy pervogo s"ezda*, pp. 27–37; *Biulleten' RODPD* 1:11 (November 1902), p. 84; *Naborshchik* 1:6 (December 8, 1902), p. 107.

recruitment standards and training deteriorated. The number of peasant children among compositors grew rapidly and approached a majority, though even after the rapid growth of the labor force at the end of the nineteenth century many apprentice compositors were recruited as before from among the children of small shopkeepers, artisans, workers, garrison soldiers, and other lower-class city dwellers.[55] This urban plebeian element among compositors was declining, but it was still larger than among most other groups of workers, even other printing workers.[56] Standards of education were also declining. Printing firms increasingly accepted as apprentice compositors youths whose literacy hardly exceeded the ability to recognize the letters of the alphabet. Already in the 1860s, a middle-aged compositor complained that "many enter into apprenticeship hardly able to read or write in Russian, to say nothing of foreign languages."[57] Still, at least minimal literacy was necessary; many apprentice compositors had attended at least a year or two at a rural or urban primary school, and some had begun secondary education.[58]

In the shops, the training of compositors had declined. One employer complained in 1895 that in many firms apprenticeship had in fact become little more than child labor, a means to get "convenient and compliant material for producing work at low prices such as could not be achieved with adult workers."[59] Many firms also hired

55. *Naborshchik* 1:3 (November 17, 1902), pp. 53–54; *Pechatnoe iskusstvo* 2:3 (December 1902), p. 98.

56. Exact calculation of urban birth is difficult. Census data record that in Moscow in 1902, 38.6% of compositors were born in the city, compared to 18.7% of press workers in typographic shops and 13.1% in lithographic enterprises. Throughout all industry, by contrast, only 10.5% of workers were born in Moscow. *Perepis' Moskvy 1902 goda*, vypusk 2, table 6. The 1881 Petersburg census indicates that 37.8% of typographic workers and 16.1% of lithographic workers were born in the city, compared to 11.7% for all industrial and trade workers; the census does not provide separate information on compositors. *S.-Peterburg po perepisi 15 dekabria 1881 goda*, vol. 1, part 2, pp. 306–07. Unfortunately, available data do not indicate whether individuals not born in the city in which they resided were born in *other cities*, a background that was likely to have been relatively common among compositors, given their high rates of geographic mobility. A survey conducted in Moscow in 1907 found that nearly a third of all compositors had lived and worked at some time in another city. Svavitskii and Sher, *Ocherk polozheniia*, pp. 11–14. Most likely, the total number of urban-born compositors was rather higher than the census figures indicate.

57. *Tipografskii zhurnal* 1:12 (December 15, 1867), p. 52.

58. *Otchet po pervoi shkole pechatnogo dela I.R.T.O. za 1885–6 uchebnyi god*, p. 6; *Naborshchik* 1:14 (February 2, 1903), p. 241; Solov'ev, *Gosudar'ev pechatnyi dvor*, p. 101; *Istoriia leningradskogo soiuza*, p. 13; Svavitskii and Sher, *Ocherk polozheniia*, table 2. By contrast, many press workers were illiterate when hired and often remained so. *Trudy pervogo s"ezda*, p. 37; *Naborshchik* 1:15 (February 9, 1903), p. 255.

59. *Trudy pervogo s"ezda*, p. 27.

nedouchki—"half-way boys," as they were called by American printers in the nineteenth century—who had quit their low-paying apprenticeships in order to earn journeymen's wages after learning only the simple mechanics of setting a line of plain type. The majority of compositors were simple line compositors (*strochnye*) who could only set plain text. Above them were highly skilled specialists: design, table, and job compositors (*aktsidentnye, tablichnye,* and *melochnye naborshchiki*).

Finally, as in the pressroom, this new hierarchy of skill included an occupation—that of the *metranpazh*—whose role was an ambiguous mix of worker and supervisor. As a worker, the *metranpazh* (a Russification of *metteur en pages*) was responsible for the final imposition of the type and for locking up these pages of type into forms for printing. Before the 1830s, this job had been well-paying work delegated by the workers themselves to older compositors. By the end of the century, employers had eliminated this form of worker control of the labor process, and *metranpazhi* were chosen only by the owner or manager. At the same time, the responsibilities of the *metranpazh* often expanded to that of foreman: he was often responsible for the discipline of "his" compositors (in larger shops there were several *metranpazhi,* each with his own work group), for the distribution of copy, for calculating the payment of wages, for training apprentices, and occasionally even for hiring and firing workers. Some *metranpazhi* acted as subcontractors, accepting an entire job at a negotiated price and undertaking full responsibility for hiring, supervising, and paying compositors—workers named the worst of these "spiders."[60]

The changing role of the *metranpazh* reflected the changing division of labor and work process in type composition, but it did not indicate the complete loss of workers' autonomy. Payment by the piece (per thousand letters set) and the individualized structure of the work process made supervisory control of compositors impractical. Fines for breaches of discipline, common among factory workers and even press workers, rarely existed.[61] The speed and manner of work remained, quite literally, in a compositor's own hands. Some compositors added a collective dimension to this workplace control, creating small "companies" (*kompanii*) that negotiated with an employer for the price of an entire job and then handled all questions of payment, discipline, and

60. Trotskii, "Ekonomicheskie i sanitarnye usloviia," part 1, pp. 84–85; Bakhtiarov, *Slugi pechati,* pp. 34–35; Kolomnin, *Kratkie svedeniia,* pp. 66–67, 388–465; *Istoriia leningradskogo soiuza,* p. 29; *Tipografiia Lenizdata,* p. 12; Vechtomova, *Zdes' pechata-las' "Pravda,"* p. 25.

61. *Istoriia leningradskogo soiuza,* p. 37.

work process internally. At many newspapers, compositors decided among themselves—usually by lot—who would set illegible texts, who would work late, who would be assigned to break down and distribute the used type in the morning, how vacation days would be distributed, and when and how workers would be punished for truancy.[62]

Wage rates in printing reflected these changes in the skill structure of the industry, though complicated by the influence of where one worked.[63] Printing masters and *metranpazhi*, who stood on the border between labor and management, received the highest wages in the industry, together with office personnel such as proofreaders and book-keepers, and a few highly skilled craftsmen in lithographic firms. Beneath these stood compositors (whose average wage was still above the average industrial wage in Russia), followed by press workers. In any given craft, however, wages ranged widely. Lower than average wages were paid to workers in smaller and economically more marginal enterprises, where, it was said, the competitive strategy was "cheap and dirty" (*deshevo, da plokho*). Such shops were also the most inclined to abuse apprenticeship, often employing more "apprentices" than adults, or even relying exclusively on the labor of boys under the direction of a single skilled adult.[64] By contrast, large enterprises (and firms specializing in quality work) often paid better wages and were more attentive to proper training.

As a result of these discrepancies, a printing master in St. Petersburg in 1900 might earn as much as 150 rubles a month or as little as 40 rubles. Similarly, a press feeder could earn as much as 30 rubles a month and a taker-up as much as 20 rubles, though many earned as little as 10 rubles or less. In many small printing shops at the turn of the century, compositors were paid piece rates of only 14 kopecks

62. Ibid., pp. 11–12, 28–32, 37, 43; TsGAOR, f. 6864, op. 1, d. 60, pp. 1, 3; *Naborshchik* 1:1 (October 20, 1902), p. 4; 1:13 (January 26, 1903), p. 213; 1:14 (February 2, 1903), p. 233; Iuferovyi and Sokolovskii, *Akademicheskaia tipografiia*, pp. 93–94; *Kratkii istoricheskii obzor tipografii L.S.P.O.*, p. 9.

63. The following discussion of wages is based on professional journals, firm publications, and a number of scholarly studies, the most useful of which were Mikhailovskii, *Otchet za 1885 god glavnogo fabrichnogo inspektora*, pp. 189–90; Davydov, *Otchet za 1885 g. fabrichnogo inspektora*, pp. 172–73; Trotskii, "Ekonomicheskie i sanitarnye usloviia," part 1, pp. 76–86; Bernshtein-Kogan, *Chislennost'*, pp. 111–12, 182–86; Svavitskii and Sher, *Ocherk polozheniia*, pp. 19–21; and *Istoriia leningradskogo soiuza*, pp. 10–46.

64. *Tipografskii zhurnal* 2:3 (August 1, 1868), p. 9; *Obzor graficheskikh iskusstv* 1878, no. 7 (April 15), p. 47; *Russkii kur'er*, September 14, 1883, p. 2; Davydov, *Otchet za 1885 g. fabrichnogo inspektora*, pp. 72–78; *Peterburgskaia gazeta*, November 29, 1894, p. 3; *Trudy pervogo s"ezda*, pp. 27, 37–38, 44–45; *Naborshchik* 1:1 (October 20, 1902), p. 19; 1:50 (October 12, 1903), p. 749; Sher, *Istoriia*, p. 55; *Istoriia leningradskogo soiuza*, pp. 59–60.

per thousand letters set—even less if they were minors—while at a large and quality-oriented printing plant such as Suvorin's, which sought to attract the most highly skilled workers, the pay was 18 to 26 kopecks per thousand letters for book work, depending on the complexity of the material, and up to 23 kopecks for newspaper work.[65] A compositor thus might earn as little as 17 rubles a month or as much as 75. Wage levels also varied by city and were generally lower in Moscow than in St. Petersburg and even lower in the provinces.[66]

In general terms, then, one can speak of a deskilling of the Russian typographic printer (and of the lithographer and binder, whose crafts were also transformed) as a consequence of commercialization and technical modernization. However, this was more a structural phenomenon than an individual human experience. In Western Europe, skilled printing workers were often able to avoid the destructive consequences of similar changes because of strong traditions of collective association and struggle.[67] Russian printers lacked such organizations and did not collectively resist this transformation of the industry, but most printers nonetheless individually avoided the experience of skill degradation. The rapid expansion of production, the growing need for supervisors, and the persistent shortage of skilled labor encouraged firms to accommodate and even promote workers with well-developed skills, while filling the lower ranks with a mass of new recruits. A highly skilled pressman could usually find a well-paying job on one of the remaining hand presses, where specialized work was still done, or as a machine master. A highly skilled compositor could often find employment as a specialist setting complex tabular or display work, which paid considerably more than simple line composition, and many were promoted to *metranpazh* or even production manager (*faktor* or *zaveduiushchii*).[68] The ranks of simple line compositors, press feeders,

65. *Kratkii ocherk izdatel'skoi deiatel'nosti A. S. Suvorina*, p. 10.
66. In 1900, average earnings among printers were more than 20% higher in St. Petersburg than in Moscow, and more than 5% higher in Moscow than the nationwide average. Varzar, *Statisticheskie svedeniia*, pp. 10–13; Bernshtein-Kogan, *Chislennost'*, p. 183; Svavitskii and Sher, *Ocherk polozheniia*, p. 19.
67. See, for example, Shorter and Tilly, *Strikes in France*, pp. 148–49, 204–05, 346.
68. For a number of examples, see *Obzor graficheskikh iskusstv* 1878, no. 17 (September 15), p. 129; *Obzor pervoi vserossiiskoi vystavki pechatnogo dela* 29 (May 29, 1895), p. 7; *Graficheskie iskusstva i bumazhnaia promyshlennost'* 1:11 (July 1896), p. 174; 2:2 (January 1897), p. 31; *Vestnik graficheskogo dela* 25 (January 31, 1898), p. 2; *Pechatnoe iskusstvo* 1:1 (October 1901), p. 27; 1:2 (November 1901), pp. 61, 63; 2:3 (December 1902), p. 108; *Naborshchik* 1:1 (October 20, 1902), p. 18; 2:10 (February 1, 1904), pp. 170–71; 2:45 (October 3, 1904), p. 710; Lisovskii, *Kratkii ocherk tipografii Glazunovykh*, p. 92; *Pechatnia R. R. Golike*, p. 3; *Ivan Dmitrievich Galaktionov, 12/II/1915*.

signature folders, and the like were filled not with deskilled craftsmen but with the children of peasants and other workers entering the industry for the first time. The image of the degraded artisan suffering the effects of industrial modernization is simply not appropriate here. Though skills were indeed falling, individuals were not.

This is not to say that individuals did not suffer. Wages, though widely varying, were for most insufficient to avoid cramped living conditions and a meager diet. A government commission studying working conditions in St. Petersburg from 1902 to 1905 calculated that an unmarried male worker needed a minimum of 21 rubles a month to cover living expenses and a married worker with children needed 32 rubles, even if other family members were employed (considering the lower wages earned by women and children). Other surveys drew the poverty line even higher.[69] At work, considerable hardship resulted not only from the long workday and harassment by foremen and managers, but simply from the physical environment in which printers labored, though these conditions were not uniform. Small printing shops were the most ruinous to a worker's health. Often located in the basements or half-basements of buildings, they were usually the most poorly ventilated and lit, hot and stuffy in the summer and in the winter producing a "grave-like cold."[70] By contrast, some large firms installed modern ventilation, replaced kerosene lighting with cleaner electric lighting, attached protective devices to machinery, opened dining halls so that workers might eat in a clean environment, and insisted on regular sanitary measures to keep the workplace clean.[71] Most enterprises lay somewhere between these extremes.

Each craft presented the health of printing workers with its own special hazards. Typographic pressmen, for example, inhaled the fumes of inks and solvents and risked injury from exposed gears, pulleys, and belts on machinery. Lithographers breathed large amounts of stone dust and chemical fumes. Type compositors worked in the most deadly environment, breathing air filled with lead dust and often thick with tobacco smoke and the stench of the shop toilet and straining their eyes

69. Semanov, *Peterburgskie rabochie*, p. 85. See also Surh, *1905 in St. Petersburg*, p. 25, and Kir'ianov, *Zhiznennyi uroven'*, esp. pp. 168–90, 259–62.

70. *Naborshchik* 1:5 (December 1, 1902), p. 88; *Obzor graficheskikh iskusstv* 1878, no. 7 (April 15), p. 47; Trotskii, "Ekonomicheskie i sanitarnye usloviia," part 2, p. 93.

71. The most notable examples were, in Moscow, the Synod press, Levenson's after 1900, and *Moskovskii listok* after 1894, and in St. Petersburg, the Synod press, the Office for the Manufacture of Government Paper after 1899, Suvorin's after 1900, and the Senate press after 1901.

reading often illegible manuscripts under poor lighting. Because they stood for nine or more hours a day with one arm held close to the chest to hold the composing stick and the opposite arm and shoulder raised to reach type from the case, they strained their legs and backs and suffered from lack of physical exertion that made their breathing shallow, slowed their circulation, and thus left them susceptible to disease. According to physicians who studied compositors, their ailments included trembling of the hands, swelling of the legs, varicose veins, rheumatism, skeletal deformities, nearsightedness, chronic conjunctivitis, lung disease, lead poisoning, and especially tuberculosis. Although lead poisoning was rarely a direct cause of death, it produced anemia, digestive ailments (worsened by workers' high consumption of alcohol and poor diet), hardening of the arteries, and generally increased susceptibility to disease.

The single most deadly effect of the compositors' work was tuberculosis. Easily transmitted in the dusty and unsanitary environment of the workplace, it attacked systems often already weakened by lead poisoning, poor nutrition, heavy drinking, and other diseases. Tuberculosis was widespread among compositors, audible in the constant coughing and expectoration heard in the composition room (which further spread the disease) and visible in workers' common paleness and emaciation. With good reason, the labor of the compositor was often described as "murderous." One study by a provincial physician in the 1890s found that the mortality rates of compositors were among the highest of all workers. Other studies, in Russia and elsewhere, confirmed his conclusions.[72] Most compositors died before they were forty, and many did not survive past their twenties.[73]

Workplace and craft may have been the most decisive determinants of working-class experience, but workers also lived in a larger social world. Most printing workers lived near the shops in which they

72. Sviatlovskii, *Truzheniki pechatnogo dela*. This was a reprint of a study that originally appeared in *Zemskii vrach*. Quoted in *Obzor pervoi vserossiiskoi vystavki* 9 (March 20, 1895), p. 4.
73. Trotskii, "Ekonomicheskie i sanitarnye usloviia," part 2, pp. 87–106; Virenius, "Gigiena naborshchika"; *Trudy pervogo s"ezda*, pp. 52–53 (report of Dr. E. R. Mossin); *Russkie vedomosti*, August 10, 1894, p. 3; *Obzor pervoi vserossiiskoi vystavki* 9 (March 20, 1895), pp. 4–5; *Trudy pervogo vserossiiskogo s"ezda fabrichnykh vrachei* (Moscow, 1910), vol. 1, pp. 119–26 (report of P. V. Beliaevskii); *Entsiklopedicheskii slovar'*, vol. 33, pp. 216–20 (F. Erisman); *Istoriia leningradskogo soiuza*, pp. 49–54; Orlov, *Poligraficheskaia promyshlennost' Moskvy*, pp. 267–68; *Tipografiia Lenizdata*, pp. 23–24. For a comparative perspective, see *Obzor graficheskikh iskusstv* 1879, no. 6 (March 15), pp. 44–45 (essay by "Amicus," based on German studies), and Hamilton and Verrill, *Hygiene of the Printing Trades*.

worked,[74] and this is where workers spent most of their rather limited free time. Memoirs of workers describe visiting local taverns and beer halls, frequenting the local bathhouse on Saturdays, attending the local church on holidays, and purchasing food and other necessities from local shopkeepers. Although memoirs recall holiday excursions out of town to fish, swim, or walk in the woods, apart from some workers' rare visits to public literary readings, lectures, or concerts, workers apparently seldom frequented other parts of the city (unless they changed jobs).

Like workers in most artisanal manufacturing and commerce, the printers' neighborhood was the inner city. As the industry expanded and larger plants were built, enterprises and workers' residences became more dispersed, but only relatively so. In St. Petersburg in 1881, 76 percent of printing workers lived in the five centermost districts of the city (Admiralteiskaia, Kazanskaia, Spasskaia, Liteinaia, Moskovskaia) and across the Neva on Vasil'evskii Island; by comparison, only 44 percent of metal and machine workers lived in these districts. By 1900, though only 51 percent of printing workers still lived in these same districts, most of the others lived nearby in the innermost wards of the Narvskaia district, where the massive Office for the Manufacture of Government Paper was located. Less than 8 percent of all printing workers lived in the heavily industrial Aleksandro-Nevskaia and Vyborgskaia districts, a growing but still relatively small proportion, and virtually none in the city's industrial suburbs.[75]

In Moscow, similarly, half of all printing workers in 1890 resided within the innermost of the city's central rings; the slightly wider range defined by the circular boulevards, where the concentric walls of the old city once stood, encompassed more than two-thirds of the residences of all printing workers. By contrast, more than three-quarters of

74. This is suggested by memoirs as well as by the high correlation between the location of the workplaces and the residences of printing workers. *Spisok zavedenii pechati* (1875); *S.-Peterburg po perepisi 1881 goda*, vol. 1, part 2; *Torgovo-promyshlennye zavedeniia Moskvy v 1885–1890 gg.*, pp. 16–19, 26–29; *Pravitel'stvennyi vestnik*, December 11(23), 1894, p. 4; *S.-Peterburg po perepisi 1900 goda*, vypusk 2, p. 12; *Spisok fabrik i zavodov* (1903), pp. 150–55; Ginlein, *Adresnaia kniga*, pp. 80–91; Pogozhev, *Adresnaia kniga*, pp. 104–08, 113–15. Detailed calculations based on these sources may be found in my "Consciousness and Conflict in a Russian Industry," tables 5.3 and 5.4. Contiguous patterns of work and residence were common among Russian workers generally in the two capitals. Bater, *St. Petersburg*, pp. 128–39, 280–95; Bradley, *Muzhik and Muscovite*, pp. 232–34.

75. *Spisok zavedenii pechati* (1875); *Pravitel'stvennyi vestnik*, December 11 (23), 1894, p. 4; Ginlein, *Adresnaia kniga*, pp. 80–86; *S.-Peterburg po perepisi 1881 goda*, vol. 1, part 2; *S.-Peterburg po perepisi 1900 goda*, vypusk 2. See also Zelnik, *Labor and Society*, pp. 215–20, 231–34; and Bater, *St. Petersburg*, pp. 91–110, 228–54.

all manufacturing workers—including 80 percent of all metal workers and 97 percent of all textile workers—lived beyond the boulevards or across the river. Gradually, large printing plants grew up in these outer districts, and workers' residency patterns shifted with them, yet the move was never very far. By 1900, although 42 percent of printing workers were employed outside of the boulevards or across the river, they worked mostly in neighborhoods nearest the center.[76]

Life in the city center meant exposure to both hardships and social and cultural diversity. In St. Petersburg, the largest concentration of printing workers was found in the districts and wards surrounding the Haymarket, the worst inner-city neighborhood—overcrowded, unsanitary, and full of disease and crime. Other residents of these districts included shopkeepers, artisanal masters, and owners of small manufactories, but mainly the poor: artisans, commercial employees, itinerant laborers, service workers, prostitutes, vagrants, and petty thieves. Printers also lived nearby in such neighborhoods as the less congested and more fashionable commercial districts beside the Nevskii Prospect or across the Nevskii in predominantly upper-class residential neighborhoods. But there they typically lived crowded together with other workers in upper floors, garrets, or cellars or around the corner in an alley or side street.[77]

In Moscow, too, most printers lived in the densely populated and socially diverse central districts of the city. As in St. Petersburg, the lower classes of the inner city included few industrial workers but large numbers of tailors, shoemakers, bakers, cabinetmakers, goldsmiths, printers, salesclerks, servants, waiters, peddlers, prostitutes, and the casual laborers, vagrants, paupers, and criminals of Moscow's notorious skid row, the Khitrov market. And as in St. Petersburg, these central districts also included fashionable shops and restaurants, the university and the conservatory, theaters and government offices, and the residences of the rich and powerful as well as more modest professionals, writers, artists, merchants, and entrepreneurs.[78]

76. *Torgovo-promyshlennye zavedeniia goroda Moskvy v 1885–1890 gg.*, pp. 16–19, 26–29; *Spisok fabrik i zavodov*, pp. 150–55; Ginlein, *Adresnaia kniga*, pp. 86–91; Pogozhev, *Adresnaia kniga*, pp. 104–08. See also Bradley, *Muzhik and Muscovite*, pp. 52–60.

77. Surh, *1905 in St. Petersburg*, pp. 38–43; Zelnik, *Labor and Society*, pp. 242–43; Bater, *St. Petersburg*, pp. 166–67, 173–75, 193–207, 342–53, 373–80, 401–06; *S.-Peterburg po perepisi 1881 goda*, vol. 1, part 1, and part 2, map 5 and table 1.

78. Bradley, *Muzhik and Muscovite*, pp. 53–55, 273–81; Laura Engelstein, *Moscow, 1905*, pp. 43–46; *Torgovo-promyshlennye zavedeniia*, table 1 and maps 2–7; *Statisticheskii atlas goroda Moskvy*, pp. 55–58, 63–64.

It has been suggested that the greater visibility of inequality in the center of the city helped to promote "class consciousness" among workers living there.[79] With equal logic it has been argued that the closer "spatial relationships among classes" of the inner city tended to narrow the social distance between classes and hence to moderate class antagonisms.[80] Ultimately, other experiences and other influences would decide how these ambiguous circumstances would be perceived and made meaningful. This was generally true of the structured conditions in which workers lived. Mechanization and a deepening division of labor had obliterated some crafts, marginalized others, created new unskilled and semi-skilled jobs, and made apprenticeship in many cases little more than a veil for child labor. However, individual workers with traditional skills often found opportunities for advancement, while the less skilled jobs were filled mainly by peasants and others entering the industry for the first time. At a certain level, there was no ambiguity in workers' position. Most workers, whatever the relative changes in their condition, remained subordinate and poor and faced long hours of daily labor in a murderous physical environment. Still, the definition of these conditions as unjust depended on matters of perception that the structures themselves did not determine.

79. Smith, *Red Petrograd*, p. 13.
80. Koenker, *Moscow Workers*, pp. 10, 28.

CHAPTER TWO

The Morality
of Authority

Karl Marx believed that it was the historic function of the capitalist bourgeoisie to "piteously" tear asunder "the motley feudal ties that bound man to his 'natural superiors,' " leaving "no other nexus between man and man than naked self-interest, than callous 'cash payment.' "[1] More often, capitalists have resisted so desanctifying social relationships. Naked self-interest has been clothed in notions of merit, responsibility, morality, and common interest. As in non-capitalist societies, relations of authority and inequality have tended to be "euphemized,"[2] to be presented as relations other than those solely of power, appropriation, and subordination.[3] This euphemization is not a simple matter of dominant groups cleverly disguising reality in order to convince subordinates that the existing order is just. Those holding power often themselves have felt a need, as Max Weber argued in explaining a function of religion, for the "psychological reassurance of legitimacy," to feel that their own authority is held by right.[4] This is also not simply a matter of self-deception. As will be seen, the euphemization of authority and inequality has entailed behavior to make these claims plausible. And these actions in turn have had unintended effects.

1. Marx and Engels, "The Communist Manifesto," in *The Marx-Engels Reader,* p. 475.
2. Bourdieu, *Outline of a Theory of Practice,* p. 191.
3. See also James Scott, *Weapons of the Weak,* ch. 8, and *Domination and the Arts of Resistance.*
4. Max Weber, *The Sociology of Religion* (Boston, 1963), p. 107; cited and discussed in James Scott, *Domination and the Arts of Resistance,* p. 68.

The need to legitimize relations of power and inequality has been especially strong during periods when new forms of social or political organization are being established. During the early years of European industrialization, entrepreneurs often presented themselves to the public in traditional moral dress. English employers, as John Stuart Mill wrote in the 1840s, often continued to insist that "the relation between rich and poor . . . be amiable, moral, and sentimental; affectionate tutelage on the one side, respectful and grateful deference on the other."[5] Such standards helped to reassure employers of their own morality and honor, but also, as Mill recognized, to ensure their workers' "obedience to the rules prescribed for them."[6]

Russian employers also often hesitated before the "icy water of egotistical calculation," and partly due to the very "philistine sentimentalism" that Marx believed it to be their historical mission to destroy.[7] Facing a society in which entrepreneurship was generally considered immoral by definition,[8] employers sought to demonstrate that their social honor was consistent with traditional values. The merchant and manufacturer Timofei Prokhorov reflected such sentiments when he argued in 1850 that "it is permissible to possess wealth only if it is used to help the needy or to assist in some way or another the spiritual and moral improvement of mankind."[9] Acting in a society still caught in the ambiguous "social space between the immobility of caste and the dynamism of class,"[10] employers were reluctant to abandon the accepted model of morally responsible authority for a still-alien ideal of social relations based on free contract between individuals.

Employers' behavior also reflected a wider cultural anxiety over the disintegrating social fabric. Many privileged Russians during the second half of the nineteenth century, including owners of a number of large industrial and commercial enterprises, expressed concern over the growing numbers of workers and poor in the cities. Criminality, disease, and moral depravity seemed to threaten the social order, a threat made tangible by the growing incidence of labor unrest. The upper-

5. *Principles of Political Economy,* vol. 2, p. 319.
6. Ibid. See also Newby, "Paternalism and Capitalism," pp. 59–73; Bendix, *Work and Authority in Industry,* pp. 46–73; David Roberts, *Paternalism in Early Victorian England;* Donald Reid, "Industrial Paternalism," pp. 579–607.
7. Marx and Engels, "The Communist Manifesto," p. 475.
8. Ruckman, *The Moscow Business Elite,* pp. 7–14; Buryshkin, *Moskva kupecheskaia,* pp. 21–47; Bill, *The Forgotten Class,* ch. 7.
9. Quoted in Ruckman, *The Moscow Business Elite,* p. 92.
10. Rieber, *Merchants and Entrepreneurs,* p. 416.

class response was above all moralistic and tutelary, focusing on charity, welfare, and reform. Organizations were established to "encourage industriousness," to "disseminate useful books," and to teach temperance among the masses. The founders of these societies wished to create, in the words of the chronicler of the Moscow Society to Encourage Industriousness, "a rational, sober, literate, honorable workingman . . . a goal dear to every Russian who values the growth and progress of our industry and productivity."[11]

Employers tended to respond to these complex challenges to their authority, honor, and self-esteem with traditional means. The owners of large enterprises, especially, in many industries assumed the part of paternal guardians of labor, offering workers free medical care, schools, libraries, and cultural activities.[12] In the printing industry, employers similarly created a network of trade institutions and workplace practices directed at improving the lives of workers and presenting themselves to the public as "humane and enlightened" individuals. In such efforts, of course, there was no simple line of division between self-interest and moral evaluation. Employers naturally and necessarily calculated on the basis of both.

Russian printing employers sought to infuse social relationships with a sense of moral community. Emile Durkheim argued that anxiety over the disintegration of traditional social bonds in the course of industrial modernization naturally led to efforts to reintegrate the individual into newer forms of community, consisting of both ties of cooperation derived from economic interdependence and the bonds of common moral values and rules.[13] This was precisely the meaning printing employers in Russia had in mind when they spoke of the workplace and the trade as a "family" united by common interests and love. And of course, like the model to which they referred, this was to be a traditional family in which affection and authority, and economic

11. *Obshchestvo pooshchreniia trudoliubiia v Moskve*, p. 277. See also Bradley, *Muzhik and Muscovite*, esp. pp. 249–354; Zelnik, *Labor and Society*; Lindenmeyr, "Charity and the Problem of Unemployment," pp. 1–22; idem., "A Russian Experiment in Voluntarism," pp. 429–51.

12. Owen, *Capitalism and Politics*, pp. 132–34; Rieber, *Merchants and Entrepreneurs*, pp. 126–28, 146, 159, 205, 420, 425; Ruckman, *The Moscow Business Elite*, pp. 163–64; Zelnik, *Labor and Society*, pp. 177, 285–89, 336–40.

13. Giddens, *Emile Durkheim: Selected Writings*, pp. 1–29, 89–107; Giddens, *Capitalism and Modern Social Theory*, pp. 66–81, 95–118. See also the discussion of "moral community" among French artisans in Sewell, *Work and Revolution in France*, pp. 32–37.

interdependence and inequality, were combined. My attention in this chapter, I would emphasize, is focused not on whether such a community actually existed—in many ways, as will be seen, it was an illusion—but on employers' efforts to create such a community, and what these efforts reveal about employers' concerns, values, and sense of social self.

EMPLOYER ACTIVISTS

Employers who sought to build such a moral community in the printing industry recognized that they constituted a minority. Most owners of printing firms, they complained, were distrustful of social activity, apathetic toward any but their own immediate interests, and exploitative of others.[14] They were probably right. The active minority of employers whose words and practices are the subject of this chapter—including owners of private enterprises, directors of corporately owned plants, and directors of state-owned firms—represented no more than one-fifth of the total number of printing enterprises in St. Petersburg and a somewhat smaller proportion in Moscow. Only seventeen employers in St. Petersburg and eleven in Moscow served as officers or made donations to one of the printers' assistance funds between the 1860s and 1904; only thirty-two employers joined the Moscow Graphic Circle in the early 1880s; only fifty firms sent apprentices to the Petersburg printing school during its busiest first decade after 1884; only fifty-two Petersburg employers and six from Moscow attended the national Congress of Printing that was held in St. Petersburg in 1895; only forty-four employers were members of the Russian Printing Society in St. Petersburg and eighteen in Moscow by 1903; finally, only eighteen printing firms in St. Petersburg and seven in Moscow left any evidence of the sort of paternalistic measures within their own enterprises that the supporters of the trade community promoted. And if we narrow the definition of employer activism to individuals involved regularly in more than one organization or activity, the circle narrows still more. (The members of this main activist cohort are listed in the Appendix.)

14. *Tipografskii zhurnal* 1:22–23 (June 1, 1868), p. 91; *Obzor graficheskikh iskusstv* 1878, no. 24 (December 15), p. 184; 1879, no. 20 (October 15), p. 113; 1880, no. 23 (December 1), p. 175; 1883, no. 9 (May 1), pp. 7–8; 1884, no. 5 (March 1), pp. 35–36; no. 22 (November 15), p. 171; *Pervaia russkaia shkola*, p. 9; *Pechatnoe iskusstvo* 1:2 (November 1901), p. 49.

What sort of minority was this?[15] In many respects, its membership resembles that of other groups of socially or culturally active entrepreneurs. Reginald Zelnik has identified as "advanced entrepreneurs" in St. Petersburg in the 1860s large-scale industrialists "either of close foreign background or . . . Russian nobles with advanced technical educations."[16] Describing activist entrepreneurs of the 1890s, Alfred Rieber similarly found a preponderance of foreigners, nobles, and technically trained "professional managers."[17] If we substitute advanced education generally for technical training, these descriptions indicate the backgrounds of many employer-activists in printing as well.

A large proportion of employer-activists were from ethnically non-Russian backgrounds, especially in St. Petersburg, where foreign entrepreneurship was more extensive than in Moscow. Of the six largest financial donors to the Petersburg printing school, two were born in Germany (Alexander Böhnke and Heinrich Schröder), two were the sons or grandsons of immigrants (Roman Golike and Josef Lehmann), and one was raised by an immigrant family (Petr Mikhailov). Ethnic non-Russians accounted for five of the seven publishers of trade journals for printers (Rudolf Schneider, Eduard Hoppe, Isidor Goldberg, Roman Golike, Josef Lehmann). And of the nineteen employers who paid 300 rubles to be considered "founding members" at the first meeting of the Russian Printing Society, ten were immigrants or their children; these also accounted for most of the officers elected to the first directing board of the society. Even in Moscow, where the numbers of foreign entrepreneurs were far smaller, such non-Russians as the Tallin-born Peter Jürgensohn and his son Boris and especially the Bavarian-born Otto Herbeck played major roles in almost all of the associations of Moscow printers. Memories of European traditions of craft association, experiences as former workers, and perhaps the moral insecurity of being both foreigner and entrepreneur in a cultural environment that distrusted both may all have contributed to the activism of these men.

In different ways, activist native Russians were also distinguished from the ordinary printing-shop owner. Many activists were members of the nobility, a status they usually gained through state service. Of the twenty-four employers who participated in discussions at the 1895 printing congress, besides the eleven who were from recent foreign

15. The preceding calculations and the following discussion are based on a data file on employer activists in the printing industry. See Appendix for a list of the major sources.

16. Zelnik, *Labor and Society*, p. 286.

17. Rieber, *Merchants and Entrepreneurs*, pp. 250–52.

backgrounds, seven were nobles (Evgenii Evdokimov, Aleksei Il'in, Spiridon Nedel'kovich, Petr Iablonskii, and Nikolai Palibin from St. Petersburg, and Ivan Kushnerev and A. A. Levenson from Moscow). Similarly, of the eighteen Petersburg employers who undertook paternalistic measures in their own firms, at least nine had noble status (or in a couple of cases were the sons of personal nobles), mostly through state service, which several continued as directors of state-owned printing plants.[18]

However, it was not so much the formal marks of status itself—or the non-noble titles of "honored citizen" (*pochetnyi grazhdanin*) that had been granted to several others—but the more substantive distinctions of education, public service, and cultural achievement that for these activist entrepreneurs were invariably associated with rank. Indeed, many of the most active printing employers, regardless of their legal status or background, may be defined as members of an entrepreneurial "intelligentsia." In addition to owning printing enterprises or directing state-owned firms, they were also publishers, editors, and writers. All four of the printing employers who participated in the planning committee for the 1895 Congress—Roman Golike, Vissarion Komarov, Aleksei Il'in, and Vasilii Vishniakov—were publishers or editors as well as owners or directing managers of print shops (and, appropriately, two were nobles and one was the son of an immigrant). Among the founding members of the Printing Society, at least ten of the nineteen employers in St. Petersburg and four of seven in Moscow were also editors, publishers, or booksellers. Some of these—such as Ivan Sytin and Peter Jürgensohn in Moscow, and Adolf Marx, S. M. Propper, Petr Soikin, and Aleksei Suvorin in St. Petersburg—were in fact better known to the public in these roles. As men whose professions were tied up with Russia's developing civic culture, these publishers, editors, and booksellers were more likely than printers whose lives were focused more narrowly on production to be attentive to society's moral standards, especially since they were also much more in the public eye, and their public was a literate and often critical one.

The visibility of employer-activists was also a function of the relatively large size of most of their enterprises. Taken together, the nineteen employers who founded the Printing Society employed more than three thousand workers, about one-quarter of the entire printing labor

18. Owners of private firms: Glazunov, Iablonskii, Il'in, Kirshbaum, and Suvorin. Directors of state enterprises: Gavrilov (Synod), Golitsyn (Office for the Manufacture of Government Paper), Markevich (Senate), Nedel'kovich (Naval Ministry).

force. This concentration of labor was even more pronounced among activists in the Moscow branch of the society, where the seven employers who founded the society employed over two thousand workers, more than one-quarter of all printing workers in Moscow. The same source of activism can be seen among supporters of the assistance funds. The seventeen employers in St. Petersburg and eleven in Moscow who served as officers of or made donations to one of the funds employed a total of over two thousand workers. Similarly, though only eighteen Petersburg employers and seven Moscow employers left evidence of organizing and subsidizing within their own firms assistance funds, schools, choirs, and libraries, those who did employed approximately forty-five hundred workers in St. Petersburg and over two thousand workers in Moscow. As owners of large enterprises, these men controlled greater resources to invest in various welfare measures for workers. They also had particular reason to be threatened by the naked exploitation often practiced by owners of marginal shops trying to compete and reason to be concerned about the hazards and costs of an ill-trained and ill-behaved labor force.

THE HONOR OF THE TRADE

Activist employers formulated their vision of social relations in the industry most commonly with the metaphor of "family." Rudolf Schneider argued in 1868 that "an enterprise can benefit everyone only when its members consider themselves to be a single family."[19] In 1903, Ivan Sytin similarly spoke of his "close, though numerous, family of employees and workers."[20] And the intervening years were filled with declarations of commitment to building a "family of printers" (sem'ia tipografov) and of admiration for its proponents.[21] Printers were not unusual in making use of such rhetoric. The metaphor of a social family was a universal image of interdependent social relations often used by Russian advocates of traditional forms of social cohesion.[22]

The notion of social family, however, was open and flexible enough to contain different meanings. Partly, these meanings changed over

19. *Tipografskii zhurnal* 2:9–10 (November 15, 1868), p. 34.
20. *Knizhnyi vestnik* 1903, no. 18 (May 4), p. 561.
21. For example, *Obzor graficheskikh iskusstv* 1883, no. 23–24 (December 15), pp. 199–203.
22. See the account of the banquet at the Putilov factory in St. Petersburg in 1870, in Zelnik, *Labor and Society,* pp. 336–40, and esp. p. 338, quoting the evaluation by *Birzhevye vedomosti.*

time. Before the 1880s, when the scale of enterprise remained relatively small, employers typically spoke of themselves and their workers alike as *truzheniki* ("workmen," though with a more respectable connotation than *rabochie* or *rabotniki*) or simply as "printers"—*tipografy* or even *tipografshchiki*. Trade journals often praised employers who treated their subordinates not as "workers" but as "colleagues in their great endeavor."[23] Employers who continued to speak in these terms in later years were frequently owners of relatively small shops and often themselves former workers. But as the structure of enterprises changed, this fraternal ideal yielded ground to more hierarchical ways of representing the family of printers. Employers increasingly came to describe themselves as benevolent "fathers" caring for their (hopefully dutiful) worker "children."[24]

This metamorphosis, and its association with the increasing size of enterprises, was far from absolute, however. Owners of large enterprises were sometimes attracted to a fraternal image of labor relations. Ivan Sytin, the owner of one of the largest printing companies in Russia, liked to portray himself as working side by side with his many hundreds of workers.[25] Sytin's lower-class origins might have influenced this ideal, but we find the same model being presented by owners from privileged backgrounds. Ivan Kushnerev, a former landowner and state official and the owner of another of Moscow's largest printing houses, similarly insisted on "the close common labor" (*druzhnoe sotrudnichestvo*) of owners and workers.[26] Conversely, paternalistic notions of social family were not limited to the owners of larger firms or to men from elite backgrounds, nor were they heard only in later years. Already in the 1860s, even a small employer from immigrant worker background, Rudolf Schneider, could envision the ideal employer as "the father of the family," extending to his workers "a helpful hand," attending to their education and welfare, and generally assuring their "well-being."[27] Sometimes, the relation between fraternal mutuality and paternalistic benevolence was simply muddled, as in the notion of

23. *Obzor graficheskikh iskusstv* 1884, no. 1 (January 1), p. 7.

24. For example, *Vestnik graficheskogo dela* 22 (November 18, 1897), p. 221; *Piatidesiatiletnii iubilei tipografii I. G. Chuksina*, pp. 4–5.

25. Dinershtein, *I. D. Sytin*, p. 177. The author speaks of Sytin being inspired by a "pathos of mutual labor."

26. *Dvadtsatipiatiletie tipografii t-va I. N. Kushnerev*, p. 17. For other examples, see *Naborshchik* 1:12 (January 9, 1903), p. 206; *Aktsionernoe obshchestvo O. I. Leman*, p. 30.

27. *Tipografskii zhurnal* 2:9–10 (November 15, 1868), pp. 34, 37; *Obzor graficheskikh iskusstv* 1878, no. 10 (June 1), p. 71; 1881, no. 18 (September 15), p. 135.

workers as employers' "younger brothers" (*men'shie brat'ia* or *men'-shaia bratiia*).[28] Even more ambiguous was the suggestion by Aleksei Suvorin in 1881 that employers ought to display "a fatherly relation to their younger brother."[29]

These apparent anomalies and ambiguities suggest the common moral logic behind this rhetoric of community. Like other entrepreneurs during times of industrialization, printers in Russia faced a society in which elites and commoners alike viewed businessmen as greedy, dishonest, and immoral. However, as manufacturers of *cultural* products printers earned a measure of respect that most other employers could not. Printing has universally been viewed as an "art" as much as a business or craft, the press as a tool of culture and civilization as much as of commerce.[30] In Russia, where the freedom of the printed word was more restricted and thus its value more appreciated, recognition of the special honor of the printing trade was especially strong. As a speaker observed in 1880 at a fiftieth anniversary celebration of the career of one Petersburg printing employer, although many other businesses have been viewed as disreputable "not a single voice has been raised against the art of printing."[31]

Society's blessing also brought a burden. Printing employers were expected to behave according to a higher moral standard. Journalists, especially, derided printers for allowing their art to become "the same as any other business, like opening an office or setting up a factory,"[32] and for often revealing a "disgraceful desire to line their own pockets."[33] These critics, as writers, may well have had professional and personal reasons for resenting the greed of printers and publishers.

28. *Obzor graficheskikh iskusstv* 1884, no. 4 (February 15), p. 29.

29. Quoted from the newspaper *Novoe vremia* in Ambler, *Russian Journalism*, p. 170.

30. Typical of such expressions were speeches made by both printers and public guests at printers' festivals held in a number of cities in the eastern United States in the mid-1800s. Brenton, *Voices from the Press.*

31. *Obzor graficheskikh iskusstv* 1880, no. 24 (December 15), p. 184.

32. A comment in the liberal-populist weekly *Molva* in 1876, quoted in *Ocherki po istorii russkoi zhurnalistiki i kritiki*, vol. 2, p. 450.

33. Article reprinted from *S.-Peterburgskie vedomosti* in *Knizhnyi vestnik* 1903, no. 49 (December 7), pp. 1571–75 (quotation on p. 1572). For similar critiques, see "Literaturnye rabochie," *Sovremennik* 89 (October 1861), part 2, p. 204; *Knigovedenie* 7–8 (September 3, 1894), p. 32; Bakhtiarov, *Slugi pechati*, pp. 37, 77–78, 184, 189–91; Lemke, *Dumy zhurnalista*, pp. 24–42. Soviet historians of publishing often judged their subject from the same moral high ground as these earlier critics, admiring "idealistic" publishers motivated by intellectual purpose and condemning "bourgeois commercial publishers" whose only goal was profit. For example, Belov and Tolstiakov, *Russkie izdateli;* Dinershtein, *I. D. Sytin;* idem, "Izdatel'skaia deiatel'nost' A. S. Suvorina."

But they articulated their complaints through widely accepted values about the proper moral behavior expected of guardians of the printing art.

Many printing employers evidently cared little what society thought of them or at least kept their values to themselves and directed their energies precisely toward the narrow concerns of business that society despised. Others, like many employers in Western countries, challenged the disrepute into which they were cast by asserting a new morality by which business would be honored. This was seen from the moment that printers acquired their own public voice, with the establishment of trade journals starting in the late 1860s. A regular feature in the trade press was the biographies of employers and managers who, it was said, had worked their way up from the shop floor by virtue of dedication, honesty, hard work, and ability.[34] Individual employers also sometimes represented themselves to others in terms of this new work ethic. At a celebration marking the opening of A. A. Levenson's new plant in Moscow in 1900, a banner proclaimed Levenson's motto: "Labor improbus omnia vincit."[35] Aleksei Suvorin, one of St. Petersburg's most successful publishers and printers, observed in a private letter written in 1881 that though he owned "a huge business, with a turnover of nearly a million [rubles a year], I have known no entertainment or pleasure, but only backbreaking labor [katorzhnyi trud]."[36] Such asceticism among the rich, according to Max Weber, was part of the "spirit of capitalism," though here, of course, it was present in the absence of Protestant faith.[37]

Most commonly, printing employers defended their moral worth by presenting an ideal of management that conformed to traditional norms of social behavior. At banquets, at professional meetings, and in their trade press, activist printing employers, from the 1860s into the

34. For example, Obzor graficheskikh iskusstv 1879, no. 13 (July 15), p. 99; 1880, no. 16 (August 15), pp. 123–24. See also sources on individual careers cited in Chapter 1. On the development of a "conscious work ethic" among Russian businessmen generally in the second half of the nineteenth century, see Ruckman, The Moscow Business Elite, pp. 66–72.

35. Levenson, Istoricheskii ocherk, p. 12.

36. Quoted in Dinershtein, "Izdatel'skaia deiatel'nost' A. S. Suvorina," p. 84.

37. There was some Protestant influence provided by immigrants, of course, though Suvorin was Orthodox and Levenson possibly Jewish. In other industries Old Believers introduced values that had an affinity with the Protestant ethic. However, partly due to restrictions on who could own a press, few if any printers appear to have been Old Believers.

early 1900s, regularly voiced their acceptance of society's condemnation of profit-minded business but carefully distanced themselves from it. Printing, these employers insisted, "is not a craft, but an *ars liberalis.*" Printers do not manufacture "commodities" but serve the "cause of progress and civilization."[38]

The familiar image of the printer as *Kulturträger* was thus adopted in defense of their own honor, but it was also used, as it was used against them, as a critical standard. Rudolf Schneider, for example, expressed his dismay at the "cold, calculating egoism" of so many of his fellow printers, who "own a printing firm only with the aim of getting the greatest profit from it." Such men, in his view, were mere "capitalists" who "defiled the honored name" of printer.[39] Other employers similarly disparaged "capitalists," insisting that the printing "art" was alien to profiteering,[40] and condemning the "insolent exploitation of labor."[41] Such moralistic anti-capitalism could be bigoted, highlighting the emotional and traditional values involved, as when blame for the problems of the industry was cast on Jews who allegedly touched "this clean trade with their filthy hands."[42]

Positive visions of social community were also steeped in a moral language. Activist employers spoke endlessly of the need to imbue social relationships with benevolence, charity, honor, and love (*blagodeianie, blagotvoritel'nost', chest', liubov'*). They spoke of these qualities when praising the public lives of other employers and in representing themselves. Aleksei Suvorin typically described himself as a "good employer," a man of "heart, goodness, and even simplicity."[43] His

38. *Sovremennye izvestiia,* April 24, 1868, p. 1; Vol'f, *K dvadtsatipiatiletiiu,* p. 14; *Obzor graficheskikh iskusstv* 1880, no. 24 (December 15), p. 184; *Trudy pervogo s"ezda,* pp. 37, 41; Bakhtiarov, *Slugi pechati,* p. 37. The very titles of most of their professional journals—from *Survey of the Graphic Arts* in the 1870s and 1880s to *Printing Art* in the early 1900s—reflected this self-image of printing as a noble art.

39. *Tipografskii zhurnal* 2:11–12 (December 15, 1868), p. 43; *Obzor graficheskikh iskusstv* 1878, no. 24 (December 15), p. 184; 1881, no. 6 (March 15), p. 42; no. 18 (October 1), p. 135.

40. *Knizhnyi vestnik* 1860, no. 10 (n.d.), p. 78; 1863, no. 16 (August 31), p. 284; 1904, no. 34 (August 29), pp. 961–64; *Tipografskii zhurnal* 2:1 (July 1, 1868), p. 2; *Obzor graficheskikh iskusstv* 1882, no. 3–4 (February 1 and 15), pp. 11–12; *Trudy pervogo s"ezda,* pp. 44, 46; Russkoe Obshchestvo deiatelei pechatnogo dela, Moskovskoe otdelenie (RODPD-MO), *Kratkii otchet,* p. 4.

41. *Knizhnyi vestnik* 1903, no. 49 (December 7), p. 1572.

42. *Obzor graficheskikh iskusstv* 1878, no. 7 (April 15), p. 50. Similar sentiments were expressed in the lead article in this issue (probably by R. Schneider) and in a letter entitled "Evrei—vragi tipografskogo dela" (Jews—enemies of printing) in *Obzor graficheskikh iskusstv* 1883, no. 21 (November 1), p. 182.

43. Dinershtein, "Izdatel'skaia deiatel'nost' A. S. Suvorina," p. 84.

assistant manager, Vasilii Terskii, agreed, judging by a panegyric poem that he read to workers describing their "loving" (*liubveobil'-nyi*) boss.[44]

Moral representations of social relations were very often efforts to euphemize domination, to show that social relations were just by framing them in traditional terms. Interested motivations need not only be inferred. Already in the 1860s, Rudolf Schneider—who had experienced the 1848 revolution in Germany as an apprentice—warned his fellow employers of the hazards of "mercenary" labor relations, pointing to the trade union struggles and strikes that were then endemic in Western Europe, including among printing workers.[45] Schneider was not alone in hoping to prevent "the emergence of a dangerous proletariat in our midst."[46] Although only a handful of small strikes by printing workers are known to have occurred in St. Petersburg or Moscow before 1903,[47] strikes by printers in Western Europe and increasingly by workers in other Russian industries suggested that a threat to employers' authority might be incipient, especially as the industry grew and changed.

Workers also presented a more immediate and everyday threat to employers' authority. As the scale of enterprises grew and large numbers of new workers entered the industry, employers began increasingly to complain of the "drunkenness of workers, their carelessness toward their duties, and the impossibility of finding good workmen who know their craft."[48] By the 1880s, as will be seen, these concerns produced an organized effort among employers to make workers more competent, sober, loyal, and responsible. The practical value in this light of greater solicitude for the worker was quite clear and stated directly. Efforts to improve workers' physical environment and training and to raise workers' literacy and general culture would produce, it was hoped, more loyal and productive workers. Warm and sympathetic relations with workers would teach them "love and respect, and zeal for work."[49] And all of these efforts were considered in the "interests" of both em-

44. *Graficheskie iskusstva i bumazhnaia promyshlennost'* 1:7 (March 1896), pp. 106–07.
45. *Tipografskii zhurnal* 2:9–10 (November 15, 1868), pp. 34, 37.
46. *Obzor graficheskikh iskusstv* 1882, no. 10 (May 15), p. 64.
47. See Chapter 5.
48. *Trudy pervogo s"ezda*, pp. 27–37, 45 (quotation), 53–54. For examples from a much earlier period, see *Tipografskii zhurnal* 1:14–15 (February 1, 1868), pp. 59–61; 1:17 (March 1, 1868), p. 71; 2:1 (July 1, 1868), p. 2.
49. *Pechatnoe iskusstvo* 1:3 (December 1901), p. 94. See also *Obzor graficheskikh iskusstv* 1880, no. 17 (August 30), p. 126; *Trudy pervogo s"ezda*, pp. 53–54; *Naborshchik* 1:6 (December 8, 1902), p. 113; Solov'ev, *Gosudarev pechatnyi dvor*, p. 100.

ployers and workers. The community of workers and employers was viewed not only as a moral community, but also as an organic "community of material interest" among workers and employers.[50]

We must not oversimplify employers' thinking. Although it is clear that we cannot accept their public presentations of their virtues at face value, we would also be mistaken to treat these self-idealizations as merely a clever mask disguising the realities of domination and self-interest. That a successful printer like Aleksei Suvorin should claim that he did not "look at money as something deserving attention,"[51] need not be believed, but the claim suggests complex motives. Moral norms and the calculation of self-interest remained bound together. The material progress of the industry was seen to depend on its "honorable [*chestnyi*] existence."[52] Exploitation was viewed as harmful because it was an "evil" that "inevitably gives rise" to other evils, such as workers' drunkenness and poor workmanship.[53] For people to live "like wild beasts, isolated from one another," as Rudolf Schneider put it, seemed both wrong and hazardous.[54] Workers and employers must live together as a community, for reasons that were as much normative as utilitarian. This imperative was voiced in employers' rhetoric, but it was also expressed in employers' efforts to realize their ideal of community in practice.

ASSOCIATIONS OF COMMUNITY

Early in the summer of 1867, Rudolf Schneider held a party in St. Petersburg's Elysium Gardens. Together with other, mainly German, printing shop owners and compositors, some of whom helped him to plan this celebration, Schneider hoped to create among Russian printers, in his words, ties of "solidarity" such as had existed among German printers "from distant times." The gathering was said to be modeled on the traditional corporative summer festival of printers in southern Germany, the Feier des Johannisfestes, dedicated to Johannes

50. *Tipografskii zhurnal* 1:19 (April 1, 1868), p. 79; 1:24 (June 15, 1868), p. 96; 2:9–10 (November 15, 1868), p. 34; *Obzor graficheskikh iskusstv* 1878, no. 13 (July 15), p. 95; no. 15 (August 15), p. 111; 1881, no. 6 (March 15), p. 42; *Obzor pervoi vserossiiskoi vystavki* 15 (April 10, 1895), pp. 7–8; 18 (April 20, 1895), pp. 6–8; 19 (April 24, 1895), pp. 7–8.
51. Dinershtein, "Izdatel'skaia deiatel'nost" A. S. Suvorina," p. 8.
52. *Obzor graficheskikh iskusstv* 1878, no. 7 (April 15), p. 48.
53. *Trudy pervogo s"ezda*, p. 45.
54. *Obzor graficheskikh iskusstv* 1878, no. 10 (June 1), p. 71.

Gutenberg the printer and John the Baptist (though Saint John's Day was also a traditional festival of the Freemasons). The affair disappointed Schneider, though the attendance was good and not limited to Germans. Schneider planned for this celebration, in the manner of the original, to combine dancing, eating, and drinking with serious consideration of professional concerns. His guests were in a more celebratory mood. They listened politely when Schneider announced that he would soon begin to publish the first professional journal for printers in Russia, but when he tried to read some poetry he had written for the occasion and to discuss other serious matters, Schneider could not even get the attention of the guests, who were too busy eating and drinking.[55]

This gathering of workers and employers, though still involving mainly non-Russians, was the most public display yet of the emerging corporative identity of Russia's printers, notwithstanding Schneider's disappointment over its tone. The trade journals that were published, with some interruptions, from 1867 until 1917, did much to encourage this process. Again, Schneider was responsible for this innovation in the professional life of Russian printing, establishing his bilingual *Tipografskii zhurnal/Journal für Buchdruckerkunst* in 1867.[56] This journal and all of its successors were published in St. Petersburg, though their publishers intended that they serve as national organs and successfully solicited subscribers in several cities. As trade publications, they informed readers about technical questions (often translating articles from foreign printers' journals), included essays on printers' economic and social concerns (often contributed from throughout the country), recounted the careers of successful printers, and reported on the activities of trade associations.[57]

55. *Tipografskii zhurnal* 1:2 (July 15, 1867), pp. 6–7; *Peterburgskii listok* 1868, no. 9 (January 20), p. 1. Ten years later, Schneider faulted French printers for a similar lack of seriousness when they organized what he hoped would be the first international congress of printers. It turned out to be "a common drinking spree by printers of various European countries." *Obzor graficheskikh iskusstv* 1878, no. 16 (September 1), p. 119. Whether Schneider was a Freemason is not known. He was unlikely to mention the Masonic tradition of St. John's Day feasts even if he were aware of it, and though he often expressed identifiably Masonic ideals of fraternity, charity, and moral improvement, these had a wider provenance.

56. A partial predecessor was *Knizhnyi vestnik,* a mainly bibliographical journal for booksellers that appeared from 1861 to 1867, and in 1866 began to include information on professional matters to attract the interest of publishers, printers, and others. *Knizhnyi vestnik* 1866, no. 1 (January 30), pp. 33–35. See Bibliography for a complete list of printers' journals.

57. The only study of these journals is the 1914 pamphlet by Galaktionov, *Zhurnaly pechatnogo dela.*

These journals also gave essential support to other institutions of trade community. The first trade association among printers in Russia, which in fact slightly predated Schneider's Johannisfest and probably helped to plan the festival and to discuss the need for a journal, originated as regular meetings in the spring of 1867 among ethnic German printing employers, foremen, and workers at "die Palme," the German artisans' club in St. Petersburg. These meetings provided German printers an opportunity to socialize and drink together and also to discuss news of their profession from Western Europe and the problems of printing in Russia. They continued these meetings for three years, attracting new participants and soon adopting a formal name: Versammlung der Buchdrucker und Schriftgeisser.[58] In 1879, Schneider tried to create a wider occupational community by organizing a series of "graphic circle evenings" at which owners, managers, and workers gathered to socialize, be entertained, and "cultivate the graphic arts." Nearly a thousand people attended the largest of these evenings, which continued for almost two years.[59] In Moscow in 1880, Otto Herbeck, a Bavarian-born owner of a printing shop and type foundry, organized a similar "Moscow Graphic Circle." During the two years that Herbeck's circle existed, it signed as members thirty-two employers, twenty-seven managers and foremen, seventy-five compositors, and forty-one other printing workers.[60]

The proclaimed purpose of these early associations was to "improve the art," which partly meant promoting better workmanship and technical innovation by means of lectures, competitions, and special exhibits. But improvement was also understood to mean ensuring what an 1878 proposal for a congress of printers called ensuring "the honorable existence" of the trade.[61] Toward this goal a variety of measures of corporative self-regulation were proposed over the years, including suggestions that typefounders be prevented from selling type to "capitalist" printers who lacked proper training in the art, that prices be regulated

58. *Tipografskii zhurnal* 1:8 (October 15, 1867), p. 34; *Peterburgskii listok* 1868, no. 9 (January 20), p. 1.
59. *Obzor graficheskikh iskusstv* 1878, no. 9 (May 15), p. 63; 1879, no. 6 (March 15), p. 43; 1879, no. 8 (April 15), p. 59; 1879, no. 21 (November 1), pp. 120–21; 1879, no. 24 (December 15), pp. 145–46; 1880, no. 3 (February 1), p. 21; Galaktionov, *Zhurnaly pechatnogo dela*, pp. 8–9.
60. *Obzor graficheskikh iskusstv* 1880, no. 23 (December 1), p. 176; 1881, no. 3 (February 1), p. 23. Several years earlier, in 1868, Herbeck had tried unsuccessfully to organize a "Society for the Improvement of the Printing Trade." *Tipografskii zhurnal* 2:2 (July 15, 1868), p. 6; *Obzor graficheskikh iskusstv* 1880, no. 23 (December 1), p. 176.
61. *Obzor graficheskikh iskusstv* 1878, no. 7 (April 15), p. 48.

in order to protect both the profits of employers and workers' wages, and even that an industry-wide "tariff" (*tarif*) be established to regulate wages, hours, and working conditions; this last proposal became especially important in later years.[62]

The issue that preoccupied the attention of these employers at meetings and in their press was the breakdown in the proper training and education of workers. The problems of apprenticeship brought together most of the concerns of activist employers: improving the techniques of production, regulating competition, developing more skilled and disciplined workers, and ensuring a proper moral foundation for social relations. The majority of activist employers agreed that the blame for the decline in proper apprenticeship training in printing lay with employers "who, like traders in their shops, care only about profit."[63] Supervisors were also blamed, because their own training was often poor and they were under pressure to produce as much as possible at the lowest cost.[64]

A variety of solutions was proposed, all involving some mechanism of corporative self-regulation: rules restricting employers from taking as apprentices boys who were under fifteen years of age or who did not have at least rudimentary formal education; rules requiring employers to issue certificates to workers who had successfully completed a proper apprenticeship and to see equivalent papers before hiring a worker; and higher wage standards in order to attract and hold better-quality apprentices and workers.[65] Some employers proposed that the trade address as a community the problem of training by establishing a printing school for apprentices. One of these proponents, the ubiquitous Rudolf Schneider, briefly opened a school for apprentices in his own apartment in 1868.[66] Several years of discussions and the encour-

62. For example, *Tipografskii zhurnal* 1:12 (December 15, 1867), p. 52; 2:11–12 (December 15, 1868), pp. 43–44; *Obzor graficheskikh iskusstv* 1878, no. 7 (April 15), p. 50; 1879, no. 6 (March 15), p. 43; 1881, no. 12 (June 15), p. 83; 1884, no. 2 (January 15), p. 14.

63. *Tipografskii zhurnal* 2:1 (July 1, 1868), p. 2 (quotation); 2:2 (July 15, 1868), p. 5; 2:3 (August 1, 1868), p. 9; *Obzor graficheskikh iskusstv* 1884, no. 3 (February 1), pp. 20–21.

64. For example, *Tipografskii zhurnal* 1:14–15 (February 1, 1868), p. 60.

65. *Tipografskii zhurnal* 1:12 (December 15, 1867), p. 52; 1:18 (March 15, 1868), pp. 75–76; *Obzor graficheskikh iskusstv* 1878, no. 6 (April 1), pp. 41–42. For an example of support for government intervention, see *Obzor graficheskikh iskusstv* 1883, no. 8 (April 15), pp. 65–66.

66. *Tipografskii zhurnal* 1:16 (February 15, 1868), p. 68; *Obzor graficheskikh iskusstv* 1878, no. 23 (December 1), p. 173; Galaktionov, *Pervaia shkola*, p. 7; *Pervaia russkaia shkola, 1884–1894*, p. 7.

agement and ultimately sponsorship of the Standing Commission on Technical Education of the Imperial Russian Technical Society resulted in 1884 in the permanent establishment of a printing school in St. Petersburg.[67]

At the same time as they formed institutions whose main purpose was to "improve the art," activist printing employers established organizations aimed at uniting workers and employers: the assistance funds (*vspomogatel'nye kassy*). The immediate purpose of such funds was to give financial aid to dues-paying members and their families when they could not work because of sickness, disability, old age, or death. The first such fund—the first mutual aid society in any industry in Russia[68] —was organized by German printers in St. Petersburg in 1838 (its charter was approved in 1840). Known among its members as the Buchdrucker-Hilfskasse—though simply called the "German Fund" by Russian printers[69]—it was open to German-speaking workers, supervisors, and employers in all printing crafts. Over time the initial German identity was diluted by the membership of other non-Russians. Toward the end of 1864, a group of Russian "typographers," as they ambiguously identified themselves, met in St. Petersburg to organize a similar fund for Russian printers, which was approved by the Ministry of Internal Affairs in 1866 as the Compositors' Assistance Fund. In Moscow in 1868, German and Russian printers united to establish a fund, which was chartered in 1869 as the Typographers' Assistance Fund. Still later, at the end of 1899, a Printers' Burial Society was founded in St. Petersburg.[70]

---

67. Galaktionov, *Pervaia shkola*, pp. 7–11; *Pervaia russkaia shkola, 1884–1894*, pp. 7–13; *Pervaia shkola pechatnogo dela, 1884–1914*, pp. 6–10. Discussions on the organization of this school appeared frequently in *Obzor graficheskikh iskusstv* from 1879 through 1884. The printing school continued in operation until 1917.

68. Excluding organizations in the Polish and Baltic regions of the Empire, which were also established by printers.

69. It was legally registered as the Assistance Fund of the Society of Printers in St. Petersburg (Vspomogatel'naia kassa "Obshchestva Tipografshchikov v S.-Peterburge"). Later it was renamed the Assistance Fund for Printers, Typefounders, Lithographers, Xylographers, and Photographers, and still later the First Fund of Working People (*trudiashchiisia*) in all Branches of the Graphic Arts. Its formal German name was the Unterstützungskasse der Buchdrucker-Gesellschaft.

70. The main sources on these organizations, in addition to the professional press, are as follows. On the German fund: *Obzor deiatel'nosti vspomogatel'noi kassy "Obshchestva Tipografshchikov v S.-Peterburge"; Piatidesiatiletie sushchestvovaniia Vspomogatel'noi kassy dlia tipografov.* On the Petersburg fund: Grents and Galaktionov, *Obzor; Otchet dvadtsatipiatiletnei VKN;* Vorob'ev, *Kratkii ocherk VKN.* On the Moscow fund: *Sbornik svedenii VKT; Po povodu tridtsatiletiia VKT.* On the burial fund (Pokhoronnaia kassa truzhenikov pechatnogo dela): *Pechatnoe iskusstvo* 1:3 (December 1901), pp. 76–87.

One may characterize these funds as workers' organizations under
the leadership and control of employers and supervisors. The overwhelming majority of members in each of these funds were rank-and-
file workers, especially compositors. But the policies and everyday
management of the funds were in other hands. The founder and leader
of the German fund for many years was Eduard Pratz, the owner of a
small printing shop; most other officers were also employers, managers,
and foremen.[71] Employers and supervisors similarly ran the Compositors' Assistance Fund in St. Petersburg, and much of its budget was
provided by the donations of employers.[72] In Moscow, the initiative for
organizing the fund came from a group of German owners and supervisors who had been socializing in a beer hall. Although rank-and-file
workers comprised on average 93 percent of members of the Moscow
fund over the next thirty years, most officers and all of the fund's directors were owners, managers, or foremen. Employers' donations also
comprised a major source of financial support.[73] These were organizations for the workers' benefit but not under their control.

The atmosphere within these funds, however, especially in the early
years, conveyed a spirit of artisanal mutuality, of the solidarity of masters and men in a fraternal "family of printers," though the tendency
was increasingly toward a more hierarchical benevolence. The German
fund, as early as the 1860s, defined its functions as "charitable"
(*blagotvoritel'nyi*).[74] The organizers of the Russian funds also increasingly began to identify them as "charitable institutions" (*blagotvoritel'-
nye* or *blagodetel'nye uchrezhdeniia*).[75] The ethos of benevolence also
pervaded the rhetoric of the leaders of the funds. They spoke, for example, of their "humane goal" to aid "the poor in need, sickness, and

71. *Obzor deiatel'nosti vspomogatel'noi kassy "Obshchestva Tipografshchikov
v S.-Peterburge"*; *Piatidesiatiletie sushchestvovaniia Vspomogatel'noi kassy dlia
tipografov*; *Tipografskii zhurnal* 1:18 (March 15, 1868) p. 76; 2:15–16 (February 15,
1869), p. 59; *Obzor graficheskikh iskusstv* 1884, no. 6 (March 15, 1884), pp. 47–48; *Pechatnoe iskusstvo* 1:1 (October 1901), p. 29; 1:7 (April 1902), p. 220.
72. Grents and Galaktionov, *Obzor*, pp. 3–25; *Otchet dvadtsatipiatiletnei VKN*, pp.
9–41; Vorob'ev, *Kratkii ocherk VKN*, pp. 5–9; *Tipografskii zhurnal* 2:4 (August 15,
1868), pribavlenie, pp. 1–2; *Obzor graficheskikh iskusstv* 1878, no. 6 (April 1), p. 45;
1880, no. 8 (May 15), p. 76; 1883, no. 13 (July 1), p. 115; 1884, no. 11 (June 1), p. 86;
Knigovedenie 1894, no. 7–8 (September 3), p. 35.
73. *Sbornik svedenii VKT*, pp. vii–xii, 12–58; *Tipografskii zhurnal* 1:21 (May 1,
1868), p. 88; 1:22–23 (June 1, 1868), pp. 93–94; 2:13–14 (January 15, 1869), p. 52; 3:1
(July 1, 1869), p. 3.
74. *Obzor deiatel'nosti vspomogatel'noi kassy "Obshchestva Tipografshchikov,"*
p. 2.
75. *Otchet dvadtsatipiatiletnei VKN*, pp. 3, 14; *Knizhnyi vestnik* 1900, no. 1 (January), p. 15.

death,"[76] and characterized one another as individuals with "exceptional love and heartfelt sympathy for working people."[77]

The employers and supervisors who led the assistance funds sought to extend this solicitude to embrace the whole life of the worker, especially his "moral and intellectual development" (nravstvennoe i umstvennoe razvitie). Hoping that the experience of membership itself would teach workers the virtue of thrift, some fund leaders suggested that employers ought to encourage their workers to participate by paying their entrance dues.[78] They also sought to encourage workers to devote less time to drink and more to moral and educational self-improvement by organizing lectures, free libraries, reading rooms, evenings of edifying entertainment, and family excursions to the countryside, and they offered educational grants to members' children. The leaders of the funds also sought to improve working conditions in the industry, though this too generally had tutelary purposes: ending work on Sundays, for example, was said to be desirable to increase church attendance and participation in the uplifting activities of the fund.[79]

In the spring of 1895, a major national exhibition and congress was held in St. Petersburg with the aim of strengthening and expanding the developing trade community among printers. During the four months that the First All-Russian Exhibition of Printing remained open, over 40,000 people visited, including most of the owners of printing firms in St. Petersburg, many from other cities, and several thousand printing workers, who were admitted without charge.[80] The weeklong First Congress of Russian Printing (pervyi s"ezd russkikh deiatelei po pechatnomu delu) attracted the participation of most of the major printing firms in St. Petersburg and many from Moscow.[81]

The exhibition and congress were planned, organized, and sponsored by the Imperial Russian Technical Society. Founded in 1866, the Technical Society brought together engineers, entrepreneurs, academ-

76. Obzor graficheskikh iskusstv 1878, no. 9 (May 15), pp. 64–65.

77. Pechatnoe iskusstvo 1:1 (October 1901), pp. 21–22.

78. Grents and Galaktionov, Obzor, p. 23; Obzor graficheskikh iskusstv 1878, no. 3 (February 15), p. 17; 1878, no. 9 (May 15), pp. 64–65; 1879, no. 17 (September 1), p. 101; 1884, no. 11 (June 1), pp. 85–86; Trudy pervogo s"ezda, pp. 48, 116, 199; Moskovskie pechatniki v 1905 godu, p. 15.

79. Otchet dvadtsatipiatiletnei VKN, pp. 3–37; Grents and Galaktionov, Obzor, pp. 11–25; Sbornik svedenii VKT, pp. viii–xxii; Pechatnoe iskusstvo 1:5 (February 1902), pp. 162–64; Knizhnyi vestnik 1904, no. 51–52 (December 31), pp. 1467–70.

80. Obzor pervoi vserossiiskoi vystavki 32 (June 12, 1895), pp. 1–3; 34 (June 15, 1895), pp. 9–10. This journal is the best source of information about the exhibition.

81. Trudy pervogo s"ezda, pp. 1–3.

ics, and government officials who shared a commitment to advancing technical knowledge in Russia. The association of a number of printing employers with the Technical Society, especially through the Society's sponsorship of the Petersburg printing school, facilitated their associative efforts, especially the organization of the exhibition and congress. But the connection with the Technical Society also influenced how printers thought about the structure and goals of association. In outlook, and partly in composition, the Technical Society was a "professional" organization, emphasizing knowledge and expertise in the service of economic modernization and rationalization.[82]

These values were becoming increasingly a part of the thinking of activist printing employers and managers. This was evident, for example, in the changing language of their self-identification. By the 1890s, activist employers tended no longer to describe themselves as *truzheniki* (workmen) or *tipografy* (printers), but increasingly as *deiateli,* a term denoting professional expertise and commitment rather than labor or occupation. This identification was the industry-level parallel to the tendency of employers within their enterprises to present themselves as benevolent "fathers" to labor. Both terms designated elites defined according to behavior and attributes that workers could not share.

This definition of the employer as *deiatel'* was reflected in the changing structure of association in the industry. The organizing committee for the Printing Congress included four owners of printing enterprises together with government officials, publishers, editors, and educators. Similarly, the congress welcomed as participants the managers and owners of printing shops, publishers, editors, writers, journalists, booksellers, lawyers, engineers, and educators—but not workers.[83] Unlike the tavern meetings and graphic circle evenings of the 1860s and early 1880s, the congress evidently no longer considered workers to be partners in "improving the art."

The establishment after the congress of a new organization—the Russian Printing Society (Russkoe Obshchestvo deiatelei pechatnogo

82. Zelnik, *Labor and Society,* pp. 284–300; Rieber, *Merchants and Entrepreneurs,* pp. 251–53, 277–78; N. G. Filippov, *Nauchno-technicheskie obshchestva Rossii,* pp. 25–41.

83. *Trudy pervogo s"ezda,* pp. iii, 1–3. According to *Istoriia leningradskogo soiuza,* p. 74, one worker, the compositor Nikolai Grosman, attended the congress as a representative of the Typographers' Assistance Fund in Moscow. It is likely, however, that Grosman was at least a supervisor by 1895, since within four years he became co-owner of a small printing shop.

dela)[84]—reinforced this associational redefinition. Although the establishment of such a society had been proposed at the congress, it was organized only in 1897—the same year that industrialists in St. Petersburg established the Society for the Assistance, Improvement, and Development of Factory Industry—and received government approval only in 1899, with a branch opening in Moscow the following year. The society, even more than the congress, was run by owners and managers of printing enterprises, who held almost all of the positions as officers.[85] In other respects, however, the Printing Society was very much a new type of association within the industry. Membership was open to government officials, writers, academics, publishers, and editors, as well as printing employers and supervisors. There were no worker members, a limitation resulting formally from high membership dues rather than stated policy but understood and accepted as appropriate. When the possibility of lowering dues so that workers might join was specifically discussed—in the Moscow branch in 1902, in St. Petersburg in 1904—most members agreed with the chairman of the Petersburg branch, who opposed the suggestion as a threat to the character of a society that had been founded to unite "independent and self-sufficient" persons who were in a position to influence the development of the art.[86]

Although the congress and the Printing Society represented a further move away from the fraternal ideal of a trade community, the purposes and motivations continued the traditions of earlier associations. As before, the primary purpose was to "improve the art" by means of corporative self-regulation, though virtually all authority within this corporative body was reserved for owners and managers. The progress of the industry was still seen to depend on improving the skills, knowledge, and moral character of workers, an improvement portrayed as in the interest not only of production but also of moral good order.

84. The organizers of the society, intending to establish links with similar associations in Western Europe, offered their own official translations of their name—Die Russische Buchgewerbe-Gesellschaft, La Société russe des arts du livre, The Russian Society of Printing Matters.

85. *Otchet soveta RODPD za 1902 g.*, addendum; RODPD-MO, *Kratkii otchet*, p. 1 and addendum. The major exceptions were the largely honorary senior positions of chairman and vice-chairman, which were usually filled by non-printer representatives of the Technical Society. In Moscow, however, the employer A. A. Levenson was elected first vice-chairman, and the director of the large Kushnerev press, Vladimir Borovik, became chairman in 1902.

86. *Naborshchik* 1:6 (December 8, 1902), pp. 108–09; 2:46 (October 10, 1904), p. 727.

The most heated discussions at the congress occurred at meetings devoted to the problem and consequences of competition.[87] Although most employers and managers accepted as a matter of principle the liberal argument that competition was beneficial to the development of industry, they condemned its "excesses," which, they said, promoted brutal business practices, including the "exploitation" of workers and apprentices, who had become the main "victims of unprincipled competition." Excessive competition was also said to be cutting into profits and generally ruining the industry. A few speakers favored government intervention to regulate the industry, but most employers preferred self-discipline. Regulating wages and especially prices was discussed, and French and German tariffs regulating labor conditions for printers were examined and endorsed as useful models.[88] But the most critical need, it was felt, was to regulate apprenticeship. Proposals included notarized contracts stipulating the mutual obligations of employers, apprentices, and their parents; rules establishing the appropriate ratio of apprentices to adult workers, the age at which they might be hired, and their working conditions; and a special supervisory bureau with the power to fine or even arrange the arrest of employers or apprentices who violated the regulations.[89]

The future Printing Society was envisioned as the agency to promote and oversee such regulation, and soon after its establishment the society began drafting and discussing detailed "Regulations on Apprenticeship." The original draft of these rules was far-reaching in its regulatory ambitions, specifying minimum age requirements, the length and manner of training, maximum hours, and the ratio of adults to apprentices. A special bureau of the society was to register all apprentices and oversee the enforcement of the rules with the assistance of the government's Factory Inspectorate. Disputes among members and concerns about government approval caused this original proposal to be watered down, but the essential goal remained: to introduce order into the conduct of apprenticeship with the sanction of both law and professional self-discipline.[90]

87. *Obzor pervoi vserossiiskoi vystavki* 14 (April 6, 1895), p. 2.

88. *Trudy pervogo s"ezda*, p. 107.

89. Ibid., pp. 27–38, 44–45, 53–54, 56–59.

90. *Otchet soveta RODPD za 1902 g.*, pp. 8, 17; *Pechatnoe iskusstvo* 1:5 (February 1902), pp. 155–61; *Biulleten' RODPD* 1:4 (March 1902), pp. 52–54; 1:11 (November 1902), p. 84; *Naborshchik* 1:2 (November 1902), pp. 40, 45. The society submitted the final draft of these rules for approval to the Ministry of Finance in January 1903.

The corporative idealists of the congress and the Printing Society did not limit their regulatory ambitions to creating rules and structures to govern the treatment of apprentices and workers. They also expected employers, as in the past, to be responsible for the inner lives of their workers as well. Employers were to look after apprentices' moral "upbringing" (*vospitanie*), teach them "diligence, good morals, and proper behavior," and shelter them from the "drunkenness and depravity" all around.[91] This attention was not to be bounded by the walls of the workplace nor limited to apprentices. Speakers at the 1895 congress proposed that apprentices be compelled to attend church, that adult workers be "obliged" to join an assistance fund (to imbue workers with a "consciousness of their moral duties"), and that all workers be offered free libraries, reading rooms, and lectures that might "divert [the worker] from harmful amusements during his hours of rest."[92] The "Regulations on Apprenticeship" that the Printing Society proposed similarly spoke of the "obligation" of employers to "watch over the behavior of apprentices" at all times and even recommended that employers or their representatives visit apprentices where they lived and make certain that they did not frequent taverns.[93] Other projects developed by the Printing Society, such as the printing school opened by the Moscow branch and a library and reading room for workers organized in St. Petersburg, similarly concerned the moral and educational "upbringing" of workers.[94] In general, organized printing employers wished to "raise [workers'] intellectual and moral level, assist them in their general and technical education, . . . and [help them] to spend their time away from work in a reasonable manner, not succumbing to bad habits such as drunkenness."[95]

Material calculations of their own interests were undoubtedly important in motivating these efforts. As we have seen, employers frequently complained of workers' poor training, drunkenness, absenteeism, and carelessness. One of the main purposes of organization was precisely the formation of a skilled, diligent, and well-behaved labor

91. *Trudy pervogo s"ezda*, pp. 27–37, 53–54; *Obzor pervoi vserossiiskoi vystavki* 15 (April 10, 1895), pp. 7–8; *Tridtsatipiatiletie t-va "Obshchestvennaia pol'za,"* p. 19.
92. *Trudy pervogo s"ezda*, pp. 46–48, 56–57, 85–86, 118–19.
93. *Biulleten' RODPD* 1:4 (March 1902), pp. 53–54; 1:11 (November 1902), p. 84.
94. RODPD-MO, *Kratkii otchet*, pp. 1–4; *Proekt ustava Obshchestvennoi biblioteki*, pp. 1–2; *Otchet soveta RODPD za 1902*, pp. 18–19. The Petersburg branch also investigated what other social organizations were doing to "aid the moral improvement of compositors." *Biulleten' RODPD* 2:3 (March 1903), p. 104.
95. *Proekt ustava Obshchestvennoi biblioteki*, p. 1.

force. Yet employers also continued to insist on the moral issues: workers were drunken and careless, they said, largely because some employers "exploited" workers and abused apprenticeship.[96] Concern for the moral behavior of workers and for their own personal relations with their workers was seen as a matter of obligation and duty as well as of rationally understood self-interest. As the Petersburg press owner Ivan Tsvetkov argued at the 1895 congress, employers must seek to "spread in our trade a morality corresponding to its high significance."[97] They wished to demonstrate, as the chairman of the Petersburg Printing School stated at the dedication of a sanatorium for printing workers in 1903,[98] that they were also "humane and enlightened" individuals.[99] There was felt to be no contradiction between their responsibilities as professionals devoted to the needs of the trade and their responsibilities to themselves and others as moral human beings; interest and morality were viewed as inseparable. Similarly, there was felt to be no opposition between the ideal of their industry as a moral community and their own workplace authority as guardians of this moral order. As it was said, without irony, they were fathers to their brothers.

WORKPLACE PATERNALISM

Employers most often presented themselves in this paternal role within their own enterprises—in the social space and to the individuals over which they had the greatest control. This workplace paternalism must be distinguished from the patriarchalism of the small traditional workshop, though that too was a model of authority that could be benevolent and sentimental as well as harsh and authoritarian. The paternalism of the activist employers represented a new phenomenon that appeared and grew together with the emergence of large-scale enterprises in printing and distinguished itself from traditional patriarchalism not only by the original forms it created but especially by its self-conscious and demonstrative moralism.

96. *Trudy pervogo s"ezda*, p. 45.
97. Ibid., p. 59.
98. The sanatorium was called the Petrine Colony of Working People of the Printing Industry of the Russian Printing Society (1903 was the tricentennial of the founding of the first periodical in Russia by Peter I). Its formation is discussed in I. D. Galaktionov, *Petrovskaia koloniia*, pp. 3–15, and in regular reports in *Pechatnoe iskusstvo* and *Biulleten' RODPD*.
99. *Pechatnoe iskusstvo* 2:8–9 (May–June 1903), p. 279. The Compositors' Assistance Fund similarly described the sanatorium as "a humane and truly Christian establishment." *Pechatnoe iskusstvo* 2:12 (September 1903), p. 350.

Among private entrepreneurs, Aleksei Suvorin stands as the model of the new paternalist, establishing for his workers a variety of what he called "charitable institutions." Lower-paid workers received free lodging in a private apartment building, which included, also without charge, heating, lighting, beds, and linen, as well as a cook, a maid, and a laundress. Starting in 1891, all workers and their immediate families received free medical care from the plant clinic and free medicine from the pharmacy. When legislation in 1897 made free medical assistance mandatory for all factories employing over fifty workers, Suvorin had already exceeded the requirements of the law and made a point of continuing to do so. He also undertook preventive health measures, such as installing electric ventilation to protect compositors from lead dust. In 1885, Suvorin established a voluntary assistance fund for his workers, to which he and his two sons donated 6,300 rubles when it was reorganized in 1897 as a more effective "savings association." A separate burial society was established to cover funeral expenses and assist a deceased worker's survivors. The centerpiece of Suvorin's paternalistic management, however, was his free school and library. Founded in 1884 as a private elementary school for printing workers, it included (after 1890) additional courses on the theory and practice of printing. Although mainly for his own apprentices, outsiders were accepted by competition, with the expectation, often realized, that graduates would come to work for him.[100] Suvorin expressed great pride in the fact that he was spending up to 3,000 rubles a year on the school.[101]

Similar benefits could be found in other large enterprises, especially in St. Petersburg, where this movement was generally more developed. Most common was simple charity—subsidized pension and assistance funds or direct payments to workers who became too sick, injured, or aged to work. Private assistance funds were established in the printing houses of Aleksei Il'in in 1884, Vladimir Kirshbaum in 1894, *Obshchestvennaia pol'za* in 1895, the *Prosveshchenie* press in 1904, and in the recently combined Golike and Wilborg press in the same year.[102] In

100. *Na pamiat' o desiatiletii "Novogo vremeni,"* unpaginated; *Tipografiia "Novogo vremeni,"* p. 2; *Kratkii ocherk izdatel'skoi deiatel'nosti A. S. Suvorina,* pp. 14, 18–21; *Shkola pri tipografii gazety "Novoe vremia"*; *Vestnik graficheskogo dela* 19 (October 18, 1897), pp. 193–94; *Pechatnoe iskusstvo* 1:5 (February 1902), p. 159; 2:8–9 (May–June 1903), p. 282; 2:12 (September 1903), p. 359.
101. See his letter to I. N. Kramskoi, quoted in Dinershtein, "Izdatel'skaia deiatel'-nost'" A. S. Suvorina," p. 84.
102. *Knizhnyi vestnik* 1884, no. 5–6 (March 1 and 15), pp. 177–78; *Dvadtsatipiatiletie kartograficheskogo zavedeniia A. Il'ina,* p. 19; *Pechatnoe iskusstvo* 1:3 (December

Moscow, in 1900, A. A. Levenson insured all of his workers in case of accident and organized a subsidized savings fund. In the same year, Ivan Sytin contributed 13,500 rubles to establish a "charity fund" for his workers.[103]

Paternalist employers also sought to improve working conditions. The connection between such improvements and the growing scale and modernization of the industry was indicated by the frequent association of improved working conditions with a company's move into quarters designed to accommodate modern machinery. When Petr Iablonskii rebuilt his large printing plant in St. Petersburg in the 1890s, he also installed electric ventilation and lighting and a heated lavatory and provided workers with free soap and towels and a special room for eating.[104] In Moscow, the Sytin firm announced in 1903 that its new factory building would house not only the "last word" in technology but also the best hygienic conditions possible, a special dining hall, a library, and a social hall for the firm's many workers.[105] Similarly, when A. A. Levenson moved his large Moscow printing firm into a new building in 1900, also designed to be the "last word in modern technique, hygiene, and architecture," dangerous and noisy motor belts were hidden beneath the floors, and cleaner electric power and lighting and mechanical ventilation were installed. In order to provide workers with "various comforts, facilities for their diversion, etc.," Levenson established a free infirmary and pharmacy, a dining hall with "exemplary cuisine" where workers could eat on credit and at low cost, a library and reading room, a singing class, and a balalaika orchestra.[106]

Libraries, classes, orchestras, and other cultural programs aimed at encouraging workers' "intellectual and moral development" were established in a number of large private firms, reminiscent of the serf orchestras and theaters organized by some members of the gentry in earlier times. At the Mamontov press in Moscow, for example, the owner—a member of a well-known family of business leaders, philan-

---

1901), p. 94; *Tridtsatipiatiletie t-va "Obshchestvennaia pol'za,"* p. 19; *Istoriia leningradskogo soiuza,* p. 87.

103. Levenson, *Istoricheskii ocherk,* p. 111; Dinershtein, *I. D. Sytin,* pp. 176–77; *Société d'édition J. D. Sytin,* p. 21; TsGIAgM, f. 2316, op. 1, d. 2, pp. 2–115 [annual reports, 1899–1905].

104. *Kratkii istoricheskii obzor tipografii L.S.P.O.,* pp. 6–7. See also *Dvadtsatipiatiletie tipografsko-izdatelskoi deiatel'nosti Soikina,* p. 10.

105. *Knizhnyi vestnik* 1903, no. 18 (May 4), pp. 559–61.

106. Levenson, *Istoricheskii ocherk,* pp. 9, 19, 27, 31, 84–85, 111 (quotation); TsGAOR, f. 6864, op. 1, d. 216, p. 6.

thropists, and art patrons—organized an orchestra, a workers' bala-laika ensemble (which even performed in Paris), and music and singing classes for his workers under the direction of an instructor from the conservatory.[107]

The directors of large state-owned printing firms, concentrated in St. Petersburg, were especially inclined to pursue protective and benevolent relationships with their workers. In presses such as those of the State Senate, the Naval Ministry, the Academy of Sciences, and the Holy Synod (which had plants in both Moscow and St. Petersburg), and in the huge Office for the Manufacture of Government Paper, we find subsidized assistance funds, free medical care, improvements in sanitary conditions, and efforts to "divert [workers] from amusements harmful to their health and morality"[108] by organizing schools, religious and secular choirs, orchestras, free libraries, lectures, and evenings of literature and music.[109]

Prince Golitsyn achieved almost legendary stature as a paternalist after he took over the Office for the Manufacture of Government Paper in 1899. He raised wages, instituted the only eight-hour day in any Russian printing firm before 1905, fitted machinery with safety devices, improved the dining hall, constructed new workers' quarters, installed electric lighting in old residences, offered a compensatory wage supplement to workers who preferred to move into private apartments, opened a subsidized food store for workers, established a nursery for workers' children, expanded the factory hospital and added a maternity ward, increased support to the pension fund that had existed since the 1860s, and opened a summer *dacha* for young workers and apprentices. Drawing attention to himself as the source of these benefits, Golitsyn regularly gave at his discretion individual grants of financial aid, clothes, and shoes to needy workers or their widows and orphans. Determined also to provide workers with "appropriate amusements

107. TsGAOR, f. 6864, op. 1, d. 216, pp. 49–50.
108. *Senatskaia tipografiia*, unpaginated.
109. In addition to the examples that follow, *Senatskaia tipografiia*; *Kratkii ocherk istorii i sovremennogo sostoianiia S.-Peterburgskoi Sinodal'noi tipografii*, p. 28; *S.-Peterburgskaia Sinodal'naia tipografiia*, pp. 14–15; TsGIA, f. 800, op. 1, d. 92, p. 1; d. 176, p. 2; d. 338, pp. 1–9; Solov'ev, *Gosudar'ev pechatnyi dvor*, pp. 100–102; *Dvukhklassnaia tserkovno-prikhodskaia shkola*; Iuferovyi and Sokolovskii, eds., *Akademicheskaia tipografiia*, p. 62; *Knizhnyi vestnik* 1896, no. 4 (April), p. 9; 1896, no. 9 (September), p. 7; *Graficheskie iskusstva i bumazhnaia promyshlennost'* 3:2 (February 1898), pp. 28–29; 3:4 (April 1898), pp. 61–62; *Biulleten' RODPD* 1:9 (September 1902), pp. 73–76; *Naborshchik* 1:3 (November 17, 1902), p. 56; *Pechatnoe iskusstvo* 2:2 (November 1902), p. 68; 2:3 (December 1902), p. 110; 2:7 (April 1903), p. 232.

[*razvlechenie*] that might counter their drinking and visiting of taverns,"[110] he expanded the schools for workers that his predecessors had established, organized a workers' choir and orchestra, opened a free library and reading room, helped workers to subscribe to journals and newspapers by allowing them to pay in installments through the company office, and constructed a special building next to the factory to house a workers' theater, concert hall, tearoom, library, and reading room.[111]

In these efforts, too, fraternalism and condescension were mixed ambiguously, reflecting in part the influence of size of enterprise, but also reflecting, in many cases, differences in employers' personal style. Whereas many large employers, such as Golitsyn, remained aloof, avoiding personal contact with their workers, others considered face-to-face relations important even in the largest enterprises. At the large Kushnerev press in Moscow, for example, in addition to providing workers with many of the usual material benefits—free bed linens, clothing, and cultural activities for apprentices, rent subsidies for adult workers—Ivan Kushnerev personally sat in a special arbor by the entrance to his plant to greet his hundreds of workers (and encourage them not to be late) as they arrived at work each morning and as they returned from their mid-day break. During the day, he often walked around the factory, chatting with his workers. In the words of the Soviet historian of this plant, Kushnerev "cleverly hid behind the mask of a 'democrat.' "[112]

Whatever the differences in manner among these paternalists, whatever mixture of mutuality and benevolence they favored, the intended effect was the same. As we have seen, employers hoped to inculcate in workers "love and respect, and zeal for work." But as this expression suggests, moral and practical considerations were thought to be in harmony, as was illustrated in 1900 when A. A. Levenson moved his five hundred workers into his new Moscow printing plant. The physical appearance of the plant, designed by the architect F. O. Shekhtel', symbolically expressed the marriage of beauty and function:

110. LGIA, f. 1458, op. 2, d. 841, p. 9.
111. Voznesenskii, *Sto let,* pp. 34–40; Mikhailovskii, *Ekspeditsiia,* pp. 17–20; Idem, *Obzor i plany,* pp. 4, 11; LGIA, f. 1458, op. 2, d. 841, pp. 15ff; d. 888, pp. 115–32; *Ustav tekhnicheskoi shkoly; Pechatnoe iskusstvo* 1:3 (December 1901), p. 73; 1:7 (April 1902), p. 233; 2:4 (January 1903), pp. 147–48; *Biulleten' RODPD* 1:6 (May 1902), p. 61.
112. *Leninskii zakaz* (Moscow, 1969), pp. 13–17 (quotation p. 14); *Dvadtsatipiatiletie tipografii t-va Kushnerev,* pp. 17–18; *Graficheskie iskusstva i bumazhnaia promyshlennost'* 1:6 (February 1896), p. 92.

stylized art nouveau decorative features, cleaner electric lighting and power, and a floorplan that hid dangerous and noisy motor belts between the floors. All of these improvements were equally essential to the modernity of the design. Similarly, the reorganization of the working life in the plant sought to unite the charitable benevolence of a paternalistic morality with the rationalistic calculations of managerial efficiency. Under Levenson's "new order," as one worker later called it,[113] workers not only received a wide range of material and cultural benefits—from cleaner lavatories to singing classes—but were given numbered cards to be used with an automatic time clock that was installed at the entrance to the plant and were encouraged to dress in identical blue work suits.[114] Like the Taylorist managerial system that Levenson's system foreshadowed, moral purpose and material benefit were inseparable.

RITES OF SOLIDARITY

Every community requires practices that symbolize, reinforce, and perhaps sanctify its order and structure.[115] In Western Europe and North America, festivals of craft community were among the most fundamental corporative traditions of pre-industrial artisans, including printers, and were frequently adapted in more modern times to the cause of occupational solidarity.[116] Although Russian industries, even when built on artisanal foundations, lacked such a heritage, printers freely borrowed, adapted, and invented rites of their own. In 1867, Rudolf Schneider simply imported the traditional religious-corporative festival of Freemasons and of German printers, the Feier des Johannisfestes. As formal organization in the industry increased, so too did the incidence, elaborateness, and originality of such festivals.

In 1880, the Compositors' Assistance Fund sponsored a mass at Saint Isaac's Cathedral in St. Petersburg, which was attended by almost

113. TsGAOR, f. 6864, op. 1, d. 216, p. 6.
114. Levenson, *Istoricheskii ocherk*, 86; TsGAOR, f. 6864, op. 1, d. 216, p. 6; *Vospominaniia rabochikh 16-i tipo-litografii Mospoligraf (b. Levenson)*, pp. 25–26.
115. Wilentz, *Rites of Power*.
116. See Hobsbawm, *Workers*, pp. 69–73; Davis, *Society and Culture in Early Modern France*, pp. 5, 16, 98, 111; Sewell, *Work and Revolution in France*, pp. 34–35, 53, 173, 184, 256–57; Rock, *Artisans of the New Republic*, pp. 128–29; Beier, *Schwarze Kunst und Klassenkampf*, vol. 1, pp. 126–28; Howe, *Passages from the Literature of the Printing Craft*, pp. 19–23; Lawrence S. Thompson, *Folklore of the Chapel*, pp. 11–13; Brenton, *Voices from the Press*, pp. 51–56, 219–35.

all of the city's printing workers and employers. The occasion was the twenty-fifth anniversary of the reign of Alexander II. But the ceremony also served symbolically to sanctify the moral community of printers by framing it in the light of both the national community led by a benevolent tsar and the family of mankind guided by a benevolent, all-powerful God.[117] Most printers' festivals marked occasions more directly associated with the industry. In 1883 in St. Petersburg, one thousand printing-shop owners, managers, foremen, compositors, and pressmen, together with their spouses and children, attended a requiem mass at the Kazan cathedral on the three hundredth anniversary of the death of Russia's "first printer," Ivan Fedorov. The next morning, workers, supervisors, and the owners of most of the printing firms in the city, joined by a handful of government officials and writers, gathered in the hall of the City Duma to listen to special readings and musical performances. The model of community represented by these celebrations of the 1880s was already less fraternal than at Schneider's earlier gathering: when it came time to eat and drink, only owners, managers, writers, officials, and other "special guests" could afford to attend the ten-ruble-a-plate banquet. Speeches continued to emphasize the inclusiveness of the "family" of printers, but its hierarchical structure was plainly evident.[118]

The assistance funds were responsible for most printers' festivals in Russia. In St. Petersburg, the Compositors' Assistance Fund organized these on numerous occasions: the millennium of the creation of the Cyrillic alphabet in 1885, the centenary of Pushkin's birth in 1899, the five hundredth anniversary of Gutenberg's birth in 1900, and important anniversaries of the fund itself. Ceremonies were also held to honor leading members of the fund.[119] In Moscow, the Typographers' Assistance Fund took part in the celebration marking the tricentennial of Ivan Fedorov's death in 1883 and began sponsoring annual memorials to Fedorov (on December 7) in 1888. Annual Christmas parties for members and their families began in the 1890s.[120]

---

117. *Otchet dvadtsatipiatiletnei VKN*, pp. 24–35. A year later, when Alexander II was assassinated, more than a thousand people attended the general meeting of the fund to take part in a mass in his memory and in honor of the new tsar. For services organized by the Moscow fund, see *Sbornik svedenii VKT*, pp. xviii–xx.

118. *Obzor graficheskikh iskusstv* 1883, no. 23–24 (December 15), pp. 199–203.

119. Grents and Galaktionov, *Obzor*, pp. 12–20, 23; *Knizhnyi vestnik* 1890, no. 1 (January), p. 45.

120. *Sbornik svedenii VKT*, pp. xviii–xx; TsGAOR, f. 6864, op. 1, d. 4, p. 2; f. 6864, op. 1, d. 216, p. 49.

Most of these festivals followed a common format. After a religious service in a local church, attended by employers, managers, workers, and often their spouses and children, secular festivities would follow, usually including speeches, musical and literary performances, and dancing. A visitor to Moscow described the Fedorov jubilee of 1897. Owners and workers stood together in prayer at the Holy Trinity in the Fields church, built near the spot where Ivan Fedorov was believed to have founded his historic press. With candles in their hands, participants knelt in memory of Fedorov and of all fellow printers who "have passed into life eternal where there is neither sickness nor worry." Following the service, a smaller group of participants attended a dinner at a nearby restaurant. On this occasion, efforts were made to preserve a certain spirit of fraternity. The manager of the Mamontov press noted in his welcoming speech (to cheers from the participants) that side by side sat "owners, directors, managers, foremen, machine operators, compositors, and others."[121]

Most such rites of community were held in the workplace. The printers' trade press was filled with accounts of workplace festivities organized by employers on religious holidays or on various anniversaries in the life of a firm. The religious component of these ritual gatherings of workers and employers should be emphasized. As a sacred link between individuals, common faith has often been invoked to sanctify secular bonds. Moreover, efforts to create a trade community in the late nineteenth century could draw to some extent on an earlier heritage of association between masters and men by evoking the religious services (*molebna*) that had been held traditionally in printing shops on the saint's day of the shop icon, on certain religious or national holidays, and sometimes on the name day of the shop's master.

Shop-based religious rites persisted into later years, even in many large enterprises. They followed a typical pattern: a priest would come to the shop to pray for the health of the owner and his family, bless the workers, offer a few words reminding everyone of their duties to serve God and the tsar, and admonish workers to serve their employers. After the service, the employer would provide workers and supervisors with food and drink, either at the shop or in a nearby tavern, and sometimes join them himself (especially in smaller shops). If the celebration was to mark an employer's name day, the religious service would be followed

121. *Vestnik graficheskogo dela* 24 (December 22, 1897), pp. 246–47.

first by speeches and presents and then by the employer-sponsored carouse.[122]

In large enterprises, especially when the owners were active in one of the trade associations, workplace rituals could become quite elaborate in their enactment of moral community. As one worker recalled, "the larger employers . . . dressing themselves in sheep's clothing would cry 'We are your benefactors.' Services were offered up to God, pleasing speeches were made, and a banquet was laid out."[123] These festivities tended to be associated less with religious holidays than with celebrations of the firm itself—anniversaries of its founding, dedication of new facilities, or career anniversaries of the owner, manager, or a foreman. The general pattern of these celebrations followed the lines of the traditional shop ritual. A religious service would be held, attended by the employer, supervisors, and workers, and often by family members, customers, and special guests. Gifts would be presented and testimonials read. Workers would be expected to have selected a representative to present their gift (which was often an icon) and to express their appreciation of the employer or honored manager or supervisor. Finally, everyone would eat and drink, usually to the accompaniment of additional toasts. The whole event would be reported in the trade press as a joyous "family celebration."[124]

As with all such expressions by employers of the ideal of trade community, the symbolic message of these rituals varied. Some employers, especially former workers and the owners of small enterprises, liked to represent the relationship between themselves and their workers in relatively fraternal terms. When Otto Herbeck celebrated the fiftieth anniversary of his working career in 1902, his banquet was attended by workers as well as by other employers.[125] But the fraternal ideal was

122. *Istoriia leningradskogo soiuza*, p. 40; Vechtomova, *Zdes' pechatalas' "Pravda,"* p. 23; Iuferovyi and Sokolovskii, *Akademicheskaia tipografiia*, p. 95; Solov'ev, *Gosudar'ev pechatnyi dvor*, p. 95; *Tipografskii zhurnal* 2:7–8 (October 15, 1868), p. 28; *Knizhnyi vestnik* 1903, no. 21 (May 21), p. 671. On the general observation of this tradition in Russian industry, see Bonnell, *The Russian Worker*, pp. 42–43.
123. TsGAOR, f. 6864, op. 1, d. 56, p. 200.
124. For examples of celebrations of the careers of managers or foremen, *Graficheskie iskusstva i bumazhnaia promyshlennost'* 1:1 (September 1, 1895), pp. 14–15; 1:9 (June 3, 1897), pp. 81–82; 4:1 (January 1899), p. 13; *Pechatnoe iskusstvo* 1:1 (October 1901), p. 26; 1:2 (November 1901), p. 61; 1:5 (February 1902), p. 164; 1:7 (April 1902), p. 233. For examples of enterprise jubilees, dedications, or career anniversaries of employers, *Pechatnoe iskusstvo* 1:4 (January 1902), pp. 125–28; 1:7 (April 1902), pp. 232–33; 2:1 (October 1902), p. 29; 2:2 (November 1902), p. 49; 2:4 (January 1903), pp. 147, 151; 2:5 (February 1903), pp. 179–80.
125. *Naborshchik* 1:1 (October 20, 1902), pp. 16–18.

used by people from quite different backgrounds, such as when Aleksei Il'in, a member of the gentry and a military officer, celebrated the twenty-fifth anniversary in 1884 of the founding of his map-printing firm. After the usual religious ceremony and presentation of gifts, Il'in treated all those present to a meal at which, it was reported, "fellow officers, friends, and colleagues of the gracious host sat indiscriminately among engravers, pressmen, and employees," giving the meal a "family character."[126]

In larger enterprises especially, these affairs normally represented the relationship between employers and workers as less ambiguously paternalistic and hierarchical, though still as communal. For example, in the celebration in 1896 of the twentieth anniversary of the founding of Aleksei Suvorin's newspaper *Novoe vremia*, an older worker, selected by the workers to represent them, "humbly" thanked Suvorin for his "care" and his "constantly good and warm relations" with his workers. Suvorin responded with a fatherly gesture, donating an additional 5,000 rubles to the workers' aid fund, for which workers reportedly began cheering and shouting "Thank you, thank you, may God grant you health!" According to custom, Suvorin then treated his employees and guests to food and drink, though not "indiscriminately": press workers ate and drank within the plant itself, while compositors, office workers, and supervisors—as more respectable "employees" (*sluzhashchie*)— were treated at a small nearby restaurant. Suvorin himself joined his journalists and other guests at an expensive restaurant.[127]

Christmas, with its sacred and familial associations, was a favorite opportunity for an employer to present himself as benevolent father within his enterprise. In the early 1900s, a number of large employers began inviting workers and their families to Christmas parties (*elki*). Food and tea would be served, the children would be given small presents, and music would be performed, often by workers themselves. Sometimes a dance for the adults would follow. On such occasions employers expected and often received expressions of gratitude from their workers, as in 1898 when "Suvorin and his wife appeared among the children" to be greeted "by deafening and unceasing applause and the

126. *Knizhnyi vestnik* 1884, no. 5–6 (March 1 and 15), pp. 177–78; *Dvadtsatipiatiletie kartograficheskogo zavedeniia A. Il'ina*, pp. 10, 19.

127. *Graficheskie iskusstva i bumazhnaia promyshlennost'* 1:7 (March 1896), pp. 106–07. Every year, Suvorin also held a smaller celebration on the saint's day chosen to mark the founding of his newspaper. *Kratkii ocherk izdatel'skoi deiatel'nosti Suvorina*, p. 21.

sincere shouts of the parents, 'thank you, thank you' [*blagodarim*]."[128]
Like other practices in which employers sought to express their ideal of
the family of workers and employers, we see at the same moment a
celebration of community and a theater of power.

128. *Vestnik graficheskogo dela* 25 (January 31, 1898), p. 3. For other examples, *Pe-chatnoe iskusstvo* 1:2 (November 1901), p. 62; 2:3 (December 1902), pp. 99, 109–10; 2:4 (January 1903), p. 150; *Kratkii ocherk izdatel'skoi deiatel'nosti Suvorina*, p. 21; *Pechatnoe iskusstvo* 1:4 (January 1902), p. 130; *Naborshchik* 1:10 (January 5, 1903), pp. 176–77; 1:11 (January 12, 1903), pp. 192–93.

CHAPTER THREE
Workers' Community

Most workers were an obstinate audience for employers' efforts to proselytize the ideal of a family of workers and employers and the values of discipline, sobriety, and gratitude. Although the public face of labor relations in the industry remained calm—until 1903, strikes and other labor disturbances by Russian printers were virtually unknown—the absence of a direct challenge to authority did not preclude more subtle forms of resistance. Rather, the everyday life of printing workers exemplified the routine sort of resistance that one often sees where domination seems secure.[1] In effect, printing workers faced employers with a moral community of their own. It was less formal and explicit than the corporative ideal promoted by employers, but its practices were more deeply rooted in workers' everyday lives, in ordinary practices of sociability and comradeship. Drinking habits and rituals, manners of speech and demeanor, and attitudes toward work and leisure defined this workers' community and especially its difference and separation from those in authority.

This was an ambiguous community, however. First, it was divided within itself. The customs and rituals of sociability that created and sustained a sense of separate identity and solidarity among workers were overwhelmingly immediate, face-to-face interactions among workmates and were therefore tied to place and craft. The connection to

1. See the discussions of "everyday forms of resistance" in James Scott, *Weapons of the Weak;* idem, *Domination and the Arts of Resistance;* Certeau, *The Practice of Everyday Life;* Luedtke, "Cash, Coffee Breaks, Horseplay," pp. 65–95.

craft potentially widened the scope of worker community beyond a single workshop, but although there were moments when skilled printers viewed themselves as sharing a common identity, such perspective did not overcome the essential boundaries of a community demarcated by skill, occupation, and gender. Workers defined their identity not only in opposition to employers but also in contradistinction to other, different workers.

This workers' community also posed only an ambiguous challenge to authority. As in other situations where workers sustain values and behaviors largely resistant to elite efforts to guide them, these forms of resistance often do not lead to any more combative dissent.[2] There was no intrinsically militant telos toward which this separate worker culture was heading. Yet the everyday solidarities of worker community did not preclude such a course and in fact offered workers both a potential foundation for collective protest and organization and a refuge within which they could satisfy their needs to feel connected with the lives of others without the dangers of directly challenging their subordination.

APPRENTICESHIP AS SOCIALIZATION

In most of the printing crafts, a worker learned the ways of the worker community as a young apprentice. During these first years, a boy learned the techniques of his trade and was also inducted into a community of workers, taught its customs, and encouraged to conform to its mores. Apprenticeship was the medium through which workers reproduced their own community and culture. Appropriately, this socialization occurred in adolescence. At a time of life subject to emotional stress and role anxiety under any circumstances, working-class youths were compelled to spend most of their waking hours for six or seven days a week laboring in the company of unrelated but demanding adults. In this crucible were shaped many of the attitudes and expectations of the adult worker.[3]

2. Gareth Stedman Jones, "Working-Class Culture and Working-Class Politics in London, 1870–1900: Notes on the Remaking of a Working Class," in his *Languages of Class*, ch. 4; and Luedtke, "Cash, Coffee Breaks, Horseplay," esp. pp. 80–89.

3. The discussion that follows is based largely on workers' memoirs, cited below. In addition, valuable descriptions of apprenticeship in the Russian printing industry may be found in *Trudy pervogo s"ezda*, pp. 27–37, 53; Trotskii, "Ekonomicheskie i sanitarnye usloviia," part 1, pp. 78–79; *Istoriia leningradskogo soiuza*, pp. 59–63; and in the contemporary trade press, especially *Naborshchik* (1902–1916).

Most printing workers experienced some form of apprenticeship, though its structure and customs were best preserved in crafts where hand work was still predominant—engraving, lithographic transferring, bookbinding, and especially type composition, on which I focus. In a certain sense, the compositor was the "typical" printing worker. Although at one time most of the workers in the industry were pressmen—before mechanization a workshop typically employed two hand pressmen and two inkers for every type compositor—by the end of the nineteenth century, with press work largely mechanized but typesetting still mainly a hand craft, one-half to two-thirds of all typographic workers were compositors, and in the larger and more extensively mechanized plants the ratio might be as high as five to one.[4] Compositors also tended to determine workers' collective life in the industry. They were the dominant presence in almost all organizations and collective actions among printers (and in 1905 and after, they were an important presence in general labor organizations).

Compositors often remembered their years of apprenticeship as distressing and even traumatic, and considered surviving apprenticeship to be their first rite of passage into the worker community. Upon entering into an apprenticeship in the 1890s in what he had imagined would be "a holy temple of thought, a printing house," one compositor recalled finding "not learning, but martyrdom" (ne uchen'ia, a muchen'ia).[5] Many apprentices felt similarly tortured during the first months. In the 1870s, Gerasim Grents "prayed to God to end [his] torment," crying at the sight of other children playing in the street outside the plant.[6] Others also recalled tears.[7] In crafts such as engraving and bookbinding, where apprentices lived with their new masters, the distress of beginning a new and difficult life was reinforced by the separation from parents. The engraver Ivan Pavlov recalled screaming for his mother and crying most of the first day of his apprenticeship after his father handed him over to the shop master.[8] But even boys who could go home did not

4. Orlov, Poligraficheskaia promyshlennost' Moskvy, pp. 57–58; Perepis' Moskvy 1902 goda, part 1, vypusk 2, table 6; Varzar, Statisticheskie svedeniia o fabrikakh i zavodakh, part 2, pp. 36–37; Kratkii ocherk izdatel'skoi deiatel'nosti A. S. Suvorina, pp. 11–15; Bakhtiarov, Slugi pechati, p. 49.

5. TsGAOR, f. 6864, op. 1, d. 56, p. 200.

6. Naborshchik 1:12 (January 19, 1903), p. 201. This is a part of the memoir by "Shilo" (Gerasim Grents), "Istoriia moego ucheniia," Naborshchik 1:10, 12, 15, 18 (January–March 1903). Grents was an apprentice in Odessa in the 1870s, working in a type foundry, a pressroom, and a composition room, before moving to St. Petersburg.

7. For example, Aleksei Kairovich in Leninskii zakaz, p. 29.

8. Pavlov, Zhizn' russkogo gravera, p. 39. Pavlov was apprenticed in Moscow in the 1880s.

always find sympathy. When M. E. Egorov, an apprentice compositor, pleaded with his father not to be sent back to the printing shop but to be apprenticed in a metal factory, his father thrashed him.[9]

These youths had reason to despair. In what many hoped would be a "temple of learning," apprentices found an environment that more resembled a "barracks" or a "prison."[10] This oppressive atmosphere was partly the effect of the physical rigors of the job on boys starting work at the age of fourteen (and sometimes as young as ten or eleven, despite the child-labor legislation of 1882 and 1897).[11] They worked from eight to fourteen hours a day,[12] for little pay,[13] in an environment that was often filthy and malodorous. Contributing greatly to the torments of this new world were the adults who inhabited it. The compositor Egorov recalled his first impressions of the Pantaleev press in St. Petersburg where he was apprenticed in the 1890s: "The smell of ink, kerosene, and soot, the pounding of machines, half-drunk compositors who permanently smelled of something foul, the slaps, the errands every minute, now for *kvas*, now for *pirog* or sausage, the crudity—all this made a strong impression on me."[14]

Like artisanal apprentices in other crafts and other countries, a young compositor spent much of the time, especially in his first year, running errands. The employer or manager might require him to stop at a bakery for fresh rolls each morning, send him out during the day with packages for customers or deliveries to the censorship office, or have him sweep the floor or clean the toilets. But the largest number of demands came from the adult workers. An apprentice would often be sent to purchase vodka, tobacco, sausages, and pastries for the workers. Since most employers and managers forbade drinking at work,

9. Vechtomova, *Zdes' pechatalas' "Pravda,"* p. 23. This work contains the memoir of Egorov, an apprentice in St. Petersburg in the 1890s.

10. *Naborshchik* 1:10 (January 5, 1903), p. 169; Vechtomova, *Zdes' pechatalas' "Pravda,"* p. 22.

11. *Ekho*, November 30, 1883, p. 3; Svavitskii and Sher, *Ocherk polozheniia*, pp. 10, 47; *Protokoly pervoi vserossiiskoi konferentsii*, p. 79.

12. Mikhailovskii, *Otchet za 1885 god glavnogo fabrichnogo inspektora*, pp. 102–03, 137–38; *Prodolzhitel'nost' rabochego dnia i zarabotnaia plata rabochikh*, pp. 91–92, 215; Bernshtein-Kogan, *Chislennost'*, pp. 130, 138, 141; Sher, *Istoriia*, pp. 47–52; TsGAOR, f. 6864, op. 1, d. 216, pp. 44–45; Vechtomova, *Zdes' pechatalas' "Pravda,"* p. 22.

13. For the first three months an apprentice usually received no pay at all. He would get a few rubles a month during the remainder of the first year, which would increase to no more than ten rubles, about one-third the pay of a regular compositor, by the final year. Trotskii, "Ekonomicheskie i sanitarnye usloviia," part 1, p. 78; Davydov, *Otchet za 1885 god fabrichnogo inspektora*, pp. 72–78.

14. Vechtomova, *Zdes' pechatalas' "Pravda,"* p. 22.

vodka had to be smuggled in without their knowledge, though fore-men, who were more directly involved in shop-floor life, were often co-conspirators. For an apprentice to refuse to run errands or smuggle in vodka was to risk ostracism: adult compositors would shun the unco-operative apprentice, perhaps refuse to teach him, and slap him for the slightest error. To succeed in the smuggling and other assignments was to become known as an "artful dodger" (*lovkach*) and to earn the re-spect of the adult workers.[15] By pleasing one's teachers, these successes also hastened the time when running errands would end and real train-ing in the skills of the trade would begin. But these social lessons were no less essential to a worker's education. Workers learned what it meant to be a comrade and also mastered the routine deceptions with which workers faced authority.

Other experiences in an apprentice's life offered additional moral lessons. Slaps and beatings (varied with ear pulling, nose twisting, and hair yanking) by both foreman and fellow workers were a pervasive fact of life for most apprentices, viewed by most adults as essential to a proper upbringing.[16] Also common were more subtle forms of abuse. Like all artisans, compositors and other skilled printers had their own special craft humor, fool's errands for the uninitiated. An innocent ap-prentice might be sent to the plant's printing shop to ask the workers there for a "*marashka*"—a typographic term for a poorly locked-up space that spoils a page by showing up in print—only to get a good-natured but still-painful and humiliating smack from a pressman.[17] Or an apprentice might be sent to a nearby store and told to ask for two kopecks' worth of "pull" (*taska*), to which request the knowing shop-keeper would pull the boy's hair and kick him out. When he returned in confusion to the workshop, the adult workers would laugh and then tell him, "That's exactly what we sent you for, stupid, now you'll be a little smarter."[18]

15. TsGAOR, f. 6864, op. 1, d. 216, pp. 45–46. From the unpublished memoir of M. A. Popov, who was apprenticed in Moscow in the 1880s.

16. Zinov'ev, *Na rubezhe dvukh epokh*, p. 11; *Naborshchik* 1:15 (February 9, 1903), p. 248; TsGAOR, f. 6864, op. 1, d. 60, p. 1 (unpublished memoir of an apprentice com-positor in St. Petersburg in the 1890s).

17. *Leninskii zakaz*, pp. 29–30; also TsGAOR, f. 6864, op. 1, d. 216, p. 44. Such ini-tiatory rites are still practiced among skilled printers in the United States. At the start of my own brief apprenticeship in a printing shop in New York, I was sent by the senior pressman to another shop in the building to ask for "a bucket of halftone dots," only to be laughed at for my ignorance when I requested this quite non-portable element of pho-tographic offset lithography, and teased even more mercilessly when I returned to my own shop, red-faced and naturally empty-handed.

18. Pavlov, *Zhizn' russkogo gravera*, p. 44.

Beatings and fool's errands served a complex function in apprenticeship. Partly, they were just what apprentices often felt them to be: the
cruelty of ignorant men looking to have a good laugh or to take out
their aggression on someone weaker. However, they were also part of
the apprentice's education—his preparation to join the community and
culture of adult workers. Fool's errands, rooted in the argot of the craft,
taught new workers its secrets, and beatings punished an apprentice
for his mistakes. Fool's errands were also practical lessons in "street
smarts" (*smekalka*), and beatings helped to ensure a certain tough resignation, both of which were needed to get by in the world.[19] Finally,
beatings and humiliating jokes were part of the customary culture of a
craft community. This reproduction of custom had its simple side: they
did this to us when we were apprentices, so we shall do the same to you.
Yet even this simple repetition of treatment suggests a rite of passage.
Like the willingness to run errands and smuggle in vodka, enduring
beatings and humiliation were requirements for acceptance. And conformity, like street smarts and fortitude, was one of the moral rules on
which this community was built.

Apprenticeship was also a forced march into adulthood. Although
most adult workers disapproved of drinking, smoking, and swearing
by apprentices—sometimes beating offenders when they were caught—
they made no effort to shelter boys from such behavior. They drank
heavily, swore bawdily, and openly bragged about sexual adventures.
This exposure to the adult world could be disturbing to a young apprentice. One compositor recalled being "terribly shocked and as-
tounded by all this sort of talk and drunkenness and decided that there
were no worse people in the world than compositors."[20] But workers
would also recall being fascinated as apprentices by adult talk—which
included discussions not only about sex but also about life in the world,
distant places, and even literature. Of special interest were the tales of
wanderers—a familiar group among compositors—who described the
lives of peasants in different regions, the work of printers in the provinces, and assorted "scandals" they had witnessed.[21]

Acculturation into this adult world was often aided by a separate
youth culture among apprentices, which mimicked many of the standards of the adults. Especially in the larger enterprises, where a number

19. A discussion by a sociologist of "socialization through insult" can be found in
Flynn, *Insult and Society*, ch. 8.
20. TsGAOR, f. 6864, op. 1, d. 60, pp. 1–2.
21. Ibid., d. 216, p. 48.

of apprentices were being trained at the same time, they often formed a community of their own. During the long midday break and after work, apprentices often spent time together—playing children's games like tag and leapfrog (*piatnashki* and *chekharda*), and also taunting passers-by and picking fights with one another.[22] Some apprentices even formed gangs that fought other gangs, imitating the sporting collective brawls that were common among both urban workers and peasants.[23]

The solidarity of this youthful community was evident from the moment a new apprentice was hired: one compositor recalled the "extremely unfriendly looks" of the other apprentices on his first day at work.[24] But a new apprentice would soon be initiated, much as an adult worker would be accepted into the larger workshop community. One compositor recalled that soon after he was hired as an apprentice at the age of twelve, the other apprentices approached him and "began to pester me, 'Let's have a smoke, got any cigarettes?' 'I don't smoke.' 'What! What sort of a comrade are you?! Here, take a puff, just so we won't think you're giving us the cold shoulder.' " When he received his first paycheck at the end of the fourth month, he was expected to treat his fellow apprentices to drinks at a local tavern.[25] Generally, young workers learned to drink and smoke in the company of their peers. Drinking and smoking, of course, were attractive as symbols of adulthood. But they also served as rituals of comradeship and conformity among apprentices.

The psychological, moral, and social impact of apprenticeship was complex and varied. Some observers worried that the main effect was to demoralize workers: "The apprentice sees nothing good, nothing that might have a salutary effect on his young spirit and preserve him from a drunken, half-starved, itinerant life. His youth is broken and spoiled."[26] But this same evidence can be read in other ways. Parents put a son into an apprenticeship with the hope of benefiting from his

22. Zinov'ev, *Na rubezhe*, p. 9. Lunch breaks for apprentices often lasted two to four hours to comply with regulations limiting the actual working time of minors to eight hours a day.

23. TsGAOR, f. 6864, op. 1, d. 60, p. 4. On the general phenomenon, see V. Lebedev, "K istorii kulachnykh boev na Rusi"; Buiko, *Put' rabochego*, p. 15; Brower, "Labor Violence in Russia in the Late Nineteenth Century," pp. 425–26.

24. *Naborshchik* 1:12 (January 19, 1903), p. 198.

25. TsGAOR, f. 6864, op. 1, d. 60, pp. 9–10.

26. *Vestnik graficheskogo dela* 15 (August 13, 1897), p. 141. The author, Aleksei Filippov, was a supervisor who had himself been a compositor.

future earnings but also hoping to "make a man of him."[27] Indeed, apprentices learned to drink, smoke, and swear, usually before they were fifteen. They also learned a measure of independence and personal responsibility. When an apprentice made mistakes, he suffered physically. If he was talented—even if only at smuggling vodka into the shop—he was rewarded. Adults complained that apprentices quickly became "inattentive and rude," finding ways to avoid doing what they were told, wasting time, sneaking away to smoke, and talking back. In a word, it was said, they began to "strut arrogantly about like adults."[28] This coming of age was psychological and personal but also social. While an apprentice, a boy learned what it meant to be a "comrade"—to be street smart and tough, to drink and smoke with one's fellows, not to be aloof. Apprenticeship taught him the values and standards of the community of adult workers, and it taught him to conform to these, contributing both to a worker's sense of self and to his identity as a member of a collective that stood apart and distinct from others.

COMMUNAL SPACE

As apprentices learned, the workplace and working time were not entirely the domain of the employers. Workers expropriated portions of working time and space—the terrain that most symbolized their subordination to others—for their own uses, for being together with one another and apart from authority.[29] They smuggled vodka into the shop, talked, drank, and swore together—certainly undermining the efforts of employers to train obedient and well-behaved future workers but maintaining a significant light-heartedness, a playful and thus less threatening expression of collective solidarity and disobedience.

This mixture of playfulness and challenge was especially evident in practices associated with alcohol. Although drink pervaded the social lives of most male workers in Russia, compositors were particularly prodigious drinkers, a subject of persistent concern among employers.

27. *Naborshchik* 1:27 (May 4, 1903), p. 444.

28. Ibid. 1:17 (February 25, 1903), p. 286; 1:20 (March 16, 1903), pp. 339–40.

29. Alf Luedtke has used the concept of *Eigensinn* to describe everyday practices in which workers "expressed a space of their own" during "expropriated bits of the time formally designated as working time." *Eigensinn* was "expressed and reaffirmed by walking around and talking, by momentarily slipping away or day-dreaming, but primarily by reciprocal body contact and horseplay." Luedtke, "Cash, Coffee Breaks, Horseplay," pp. 79–80. See also James Scott, *Domination and the Arts of Resistance*, ch. 2 ("Making Social Space for a Dissident Subculture"); Certeau, *Practice of Everyday Life*, pp. xix, 34–39.

A letter to the trade journal *Tipografskii zhurnal* in 1867 complained that when compositors receive their wages on Saturday, "these people know no moderation" but spend the entire weekend drinking so much that they are often unable to work on Monday.[30] Employers and managers, but also temperance advocates among the workers, focused on the excesses: drunken binges after payday, absenteeism on Mondays and even Tuesdays, the dissipation of a week's earnings or more on a single weekend, and the resultant suffering of their families.[31] Periodic bouts of severe drunkenness were certainly common to most printing workers, but alcohol also held a more constant and measured place in their lives. Most compositors drank (usually surreptitiously) during their midday meal break, many drank occasionally throughout the day, and many spent at least a few weekday evenings at the local tavern.

Compositors drank for many reasons. They drank for their health, believing, as many contemporaries did, that alcohol was beneficial to good health, and specifically that it fortified the body against the ill effects of lead dust.[32] They drank to escape—"to forget, not to think, not to feel."[33] Finally, though not least in importance, they drank for the sake of sociability and community. Drink was so much a part of the customary life of the workshop that compositors had their own special vernacular to describe the many occasions on which they drank. Ordinary drinking, especially if heavy, was simply *balda*—a term suggesting stupefaction (literally, a heavy hammer or a stupid person). *Khlopoty* (sometimes *khlopochi*) also referred to everyday drinking, but in a restricted sense more directly tied to the associational life of the workshop.

In normal usage, *khlopoty* refers to troubles and worries and also busy activity. Among printers, it described the daily, and illegal, process of collecting money from all the workers for the purchase of vodka and snacks, begging an advance from the owner or a loan from the foreman if cash was short (such loans were known as payment "by the hatchet"—*vydacha "na topor"*—since they required repayment at substantial interest), and dispatching an apprentice off to the local tavern. When an employer succeeded in effectively barring apprentices from

30. *Tipografskii zhurnal* 1:8 (October 15, 1867), p. 34.
31. *Trudy pervogo s"ezda*, p. 56; *Naborshchik* 1:20 (March 16, 1903), p. 326; 1:47 (September 21, 1903), pp. 702–04.
32. *Naborshchik* 1:7 (December 15, 1902), p. 119.
33. Ibid 1:27 (May 4, 1903), pp. 451–53. See also *Obzor graficheskikh iskusstv* 1879, no. 4 (February 15), pp. 26–27; *Naborshchik* 1:6 (December 8, 1902), pp. 104–05; 1:18 (March 2, 1903), pp. 293–94; 1:23–24 (April 6, 1903), pp. 381–82; 1:25 (April 20, 1903), pp. 412–13.

leaving the shop, workers would appeal to the plant doorman, to workers delivering paper or supplies, even to passers-by on the street to purchase vodka for them. In some shops workers planned ahead and organized special drinking funds. All this was in preparation for the midday break, when compositors would drink, eat, talk, and play cards.[34]

In addition to this everyday drinking, there were ritual occasions requiring organized and sponsored drinking, either at the workplace or at a local tavern. Drinking was essential to the rite by which an apprentice, after completing his training, was initiated into the community of adult workers. One does not find in Russia the elaborate ceremonies by which artisans in Western Europe initiated a new journeyman into their company—mock baptisms with water, wine, or beer, bestowing of "titles," speeches stylized according to familiar custom, which reflected well-established corporative structures not found among Russian craftsmen. Russian printers, in particular, possessed no equivalents to the "chapels" of English compositors and pressmen or the brotherhoods of journeymen printers in France, which had since "time out of mind" enforced order in the trade and facilitated fellowship, professional identity, and mutual assistance.[35] In general, such corporative customs were little developed among Russian workers. However, at least among Russian printers—engravers, hand lithographers, typefounders, and especially type compositors—customs of solidarity, though less formal and rooted more in the workplace than in a larger craft community, nonetheless effectively expressed the existence and sense of collectivity.

Some compositors staged relatively elaborate initiation rituals. In shops where immigrant German compositors predominated, the traditional German *Gautschfest* was practiced as late as the early 1900s.[36] Russian ceremonies may have been influenced by immigrants, though the forms suggest inventiveness as much as borrowing. For example, at the State press in St. Petersburg in the 1890s, on the first payday after an apprentice compositor completed his training, all the compositors

34. See especially TsGAOR, f. 6864, op. 1, d. 60, pp. 2–3; Vechtomova, *Zdes' pechatalas' "Pravda,"* p. 23; *Istoriia leningradskogo soiuza*, pp. 38–39.

35. Howe, *The London Compositor*, pp. 23–32 (quotation, p. 23); Child, *Industrial Relations in the British Printing Industry*, pp. 35–39; Davis, "A Trade Union in Sixteenth-Century France," pp. 48–69; idem, "Strikes and Salvation at Lyon," in *Society and Culture in Early Modern France*, pp. 1–16; Sewell, *Work and Revolution in France*, pp. 42–47, 55–56.

36. *Naborshchik* 1:36 (July 6, 1903), p. 562.

would gather together, someone would put an old top hat or paper fool's cap on the former apprentice's head, and the oldest worker would ceremoniously lead him around the composition room.[37]

For most Russian compositors it was enough to mark the completion of apprenticeship with drink, for which the former apprentice would pay (sometimes, especially in smaller workshops, with the help of a contribution or a loan from the employer). This sponsored drinking had its share of ceremonial and even symbolic elements. To distinguish this rite from ordinary drinking, the event was named: an apprentice compositor was said to be "cleaning the heels" (*chistit' kabluki*) of his new comrades (typefounders called it "milking the cow"). Humorous speeches would sometimes be made welcoming the former apprentice into the brotherhood of craftsmen. This ceremonial completion of apprenticeship also signified the passage into adulthood. As one compositor recalled, "I was consecrated [*posviatili*] as a compositor with vodka, beer, and cigarettes, which for the first time I was allowed to smoke in the presence of the older comrades."[38]

There were other occasions when a worker was expected to "clean the heels" of his comrades at the local tavern: when he was hired in a new shop (on the first day of work or after he received his first wages), on his name day, when he was married, and when his children were christened. These occasions of sponsored collective drinking were signs of the integration of a worker's whole life into the shop community and as such were treated as moral duties. The symbolic importance of these ceremonies was expressed in their enforced camaraderie. Although *kabluki* typically cost a worker from 1 to 3 rubles and could cost more (out of a typical monthly wage of 30 rubles for a compositor in 1900), to refuse was to knowingly stand outside the collectivity and invite ostracism. A worker who refused the often-expensive custom of treating his shopmates, one recalled, "would not be accepted as a comrade."[39]

This everyday community among workers was in important respects a community of men. At the start of the twentieth century, women still comprised only about 5 percent of the total number of typographic

37. TsGAOR, f. 6864, op. 1, d. 60, p. 2.
38. Ibid., d. 216, p. 50. See also ibid., d. 60, p. 2; *Naborshchik* 1:7 (December 15, 1902), pp. 118–19; Vechtomova, *Zdes' pechatalas' "Pravda,"* pp. 23–24; *Istoriia leningradskogo soiuza,* pp. 38, 427.
39. TsGAOR, f. 6864, op. 1, d. 60, p. 2. See also Iuferovyi and Sokolovskii, *Akademicheskaia tipografiia,* p. 95; Vechtomova, *Zdes' pechatalas' "Pravda,"* p. 24; Zinov'ev, *Na rubezhe,* pp. 16, 18, 22–23; Galaktionov [Shponik], *Lebedinaia pesn',* p. 5; *Naborshchik* 1:12 (January 19, 1903), p. 206; *Istoriia leningradskogo soiuza,* p. 38.

workers (5.7 percent in St. Petersburg in 1900, 4.2 percent in Moscow in 1902), almost all of whom worked either as proofreaders or in semi-skilled jobs in binding departments, mainly folding and sewing signatures.[40] Composition work, typefounding, and machine work remained male preserves. In the few instances when women were hired as compositors before 1906—when their numbers began to grow—they were put to work in separate rooms.[41]

This circumstantial exclusion of women from the workplace facilitated the importance that gender came to occupy in the solidarity and identity of these worker communities.[42] Workers' common sexual identity—at least its presumption—was one of the bonds that united them. For example, when work was slow, compositors might gather around a shop window "enjoying and rating the legs of the women passing by."[43] Everyday talk also often had a certain locker-room quality. As one Petersburg compositor recalled:

> Foul language . . . was used for almost everything, in every situation, without the slightest modesty before the young apprentices (there were still no women). Stories and talk to apprentices were always seasoned with street-corner swearing. And when they swore, they swore strongly, with force, using triply compounded obscenities, facetious sayings, and proverbs all in the same breath. It was a kind of game. . . . For the most part, the talk among workers was about boozing and about various adventures with women and sexual encounters. All was spoken openly, shamelessly, down to the last detail.[44]

This was indeed "a kind of game"—competitive, personal, rooted in stereotypically masculine behavior, and demanding conformity if one wished to be considered a "comrade." Sometimes this play went beyond talk. After a new worker received his first paycheck, and after the customary drinking party, he might be taken whoring: "Whoever did not wish to go along would be laughed at. It was necessary to conceal not debauchery but self-restraint, or one would be mocked."[45] Heavy

40. *Perepis' Moskvy 1902*, vypusk 2, tables 6–8; *S.-Peterburg po perepisi 1900 goda*, vypusk 2, table 2.
41. For example, Levenson, *Istoricheskii ocherk*, pp. 20, 25, 49.
42. For an important argument about the relevance of gender for interpreting expressions of collective identity, among men as well as women, see Joan Wallach Scott, *Gender and the Politics of History*, esp. chs. 2–3.
43. *Naborshchik* 1:51 (October 19, 1903), p. 768. As printing shops were often located in basements with high windows near the street, workers thus turned the physical disadvantages of their position to their own uses.
44. TsGAOR, f. 6864, op. 1, d. 60, pp. 1–2.
45. Ibid., p. 2.

drinking, coarse swearing, physical roughness, and competitive sexuality were bonds that united these individuals as men as well as workers.[46]

In a different way, female relatives also represented figures against whom this male worker community defined itself. On paydays, wives, sisters, and mothers were often seen standing outside of printing shops waiting to pull their husbands, brothers, or sons home before they could escape to the tavern, or at least to take part of their pay for household expenses. Workers habitually ridiculed these women "tugboats" (*buksiry*) and sometimes ignored them. "If a 'tugboat' is late or the husband succeeds in slipping away unnoticed," an observer wrote in 1903, "it means grief for his unfortunate family—only a memory remains of a two-week wage."[47] In the face of a definition of worker identity and community rooted in workplace and craft, female relatives represented competing identities of family, kin, and perhaps neighborhood, and were often spurned.

Death is a final rite of passage that can define a community and its self-image. In the more developed craft communities of Western Europe, the collective and ritualized response of a community to the death of a member was an important expression of its identity as a corporative body.[48] Less formally, Russian compositors felt a similar communal obligation to help bury their own and to use this occasion to recall the ties between them. It was common for a widow to turn to her husband's former comrades for money in order to bury him, and it was expected that workers would pay. If the dead worker had been single, a friend or other relative might initiate the collection; sometimes the dying worker himself might turn to his comrades for help. Often this money would be collected as a "subscription" paid out by the plant office on credit against workers' future wages. Even after the establishment of assistance funds and burial societies, this custom, "the origins of which are lost in the distant past," persisted.[49] Attendance at a

46. Without accepting Lionel Tiger's biological determinism or the normative implications of his arguments about male social bonding (for which he has been criticized as a "theorist of patriarchy"), there is still value in his discussion of male-only social relationships as an important and distinctive form of collective solidarity. Tiger, *Men in Groups*. See also Stearns, *Be a Man: Males in Modern Society*.

47. Trotskii, "Ekonomicheskie i sanitarnye usloviia," part 2, p. 96.

48. See, for example, Sewell, *Work and Revolution in France*, p. 36.

49. *Vestnik graficheskogo dela* 28–29 (April 2, 1898), p. 52 (quotation); *Graficheskie iskusstva i bumazhnaia promyshlennost'* 1:11 (July 1896), p. 173; *Naborshchik* 1:17 (February 25, 1903), pp. 286–87; 1:48 (September 28, 1903), p. 720; Galaktionov [Shponik], *Lebedinaia pesn'*, p. 8.

worker's funeral was more contingent on how well-known an● liked a man was.

Behavior at funerals expressed how workers perceived and wished to represent their mutual relationships. Some funerals were solemn and dignified expressions of collective loss. These, naturally, were the ceremonies most often described in the professional press, which wished to encourage greater decorum. When a compositor at Suvorin's *Novoe vremia* press died in 1903, a large crowd of his fellow workers followed his coffin as it was drawn in a hearse to the cemetery. After prayers in the chapel, workers carried their late comrade's coffin to the grave. Following the burial, one compositor read a poem he had written for the occasion:

> Our friend is buried, he is with us no more
> One less comrade is among us . . .
> Gathering to pay our last respects
> We are comforted to see the circle in which the departed once lived.

Hymns were then sung and wreaths from his co-workers and his family were placed around the grave.[50]

Other funerals presented a different face of the community of compositors. Half of the money collected for a worker's funeral would often be set aside for vodka.[51] And "instead of speeches," one critic complained, "they sing obscene songs."[52] It is not necessary to prettify workers' drunkenness and coarseness to recognize here too a contribution to their solidarity as a collectivity. It was only fitting that at the death of a compositor, as on his initiation into this community, drink should define the customs of observance.

This worker community should not be viewed as more harmonious than it was. The everyday solidarity of workers was a rough sort of community that did not erase the tenacious individualism that set workers apart not only from employers but also from one another. Many of the practices that brought workers together remained ambiguous. Collective drinking, for example, expressed not only comradeship but also, as drunkenness increased, the withdrawal of the individual into himself. Sexual bragging was a collaborative game but also a

50. *Naborshchik* 1:21 (March 23, 1903), p. 356.
51. *Trudy pervogo s"ezda*, p. 48.
52. *Vestnik graficheskogo dela* 28–29 (April 2, 1898), p. 52. This may have been a reflection of peasant traditions in urban industry. On *radunitsa*, the traditional day of the dead in Russia, peasants customarily blended "funeral motifs, lamentations, wailings, and other kinds of expression of grief for the deceased, with outbursts of unrestrained merriment, gluttony, drunkenness and debauchery." Sokolov, *Russian Folklore*, p. 166.

competitive contest of egos. As has been suggested in a study of German machine workers, the everyday practices within the workshop by which workers defined time and space of their own simultaneously evoked "being-with-the-other" and "being-with-oneself."[53]

This ambivalence was made stronger by the very structures of workers' lives, which similarly pushed them apart even as they brought them together. In the composition room, especially, personal interaction was encouraged by the absence of noisy and demanding machinery, by the uneven pace of work where "rushes" and overtime alternated with enforced idleness as workers waited for new manuscripts, and generally by a high level of direct control by compositors over the pace and process of their labor, facilitated by payment by the piece. These conditions gave compositors a high degree of natural autonomy at work, and thus the opportunity to create the customs and rituals of community.

Simultaneously, however, this autonomy reinforced the individual's isolation. The work process in type composition—as well as in typefounding, bookbinding, and much handpress work—was individualistic, requiring acts of separate labor before one's own type case. This fragmentation of the work process itself was reinforced by piece rates (which are only possible when work has this individual character). These work structures separated workers within a common craft by levels of skill, earnings, and prospects for advancement. But even among workers with identical skill and earnings, reliance on piece rates encouraged conflicts between workers. When, for example, a compositor had to search several type cases to find a needed typeface or more leading—spacing material of which one needed large quantities—he disturbed the work of other compositors as well as causing a loss of his own wages. On such occasions, annoyance might escalate into arguments and even fist fights.[54] Even efforts to overcome the divisive effects of piece rates sometimes created new ones: when compositors formed "companies" to work collectively at a set price for a job, they became competitors of other "companies" of compositors, each trying to offer the lowest price.[55]

These tensions and conflicts persisted beside the rituals of conformity and comradeship. For workers who viewed this ambiguous reality from the standpoint of the ideal, community seemed hardly to exist at

53. Luedtke, "Cash, Coffee Breaks, Horseplay," pp. 80–82.
54. *Istoriia leningradskogo soiuza*, pp. 24–25; *Naborshchik* 1:3 (November 17, 1902), p. 53; Rossiiskaia sotsial-demokraticheskaia rabochaia partiia, Moskovskii komitet, *Pis'mo k moskovskim naborshchikam* (1899), p. 2; Zinov'ev, *Na rubezhe*, p. 16.
55. Orlov, *Poligraficheskaia promyshlennost' Moskvy*, p. 274.

all. Memoirs recall "coolness and hostility" among workers and a lack
of solidarity or " 'comradeship' in the best and most sincere meaning
of the word," but only a "splintered and motley" collection of individuals.[56] In fact, solidarity and difference often coexisted.

Workers' sense of community often reached beyond the limitations
of workplace and even craft. The immediate, face-to-face interactions
among individuals with similar skills, which defined and sustained the
workplace community, also implied a larger craft identity. And this often merged with a wider identification as "printer" (*tipograf, tipograf-
shchik, pechatnik*), as sharing an identity with all *skilled* crafts. This
wider occupational community found its own structures to sustain it.
The assistance funds provided one locale for wider association. In St.
Petersburg and Moscow, several hundred compositors, pressmen, typefounders, and bookbinders joined the assistance funds and participated
in their various organized activities.[57] More commonly, the tavern
served as a gathering place for printers from different shops and crafts.
Two types of taverns can be distinguished: neighborhood bars where
workers from nearby shops would gather regularly during the midday
break and after work (and where they could usually drink on credit),
and special taverns that brought together printers from throughout the
city to socialize and also learn of job openings, such as the *Gong* and
the *Maidan* in St. Petersburg, and the *Golubiatnia* ("Dovecote") and
Tsarskoe selo in Moscow.[58] Both kinds of drinking places brought together workers from diverse crafts.

We do not know the complex lines of fraternization that may have
occurred within the walls of these taverns or at gatherings organized by
the assistance funds. What is evident, however, is that perceptions of
skill often determined association and thus the perceived boundaries of
(and exclusions from) this larger community. Compositors, notably,
were often openly contemptuous of less skilled printers. They referred
to ordinary press workers, for example, simply as "workers" (*rabochie*
or *chernorabochie*) or even as "peasants" (*muzhiki*). They would welcome a printing master into their company, drinking with him at the

56. *Naborshchik* 1:34 (June 22, 1903), p. 534; *Tipografiia Lenizdata: K 175-letiiu so
dnia osnovaniia tipografii imeni Volodarskogo Lenizdata*, p. 21.
57. Workers' involvement in these funds is discussed in Chapter 4.
58. TsGAOR, f. 6864, op. 1, d. 216, p. 46; Zinov'ev, *Na rubezhe*, pp. 13, 17,
20–21; Vechtomova, *Zdes' pechatalas' "Pravda,"* p. 23; Galaktionov [Shponik],
Lebedinaia pesn', p. 6; *Ekho*, November 30, 1883, p. 3; *Naborshchik* 1:28 (May 11,
1903), p. 452.

tavern or even at work,[59] but they avoided socializing with less skilled workers, including all women working in the industry, and generally treated them rudely.[60]

> I will not be guilty of excessive exaggeration if I say that most compositors consider it beneath them even to speak with a press feeder, to say nothing of the fact that when addressing them they always use the informal *ty*.[61]

This haughtiness extended to workers in other industries. A Petersburg compositor recalled that if compositors "heard that there was a strike in some factory, they would say, 'the workers are demanding something,' and would show no further interest, since they did not consider themselves to be workers, but something in between workers and intellectuals."[62]

EVERYDAY CULTURE

As this last comment suggests, collective identity among printing workers, especially compositors, was defined not only by levels of skill, common craft, or place of work, all of which were nonetheless essential to workers' calculations as they drew the boundaries of community around themselves. Also important were the practices by which workers defined themselves when they were not at work.

The characteristics of this everyday worker culture, and its limits, can be seen by viewing its margins. At one extreme stood workers known in printers' jargon as "Italians"—homeless tramps who alternated between intense work and vagabondage. They were easily recognizable by their appearance: "pale and thin, with haggard faces, and a continual cough. Their clothing was filthy and torn: a cap made of paper; trousers so threadbare that they would stuff in paper and hold them up with cord; a shirt made of sackcloth, patched in several places; ragged footwear, and sometimes even bast shoes."[63] They were also

59. See, for example, Egorov's memoir in Vechtomova, *Zdes' pechatalas' "Pravda,"* p. 23.

60. *Obzor graficheskikh iskusstv* 1878, no. 13 (July 15), p. 95; *Naborshchik* 1:8 (December 22, 1902), pp. 134–35; 1:23–24 (April 6, 1903), p. 382; TsGAOR, f. 6864, op. 1, d. 60, p. 5; *Istoriia leningradskogo soiuza,* pp. 11–12; Iuforovyi and Sokolovskii, *Akademicheskaia tipografiia,* p. 94.

61. *Pechatnyi vestnik* 1905, no. 8 (August 21), p. 8.

62. TsGAOR, f. 6864, op. 1, d. 60, p. 5.

63. From the unpublished recollections of M. V. Levin, quoted in Vechtomova, *Zdes' pechatalas' "Pravda,"* p. 27.

distinguished by their habits. During the summer they would often travel about the country, sleeping in barns or open fields, taking temporary jobs in provincial towns, earning a little money and then quitting until destitute again. Most drank heavily. When in town, they slept on the floors of printing shops when they were employed, and when they were without work they slept in flophouses (*nochlezhnye doma*) in city slums such as the "Viazemskaia lavra" in St. Petersburg or the Khitrov market in Moscow. They also sometimes begged at churches. When they worked, they accepted lower wages than average—even though some were quite skilled—and often did not leave the shop for days, working as many hours as they could and sleeping by their type frames. After a time, when enough money was saved, they would quit work and move on.[64]

At the opposite end of the scale were "aristocrats," generally better-paid compositors who, it was said, "liked to dress well, in the summertime arrived at work on a bicycle, always wore starched linens and worked in their own smocks, wore fancy hair styles, attended theaters and dances, went to the races, were interested in sports, frequented clubs, and generally maintained a *bon ton*."[65] They typically joined mutual assistance funds or burial societies in order to protect themselves and their families in the event of sickness, retirement, or death, and tended toward sobriety. Many also sought to improve themselves culturally. Ivan Galaktionov recalled being invited in the late 1880s to the apartment of an older compositor named Ivolgin, where "the walls of his two small rooms [a sizable apartment for a compositor] were positively covered by shelves filled with books," including many of the classics of Russian literature and criticism.[66] Another compositor recalled a "respectable elder compositor" regularly reading poetry to apprentices after work.[67] Occupying the margins of working-class life, such workers felt alienated from most of their fellow workers, who, they complained, were interested in nothing except "boozing and scandals" and sought "consolation and diversion only in vodka and the

---

64. *Istoriia leningradskogo soiuza*, pp. 15–16, 27; Trotskii, "Ekonomicheskie i sanitarnye usloviia," part 1, pp. 96–97; TsGAOR, f. 6864, op. 1, d. 216, p. 47; Vechtomova, *Zdes' pechatalas' "Pravda,"* pp. 26–27; Zinov'ev, *Na rubezhe*, pp. 20–21. There was an extended discussion from May 1902 through August 1903 of the problem of *ital'ianshchina* in *Pechatnoe iskusstvo* (1:8 and 9) and *Naborshchik* (1:13, 20, 21, 22, 30, 34, 38–39, and 41–42).
65. *Istoriia leningradskogo soiuza*, p. 15.
66. Galaktionov, *Besedy naborshchika*, p. 7.
67. *Po povodu tridtsatiletiia VKT*, pp. 5–6.

tavern."[68] But their testimony may reveal more about their own high standards than about the actual interests of their fellows.

Most compositors, in various degrees, combined in their lives elements of both "aristocrats" and "Italians." The pattern of work of most compositors suggested, in a less exaggerated manner, the cycle of fitful work and extended unemployment of the "Italians." During rushes, piece-rate compositors might work several days of overtime, work during meals, and even sleep at the shop; on other occasions they might fail to return to work for days, especially after a particularly inebriated weekend.[69] Similarly, the perpetual mobility of "Italians" was only an exaggerated form of the wanderlust of most compositors. A typical compositor, it was said, was "a common migrating bird," a "free Cossack" with an inherent "tendency for vagrancy."[70] A survey conducted in Moscow in 1907 found that only one-quarter of all compositors had been working in the same enterprise for more than five years, and that nearly one-third had worked in two or three different cities.[71] Piece rates and a high demand for labor facilitated this itinerancy. So did recurrent temporary unemployment: each summer, as business slowed, some workers would be laid off until the fall,[72] and every decade or so—in 1867, 1878–1881, and 1902–1903—recessions put thousands of compositors out of work.[73] But vagabondage was also a matter of inclination. It was, some said, "in the compositor's blood."[74] M. A. Popov was not unusual in joining a "company" of traveling compositors that contracted for jobs in various cities, then

68. *Naborshchik* 1:34 (January 22, 1903), p. 534; Galaktionov, *Besedy naborshchika*, p. 6; Zinov'ev, *Na rubezhe*, p. 32.

69. For one example, TsGAOR, f. 6864, op. 1, d. 216, p. 47.

70. *Vestnik graficheskogo dela* 17–18 (September 25, 1897), p. 176; Trotskii, "Ekonomicheskie i sanitarnye usloviia," part 2, p. 95; *Naborshchik* 1:6 (December 8, 1902), p. 104; 1:14 (February 14, 1903), p. 233; *Trudy pervogo s"ezda*, p. 118.

71. Svavitskii and Sher, *Ocherk polozheniia*, pp. 11–14.

72. Orlov, *Poligraficheskaia promyshlennost' Moskvy*, p. 217; *Obzor graficheskikh iskusstv* 1878, no. 18 (October 1), p. 135.

73. In 1867, 7% of compositors in St. Petersburg were unemployed and 10% were working part time, and unemployment was also reported in Moscow. In 1878, "thousands" of compositors were said to be out of work. In 1900–1903, unemployment among compositors may have been as high as 20%. These economic crises were made worse by an influx of workers from the provinces who believed that at least in Moscow and St. Petersburg there would be work. *Tipografskii zhurnal* 1:8 (October 15, 1867), p. 34; 1:9 (November 1, 1867), p. 37; *Obzor graficheskikh iskusstv* 1878, no. 18 (October 1), p. 135; 1881, no. 16 (August 15), p. 103; *Pechatnoe iskusstvo* 1:8 (May 1902), pp. 259–60; *Naborshchik* 1:1 (October 20, 1902), pp. 6–7; 1:13 (January 26, 1903), p. 213; 1:36 (July 6, 1903), p. 561; 1:46 (September 14, 1903), pp. 685–86; Trotskii, "Ekonomicheskie i sanitarnye usloviia," part 1, pp. 78, 81.

74. *Istoriia leningradskogo soiuza*, p. 33.

settling briefly in Samara, moving next to St. Petersburg, and then undertaking to walk to Moscow and observe country life along the way. "I was all the time searching for something," he wrote, "I could not sit still."[75] Whether the "something" being searched for was transcendent or something as plain as higher pay, a better boss, more compatible workmates, or simply a change of pace, large numbers of compositors were on the move.[76]

Also like the "Italians," most workers defied society's efforts to define and control workers' everyday behavior. Coarseness and profanity, we have seen, ruled in the shops. Workers occasionally joked about their defiant rowdiness: "Compositors are unmanageable," a foreman was said to have complained to a press owner, "abuse, abuse, and more abuse. You can't even walk through the composition room. One even just sent me to the devil!" "Then why," the owner responded, "are you coming to me?"[77] Managers and employers discovered how deeply this unmanageability ran when they tried to "improve" workers—to make them drink less, become better mannered and knowledgeable, work more assiduously, and change jobs less often.

At the same time, many compositors did in fact share the desire of "aristocrats" to be more respectable and cultured. Middle-class observers, and many compositors themselves, frequently suggested that the work of the compositor led him naturally toward self-cultivation. As the "first reader" of every work, the compositor was said to have been made more cultured and educated through the very process of his work.[78] A poem by Nikolai Nekrasov, set in the voice of a compositor, was often quoted as an expression of this belief:

> Compositors are at times
> Philosophers. . . .
> They encounter essays
> They encounter intellects—
> Useful ideas
> We are mastering.[79]

75. TsGAOR, f. 6864, op. 1, d. 216, pp. 50–52.

76. Ibid., pp. 46–48; *Istoriia leningradskogo soiuza,* pp. 32–33; Trotskii, "Ekonomicheskie i sanitarnye usloviia," part 2, p. 95; *Naborshchik* 1:4 (November 24, 1902), p. 77; 1:57 (October 19, 1903), pp. 768–69; Zinov'ev, *Na rubezhe,* pp. 14–29.

77. *Naborshchik* 1:1 (October 20, 1902), p. 22.

78. Bakhtiarov, *Slugi pechati,* p. 3; Trotskii, "Ekonomicheskie i sanitarnye usloviia," part 1, p. 77; *Peterburgskii listok,* January 20, 1868, p. 1; *Ekho,* November 30, 1883, p. 3; *Obzor pervoi vserossiiskoi vystavki* 4 (March 2, 1895), p. 7; *Naborshchik* 1:1 (October 20, 1902), p. 7; 1:3 (November 17, 1902), p. 54; 1:12 (January 19, 1903), p. 196; 1:17 (February 25, 1903), p. 280.

79. From "Naborshchiki," a section of "Pesni o svobodnom slove" (1866), in N. A. Nekrasov, *Polnoe sobranie sochinenii i pisem,* vol. 2 (Leningrad, 1981), p. 214.

Skeptics, including some compositors, viewed such notions as flattering but naive. The work of the compositor, they argued, was "mechanical." Most compositors lacked the education to understand much of what they set into type, and at any rate rarely did they have before them more than a fragment of a larger work. Even if a compositor could understand the sense of a text, trying to do so would have slowed his pace and thus reduced his earnings.[80] Still, even critics often conceded that compositors acquired "scraps of knowledge" through their work.[81] Just as important, the myth of the compositor as "philosopher" itself encouraged a self-image that many compositors sought to justify in practice.

For many workers, the obstacle to becoming a worker "aristocrat" was mainly money: "To attend theaters and dances regularly is beyond my means," one compositor wrote in 1903.[82] Within this limitation, many compositors did all they could to cultivate a more mannered lifestyle. They sprinkled their vocabulary with intellectual-sounding phrases and referred to one another as "colleagues,"[83] and they dressed on special occasions and sometimes even at work in starched shirts and neckties.[84] Some workers attended free public literary readings, lectures, and concerts.[85] Most of all, workers read. In almost every printing shop, compositors subscribed collectively, usually on credit, to an inexpensive popular newspaper, borrowed books from public libraries, or bought cheap used books. A compositor writing in 1903 estimated that half of all compositors read books or periodicals in their leisure time, though most preferred newspapers to the "thick journals" and preferred popular (*lubochnaia*) literature, such as the tales of the bandit Churkin (serialized in *Moskovskii listok* in the 1880s), to belles lettres.[86]

80. *Istoriia leningradskogo soiuza*, p. 14; Trotskii, "Ekonomicheskie i sanitarnye usloviia," part 1, p. 78; TsGAOR, f. 6864, op. 1, d. 216, p. 49; *Obzor pervoi vserossiiskoi vystavki* 4 (March 2, 1895), pp. 7–8; *Naborshchik* 1:1 (October 20, 1902), p. 3; 1:13 (January 26, 1903), p. 213; 1:20 (March 16, 1903), pp. 328–29.

81. *Naborshchik* 1:20 (March 16, 1903), p. 329. Of interest in this regard is the conclusion of two Soviet psychologists who studied compositors: "The fact of continual—though admittedly external—contact [*obshchenie*] by compositors with diverse literary materials cannot but have an influence on the psycho-physical apparatus of the workman." Gellershtein and Ittin, *Psikhologicheskii analiz professii naborshchika*, pp. 16–17.

82. *Naborshchik* 1:21 (March 23, 1903), p. 358.

83. Ibid. 1:13 (January 26, 1903), p. 213.

84. Zinov'ev, *Na rubezhe*, p. 30; *Obzor pervoi vserossiiskoi vystavki* 13 (April 3, 1895), p. 4; *Naborshchik* 1:7 (December 15, 1902), p. 128.

85. Sher, "Moskovskie pechatniki v revoliutsii 1905 g.," in *Moskovskie pechatniki v 1905 g.*, p. 12; *Leninskii zakaz*, p. 23; *Naborshchik* 1:34 (January 22, 1903), p. 535; *Istoriia leningradskogo soiuza*, pp. 91, 429; Zinov'ev, *Na rubezhe*, p. 32.

86. *Obzor graficheskikh iskusstv* 1880, no. 23 (December 1), p. 176; *Naborshchik* 1:13 (January 26, 1903), p. 213; Trotskii, "Ekonomicheskie i sanitarnye usloviia," part

Common work and common subordination did not efface the persistent differences and tensions that kept workers apart. The culture of "boozing and scandals" coexisted with the pursuit of respectability partly as expressions of different workers. But these alternatives also reflected the ambivalent values and desires of most workers: the wish to be a good "comrade" but also to escape, if only privately, from the smells, filth, monotony, and coarseness of the workplace; the wish to live according to rules and norms not set down by those in authority, but also to be recognized as no worse than other people by adopting these same standards and manners. This ambivalence had its limits. As will be seen, even workers who sought to uplift themselves culturally and morally expressed perceptions of themselves and the world around them that challenged established structures of authority and subordination, that defined the starched shirt and necktie, the volume of Nekrasov's poetry beneath the workbench or typeframe, or even the refusal to get drunk, at least partly as defiant gestures.

2, p. 97; TsGAOR, f. 6864, op. 1, d. 216, p. 46; Galaktionov, *Besedy naborshchika*, p. 10. See Brooks, *When Russia Learned to Read*, on lubochnaia and street literature generally.

CHAPTER FOUR

A Moral Vanguard

Among the owners of graphic enterprises there are monsters [*urody*] who trample upon the human dignity that by right belongs to their workers. Happily, these isolated types exist almost unnoticed, leaving hardly a trace in the mass of our more or less humane employers, the majority of whom have begun to treat us not as workers, but as collaborators in their great endeavor, for which we are extremely grateful.

Ivan Loginov, a compositor, speaking at a printing festival in 1883

A sense of marginality before both society and other workers may encourage in workers feelings of both alienation and anger. This perception may result from the acquisition of craft skills, especially in a society where these skills are still scarce, or from intellectual encounters with provocative ideas about the individual and society, or simply from personal inclination; frequently all of these influences are present. Their effect is often painful self-awareness: resentful feelings of being excluded and humiliated by employers and by society in general but also alienation from the often rough and drunken ways of worker sociability. Such estrangement has led some workers to seek an escape into a more attractive world of literature and manners, and perhaps also to flee from their working-class jobs. But marginality has also led paradoxically to collective protest, association, and leadership.[1] Among Russian printing workers in the decades before the first open conflicts of 1903 and 1905, we see the emergence of just such an alienated, and increasingly critical, elite.

For printers, in Russia as elsewhere, the self-perception of being on the social margins was encouraged by the distinctive product of their labor. Type compositors, especially, tended to feel that their work gave them a special worth, since their skillfulness lay not in muscular

1. For an illustration from a quite different social and political setting, see Rancière, *Nights of Labor.*

strength or knowledge of machinery but in their ability to handle letters and words, tools of culture. "A compositor is not a common worker," Russian compositors often asserted, in words like those heard among printers in many countries, "but a semi-intellectual man of labor" (*truzhenik-poluintelligent*).[2] Such status pride could lead workers to challenge their subordination and poverty as offensive to their natural honor. But work experience itself was only a part of the source of this critical self-esteem. Their intellectual sensibility had more to do with encounters with new ideas and values than with the steady accumulation of everyday experience. In this, these printers had less in common with many workers in their own craft than with the minority of workers in diverse industries and occupations who considered themselves "conscious."[3]

Although some of these workers withdrew into a kind of "internal exile,"[4] in which personal cultivation and the world of literature became a barrier between them and all but a few like-minded workers, many defined themselves as exemplars and guides, setting themselves up, as it were, as a vanguard. The conventional model of the vanguard worker, of course, was the class-conscious socialist influenced by and often associated with the radical intelligentsia. Such types were found only rarely among printers before the coming of mass strikes in the early 1900s. When reading the reminiscences by even the most politicized printing workers of later years, often written in the 1920s when connections to the socialist movement were usually emphasized, one is struck by the evident paucity of Social Democratic influence before 1903 in Moscow and 1905 in St. Petersburg.[5] This was largely because Social Democrats, especially in Moscow and St. Petersburg, had less interest in printers than in workers in the large textile and especially metal factories, who were more conveniently concentrated and more visibly restive.

Nonetheless, individual printing workers became involved in socialist groups. In several printing houses in St. Petersburg, small groups of compositors established political self-education circles (*kruzhki*), where they met together to read and talk and sometimes stole type and ink for

2. *Naborshchik* 1:9 (December 29, 1902), p. 160.

3. See McDaniel, *Autocracy, Capitalism, and Revolution,* esp. ch. 8; Bonnell, *Roots of Rebellion;* Zelnik, "Russian Bebels"; Zelnik, *A Radical Worker in Tsarist Russia.*

4. McDaniel, *Autocracy, Capitalism, and Revolution,* p. 203.

5. Similarly, histories of Russian printing workers, also written mainly by participants, mention little or no contact between printing workers and the socialist intelligentsia. Sher, *Istoriia; Istoriia leningradskogo soiuza; Materialy po istorii professional'nogo dvizheniia rabochikh poligraficheskogo proizvodstva.*

underground party organizations.[6] In the 1890s, a group of Social Democrats led by the student M. I. Brusnev organized a small circle for Petersburg lithographic printers, which included several workers who would in 1904 be active in the Gaponist movement and in 1905 help to establish a lithographers' trade union.[7] In Moscow, too, scattered evidence suggests at least irregular contacts between workers and *intelligenty*. For example, an agitational letter to Moscow compositors, which was evidently written by a compositor and which mentioned a printers' club that sought legalization, was issued by the Moscow committee of the Russian Social Democratic Workers' Party and reprinted in 1899.[8] Later, the rhetoric of some of the leaders of the Moscow printers' strike in 1903 would echo the language of Social Democracy.[9]

It must be noted that printers in Moscow and St. Petersburg were paradoxically in a political backwater compared to printers in many provincial cities. In smaller and more economically traditional towns, the relative smallness of the factory proletariat caused Social Democrats to pay more attention to workers such as printers and to organize circles among them and distribute radical literature.[10] Such activity in the provinces did affect the capitals, however. The migration of printing workers around Russia, and often to Moscow and St. Petersburg, meant that socialist workers themselves were often the main carriers of socialist ideas to other printers.[11]

This chapter focuses attention on a different vanguard, which was larger and more influential. Its members were found not in illegal circles with ties to the radical intelligentsia but in legal assistance funds sponsored by employers. They read and wrote not for underground socialist publications but for legal trade journals and especially for the first legal workers' journal in Russia, the weekly *Naborshchik* (*The Compositor*). Most importantly, their message was in many ways

6. *Istoriia leningradskogo soiuza*, p. 78.

7. Karelin, "Deviatoe ianvaria i Gapon," p. 106; idem, "Soiuz litografskikh rabochikh," p. 13. See Chapter 6.

8. Rossiiskaia sotsial-demokraticheskaia rabochaia partiia, Moskovskii komitet, *Pis'mo k moskovskim naborshchikam* (1899), pp. 1–9.

9. See Chapter 5.

10. Degot', "Odesskie pechatniki v revoliutsionnom dvizhenii (iz lichnykh vospominaniia)," p. 236; Poliak, "Na zare rabochego dvizheniia v Zapadnoi Rossii (iz vospominaniia)," 13–14.

11. This was the case, for example, of Ivan Liubimtsev, the only compositor known to be a Social Democrat among the workers who organized the printers' union in St. Petersburg in 1905, and of A. Goloveshkin, a compositor who led one of the major Social Democratic circles among printers in St. Petersburg in the 1890s. Both men came from Nizhnii Novgorod. *Istoriia leningradskogo soiuza*, pp. 78, 438.

opposed to that of the class-conscious socialist vanguard. They openly
cherished paternalistic management and shared employers' dreams of a
trade community uniting masters and men in moral solidarity. But the
opposition between these two groups was not absolute. When workers
thought about a moral community, what they imagined was more than
a simple reflection of the ideal of employers and managers. Although
they joined their social superiors in preaching to their fellow workers
the virtues of thrift, sobriety, and intellectual cultivation, they did so to
remind workers of their human worth, so that society would show
workers more honor. And though they accepted the social power that
employers had over them, they did so because they thought it could
be made more humane and moral. In challenging authority these workers were still amicable and sympathetic, but they were challenging it
nonetheless.

ORGANIZING SELF-IMPROVEMENT

Although mutual assistance funds among printing workers were the
oldest and most highly developed workers' aid organizations in Russia,[12] most printing workers never participated in a fund. In 1900 in St.
Petersburg, out of nearly 12,000 workers in typographic and lithographic printing firms, only about 1,200 were members of either the
Compositors' Assistance Fund or the smaller German fund. A larger
number of workers joined funds that required less active involvement:
approximately 1,600 joined the Printers' Burial Society after its formation in 1899, and another 2,000 may have participated in funds established in individual printing plants. In Moscow, the level of involvement was even lower: out of approximately 7,300 printing workers in
1902, only 485 belonged to the Typographers' Assistance Fund, and enterprise funds were only beginning to appear (see table 4). Even if we
add to these totals the several hundred workers who had joined a fund
but had to be excluded for not paying their dues,[13] we can estimate, for
the early 1900s, that somewhat less than half of all printing workers in

12. On the general development of workers' mutual aid in Russia, see Prokopovich,
K rabochemu voprosu v Rossii, pp. 8–22; Sviatlovskii, "Iz istorii kass i obshchestv vzaimopomoshchi rabochikh," pp. 32–46; Bonnell, *Roots of Rebellion*, pp. 76–79.
13. Between 1866 and 1904 in St. Petersburg, 1,448 fund members were excluded, as
were 651 in Moscow from 1869 to 1901. Subtracting 25 percent of these as likely to have
moved to another city (an informed guess) and 10 percent as having died (the proportion
of *members* who died in these years) leaves a residual of 900 former members remaining
in St. Petersburg and 375 in Moscow.

St. Petersburg and only one-seventh in Moscow had any experience at all in organized mutual aid.[14]

The level of participation was higher among some groups than others. Skilled workers, and especially compositors, showed the greatest interest, reflecting in part the intentional exclusion of the less skilled. In St. Petersburg, the Compositors' Assistance Fund did not, after its early years, restrict membership to compositors, but its charter implied that only skilled workers were welcome—the list of potential members included, besides compositors, "printing masters, engravers, lithographers, and typefounders."[15] The charter of the Moscow fund stipulated no such restrictions, yet we find a similar imbalance. Of the 1,013 identifiable workers who joined the fund between 1869 and 1901 (excluding owners, managers, and office employees), 54 percent were compositors, 16 percent were press masters or skilled hand press workers, and 13 percent were skilled typefounders (see table 5). Although no detailed statistics are available on the craft structure of the industry as a whole, using estimates of contemporaries we can calculate that compositors made up about one-quarter of all printers in Moscow (less than in St. Petersburg, where the proportion was closer to one-half, probably because of the more extensive mechanization of press work in the capital),[16] and skilled press workers, as we have seen, were increasingly outnumbered by takers-up and feeders. Thus, even the more open Moscow fund drew disproportionate support from skilled labor.

Those willing to serve as elected officers of a fund, a choice suggesting a deeper commitment to the ideals of the organization than simple membership, were drawn from a still narrower and still more marginal social stratum. In St. Petersburg between 1866 and 1905, of the nineteen most active members and officials of the Assistance Fund whose occupations are known, eleven were promoted workers, mostly compositors who had advanced to positions either as senior compositors (*metranpazhi*) or production managers. All of the nine directors of the

14. Grents and Galaktionov, *Obzor*, p. 27; *Sbornik svedenii VKT*, p. x.
15. *Ustav vspomogatel'noi kassy naborshchikov v S.-Peterburge*, p. 6; Grents and Galaktionov, *Obzor*, p. 24.
16. *Trudy pervogo s"ezda*, p. 118. Speakers at the congress believed there to be about 4,000 compositors in St. Petersburg and 1,500 in Moscow in 1895. The 1897 census counted 8,160 printing workers in St. Petersburg and 5,990 in Moscow (counting typographic, lithographic, engraving and similar crafts). *Chislennost' i sostav*, vol. 2, part 1, pp. 178–79, and part 2, pp. 22–33. This ratio is confirmed for Moscow, and some change is indicated, by a *partial* count of printing workers by craft in the 1902 census, which identified 1,887 compositors and 3,589 other typographic or lithographic workers (in other words, 34% compositors). *Perepis' Moskvy 1902 g.*, pt. 1, vypusk 2, table 6.

TABLE FOUR   MEMBERSHIP IN ASSISTANCE FUNDS, 1869–1904

	St. Petersburg				Moscow
	German Fund (from 1838)	Compositors' Fund (from 1864)	Burial Society (from 1899)	Enterprise Funds	Typographers' Fund (from 1869)
1869–70	115	204	–	–	342
1877–82	120	305	–	–	156
1890	–	505	–	–	291
1901–04	ca. 300	924	1,600	ca. 2,000	485

SOURCES *Otchet dvadtsatipiatiletnei deiatel'nosti VKN*, pp. 4, 46; Grents and Galaktionov, *Obzor*, p. 27; *Obzor deiatel'nosti vspomogatel'noi kassy "Obshchestva tipografshchikov*," p. 2; *Sbornik svedenii VKT*, pp. viii–ix; and reports in the professional press and publications by individual firms on their activities. The number of members in private funds is estimated using a ratio of 60 percent of the labor force in these firms, which approximates the ratio in enterprises where membership is known. See similar figures in *Istoriia leningradskogo soiuza*, pp. 87–88.

TABLE FIVE   OCCUPATIONAL COMPOSITION OF THE
TYPOGRAPHERS' ASSISTANCE FUND, MOSCOW, 1869–1899

Compositors	543
Skilled workers:	
Hand printers (typographic)	60
Machine printers (typographic)	33
Lithographers	17
Engravers and designers	29
Other	27
	166
Semiskilled and unskilled:	
Press takers-up	86
Press feeders	46
Hand-press inkers	25
	157
Typefounders	128
Bookbinders	19
Managers:	
Production managers (*faktory*)	28
Directors and senior managers	15
Office personnel	17
Owners	22
Others	81
Total	1,176

SOURCE *Sbornik svedenii VKT,* pp. xi, xxv, 12–49.

fund in these years were managers or employers, but at least four were
former compositors. Promoted workers also proved to be the most
committed and influential: the directors of the fund (initially named
treasurers) for at least twenty-nine out of the first forty years were
former compositors.[17] In Moscow, skilled and promoted workers also
played the leading role: of the twenty-three senior officers and leading
activists of the fund from 1869 through 1899, nine were skilled workers

17. Those identified as "most active members" include treasurers, officers who held
office for five or more years, and other individuals described in the sources as exceptionally active but exclude those serving only as financial donors. Of a total of 37 such individuals, the occupations of 19 (the most active) are known. Based on the evidence from
Moscow, it is probable that these unknowns were compositors or other skilled printing
workers. Grents and Galaktionov, *Obzor,* pp. 3–23; *Otchet dvadtsatipiatiletnei deiatel'-
nosti VKN,* pp. 9–41; Vorob'ev, *Kratkii ocherk VKN,* pp. 5–9; *Tipografskii zhurnal* 2:4
(August 15, 1868), pribavlenie, pp. 1–2; *Obzor graficheskikh iskusstv* 1878, no. 6 (April
1), p. 45; 1880, no. 8 (May 15), p. 76; 1883, no. 13 (July 1), p. 115; 1884, no. 11 (June
1), p. 86; *Knigovedenie* 1894, no. 7–8 (September 3), p. 35.

(seven compositors, including one *metranpazh,* and two typefounders), three held the position of production manager, a job usually filled by promoted compositors, and two were employers who had once been workers. An additional four were white-collar workers (mostly book-keepers) employed in press offices.[18]

The salience of skilled and often socially mobile workers in the funds partly reflects one of the important obstacles to membership—high dues. For most unskilled and semi-skilled workers, the 2-ruble initiation fee and 1-ruble monthly dues (60 kopecks in Moscow) were simply too costly.[19] Most unskilled and less-skilled printers, as we have seen, earning between 10 and 30 rubles a month, but also some compositors, fell beneath normal subsistence levels.[20] Although their need for assistance was greater, self-help through organized thrift was simply not a realistic possibility.[21]

Activists recognized that high dues were often an obstacle to membership. In 1899, though the compositors' fund already insured members in case of death, a separate Burial Society was organized in St. Petersburg, which required only a 1-ruble initiation fee and no monthly dues; when a member died, other members paid 25 kopecks toward his burial. It was hoped by the organizers that such "unburdensome dues" would allow "every servant of this honored art of printing to ... rest assured that when the moment of his departure to a better world comes, his family, so oppressed with grief, will not be faced with the additional anguish and care of the required expenses of a funeral for their dear departed."[22] And indeed, more than 700 workers joined the Burial Society during its first month. The charter, which allowed no more than 1,000 members, soon had to be revised in order to admit the many workers who wished to join.[23] Yet membership was still far from embracing "every servant."

18. *Sbornik svedenii VKT,* pp. ix–xii, 12–58. This list counts individuals who served as treasurer or assistant treasurer, held office as *upolnomochennyi* or *revizor* for ten or more years, or were described by contemporaries as particularly active (unless only as financial supporters).

19. *Trudy pervogo s"ezda,* p. 47; Trotskii, "Ekonomicheskie i sanitarnye usloviia," part 2, p. 104; *Pechatnoe iskusstvo* 1:1 (October 1901), p. 27.

20. Semanov, *Peterburgskie rabochie nakanune pervoi russkoi revoliutsii,* p. 85.

21. See the discussion of wage levels in Chapter 1. Although there are no direct data on the wages of fund members before 1905, unpublished data for 1907 show that three-quarters of all members in the Moscow fund earned wages above industry averages. Sher, *Istoriia,* pp. 79–80.

22. *Pechatnoe iskusstvo* 1:3 (December 1901), p. 86.

23. *Biulleten' RODPD* 1:4 (March 1902), p. 55; *Naborshchik* 1:46 (September 14, 1903), p. 685.

Even most compositors did not join. In 1895, it was estimated that only 15 percent of compositors in St. Petersburg and 10 percent in Moscow belonged to an assistance fund (excluding members of enterprise-based funds).[24] Part of the problem was simple ignorance; many workers apparently did not even know that the funds existed or what their purposes were.[25] Information about the funds was usually spread by employers or managers, many of whom did not especially care whether their workers joined a fund and thus made no effort to inform workers of their existence, much less encourage membership as activists hoped they would. Consequently, 85 percent of the members of the Typographers' Assistance Fund in Moscow (we have no equivalent data for St. Petersburg) worked in only eleven firms, all of which had owners or managers who actively supported the fund.[26]

In the opinion of many fund activists, however, the main reason a worker participated or did not participate in a fund was not his knowledge of its existence and goals or his ability to afford membership but his perception of its value. The real obstacle keeping most workers out of the funds, or causing them to leave after a brief membership, these activists repeatedly argued, was "thoughtlessness and unconcern" (*legkomyslie i bespechnost'*) about their future, a preference for the immediate solace of drink to the sense of future security that membership in a mutual aid fund would provide.[27] As such, membership implied above all a different mental outlook among workers. Higher levels of skill and income and, for some, the experience of greater social mobility, may have contributed to this outlook by already positioning them apart from both employers and most workers. But as the non-participation of many skilled or socially mobile workers indicates, participation in mutual aid funds delineated not simply a social elite but also an intellectual and cultural elite or, to use words that correspond more closely to their own self-perception, a moral vanguard.

The employers and managers who helped to run and financially sustain the funds, we have seen, viewed the material aid provided to workers as inseparable from the tutelary goals of the funds: raising workers' cultural level and encouraging their moral virtue. The workers and

24. *Trudy pervogo s"ezda*, pp. 47, 118.
25. Ibid., p. 47.
26. *Sbornik svedenii VKT*, p. xi.
27. *Trudy pervogo s"ezda*, pp. 48 (quotation), 117–18; *Po povodu tridstatiletiia VKT*, p. 4; Galaktionov [Shponik], *Lebedinaia pesn'*, pp. 6–12; *Obzor graficheskikh iskusstv* 1878, no. 3 (February 15), p. 17; 1878, no. 9 (May 15), p. 64; *Pechatnoe iskusstvo* 1:5 (February 1902), p. 162; *Naborshchik* 1:6 (December 8, 1902), pp. 111–12.

promoted workers who were attracted to the funds often shared these goals. They often saw the very decision to join a voluntary mutual aid fund as an act of moral responsibility and commitment.[28] The compositor Stepan Tsorn associated mutual aid with the social ideals of Samuel Smiles, the Victorian British author of *Self-Help, Character, Thrift,* and *Duty.*[29] And he was not alone in sharing Smiles's high valuation of "diligent self-culture, self-discipline, and self-control" in a context of mutually respectful cooperation between masters and men.[30] "Self-help," another compositor wrote, was a "moral obligation" but also a matter of personal dignity: why "suffer the humiliation" of begging from one's fellow workers in times of need, when one could preserve "self-esteem" for only a ruble a month as a member of an assistance fund?[31]

The outlook of these advocates of organized mutual aid, as these examples suggest, expressed not only a different sense of self but even a different relationship toward time. Ivan Galaktionov, a compositor promoted into lower management, recalled that when he was a young worker in St. Petersburg in the 1880s, an elderly compositor tried to persuade him to join the Compositors' Assistance Fund because "it would be better to lay aside our hard earned money for a dark day" than to spend it drinking with one's fellows. It was wrong, this longtime member of the assistance fund proclaimed, to "live only for today."[32] That he should think so suggests not only a greater attentiveness to the passage of time but a greater confidence that he could master his own fate.

Although material security in the future was the primary reason for membership in an assistance fund, many members were also attracted by the efforts by the funds, especially in St. Petersburg, to "raise the level of development of working people in printing."[33] Each year, starting in 1877, several hundred members, spouses, and guests attended the "music and dance evenings" organized by the Compositors' fund in St. Petersburg. In Moscow, the Typographers' fund began organizing simi-

28. *Naborshchik* 1:8 (December 22, 1902), pp. 137–38; 1:19 (March 19, 1903), p. 313.

29. Ibid. 1:19 (March 19, 1903), p. 313.

30. Smiles, *Self-Help,* p. xi. See also Bendix, *Work and Authority in Industry,* pp. 109–13.

31. *Naborshchik* 1:22 (March 30, 1903), pp. 361–62.

32. Galaktionov [Shponik], *Lebedinaia pesn',* pp. 5, 7. See also *Obzor graficheskikh iskusstv* 1878, no. 9 (May 15), p. 64.

33. *Otchet dvadtsatipiatiletnei deiatel'nosti VKN,* p. 5.

lar evenings after 1900.[34] The cost of these annual affairs was high: 1 ruble for members in the early years (non-members paid 2), and between a ruble and a half and 3 rubles by 1902. Most of the participants were compositors accompanied by their wives or female guests, though some of these compositors had become senior compositors or production managers. Employers often purchased tickets to these events to support the fund, but few actually attended.[35] The large part that employers and managers played in their planning should caution us against viewing them as unambiguous expressions of a worker culture, but they do indicate a desire among some workers to enjoy more respectable entertainment and a willingness to define this respectability— in their term, *kul'turnost'*—in ways that employers seemed to share.

Fund members and guests dressed in their finest clothes for these evenings: "It is impossible not to observe," noted a somewhat condescending but accurate report in a trade paper about the 1897 evening, "that the dress of the 'printing ladies,' though not particularly luxurious or expensive, was in most cases elegant and charming."[36] Workers who attended the evenings sought to distinguish themselves not only in appearance but also in manner of entertainment. Unlike most of their comrades, it was said, they sought to "forget their hard daily labor" not through "the inspiration of Bacchus" but "in the whirl of a waltz or a polka."[37]

The evenings began in a rather formal manner. Everyone would sit with a printed program in hand—decorated with a portrait of Gutenberg, a coat-of-arms made of symbols reflecting the work of a printer, or some other appropriate embellishment—and watch a rather eclectic mix of entertainment that might include scenes from plays or one-act comedies, portions of a ballet, excerpts from Russian or foreign operas, chamber music, folk songs, and vaudeville.[38] Most of the performers were hired professionals, but some were workers:

> On stage they appear, one after the other, with balalaikas in their hands, mostly attractive young people, dressed in frock coats and white ties. Mod-

34. *Pechatnoe iskusstvo* 1:9 (June 1902), p. 282; *Naborshchik* 1:38–39 (July 20, 1903), p. 586.
35. *Vestnik graficheskogo dela* 24 (December 22, 1897), pp. 249–50.
36. *Graficheskie iskusstva i bumazhnaia promyshlennost'* 2:2 (January, 1897), p. 32. See also *Obzor graficheskikh iskusstv* 1883, no. 5 (March 1), p. 42.
37. *Vestnik graficheskogo dela* 24 (December 22, 1897), p. 249; *Graficheskie iskusstva i bumazhnaia promyshlennost'* 2:2 (January 1897), p. 31.
38. *Obzor graficheskikh iskusstv* 1878, no. 9 (May 15), p. 65; 1882, no. 10 (May 15), p. 65; 1883, no. 5 (March 1), p. 42; *Graficheskie iskusstva i bumazhnaia promyshlennost'* 4:3 (March 1899), p. 50; *Pechatnoe iskusstvo* 1:3 (December 1901), p. 85.

est, even a bit embarrassed, they sit on their chairs and begin to play. . . .
When they finish—an uncontainable outburst of delight seizes the listeners.
And how can they not be in raptures! . . . After all, these balalaika players
are members of their very own corporation—they are compositors.[39]

Following the performances, food and drink were sold—a further expense of attending these evenings—and dancing would begin. Young
workers and their guests would dance until well past midnight, while
older workers would dance a little but mainly eat, drink, listen to the
orchestra, and talk among themselves.

In May 1903, a group of members of the Compositors' Assistance
Fund of St. Petersburg—compositors, former compositors who had
been promoted into supervisory positions, and a few sympathetic employers—announced the formation of a Typographers' Music and
Drama Circle. Although the club proved to be a failure—legal restrictions on its activities, the expense of the entertainments, and the admission of officers, university students, and others such that even press
managers admitted feeling out of place combined to make it into little
more than a dancing club, and one in which workers took little
part[40]—the original plans for the circle accurately reflected the tastes
and aspirations of the cultural vanguard of St. Petersburg printers.
Members and their families were to be "given the opportunity to spend
their leisure time usefully, comfortably, and pleasantly." The circle was
to organize "various sorts of walks, readings, concerts, operatic and
theatrical shows, and technical discussions," as well as amateur orchestras and choirs, gymnastics, and games, and on its premises it planned
to establish a library with a permanent reading room and a tea room.[41]
In the Music and Drama Circle, it was hoped, cultivated printing workers could create a haven of "useful and healthy" activity, away from the
oppressive atmosphere of the shops and from the crudity of their fellow
workers.

The organizers of assistance funds sought not only to encourage personal cultivation among workers but to link it to the social ideal of a
moral community. Workers were encouraged to find healthy entertain-

39. *Graficheskie iskusstva i bumazhnaia promyshlennost'* 2:2 (January 1897), p. 31.
See also *Pechatnoe iskusstvo* 2:2 (November 1902), p. 68; *Naborshchik* 1:7 (December
15, 1902), p. 128.
40. *Naborshchik i pechatnyi mir* 1905, no. 106 (February 10), p. 85; *Istoriia leningradskogo soiuza*, p. 91.
41. *Naborshchik* 1:31 (June 1, 1903), p. 504.

ment in the company of like-minded workers and to feel the guiding presence of benevolent authority. Descriptions of music and dance evenings invariably mention some notable employer "sitting in the front row."[42] Their presence was even more apparent at events such as the annual summer excursions organized by the Petersburg compositors' fund in the 1890s. As described by Andrei Filippov, a compositor promoted into lower management, the 1899 outing was a perfect example of the familial atmosphere and respectable behavior that the fund always tried to encourage. On a steamboat hired by the fund and decked out with national flags, men wearing "frock coats, jackets, and workers' blouses" and women "in elegant summer toilette and in simple dresses" traveled to a country picnic and dance. At the symbolic center of the voyage was Petr Mikhailov, co-owner of the Lehmann typefoundry and a leading patron of the fund, to whose summer home in Schlüsselburg the boat was heading. He led this workers' excursion dressed in an elegant frock coat and wearing his state decorations. During the meal, workers toasted the health of their employers and the officers of the fund.[43]

Participation by workers in a mutual aid fund may have reflected little more than a desire to gain a modicum of economic insurance for themselves and perhaps for their families in case of sickness, disability, or death. But at least for the minority who articulated the meaning of their membership, and probably for many of those who took part in the cultural activities of the funds, even the desire to ensure one's material security reflected a deeper moral consciousness, a higher level of "self-awareness and self-activity."[44]

But what sort of "self-awareness" was this? A case may be made for identifying this activist minority as a "labor aristocracy." Many members of the aid funds belonged to that elite of workers that compositors themselves called "aristocrats." And they shared social traits with the labor aristocrats of the classic definition: they were skilled and often upwardly mobile, earned higher than average wages, were devoted to personal cultivation, held themselves aloof from the mass of workers (sometimes refusing, for example, to take part in the traditional *kabluki* for a new worker at a local tavern),[45] and were seemingly satisfied

42. For example, ibid. 1:7 (December 15, 1902), p. 128.
43. *Vestnik graficheskogo dela* 15 (August 13, 1897), p. 154.
44. *Naborshchik* 1:43 (August 24, 1903), p. 642.
45. Galaktionov [Shponik], *Lebedinaia pesn'*, pp. 5–12. Originally appeared in *Naborshchik* 2:13 (February 22, 1904).

with existing authority relationships in the industry.[46] The large trea-
suries accumulated by the funds[47] may have reinforced conservative
and elitist attitudes. In the view of Vasilii Sher, a socialist intellectual
later active among Moscow printers, "the hundred-thousand-ruble
capital of the organization was transformed into a golden chain, which
bound members firmly to the fund. Concern about the integrity of the
cash reserve, though accumulated by the hands of workers, created a
clannish, conservative mood among the majority, who avoided every
change and wished for only one thing—that everything remain as of
old."[48] Large donations to the funds by employers may have further encouraged workers to feel gratitude toward their employer "benefactors" and to be conscious of their own dependence.

Such evidence has to be weighed against the general failure, often
noted, of a labor aristocracy in Russia to play the same conservative social and political role that it is said to have played in England and other
countries. As will be seen, printers, including many who had participated in mutual aid, would engage in mass strikes—including political
strikes—and establish their own industrial unions and alliances with
other workers. The militance of Russian craft workers has been explained by a number of structural conditions: the absence of a legacy of
traditional craft guilds; the lack of civil and political rights for workers, which hindered effective craft unionism and made political incorporation virtually impossible; a generally backward economy that severely restricted the capacity of industrialists to buy off a stratum of
workers; and the pervasive and early influence of socialist intellectuals
among workers as they began to organize.[49] These obstacles to labor
conservatism were all present among compositors. In addition, for
compositors and some other craft workers in the industry, payment by

46. The classic definition, partly following the earlier formulations by Engels and Lenin, is E. J. Hobsbawm, "The Labour Aristocracy in Nineteenth-Century Britain"
(1954), reprinted in his Labouring Men, pp. 272–315.
47. The Moscow fund had more than 60,000 rubles of invested capital in 1899.
Sbornik svedenii VKT, p. 3. Although the amount of savings of the Petersburg fund is not
known, between 1864 and 1891 the fund earned 24,000 rubles in interest on its invested
capital. Otchet dvadtsatipiatiletnei deiatel'nosti VKN, p. 6.
48. Sher, Istoriia, p. 90.
49. Netesin, "K voprosu o sotsial'no-ekonomicheskikh korniakh i osebennostiakh
'rabochei aristokratii' v Rossii," pp. 192–211; Zelnik, "Russian Bebels," pp. 262–63. Although not addressing the problem of the "labor aristocracy" directly, recent discussion
of the sources of radicalism among Russian workers by Victoria Bonnell, Tim McDaniel,
and others—McDaniel refers to a "structural radicalism"—similarly identifies obstacles
to social conciliation among even the most skilled and privileged workers. McDaniel, Autocracy, Capitalism, and Revolution in Russia; Bonnell, Roots of Rebellion.

the piece discouraged their becoming a conservative worker elite by precluding the regular earnings usually identified with this stratum.

There is yet another, and more important, reason for doubting the usefulness of the notion of labor aristocracy to characterize workers such as the printers who were active in mutual aid. Notwithstanding Lenin's influential view of widespread labor "opportunism," even in countries where all of the structural conditions for a labor aristocracy were in place—as in nineteenth-century England—there is reason to doubt that these conditions consistently produced a truly conservative worker elite. Skilled craft workers in "aristocratic" trades rarely passively echoed the values and beliefs of the dominant classes. They found ways to impose their own, often subversive, meanings upon the cultural standards they embraced. Even the pursuit of "respectability" often implied the demonstration of workers' dignity and worth and thus implicitly challenged the social conditions of their subordination.[50]

In Russia, too, skilled craft workers such as printers actively shaped the message of mutual aid, producing an often-ambiguous language of social advocacy, which blended notions of self-help with ideals of social mutuality, images of paternalistic benevolence with visions of the fraternal collaboration of equals. Like English workers who aspired for "respectability," Russian printers pursued *kul'turnost'* as an expression of a desire for recognition as social equals even if still largely within the limits of the existing order. Some worker members of the funds seemed to read the message of mutual aid in an even more combative manner. "What is the mutual aid fund in the present times?" asked a member of the Moscow fund in 1903.

> It is the only legal institution that can penetrate with light the dark kingdom of the printing plant. Only from it can resound the bold voice of truth, testifying to the conditions of life of its members as citizens of the Russian empire. . . . Under the banner of the fund, the center of the living activity of typo-lithographers, the entire typo-lithographic host will gather and unite in a struggle for existence.[51]

Without challenging the structure or central values of the trade community that many employers were trying to build, these activist workers were beginning to contest its terms, or at least to appropriate them to

50. Alastair Reid, "Intelligent Artisans and Aristocrats of Labor," pp. 171–86; Gray, *The Labour Aristocracy in Victorian Edinburgh;* Crossick, *An Artisan Elite in Victorian Society.*

51. *Naborshchik* 1:43 (August 24, 1903), p. 642.

their own ends. After 1902, with the appearance of a legal journal for printing workers, this developing clash of meanings found a wider arena.

NABORSHCHIK: PREACHING VIRTUE

The journal *Naborshchik* was printed weekly in St. Petersburg from October 1902 until 1905 and then monthly until the end of 1916. When it first appeared, it was something quite new in the cultural life of Russian workers. Unlike earlier underground publications that had been produced mainly by radical intellectuals and directed at workers, *Naborshchik* was a legal publication, produced solely by workers and by workers promoted into supervisory positions.[52] As Russia's first craft paper, it was a predecessor of the trade-union papers that would appear only in 1905 and after, though its perspective differed in important ways.

Naborshchik was not the first journal to try to appeal to printing workers. In the 1860s, Rudolf Schneider proclaimed *Tipografskii zhurnal* as a journal for all "comrades of the art and the craft," from employers to workers,[53] and more than one-quarter of his 224 subscribers in 1868 were working compositors.[54] But his relative success in the 1860s would not be repeated. Schneider's own *Obzor graficheskikh iskusstv,* established in the late 1870s, attracted fewer worker readers than *Tipografskii zhurnal,* though it had twice the total number of subscribers.[55] In the 1890s, despite a special discount offered to worker-subscribers, Isidor Goldberg's *Graficheskie iskusstva i bumazhnaia promyshlennost'* apparently attracted no great response.[56] Josef Lehmann had somewhat greater success in attracting worker readers to *Pechatnoe iskusstvo,* by actively soliciting worker subscribers, offering discounts, and including essays written by workers.[57]

52. I have discovered no evidence that non-printer intellectuals were involved in the publication of *Naborshchik* until after 1905.

53. *Tipografskii zhurnal* 1:1 (July 1, 1867), p. 1.

54. Ibid. 2:1 (July 1, 1868), p. 4.

55. *Obzor graficheskikh iskusstv* 1879, no. 4 (February 15), p. 27; no. 7 (April 1), p. 53.

56. *Graficheskie iskusstva i bumazhnaia promyshlennost'* 3:1 (January 1898), p. 1. See also the statement of aims in ibid. 1:1 (September 1, 1895), pp. 1–2.

57. *Pechatnoe iskusstvo* 1:1 (October 1901), p. 1; 1:2 (November 1901), p. 49; 1:7 (April 1902), p. 215. The most important of these worker-essayists was Stepan Tsorn, who later wrote for *Naborshchik* and in 1905 became a leader in the St. Petersburg printers' union.

None of these papers attracted the worker readership of *Naborshchik*. Subscription data are not available, but such data would be of limited value in any event as a measure of worker readership, because workers often subscribed collectively to periodicals, sharing copies or reading them aloud in their shops.[58] One measure of worker support is provided by a fund-raising campaign that *Naborshchik* organized in 1903 for the sanatorium established by the Printing Society: the editorial offices received donations from approximately 1,500 workers, mostly compositors, employed in thirty-four Petersburg printing firms, as well as from a couple of hundred managers, white-collar employees, and owners.[59] If we assume that these fifteen hundred workers reflected the minimum extent of *Naborshchik*'s worker readership in the capital, we may estimate its readership as encompassing at least 13 percent of all printing workers, though closer to one-third of all compositors, working in 12 percent of the city's enterprises (also suggesting an uneven distribution of readers by size of firm). Letters to the paper show that *Naborshchik* was read by workers in Moscow, Odessa, and other cities.[60]

The reason for this relative success among workers is not difficult to discover. *Naborshchik* addressed the concerns of workers first. The name itself was part of its attraction. "Before me lies the journal *Naborshchik*," wrote a worker in a letter that the editor described as typical of many he received soon after the first issue appeared:

> Joyfully this word resounds and pride fills our hearts at the sight of this journal. *Naborshchik*, the Compositor, this is me, a printing worker, an insignificant person, unnoticed by society or literature, although I stand near both. But cloaked in the mantle of this journal, I loudly declare my existence.[61]

As this letter indicates, *Naborshchik* found an untapped reserve of articulate concern with the position of printing workers in society. The editor and publisher, Andrei Filippov, together with his co-editor, Zoia Voronova, sought to mobilize these sentiments and encouraged workers to write to the paper, reminding them that "Franklin and Edison

58. *Naborshchik* 1:19 (March 9, 1903), p. 321.

59. Reported in issues numbered 19 through 52.

60. It is also suggestive of *Naborshchik*'s success that the publisher was the first publisher of a printers' paper not to complain about the lack of reader support, and even to express satisfaction. *Naborshchik* 1:49 (October 5, 1903), p. 733.

61. Ibid. 1:8 (December 22, 1902), p. 143. For other examples, 1:2 (November 10, 1902), p. 46; 1:5 (December 1, 1902), p. 96; 1:12 (January 19, 1903), p. 197; 1:17 (February 25, 1903), p. 277.

were compositors"[62] and recruiting the most articulate as regular and sometimes paid correspondents.

Like Franklin and Edison, the editors were themselves workers only marginally. Filippov began his working life with an apprenticeship as a compositor, but he quickly rose through the ranks to become a *metranpazh*—for a number of years at Suvorin's *Novoe vremia* press—and then in 1902 became the manager (*zaveduiushchii*) of the newly opened printing plant of the city government.[63] Zoia Voronova occupied a still more marginal position among printing workers, even apart from her status as the only woman visibly involved with *Naborshchik*. What little we know of her background and career—she occupied a relatively demure position among the activists in the industry—suggests that she was as much an intellectual as a worker. Although she apparently worked as a proofreader in the industry, Filippov would describe her in 1905 as having for the previous ten years been living "by her literary and scholarly work," notably her involvement in the publications of the Imperial Russian Historical Society.[64] Even as a proofreader she occupied an elite position among workers, distinguished in literacy and pay even from most male compositors, and certainly from other women employed in the printing industry, who worked mainly as relatively unskilled and low-paid signature-folders and sewers in binding departments, and totaled between 4 and 6 percent of workers in printing firms around 1900.[65]

Like Filippov, a number of correspondents were also no longer rank-and-file workers. Gerasim Grents, who contributed regular articles on mutual aid and other questions (and was also an officer in the Compositors' Assistance Fund), was by then the manager (*upravliaiushchii*) of the Tile printing house. Ivan Galaktionov, another regular correspondent and also an activist in the assistance fund, was a former compositor who had gradually moved through the ranks to senior compositor and then to production manager at Roman Golike's press.[66] Grents, Galaktionov, and others like them, were, like Filippov, former composi-

---

62. Ibid. 1:2 (November 10, 1902), p. 30.
63. *Pechatnoe iskusstvo* 1:7 (April 1902), p. 233.
64. *Naborshchik i pechatnyi mir* 105 (January 19, 1905), p. 7.
65. *Perepis' Moskvy 1902*, part 1, vypusk 2, tables 6–8; *S-Peterburg po perepisi 1900 goda*, vypusk 2, table 2. A larger number of women were employed separately in the binding industry.
66. *Ivan Dmitrievich Galaktionov, 12/II/1915; Ivan Dmitrievich Galaktionov, 1880–25/II-1925.* In 1905, he became manager of the press of the Ministry of the Interior.

tors who had been working in the industry, and often in the same shop, since the late 1870s or early 1880s.

Many other regular correspondents to *Naborshchik,* however, were still rank-and-file compositors. Stepan Tsorn, a compositor working in Ekaterinoslav where he had helped to organize a mutual-aid fund for printers, contributed a regular column of varied social commentary. August Tens offered a series of columns, "The Russian Worker Abroad," describing his experiences working as a compositor in Western Europe.[67] G. Baranskii recounted his experiences working in various Russian cities in a column entitled "From the Notebook of a Traveling Compositor." From Moscow, K. Morozov wrote a column called "Our Problems" (*Nashi bol'nye mesta*), which dealt with issues ranging from the economic problems facing printers to their moral standards.

As senior editor and publisher of *Naborshchik,* Andrei Filippov set its intellectual tone. For many years before starting the paper, Filippov had presented himself as an advocate of workers' needs. In 1895, on the eve of the printing congress, he wrote a letter to *Novoe vremia* complaining about the lack of attention in the program of the congress to the "interests of the many thousands of typographic workers." He reminded readers of the "impossible" hygienic conditions and low wages suffered by most printing workers and accused most employers of being concerned only with "their own personal interests."[68] At the congress itself, which he attended as a representative of the Suvorin firm, Filippov continued to speak forcefully about the "arbitrariness" of wage levels in the capital. Generally his criticisms were welcomed, at least until he began naming names, identifying specific employers who paid below-average wages. Then the employer who was chairing the meeting, Vasilii Vishniakov, made Filippov stop and warned him to avoid "personal" references. Filippov indignantly refused to continue under such restrictions.[69]

After the congress, Filippov became still more critical of employers. When it was announced in 1897 that employers were planning a sanatorium for printing workers, Filippov wrote scornfully that such a noble achievement would never result "from purely maternal [*sic*] care on the part of press owners," and that any owner who suggested such

---

67. Published also as a separate book: Tens, *Russkii rabochii zagranitsei.*
68. *Novoe vremia,* March 22 (April 3), 1895, p. 3.
69. *Trudy pervogo s"ezda,* p. 107.

a "daring" notion to his colleagues was sure "to be considered mad," since employers would never voluntarily give up money to help their workers.[70] Over the next several years, Filippov frequently wrote and spoke of the harsh conditions within many enterprises, of the exploitation of apprentices, and of the selfishness of most employers.[71] In 1899, Filippov was asked to speak at a celebration of the five hundredth birthday of Gutenberg. Before a hall filled, in his own words, "with ladies in their elegant toilette and gentlemen in formal dress, adorned with all manner of Russian and foreign decorations—in a word, magnificence and wealth," Filippov broke with the convention established by the many speeches that had preceded his and spoke not about the greatness of Gutenberg, but about the "main bearer into the world of ideas of happiness, goodness, and all that elevates and ennobles the soul . . . Gutenberg's stepson—the compositor."[72]

Notwithstanding Filippov's often-challenging stance before authority, his was not an ideology of social conflict, much less of class organization or struggle. On the contrary, he admired the ideal of trade community and participated in almost every associative effort initiated by printing employers, especially after 1900: he was an elected officer in both the Compositors' Assistance Fund and the Burial Society, an active member and officer of the Russian Printing Society (where he supported proposals to expand the membership to include workers), an organizer of the sanatorium for printers—despite his initial skepticism— and a member of its oversight committee, and a judge in periodic typesetting competitions organized by employers, where he represented a school for workers run by the Imperial Philanthropic Society, at which he taught a printing course.[73]

Although Filippov often bitterly admonished employers for their selfishness and lack of concern for workers, he believed that such attitudes reflected the personal moral failings of individuals not an inherently exploitative social relationship. Much of his rhetoric, therefore, was directed at awakening employers to their moral duties, and he often accompanied his denunciations of employer greed and exploitation

70. *Vestnik graficheskogo dela* 13 (July 10, 1897), p. 117.
71. Ibid. 1 (March 14, 1897), pp. 3–4; 2 (March 21, 1897), pp. 12–13; 13 (July 10, 1897), pp. 117–18; 26 (February 21, 1898), pp. 18–19; *Pechatnoe iskusstvo* 1:4 (January 1902), p. 130; 1:5 (February 1902), pp. 155–61.
72. *Naborshchik* 1:4 (November 24, 1902), p. 69. Unpublished at the time, Filippov later printed his own speech.
73. Filippov's activities have been identified mainly from numerous references in the trade press (especially *Pechatnoe iskusstvo* and the bulletin of the Printing Society).

with praise for "enlightened, educated, and humane" employers who "warmly concern themselves with the needs of printing workers and pay well for their labor."[74]

Filippov carried both his advocacy of workers' needs and his faith in the ideal of moral community into his journal *Naborshchik*. Numerous editorials and articles admired employers who showed concern for the needs of workers.[75] But praise of benevolent virtue often served a critical purpose. Workers, Filippov maintained, had a "moral right to expect support from the society that they serve with their difficult labor."[76] Readers were advised that the Russian legal code itself stipulated that the purposes of industrial enterprise included "improving the condition of workers" and "protecting them from poverty" when they became ill or permanently disabled.[77] As before, Filippov did not confuse the ideal of moral entrepreneurship with reality. He admitted that although "here and there in some enterprises good things were done," such as worker assistance funds, they were only a "drop in the ocean." "Miserable conditions" still led most compositors "to an untimely grave."[78]

Although combative, Filippov's social ideal rejected collective struggle by workers against employers as a strategy to improve workers' lives. To be sure, Russian press laws would have prohibited him from advocating strikes or other such actions. But he could have simply ignored such a possibility. Instead, he directly warned workers of the hazards of one-sided struggle. One editorial, for example, which noted the "excessive spread in recent times of strikes" among Western European printing workers (the law prohibited mentioning strikes in Russia), advised workers that these were having "a sad and terribly harmful effect on the pocketbooks of workers in particular." Strikes were also morally flawed, according to Filippov, for they were motivated by "harmful

74. *Pechatnoe iskusstvo* 1:5 (February 1902), p. 158; *Novoe vremia*, March 22 (April 3), 1895, p. 3. See also *Obzor pervoi vserossiiskoi vystavki* 15 (April 10, 1895), p. 6; *Vestnik graficheskogo dela* 15 (August 13, 1897), pp. 141–42; *Pechatnoe iskusstvo* 1:3 (December 1901), p. 94.

75. See, for example, *Naborshchik* 1:6 (December 8, 1902), pp. 105–06; 1:14 (February 2, 1903), pp. 235–36; 1:18 (March 2, 1903), pp. 298–300; 1:20 (March 16, 1903), p. 331; 1:52 (October 26, 1903), pp. 782–85. These contributions are by Filippov or by corresponding managers or supervisors. For references by rank-and-file workers, see below.

76. *Naborshchik* 1:47 (September 21, 1903), pp. 703–05. These words were from an essay that originally appeared in the newspaper *Grazhdanin*, September 7, 1903, pp. 3–4, that Filippov reprinted in *Naborshchik* with "great satisfaction."

77. *Naborshchik* 1:3 (November 17, 1902), p. 53. See also 1:17 (February 25, 1903), p. 281.

78. Ibid. 1:5 (December 1, 1902), pp. 86–87.

ideals based not on the principle of justice but on the principle of terror."[79] Reinforcing these arguments, Zoia Voronova contributed a two-part article on "The Goals and Tasks of Typographic Societies and Unions Abroad," a treatise, in fact, on the *proper* goals of organization. Referring to the principle "in unity is strength," she insisted that this must be unity of the widest scope, embracing not only all printing crafts but employers as well. Each social group, she argued, is "unimaginable without each other, their interests are too indivisible, too closely bound."[80]

This ambiguous mixture of combative labor advocacy and collaborative moral idealism was at the heart of the social vision Filippov directed at workers in *Naborshchik*. He continually argued that employers ought to "care for their workers," to "uphold their interests," and "introduce light, warmth, and love" into their lives.[81] He appealed for "more goodness" in social relationships and reminded employers "that the love of mankind is one of the principal virtues."[82] He insisted that employers ought to help "the needy" and unite with workers in "one family, one host," guided by the "sacred truth of love of one's neighbor" and the principles of "justice and honor." He saw no other way to free the industry from the "abnormal mutual relations" under which workers suffered the most.[83] The only solution, in the words of the leading essay in the first issue of *Naborshchik,* was "consciousness of moral responsibility . . . mutual and reciprocal honor . . . starting with the employer and ending with the simplest laborer."[84]

SELF AND SOCIETY

It is perhaps not surprising that workers promoted to positions as foremen or managers should be inclined toward notions of social conciliation. But most of *Naborshchik*'s correspondents and readers were still workers and they shared the journal's common vision of social collaboration. Workers writing to *Naborshchik* joined in the praise of the pa-

79. Ibid. 1:27 (May 4, 1903), p. 443. See also 1:35 (June 19, 1903), p. 545.
80. Ibid. 1:2 (November 10, 1902), pp. 31–33; 1:4 (November 24, 1902), pp. 70–73.
81. Ibid. 1:1 (October 20, 1902), p. 6; 1:3 (November 17, 1902), p. 53; 1:10 (January 5, 1903), p. 168.
82. Ibid., 1:17 (February 25, 1903), p. 277.
83. Ibid., pp. 288–89; 1:32 (June 8, 1903), p. 509; 1:38–39 (July 20, 1903), p. 581; 1:44 (August 31, 1903), p. 657.
84. Ibid. 1:1 (October 20, 1902), p. 7. See also 1:2 (November 10, 1902), p. 30; 1:10 (January 5, 1903), pp. 165–68.

ternalistic ideal of benevolent authority.[85] For example, the compositor
Stepan Tsorn responded in early 1903 to a letter to *Naborshchik* from
Vera Fedoseevna Fesenko, the owner of a printing shop in Odessa, in
which she had suggested that from her own experience piece rates were
the main cause of homelessness, drunkenness, and vagrancy among
compositors.[86] Tsorn suggested that Fesenko was too modest. "Why do
you have no drunkards?" Tsorn asked rhetorically. "Because you, Vera
Fedoseevna, surround each of the employees of your large and, in the
broadest sense, well-run printing house with humane treatment and
motherly love."[87] Tsorn was not alone in expressing such admiration
for "humane" employers. "From the depths of our souls," wrote a Petersburg compositor, "compositors of the distant North send [Fesenko]
their heartfelt greetings of thanks." Another correspondent described
the "delight and happiness" felt by the sixty compositors with whom he
worked as they listened to one of their fellows read Tsorn's article on
Fesenko.[88] The periodic celebrations that employers staged to mark anniversaries of their own firms were occasions on which workers often
thanked their own Fesenkos. A spokesman for compositors at Moscow's *Russkie vedomosti* press, for example, thanked their employer
for his "truly parental solicitude" for their needs.[89] Of course, such
professions of faith may not have been as innocent as they appear. Only
a week after compositors at the *Russkie vedomosti* voiced their appreciation of their employers' attention to their needs, they joined a general
strike by printing workers in Moscow to demand much more attention.

Just as Filippov's advocacy of moral community differed from that of
even the most "enlightened" employers in tone and emphasis, so did the
views of many of his worker-correspondents suggest yet further reworking, further sharpening of its critical edges. As for Filippov, gratitude itself cut two ways. Workers seem often to have been using the paternalistic ideal as a moral standard for judging employers, as a means
to chastise the heartless majority with the benevolence of the few.
When Stepan Tsorn praised Vera Fesenko, he presented her as a rarity,
and his readers understood the moral of his tale. The sixty workers who
listened to Tsorn's account with such "delight and happiness" also re-

85. In addition to the references that follow, see also ibid. 1:13 (January 26, 1903),
p. 222; 1:23–24 (April 6, 1903), p. 389; 1:30 (May 25, 1903), p. 489; 1:52 (October 26,
1903), pp. 782–85.
86. Ibid. 1:13 (January 26, 1903), p. 224.
87. Ibid. 1:15 (February 9, 1903), p. 251.
88. Ibid. 1:19 (March 9, 1903), p. 321.
89. Ibid. 1:46 (September 14, 1903), p. 694.

called that she was "unique in Russia" and found themselves "staring in wonderment. . . . From sixty men was heard this exclamation: 'Lord, if only a third of our employers were such as she—oh, how we would live!' "[90]

Workers not only sought to hold employers morally accountable, they defined virtue to make it of more benefit to themselves. First, workers typically measured good on a practical scale. The pages of *Naborshchik* were filled with accounts of the appalling hygienic conditions in print shops, the exhausting seven-day work week of newspaper workers, endemic poverty, abuses of apprenticeship, and the harmful effects of piece rates. Good employers were defined against this background: they paid good wages and offered regular raises, improved hygienic conditions in the shops, offered financial aid during sickness, and gave pensions to widows and orphans.[91] What impressed workers like Stepan Tsorn about Vera Fesenko was less her humane spirit than the tangible financial assistance she gave to sick workers, her voluntary reduction in the length of the workday, and the relatively high wages she paid (and on time).[92] Like Filippov, not words but practice were the measure of virtue. Indeed, worker-correspondents like Stepan Tsorn openly expressed contempt for "false friends of the working people" who substituted "winged words" of "kindness and condescension" for practical measures.[93]

It was not only the hypocrisy that offended, however, but also the condescension. The rhetoric of worker correspondents to *Naborshchik*, like that of Filippov and other promoted workers, was pervaded by an insistence on workers' identity as human beings and hence their natural rights to be treated well: "Employers must look upon compositors from a humane point of view and remember that they are people like any other." "A compositor is a man and not a machine." "The rights of the worker, as a human being, must not be trampled upon." Or simply and directly, employers should "look upon the compositor as an equal."[94]

Subordinate groups in many settings have laid claim to the idea of their natural equality as human beings when challenging their social in-

90. Ibid. 1:19 (March 9, 1903), p. 321.

91. Ibid. 1:46 (September 14, 1903), p. 694. For earlier examples, *Pechatnoe iskusstvo* 1:5 (February 1902), p. 158; *Novoe vremia*, March 22 (April 3), 1895, p. 3.

92. *Naborshchik* 1:15 (February 9, 1903), p. 251.

93. Ibid., p. 248. These words were quoted by Tsorn from a letter written by a worker to the newspaper *Baku*.

94. Ibid. 1:5 (December 1, 1902), p. 89; 1:8 (December 22, 1902), p. 134; 1:15 (February 9, 1903), p. 251; 1:19 (March 9, 1903), p. 313; 1:46 (September 14, 1903), p. 694. Many such examples could be cited.

feriority and exclusion. It may well be that the feeling of offense to one's worth as a person is a natural and universal response to subordination. Even when indignation is not voiced publicly, there is reason to believe that the injuries of class are felt no less sharply.[95] Public protest against subordination and ill treatment, however, seems to require both an explicit definition of these as unjust and an expectation that one's actions might effect some change. In many situations, the perception and expression of moral outrage at violations of human dignity have occurred when superordinate groups have violated accepted norms of behavior—"implicit social contracts."[96] In the Russian printing industry, employers' "winged words" of paternal concern for workers—the unfulfilled promises of the moral community—may represent such a violation of an implied social contract. However, this only begins to explain workers' claims and challenge to employers.

Moral indignation may also result when subordinate groups acquire vocabularies of judgment and value that allow nascent feelings of moral offense to be articulated, as often happens in the course of workers' ongoing encounter with the culture around them and its refraction through their own experiences and needs. Workers have often given expression to their hardships and their hopes for emancipation by "reading and recopying, decomposing and recomposing" ideas and texts appropriated from the larger society.[97] We see reflections of such an encounter in the vocabulary of activist printing workers. The ideal of a community of employers and workers united by bonds of moral responsibility was itself an important source of ideas and values that workers could use in various ways. This appropriation in turn reflected the influence of other ideas.

The notion that was most central to the social thinking of activist printing workers was the intrinsic worth of all human beings. Its provenance was partly religious. When the editors or correspondents of Naborshchik wrote of social community, they often envisioned it explicitly as founded on the ideal of Christian "love." Christ and the saints, they insisted, taught compassion and love.[98] Some proponents, though especially former compositors like Gerasim Grents, read this ethical teach-

---

95. Sennett and Cobb, Hidden Injuries of Class; James Scott, Domination and the Arts of Resistance.
96. Moore, Injustice. See also the critical review by Reginald E. Zelnik, "Passivity and Protest in Germany and Russia," pp. 485–505.
97. Rancière, Nights of Labor, p. 165.
98. See, especially, comments by Filippov, Grents, and Tsorn in Naborshchik 1:23–24 (April 6, 1903), pp. 377–79.

ing as a counsel of toleration and quietism: "Love, endure, suffer, and forgive the evil of your enemies."[99] But the principle of moral love also drew upon the radicalism in its origins. Christ's commandment, readers of *Naborshchik* were often reminded, was to "love your neighbor *as yourself*," a "sacred" principle, which embodied the Christian faith in a future when "on Earth will reign . . . truth, justice, and goodness."[100]

Probably of more direct influence—though also shaped by Christian ethics—were contemporary discussions about the natural dignity and rights of the human person (*lichnost'*). Since the early nineteenth century, public discussion of social ethics and philosophy in Russia, as in the West, had focused increasingly on the innate worth and value of the human person and on the natural rights that this entailed.[101] The free development of the human person and the view that "individual dignity is maintained only by upholding the dignity of all" were values central to the social thought of the Russian intelligentsia.[102] The same concerns were also to be found more generally in the periodical press, especially liberal-democratic journals and newspapers, as well as in much popular fiction around the turn of the century.[103] Many literate workers were

99. "Liubi, terpi, stradai / i zlo vragam svoim proshchai." Ibid., p. 377.

100. Ibid. 1:32 (June 8, 1903), p. 509; 1:23–24 (April 6, 1903), pp. 377–78. See also 1:23–24 (April 6, 1903), p. 389; 1:33 (June 15, 1903), p. 521.

101. *Lichnost'* has been defined as "the totality of inner features and characteristics inherent in man as a social being; the personal, individual essence of a human being." *Slovar' sovremennogo russkogo literaturnogo iazyka,* vol. 6 (Moscow, 1957), p. 295. Writing in the 1890s, the philosopher Vladimir Solov'ev offered a definition that was more explicit about its ethical implications: as "the intrinsic definition of the independence of an individual being as the possessor of reason, will, and a distinctive character . . . human *lichnost'* has, in principle, unconditional dignity, upon which are founded inalienable rights, which have been increasingly recognized in the course of historical progress." *Entsiklopedicheskii slovar,* vol. 17a, p. 868. The term is usually translated into English as personality, individual, or individuality.

102. Lavrov, *Istoricheskie pis'ma,* pp. 51, 55–56. Articulating a view that was widespread among Russian radicals since Herzen, Lavrov defined progress as "the development of *lichnost'* in its physical, intellectual, and moral aspects, and the incorporation of truth and justice in social forms" (p. 51). Even some Marxists would embrace this ethical viewpoint, especially neo-Kantian socialists such as Mikhail Tugan-Baranovskii, who argued that the dignity of the human personality ought to be the normative standard by which the existing order is criticized, and that socialism could be seen as comparable to Kant's "kingdom of ends." Grier, *Marxist Ethical Theory in the Soviet Union,* chs. 1–3.

103. *Ocherki po istorii russkoi zhurnalistiki i kritiki,* vol. 2, pp. 384–85, 390–92, 406–07, 478, 484. The work of one journalist popular among workers, N. V. Shelgunov, has been described as challenging above all else the "humiliation of the human personality." Esin, *N. V. Shelgunov,* esp. p. 42, and Slabkin, *Mirovozrenie N. V. Shelgunova,* esp. p. 117. Concern with the dignity and humiliation of the human personality is evident in the works of "classic" authors widely read by workers, such as Nekrasov, Turgenev, Saltykov-Shedrin, Tolstoy, Gorky, and Chekhov, but also in much popular commercial literature, where, Jeffrey Brooks has argued, a new respect for the individual was to be found. Brooks, *When Russia Learned to Read.*

aware of these larger cultural discussions, as one compositor testified when he pointed to "the principle of justice and recognition of the human person about which we read and set type every day."[104] Also, the language with which workers contributing to Naborshchik and earlier journals expressed their developing awareness of self was filled with the terms that also pervaded these larger discussions: honor, dignity, personality, and culture (chest', dostoinstvo, lichnost', kul'turnost').[105]

This developing perception of self-worth was reinforced and further legitimated by the immediate influences of workers' labor, by pride in skill, craft, and profession. Acquisition of skill has often provided workers with the psychological as well as material resources to assert their needs and interests. In Russia especially, where most workers remained semiskilled or unskilled, skill "gave workers a feeling of mastery, self-respect, and control over the labor process" that made them more likely to chafe at insults to their dignity and at the subordination and powerlessness that underlay these.[106] For printing workers, pride in skill was reinforced by a distinctive professional honor that was nearly universal among printers. Like journeymen printers in sixteenth-century France who viewed themselves "as free men working voluntarily at an excellent and noble calling" or printers in the United States who proclaimed themselves "professors of [a] Heaven-born art,"[107] Russian compositors represented themselves as "free men" engaged in "noble" (blagorodnyi) labor, as a "link in the chain uniting literature with society," as "masters" "of a great art whose banner [they] must carry with honor and dignity."[108]

These professions of pride in skill and craft, however, were unlikely to have derived directly from the satisfaction and pleasure workers got from their labor. Their actual working life was a cycle of exhausting and often painful physical labor, of ever-present disease and approach-

---

104. Naborshchik 1:52 (October 26, 1903), 796. See also 1:19 (March 9, 1903), p. 313.

105. For some typical examples, Obzor graficheskikh iskusstv January 1, 1884, p. 7; letter by a compositor to Ekho, January 2 (14), 1884, pp. 2–3; Naborshchik 1:19 (March 9, 1903), p. 313; 1:28 (May 11, 1903), pp. 450–51.

106. Bonnell, Roots of Rebellion, pp. 52, 71–72. Semen Kanatchikov recalled that after he had completed his apprenticeship as a patternmaker in the machine industry he strongly felt his "own worth." Zelnik, A Radical Worker in Tsarist Russia, p. 64.

107. Davis, Society and Culture in Early Modern France, p. 5; Rock, Artisans of the New Republic, p. 140. See also Brenton, Voices from the Press, pp. 51–56, 149–61, 300; Beier, Schwarze Kunst und Klassenkampf, vol. 1, p. 141.

108. Naborshchik 1:1 (October 20, 1902), p. 3; 1:5 (December 1, 1902), pp. 96–97; 1:8 (December 22, 1902), pp. 136, 143; 1:12 (January 19, 1903), p. 197; 1:17 (February 25, 1903), p. 277; 1:32 (June 8, 1903), p. 510; 1:36 (July 6, 1903), p. 557.

ing death, and of days spent in an often-filthy and foul-smelling environment.[109] Talk of the honor of the trade, therefore, may have been yet another way of identifying "winged words" without substance, a notion of worth that helped workers interpret their everyday conditions as unjust more than the product of those conditions. But whatever the source of workers' perception, the discrepancy between the professional honor of the printer and the real conditions of his life often appeared in formulations of protest: "Everywhere for our noble labor we are paid ignobly"; though contributing to "society and literature" we are "unnoticed"; "In this noble and elevated field of activity, labor the living machinery of printing . . . simple, dying, and forgotten by all."[110] Such language was a plea for compassion, but it was also a demand for justice.

The ambivalence of workers' developing perception of self-worth should not be overlooked. For workers to challenge employers to treat a worker "as a man not a machine," not "to trample" on the "rights of the worker as a human being," was still far from expressing a notion of class identity. The very universalism of this ethic, its assumption of a natural community that embraced all classes, indeed that implicitly denied the moral legitimacy of class, drew workers toward employers. So did the idea of the special honor of the printing profession.

Even more debilitating of suggestions of class identity in these protests against offenses to workers' dignity was the alienation this worker vanguard felt from many other workers. Paradoxically, but like many "conscious" workers and not only in Russia, this moral vanguard often defined its own dignity and humanity precisely in opposition to other workers. Printers were dismissive of workers in less "noble" trades: "A person who spends his entire life within the walls of a printing house cannot be compared with a carpenter, metalfitter, or other professions that have nothing in common with printing,"[111] for "he is in every respect superior to the latter."[112] Many compositors did not consider themselves ordinary "workers" at all. As was typical among skilled workers in Russia, compositors before 1905 generally identified themselves as *truzheniki* or occasionally as *rabotniki,* terms that embraced

109. See Chapter 1.
110. *Naborshchik* 1:23–24 (April 6, 1903), p. 387; 1:8 (December 22, 1902), p. 143; 1:32 (June 8, 1903), p. 510. See also 1:9 (December 29, 1902), p. 160; 1:10 (January 5, 1903), p. 170; 1:12 (January 19, 1903), p. 197; 1:17 (February 25, 1903), p. 277.
111. Ibid. 1:30 (May 25, 1903), p. 484. See also 1:25 (April 30, 1903), p. 404; 1:52 (October 26, 1903), p. 796.
112. Ibid. 1:38–39 (July 20, 1903), p. 590.

every manner of work from the simplest manual labor to scientific research, but never as mere "workers" (*rabochie*).[113] Compositors, of course, made it clear what sort of *truzheniki* they were: "intellectual workers" (*intelligentnye truzheniki*) or even "semi-intellectual working men" (*truzheniki-poluintelligenty*).[114]

At stake here was much more than the honor associated with skill or craft, for boundaries were drawn even among skilled workers of the same craft. Ironically, the humanistic sense of self that enabled the most self-conscious workers to voice moral outrage at indignity and inequality also led them to view with moral opprobrium the workers whose humanity was most degraded. In Russia as elsewhere, "conscious" workers often defined themselves in distinction to workers whom they viewed as ignorant and morally degraded.[115] The pages of *Naborshchik* were filled with descriptions—some written by former workers like Filippov but many by working compositors—of the ignorance, drunkenness, immorality, and irreligiosity of the average printing worker.[116] One self-described "rank-and-file" compositor, who was becoming increasingly well known among compositors for his contributions to *Naborshchik* and other Petersburg papers, maintained that most of his fellow workers lacked any "spiritual and intellectual interests or aspirations" at all.[117] Although condescending, these criticisms also contained implications of solidarity with other workers. As we have seen, such workers often appealed to their less conscious fellows to join a mutual aid fund to better themselves materially and morally. In general,

113. *Slovar' sovremennogo russkogo literaturnogo iazyka* (Moscow and Leningrad, 1948–1965), vol. 12, pp. 20–28; vol. 15, p. 1051; V. I. Dal', *Tolkovyi slovar' zhivogo velikorusskogo iazyka* (Moscow, 1978–1980; reprint of 1880–1882 edition), vol. 4, pp. 6, 437. For a discussion of the language of self-identification among skilled workers generally, see also Bonnell, *Roots of Rebellion*, p. 48. Bonnell has suggested that a "distant echo" of the etymological root of *rabochii* in the Russian word for *slave* (*rab*) could account for the disdain skilled workers felt for the term, but this explanation is brought into question by the willingness of skilled compositors to identify themselves as *rabotniki*. Developed usage in context was likely more important than meanings linguistically embedded in the form of the word itself.

114. *Naborshchik* 1:3 (November 17, 1902), p. 63; 1:9 (December 29, 1902), p. 160; 1:27 (May 4, 1903), p. 435; 1:30 (May 25, 1903), p. 484.

115. Bonnell, *Roots of Rebellion*, p. 60; McDaniel, *Autocracy, Capitalism, and Revolution*, pp. 206–08. See also Rancière, *Nights of Labor*, ch. 10.

116. *Naborshchik* 1:6 (December 8, 1902), p. 113; 1:9 (December 29, 1902), p. 156; 1:13 (January 26, 1903), p. 213; 1:23–24 (April 6, 1903), p. 382; 1:27 (May 4, 1903), p. 438; 1:28 (May 11, 1903), pp. 450–53; 1:34 (June 22, 1903), pp. 533–34.

117. Ibid. 1:34 (June 22, 1903), p. 534. The author of these lines, G. Baranskii, wrote frequently not only for *Naborshchik* but also for general interest papers like *Birzhevye vedomosti*. A compositor by occupation, he was killed on Bloody Sunday, January 9, 1905.

the mission of workers associated with *Naborshchik* was to uplift their fellow workers, to convince them to turn away from the oblivion they sought in the tavern and live a "conscious life," aware of "thought, art, and literature," of their "individual dignity," and of their "obligations and rights."[118]

This was not an appeal for class pride. Just as these workers blamed exploitation on the sins of individual employers and not on social structures of domination, so did they often view workers' moral degradation as personal failings. Drunkenness was condemned both as debasing the worker and as a cause of his degradation. In the words of one worker, drunkenness was "a great and powerful evil, tongs, which once they grab hold of a man disfigure [*urodiut*] him, toss him into the lower depths, and deprive him of his physical, material, and moral strength."[119] Conscious workers wished to uplift and enlighten their fellows, but this goal did not lessen the condescending and dismissive feelings they had for them. That these conscious workers preferred association with socially mobile former workers like Filippov also suggests that much social distance remained.

Illustrating this complex encounter between ideas and social experience were the efforts by these workers to produce their own literary works, especially poetry. When compositors wrote poems, which they often read aloud to their fellows before they were sent to *Naborshchik* or elsewhere for publication, they self-consciously emulated the styles of the poets they liked best, and almost without exception, like other Russian worker-poets of the turn of the century, they took as their models the socially conscious "civic" poets of the nineteenth century, such as Nikolai Nekrasov, Ivan Nikitin, and Semen Nadson.[120] The choice was not surprising—writing in a style that was both realistic and sentimental, these poets sought to evoke sympathy, in Nekrasov's words, for "the sufferings of the people."[121]

The poems of Russian workers were not simply weak imitations of this nineteenth-century civic poetry (though they were that, too). Worker-poets, as Soviet scholars have argued, selected and emphasized certain themes: naturalistic description of the hardships of labor, ide-

118. Ibid. 1:3 (November 17, 1902), p. 63; 1:34 (June 22, 1903), p. 534; 1:27 (May 4, 1903), p. 436; 1:28 (May 11, 1903), pp. 450–51; 1:44 (August 31, 1903), p. 657. See also 1:8 (December 22, 1902), pp. 134–38; 1:14 (February 2, 1903), pp. 241–42; 1:20 (March 16, 1903), pp. 325–26.

119. Ibid. 1:34 (June 22, 1903), p. 534.

120. See Maxim Gorky's observations on the same literary sources for workers' poetry in later years. M. Gorkii, "O pisateliakh-samouchkakh," p. 111.

121. D. S. Mirsky, *A History of Russian Literature* (New York, 1958), p. 240.

alization of suffering, pleas for compassión and aid from privileged society.[122] Uniting these themes was a tragic sense of human beings mired in poverty, illness, and premature death. For compositors, this tragedy was made more poignant by the perceived nobility and significance of their labor.

This evocation of suffering, the leitmotif of compositors' poems, expressed an ambiguous message. Often, workers' poems counseled resignation: verses spoke of "bowing before fate,"[123] of the honor that came from suffering in the service of "enlightenment,"[124] and, of course, of escape—to the tavern occasionally, but especially into the comforts of nature or of the poetic imagination itself:

> This prophetic Bard
> Pours forth a magical freedom
> And, like a curative balm
> The people attentively
> Drink the miraculous sounds
> With all of their soul.[125]

Poems spoke of hope for help from on high, for "passing notice" from "powerful persons."[126] But the only sure salvation, often mentioned, was death—not as a doorway to heaven but as the ultimate oblivion.[127]

In these descriptions of stoic suffering, however, and even in the pleas for sympathy, there is an undercurrent of reproach and even a suggestion, more or less veiled, of battles to come. A hint of hidden militance was the dedication of the poem quoted above in praise of the "prophetic Bard" to the "august poet K. R." If this referred, as is likely, to the martyred Decembrist poet-revolutionary Kondratii Ryleev, the implications of such phrases as "magical freedom" may have had quite a different resonance than the soothing tone might at first suggest.

This implicit combativeness can also be discerned lexically. As is typical of moral discourse, compositors often described the world in binary terms. The language of their poetry, but also of their prose, was full of Manichaean distinctions: good and evil, truth and lies, honor

122. "Proletarskaia poeziia," in *Istoriia russkoi literatury*, vol. 14 (Leningrad, 1983), pp. 396–97; Os'makov, *Russkaia proletarskaia poeziia, 1890–1917*, pp. 50, 69–70.
123. *Naborshchik* 1:30 (May 25, 1903), p. 484.
124. Ibid. 1:34 (June 22, 1903), p. 533; 1:45 (September 7, 1903), p. 682.
125. Ibid. 1:33 (June 15, 1903), pp. 523–24. The author was a Moscow compositor. The poem was read publicly.
126. Ibid. 1:45 (September 7, 1903), p. 682. See also 1:34 (June 22, 1903), p. 533.
127. Ibid. 1:41–42 (August 10, 1903), p. 635; 1:30 (May 25, 1903), p. 484; 1:49 (October 5, 1903), p. 745.

and deceit, dignity and humiliation, justice and arbitrary power. Most pervasive was the image of darkness and light. The symbolic meaning of this opposition was partly shaped by the metaphoric language of workers' Christian culture, in which darkness had come to represent ignorance, misfortune, spiritual need, evil, and death, and light was the sign of knowledge, morality, love, spiritual life, and even of the divine in man. However, reference by workers to the darkness and light in their lives was not entirely metaphoric. When correspondents to *Naborshchik* wrote of the "dark kingdom of the printing plant,"[128] they also invoked a visible reality. Printing workers often literally toiled in partial darkness, "in workplaces where not only does a ray of sunlight seldom penetrate, but where even ordinary light only reluctantly finds its way to the composing cases."[129] Here, workers' actual experience became inseparable from the image with which it was represented. The visible reality of workers' lives encouraged worker-poets to use the language of darkness and light, while these conditions became a symbol of the deeper meanings of that experience.

That meaning, however, remained ambiguous. In part, the separation of the world into opposing spheres was a moral challenge:

> My life has passed wretchedly
> Amidst evil and lies, grief and misfortune. . . .
> But I have lived with hope, and now
> The reward, vague dreams fulfilled. . . .
> In the ranks of the lead army is heard a joyous noise:
> A longed-for guest has appeared.
> *Naborshchik*! It loves truth,
> And is prepared always to serve it incorruptibly,
> To brand with accusations from all sides
> Perfidy, evil, and arbitrary power.[130]

This poem is more combative than most. Yet the pervasive view by worker-writers of their fate as set in a matrix of good and evil—a representation not restricted to their poetry, though appearing there most starkly—suggests at least a prefiguring of moral outrage.

But the promise to bring "light" to the "dark" world of the worker was not entirely a call to battle. Much of the attention by worker correspondents to *Naborshchik*, as by Filippov, was focused on simply

128. For example, ibid. 1:25 (April 20, 1903), p. 404.
129. Ibid. 1:38–39 (July 20, 1903), p. 589.
130. Ibid. 1:5 (December 1, 1902), p. 96.

bringing "more light, knowledge, and love to printers."[131] Printing workers, it was said, had morally and culturally "fallen."[132] Salvation from this moral and spiritual fall demanded "light, more light."[133] This meant good books, dances, lectures, and the moral benefits of sobriety and thrift no less than it meant "branding with accusations . . . perfidy, evil, and arbitrary power."

Differences between employers, managers, and workers in understanding morality and community were still matters of degree and emphasis. But they suggested a coming schism. When a worker asked Andrei Filippov whether he thought that "the exploitation of labor is just," Filippov answered characteristically that it was not just but that the question ought to be how properly to understand "exploitation."[134] The correct understanding, for Filippov as for many other managers and employers, assumed a recognition that individual will, not social structure, was to blame for social evil and that exploitation could be eradicated only within a social community united on the basis of mutual responsibility and affection. Language is not so malleable that words do not also bring possibly undesirable meanings into a discussion. Thus, although Filippov agreed that exploitation of labor was unjust, he still preferred not to use the word himself. Workers, however, were increasingly less reluctant to speak of "exploitation" by name, even in the pages of *Naborshchik*.[135]

There were other indications that some worker-supporters of Filippov and *Naborshchik* were straying beyond the fold, or perhaps had never quite been penned in. The compositor Stepan Tsorn, by his own accounting, had by 1903 been "fired eighteen times for defending the just and vital interests of compositors."[136] The compositor August Tens wrote of his experiences in Western Europe as a member of the Fédération française des travailleurs du livre in Paris and of the London Society of Compositors, praising—as much as he might, given the restrictions of Russian censorship and the editorial policies of *Naborshchik*—these unions' "defense of their members' interests in all possible

131. Ibid. 1:17 (February 25, 1903), p. 278. See also 1:14 (February 2, 1903), pp. 230–31.

132. Ibid. 1:14 (February 2, 1903), p. 230.

133. Ibid. 1:34 (June 22, 1903), pp. 534–36; 1:38–39 (July 20, 1903), p. 586. The reference was to words ascribed to the dying Goethe.

134. Ibid. 1:28 (May 11, 1903), p. 461.

135. For example, ibid. 1:5 (December 1, 1902), pp. 88–89; 1:21 (March 23, 1903), pp. 345–47; 1:47 (September 21, 1903), pp. 702–04. For an earlier example, *Obzor graficheskikh iskusstv* 1878, no. 6 (April 1), p. 43.

136. *Naborshchik* 1:22 (March 30, 1903), p. 363.

circumstances" and their "advocacy of members' demands before employers."[137] Such indications of a readiness for collective struggle should not be exaggerated. Much ambivalence remained. Even to workers like Tsorn and Tens, it still seemed unnecessary to reject the moral idealism of the trade community in order to sustain a challenge to the practices of most employers. This ideal itself seemed adequate to challenge "evil and lies, grief and misfortune." This adequacy would not hold much longer.

137. Tens, *Russkii rabochii zagranitsei*, pp. 26–32, 64. Tens's essays originally appeared in *Naborshchik* 1:11, 13, 16, 19, 21, 26, 33, 37, 48, 50, 51 (January–October 1903).

Above left, A. S. SUVORIN (*Istoricheskii vestnik* April–June 1901); *above right,* R. R. GOLIKE (*Pechatnoe iskusstvo*, January 1902); *below left,* I. D. SYTIN (*Pechatnoe iskusstvo*, October 1901); *below right,* A. A. LEVENSON (*Polveka dlia kniga, 1866–1916*, Moscow, 1916)

Members and guests of the Russian Printing Society at the dedication of the sanatorium for printing workers in 1903. Aleksei Filippov stands in the front row, second from the left. (*Pechatnoe iskusstvo*, May–June 1903)

Above left, S. G. KHRENKOVA; *above right*, A. B. MEDVEDEV; *below left*, M. A. POPOV; *below right*, D. K. KOMKOV (*Moskovskie pechatniki v 1905 godu*, Moscow, 1925)

Above left, V. S. KAIROVICH; *above right,* S. I. RESHETOV; *below left,* N. I. CHISTOV; *below right,* V. V. SHER (*Moskovskie pechatniki v 1905 godu,* Moscow, 1925)

CHAPTER FIVE

The Moscow Strike

For four days in September 1903, the printing industry in Moscow was all but shut down by workers demanding improvements in wages and working conditions. Nothing like it had ever happened before. Before 1903 in Moscow and before 1905 in St. Petersburg, only a handful of strikes are known to have occurred in the printing industry, all reactive in immediate purpose and small in scale. In the 1880s, compositors at the Dobrodeev press in St. Petersburg walked out when the owner announced changes in the calculation of piece rates that would have resulted in a reduction of workers' pay; after failing to find replacements, Dobrodeev agreed to rescind the new rates.[1] In 1897, the compositors in the jobbing department of Iablonskii's printing firm in St. Petersburg struck when the manager tried to postpone the distribution of wages; after the intervention of a factory inspector, the workers were paid.[2] Two years later, compositors working in printing shops of the Ministry of the Interior led a brief but unsuccessful strike against overtime work on New Year's Eve.[3] During 1903 and 1904, there were brief and successful strikes by workers at the Petersburg newspapers *Znamia, Zaria, Vecherniaia gazeta,* and *Slovo.*[4] In Moscow, the only known strike to have occurred before 1903 was at the large Sytin printing firm in 1902, when bindery workers successfully demanded higher piece rates to

---

1. Zinov'ev, *Na rubezhe,* pp. 13–14.
2. *Kratkii istoricheskii obzor tipografii L.S.P.O.,* pp. 11–12.
3. *Tipografiia Lenizdata,* pp. 25–27.
4. Severianin, "Soiuz rabochikh pechatnogo dela," p. 55.

compensate for declining earnings because of the falling quality of available work.[5] Compared to the increasing unrest and strikes among metal and textile workers, strikes by printers were, as described by a government official, "insignificant."[6] However, printers were not exceptional. Until the early years of the twentieth century, the overwhelming majority of strikes were limited to the metalworking and textile industries.[7]

One might expect printing workers to have acted more aggressively in promoting their interests. In Western Europe and the United States, printing workers were among the earliest workers to strike and organize collectively, and they remained at the forefront of the organized labor movement into the twentieth century.[8] In Russia, in 1905 and after, printers would similarly be distinguished by their strike propensity, effective solidarity, and politicization. This militance is easier to explain than its absence. Printing workers, especially compositors and workers in smaller skilled crafts, possessed most of the traits usually associated with a capacity for collective protest: high levels of skill, urbanization, and literacy; traditions of informal workplace community; and even formal structures of craft association. Russian printers further benefited from a relative shortage of skilled labor, which gave them a strong bargaining position.

Why, then, did printing workers so rarely use these advantages in collective struggle before 1903? The peculiar structure of economic development in the industry provides part of the answer. Although printing workers experienced plentiful hardships—low wages, long hours, unhealthy workplace conditions, occasionally brutal treatment by those in authority—there was no massive assault on their livelihood or status. As I have argued, deskilling in Russian printing was a structural phenomenon rather than an individual experience. As the industry modernized and expanded, individual workers with traditional skills

5. TsGIA, f. 23, op. 17, d. 311, p. 18; op. 30, d. 13, p. 154. For less elegant bindings, workers were paid lower rates. The two historians of Moscow printing agree that there were probably few if any strikes before 1903. Sher, *Istoriia*, pp. 108–09; Orlov, *Poligraficheskaia promyshlennost' Moskvy*, p. 277.

6. Varzar, *Statisticheskie svedeniia o stachkakh rabochikh*, p. 30.

7. Balabanov, *Ocherki po istorii rabochego klassa v Rossii*, vol. 3, pp. 183–88; Kir'-ianov, *Perekhod k massovoi politicheskoi bor'be*, pp. 63, 92–105.

8. Davis, "A Trade Union in Sixteenth-Century France," pp. 48–69; Sales, *Les Relations industrielles dans l'imprimerie française*, pp. 31–88; Child, *Industrial Relations in the British Printing Industry*, pp. 15–218; Claes, *L'Organisation professionelle et le contrat collectif de travail des imprimeurs allemands*, pp. 1–82; Lipset, Trow, and Coleman, *Union Democracy*, pp. 17–40.

found opportunities for advancement, whereas the less skilled jobs were filled with peasants and others entering the industry for the first time.[9]

Yet the degree of labor satisfaction must not be overstated. Printing workers seldom struck partly because they had alternative methods of defending their interests and improving their conditions. Individual social mobility, as we have seen, was an alternative for some. Much more accessible was geographic mobility. Indeed, the most common response of a dissatisfied printing worker was simply to quit his job and take another.[10] Workers also found ways to confront employers, both individually and as a collective, without having to resort to illegal and dangerous strikes. On occasion, workers brought lawsuits against employers or supervisors, generally for failure to pay wages on time, though in at least one instance a worker sued an employer for addressing him with "insulting words and threats."[11] Workers sometimes appealed to the publishers whose work they printed, or even to the reading public, to use their influence to force the owner of a printing shop to improve conditions.[12] Workers also appealed for support to the local police or the factory inspector when wages were not paid on time or when a worker or a popular foreman was unjustly fired.[13] Even direct action was resorted to—workers sometimes opposed, for example, requirements to work overtime simply by quitting work at the customary time.[14] They also sometimes threatened employers with what amounted to a legal strike—to quit en masse and find better jobs.[15] Finally, as we have seen, many of the most active and articulate workers sought better conditions throughout the industry by joining employers in building an organized community of employers and workers.

Why did printers behave differently in 1903? Although the economic recession of 1900 to 1903 had not seriously affected the printing indus-

9. See Chapter 1.

10. For example, see M. A. Popov's memoir, TsGAOR, f. 6864, op. 1, d. 216, pp. 46, 48, 52.

11. Naborshchik 1:10 (January 5, 1903), p. 169; 1:29 (May 18, 1903), p. 474. I have not been able to discover the outcome of these suits.

12. Istoriia leningradskogo soiuza, p. 58; "Vopl' naborshchikov," Slovo, March 3, 1904, p. 2.

13. Examples from St. Petersburg: Istoriia leningradskogo soiuza, p. 58; TsGIA, f. 20, op. 15, d. 108, pp. 2–3; LGIA, f. 1229, d. 228, pp. 16–17; d. 560, p. 7. Moscow: Sher, Istoriia, p. 64; Vestnik graficheskogo dela 17–18 (September 25, 1897), p. 175; TsGIA, f. 20, op. 13a, d. 2, pp. 98–99.

14. Zinov'ev, Na rubezhe, p. 24.

15. Istoriia leningradskogo soiuza, p. 58; Kratkii istoricheskii obzor tipografii L.S.P.O., pp. 12–13.

try directly, inflation in consumer prices had somewhat reduced the real wages of printing workers.[16] More important, however, than this slight worsening in material conditions were many encouragements to increased standards and expectations. The knowledge, brought by traveling workers, that higher wages were paid to printing workers in St. Petersburg than in Moscow would become the initial stimulus to organizing among printers in Moscow. The establishment in Moscow of a branch of the Printing Society in 1900 may have suggested that employers were themselves ready to improve conditions; as we shall see, striking workers addressed themselves to the society. The appearance of the journal *Naborshchik* at the end of 1902, with its constant criticisms of low wages and unhealthful working conditions and its praise of benevolent employers, may also have encouraged some workers to adopt more critical standards and feel confident that demands for change were legitimate; some of the organizers of the strike, as will be seen, were among its readers. Paradoxically, the relative weakness of efforts to establish a trade community in Moscow—fewer employers were involved in the Printing Society than in St. Petersburg, workplace paternalism was much less developed, and organized mutual aid involved far fewer employers or workers—also may have encouraged workers' readiness to challenge employers by weakening the alternative attraction of this collaborative ideal, especially for potential leaders of collective action.

One might also speculate about the influence of unrest in other industries and in society generally. It is not known what impact the massive student demonstrations in 1901 in Moscow had on printing workers, though striking metal workers joined in, and the marches occurred in the center of the city where most printing shops and workers' residences were located. However, even the most militant printing workers of 1903 do not mention this or other expressions of social or political unrest in their memoirs.

The outbreak of strikes in the summer of 1903 in southern Russia, the Ukraine, and the Caucasus, more certainly influenced Moscow printers. Not only was this the largest strike wave to occur in the Russian empire before the revolution of 1905, but unlike earlier strike movements (with the exception of the Rostov strike of December 1902), these were multiple-industry strikes involving a wide range of workers, most of whom had not struck before, and including large numbers of

16. Sher, *Istoriia*, pp. 45–46; Kir'ianov, *Zhiznennyi uroven' rabochikh Rossii*, p. 131; TsGAOR, f. 63, 1903, d. 667, vol. 1, p. 245.

printers. In July and August, printers joined strikes in Odessa, Tiflis, Kiev, and Ekaterinoslav. In Kiev, in late July, almost all of the city's printing workers struck for ten days, and successfully won demands for a nine-hour day, a 10-percent raise, and sick pay.[17] As will be seen, although plans for a printers' strike in Moscow preceded the news of these strikes, printing workers discussed these strikes at their meetings and even borrowed from them some demands.

Politics may also have affected the thinking of some printing workers, encouraging them to act more boldly than they had before. There is evidence, as already seen, of at least some influence among printing workers by Social Democratic intellectuals and publications. Although socialists generally ignored printing workers until after the Moscow strike, individual workers, including some of the leaders of the strike, as suggested by their rhetoric, had at least some familiarity with socialist literature.

Much more important than the political influence of Social Democrats was that of policies and agents of the autocratic government. On several occasions during the 1903 strike, printers referred to government-mandated standards: the legal maximum of working hours and especially the law of June 1903, which established the possibility for factory workers to elect representatives (*starosty*) to express their needs to employers. Workers often poorly knew the details of labor legislation and thus often exaggerated its content, giving it all the more psychological importance. The occasional intervention of the state in labor relations on the workers' side may also have encouraged workers to think of the government, as some members of the government expressly thought of themselves, as workers' "just and merciful protector."[18] Finally, the government even appeared to sanction labor organization to improve workers' material and cultural position in the efforts by Sergei Zubatov, chief of the Moscow office of the secret police (*Okhrana*), to organize legal trade associations for workers in Moscow beginning in 1901.[19]

Although printers were not targeted by Zubatov until after the 1903 strike, they were well aware of these organizations. Early in the discussions that led to their strike, some of the most active printing workers

17. Koz'min, *Rabochee dvizhenie v Rossii do revoliutsii 1905 goda*, pp. 157–59; Bender, "K stachechnomu dvizheniiu na Kavkaze v 1903 g," part 2, pp. 26–27; idem, "K stachechnomu dvizheniiu na iuge Rossii v 1903 g," pp. 183–85.

18. A representative of the Ministry of Internal Affairs, quoted in McDaniel, *Autocracy, Capitalism, and Revolution*, p. 58.

19. Schneiderman, *Sergei Zubatov and Revolutionary Marxism*, pp. 103–92.

turned for assistance to the Zubatovist Mutual Aid Society of Workers in Mechanical Factories. State intervention in labor relations in its traditional paternalistic role of supraclass mediator, and especially its apparent approval of economic self-organization, may well have encouraged workers to feel more certain of the justice of their own demands.

This conjuncture of conditions and influences may have made a strike by Moscow printers increasingly likely, but it did not *cause* the strike. Nor was there any particular action by employers or sudden change in conditions that precipitated it. The strike emerged, as will be seen, out of a complex set of indeterminate considerations and actions, often by individuals, that just as easily might have led in quite a different direction. My purpose in this chapter is, therefore, less to explain why the strike happened than to suggest what it meant to the workers involved.[20]

ORGANIZING FOR UNCERTAIN ENDS

Early in 1903 two compositors, Mitrofan Biriukov and Nikita Potashev, were hired at the printing firm of Lissner and Geshel', an enterprise employing forty compositors and eleven press workers[21] at a shop near the center of Moscow on a small side street off Arbat square, a socially mixed neighborhood with a large concentration of printing shops. The two new men joined the usual discussions among the compositors at a local tavern. Biriukov described his travels around Russia and working conditions in other cities, especially in St. Petersburg, which he had just left and where wages were higher than in Moscow. Potashev had a less familiar message. According to Biriukov, Potashev often spoke about the workers' struggles against the "capitalists" in Western Europe.[22] The effect of these barroom chats was an unprecedented decision by Lissner compositors to draft a letter to all of the compositors in Moscow suggesting a common effort for higher wages and a shorter workday.

---

20. The following account is based mainly on archival sources, particularly those of the Moscow Okhrana, the political section (*Osobyi otdel*) of the Department of Police, and the Factory Inspectorate, supplemented by published recollections by participants. The only previous studies of this strike are by V. V. Sher, a socialist later active among Moscow printers. Sher, *Istoriia*, pp. 108–27; Sher, "Moskovskie pechatniki v revoliutsii 1905 g.," pp. 16–33.

21. TsGAOR, f. 63, 1903, d. 667, vol. 3, p. 44. Other contemporary sources list as many as 90 workers employed there.

22. Ibid., vol. 2, part 1, p. 235. This was part of Biriukov's testimony during his later interrogation by police. See also Reshetov, "Stachka tret'ego goda," pp. 140–41.

Whether or not such a letter was ever actually drafted (it was not discovered by the police), the plan to unite with workers from other shops resulted in a series of Sunday-morning meetings during the spring and summer of 1903. The first meetings, at the end of April, were held in the woods outside of town, though they were soon moved to a more familiar and open locale, the Golubiatnia ("Dovecote") tavern, a traditional gathering place for printers, which was located on Ostozhenka Street (near the Cathedral of Christ the Savior) only a few blocks south of the Lissner and Geshel' press. About seventy workers attended the first meeting at the Golubiatnia. By late June or early July, when the fourth meeting was held at the Golubiatnia tavern, four hundred compositors showed up.

Conduct at these meetings was serious and even formal. Meetings at the Golubiatnia were held before drinking hours, so that only tea could be served. The main activity was listening to what a participant recalled as "vague and pedantic" speeches.[23] Biriukov would talk about the need to raise wages and the inevitability of concessions by owners if workers acted together. Potashev would report on the growing unrest among workers in the south and describe the relative freedom that workers in Western Europe had to form trade unions and to struggle to improve their conditions.[24]

Police soon took notice of these meetings and warned the owner of the Golubiatnia not to allow any further gatherings by printing workers at his establishment. The meetings then moved back beyond the Arbat to the Zheltov tavern on Bol'shaia Nikitinskaia street, but after that tavernkeeper was also issued a warning[25] the organizers decided to seek official permission for their meetings and asked the leaders of the government-sponsored Mutual Aid Society of Workers in Mechanical Factories to intercede with the authorities on their behalf. The chairman and secretary of this Zubatovist society agreed to cosign an appeal, which was submitted to Chief of Police Dmitrii Trepov in the middle of July, requesting permission to meet at the Zheltov tavern on Sunday mornings for the purpose of discussing "matters relating to the consideration of the general needs" of printing workers. Trepov rejected this request as "too vague" and added that printers already had their own legal organizations that could address their problems—the Typographers' Assistance Fund and the Moscow branch of the Printing

23. Medvedev, "Pervaia zabastovka," p. 134.
24. Reshetov, "Stachka tret'ego goda," pp. 140–41.
25. Sher, Istoriia, pp. 116–17; Medvedev, "Pervaia zabastovka," p. 136.

Society.[26] The organizers submitted a second request, again with the backing of the Zubatovists, in which they insisted that the goals of the Typographers' Fund were too limited and that the Printing Society was too expensive for workers to join. Unmoved, Trepov denied this request as well.[27]

The subsequent course of events may be seen as a response by printers to frustrated efforts to seek legal redress of their grievances, a pattern characteristic of the process of labor radicalization in Russia. However, the actions of the authorities alone cannot explain the decision to strike. Even before their meetings were blocked, many of the organizers and active participants, who had already begun meeting separately to discuss strategies, raised the possibility of a strike. The idea that a strike might be necessary was apparently first suggested by Aleksei Medvedev, a senior compositor at a small printing house. Most of the members of the informal leadership agreed, though Mitrofan Biriukov, one of the original organizers of these meetings, vehemently opposed such an extreme course of action, favoring only an organized presentation of demands.[28]

As plans for a strike developed, it was decided that more formal leadership was needed. Aleksei Medvedev again took the lead and proposed establishing a "union." This suggestion was apparently made in late July or early August, after it became clear that printers were not going to be able to obtain legal sanction for their meetings.[29] Most of the workers who were meeting separately as the informal leadership agreed with Medvedev's proposal, though again Biriukov objected to the formation of what amounted to a strike committee. Medvedev drafted a charter for the union, which he called the Union of Typographical Workers for the Struggle to Improve the Conditions of Labor.

The structure of the union, as outlined in the charter, mixed together tendencies toward conspiratorial centralism with elements of democratic participation. The leaders of the organization, now to be formalized under the name of "council" (sovet) of the union, were to remain

26. TsGAOR, f. 63, 1903, d. 667, vol. 1, p. 1. See also vol. 1, p. 217; vol. 2, part 1, p. 228; vol. 5, p. 435; TsGAOR, f. 102, OO, 1898, d. 4, ch. 2, lit. E, pp. 1, 45.

27. TsGAOR, f. 63, 1903, d. 667, vol. 1, p. 230; vol. 2, part 1, p. 229.

28. Ibid., vol. 1, p. 2; vol. 2, part 1, pp. 228–29, 234–35, 254, 262; vol. 5, p. 435; Medvedev, "Pervaia zabastovka," p. 133; Reshetov, "Stachka tret'ego goda," p. 142.

29. My estimate of when the idea of unionization was proposed is based on evidence found during police searches, statements made during interrogations, and the later recollections by Medvedev and other participants.

self-appointed. To protect them from arrest, their identities were to be kept secret. But the council was not a closed circle. Rank-and-file members were to elect deputies at their workplaces who would represent them at council meetings and participate fully in major decisions. Also, whenever possible, the council would hold general membership meetings to decide important questions. In addition, every member of the union was authorized to act, "on his own good will," as a representative of the union: to disseminate the idea of organization, to recruit new members, to form local circles of members, and to collect money for a strike fund. Membership was open to "anyone working in a printing firm in the city of Moscow."[30]

The union council continued holding organizational meetings on Sundays and holidays, though now they had to be held outside the city limits.[31] In early August, 150 workers attended a meeting in the woods east of town near the Kuskovo railroad station. On August 17, approximately 200 workers responded to an invitation to "all compositors and pressmen who sympathize with the goals of the Union" to attend a second meeting (near the Perovo and Chukhlinka railroad stations) to discuss "important questions."[32] A week later, 150 printing workers attended a meeting in a large tavern in Mar'ina Roshcha, a suburb north of the city where the large Chicherin press was located. Finally, on August 29, 600 printing workers met in the woods north of town near Ostankino. Most of the workers who attended these meetings were compositors, mainly from the larger plants, though typographic press workers, lithographers, and binders also began to appear in small numbers. Some workers later told the police that they believed these meetings had been approved by the authorities,[33] though most understood that their actions were illegal; police reported workers getting on and off trains and going in various directions in order to evade police observation.[34] Workers learned of these meetings by word of mouth or from hectographed or hand-copied leaflets distributed by supporters of

30. TsGAOR, f. 63, 1903, d. 667, vol. 1, pp. 20, 22.
31. The following description of these meetings is based on police reports, interrogations, confiscated leaflets, and recollections. TsGAOR, f. 63, 1903, d. 667, vol. 1, pp. 2, 5, 8, 10–11, 18–19, 31, 36–38, 150, 218; vol. 2, part 1, pp. 229, 237, 241, 254, 262; vol. 2, part 2, pp. 32, 40; f. 102, OO, 1898, d. 4, ch. 2, lit. E, pp. 1, 7; f. 6864, op. 1, d. 216, pp. 53–56; Medvedev, "Pervaia zabastovka," pp. 136–37.
32. TsGAOR, f. 63, 1903, d. 667, vol. 2, part 2, p. 32.
33. Ibid., vol. 2, part 2, p. 218; vol. 2, part 2, p. 40.
34. Ibid., vol. 1, p. 2.

the union.[35] This direct and familiar means of communication prevented police from learning of the movement for some time and
blocked their efforts to locate and break up meetings. But it also restricted the circle of workers who knew what was being planned.

Like earlier meetings at the Golubiatnia tavern, these outdoor gatherings, presided over by a member of the union council or a shop delegate, were run with considerable formality. Here workers learned
about the new union, received copies of its charter, and paid their dues.
Vladimir Kairovich, a member of the union council, would usually report on the participation of printing workers in the strikes then spread-
ing throughout southern Russia and would read letters about the
strike, its demands, and its successes, sent by his brother Aleksei, an
army compositor working in Kiev.[36]

But most of all, workers at these meetings discussed what was to be
done in Moscow. On August 17, Medvedev read a list of demands,
drafted by Biriukov, to be presented to employers. They were discussed
and approved unanimously. It was also agreed, despite Biriukov's continued opposition, that if these demands were rejected, all of the workers in Moscow printing firms should strike.

Although the organizers, anxious to ensure unanimity, were unwilling to have workers present demands to employers until this could be
assured, the mobilizing effects of their agitation were beginning to be
felt in individual workplaces. At the large Iakovlev printing plant, for
example, compositors presented demands for higher wages in early August. Later that month, at the small Chuksin printing house (forty-five
workers), compositors and pressworkers requested a reduction in their
working day with no loss of wages.

Although these actions suggest a growing militance among workers,
a closer look indicates a more uncertain mood. At Iakovlev, when the
manager refused workers' demands and advised them to quit if they
were not satisfied, the workers quietly returned to work. Workers were
more successful at Chuksin, but not because they were more combative.
The owner, D. V. Troitskii, called for help from the factory inspector,
who tried to convince the workers that the eleven-and-a-half hours that
they worked was the legal maximum. The workers answered, perhaps
deviously, that they could not believe this since they had read in the
conservative journal *Druzheskie rechi,* which was "written by a

35. An example of one such leaflet is ibid., vol. 2, part 2, p. 32.
36. A copy of one of Aleksei Kairovich's letters to his brother is in TsGAOR, f. 63,
1903, d. 667, vol. 1, p. 224.

prince" (V. P. Meshcherskii was its publisher), that ten hours was the legal maximum. When the inspector recommended that if they were unhappy they should give notice, the workers told him that they would prefer that he "appeal to the authorities for them." In the end, they agreed to negotiations with their employer in the inspector's presence, which was sufficient to convince Troitskii to agree to their demands.[37] Had this movement been left to run its course, it is possible that it might have been dissipated in individual conflicts such as these.

There is another reason to believe that a major strike might have been avoided. As the agitation among workers for higher wages and shorter hours became known, employers in the Moscow branch of the Printing Society sought to prevent conflict by agreeing in advance to some of the demands. Since the fall of 1902, in fact, members of the society had been working on regulating prices for printed work as a first step toward setting "normal wages" in the industry.[38] On September 5, the Printing Society announced that it would hold a meeting on September 9 for the owners of all printing enterprises in Moscow to discuss raising wages and shortening the workday. To demonstrate the leaders' commitment to making improvements, Vladimir Borovik, the chairman of the society and the director of the large Kushnerev press, immediately raised wages and reduced hours for his own workers.[39]

The local political authorities in Moscow were unwilling to leave this conflict in the hands of workers and employers. Although the municipal governor had informed the Department of Police at the beginning of September that "workers at these meetings have not in any way or at any time violated the external order," he feared that events "might take on a quite dangerous character."[40] It was decided, therefore, to arrest as many of the leaders as could be identified. The raid on the leadership began late at night on September 6. Gendarmes and officers of the secret police entered the apartments of Mitrofan Biriukov, Vladimir Kairovich, Nikita Potashev, and several others, searched their belongings, and placed them under arrest. On the following day, the police for the first time knew in advance the location of a meeting of

37. Ibid., p. 13; TsGIA, f. 23, op. 30, d. 13, p. 347.
38. Russkoe obshchestvo deiatelei pechatnogo dela, Moskovskoe otdelenie (RODPD-MO), *Kratkii otchet o deiatel'nosti za 1902–3*, pp. 1–4; *Knizhnyi vestnik* 1902, no. 41 (October 13), p. 1325; *Naborshchik*, 1:1 (October 20, 1902), p. 5; 1:2 (November 10, 1902), p. 37; 1:15 (February 19, 1903), pp. 255–56; Orlov, *Poligraficheskaia promyshlennost' Moskvy*, pp. 219–22.
39. TsGAOR, f. 63, 1903, d. 667, vol. 1, pp. 29–30, 61, 73, 98; TsGIAgM, f. 212, op. 2, d. 30, p. 10.
40. TsGAOR, f. 102, OO, 1898, d. 4, ch. 2, lit. E, p. 8.

printing workers and were on hand to stop the meeting and arrest an additional twenty-eight workers. This crisis forced the few remaining organizers to improvise. Aleksei Medvedev, still free, managed to find one other member of the union council, and together they decided to inform as many workers as they could that the "union" had declared a strike for September 9. Although police prevented a meeting planned for Monday, September 8, and arrested Medvedev on September 9,[41] the strike began that day as announced. In retrospect, the Moscow governor felt that arresting the leadership may have been a mistake, depriving the movement, in his estimation, of its organizational "restraint and cool-headedness."[42]

THE STRIKE

At the hour that work would normally have begun on September 9, printing workers throughout the city presented their employers with handwritten lists of demands and walked out.[43] By midday, approximately 3,000 printing workers were on strike. By evening, nearly 6,000 workers in seventy firms were striking, and the number continued to increase the following day. Before the strike ended on September 12, more than 6,500 workers in eighty-seven firms had taken part. The police estimated that 80 percent of all printing and binding workers in Moscow struck, affecting 60 percent of the city's printing and binding firms.

Although firms of all sizes were affected, the largest plants were the first and most likely to be struck. Twelve of the thirteen printing plants in Moscow with over 100 employees were shut down (the exception was the Holy Synod Press). Excluding the Synod press, the average nonstriking firm employed only 18 workers. By contrast, the average striking enterprise employed 75 workers, and more than half of all striking workers were employed in enterprises with over 200 employees.[44]

41. TsGAOR, f. 63, 1903, d. 667, vol. 1, pp. 23–24, 33, 218–19; f. 102, OO, 1898, d. 4, ch. 2, lit. E, pp. 10, 43; Medvedev, "Pervaia zabastovka," pp. 137–38.

42. TsGAOR, f. 63, 1903, d. 667, vol. 1, pp. 219–20.

43. My account of the strike is based mainly on official reports and seized documents located in the archives of the Moscow Okhrana (TsGAOR, f. 63, 1903, d. 667, vols. 1–6) and the Factory Inspectorate (TsGIA, f. 23, op. 30, d. 13, pp. 348–436). Some relevant documents have been reprinted in *Rabochee dvizhenie v Rossii v 1901–1904 gg*, pp. 178–82. Also useful is the account, also based in part on archival documents, in Sher, *Istoriia*, pp. 119–26.

44. A detailed list of striking and non-striking firms is in TsGAOR, f. 63, 1903, d. 667, vol. 1, pp. 137–41.

The demands that striking workers presented were almost invariably those that had been drafted by the union and discussed at earlier meetings.[45] The main demands concerned wages and hours:

Reduction of the workday by two hours to nine in the daytime and eight at night.

A 20 percent increase in monthly wages, and larger increases in piece and day rates.

Payment of wages on the first and the fifteenth of each month "without fail."

The limitation of overtime work to two hours a day, and a bonus of 30 kopecks for each hour of overtime.

A number of demands reflected workers' concerns about the ill effects of their labor on their health:

Adequate lighting and ventilation and regular cleaning of the shops.

A free medical clinic and a pharmacy dispensing medicine free of charge, staffed by a medical assistant (fel'dsher) and visited by a doctor at least once a week, in every enterprise with 15 or more workers.

Sick leave paid at the rate of one-half of a worker's regular wage.

Several demands concerned the internal order of the enterprise, going beyond unambiguous "economic" demands to encompass sensitive matters of control and social relations:

Cessation of physical searches of workers as they leave work.

Replacement of direct fines for lateness by deductions from wages.

Use of "polite address" (vezhlivoe obrashchenie) by employers and managers.

Implementation of the law of June 10, 1903, on the election of workers' representatives (starosty).

Compositors added further demands designed to end many of the abuses of apprenticeship, which also threatened the position of adult workers:

45. The following list is paraphrased from lists of demands in TsGAOR, f. 63, 1903, d. 667, vol. 1, pp. 235–37; vol. 2, pp. 398–405; vol. 3, pp. 39, 117–19, 385; TsGIA, f. 23, op. 30, d. 13, pp. 390–93, 409–11. When quotations are indicated, these are words that appear consistently in the majority of lists.

Four years of mandatory apprenticeship, after which an apprentice must pass an examination before receiving a diploma, without which he could not be hired as a compositor.

Substantial increases in the minimum wages of apprentices.

Limitation on the number of apprentices, based on the total number of compositors in each shop.

Use of apprentices only for the jobs for which they were being trained; specifically, the end of the custom of having apprentices sweep floors and run errands.

Finally, to assure that these demands created uniform conditions throughout the city, each list concluded by stipulating "no negotiations with individual employers" and insisting that the answer "must be given by the Printing Society, over the signatures of the employers and of the factory inspector."

The senior factory inspector in Moscow was impressed by the "unusual discipline and unanimity" among printing workers, especially compositors, during the strike. In his view, discipline was "the characteristic feature" of the entire strike.[46] It was visible in the identical demands presented in almost all enterprises. It was also evident when workers struck explicitly to demonstrate their solidarity with other workers, as at the Kushnerev plant, where despite the fact that most demands had been satisfied before the strike began workers insisted that they would remain on strike until the demands of workers in other shops had been met.[47] Similarly, in plants where employers made concessions early in the strike, workers often refused to return to work until the decision of all of the city's printing employers had been announced.[48] As the workers of the Levenson plant explained to a factory inspector, no matter what concessions Levenson offered they could not resume work because "the matter affected not only themselves but the workers of all printing firms."[49]

This "discipline and unanimity" was not always voluntary. Many workers, especially in the smaller plants, told the police that they were "forced" to join the strike by threatening crowds of striking workers.

46. TsGIA, f. 23, op. 30, d. 13, p. 408. These statements repeated words from the district factory inspector's report to the senior inspector. Ibid., p. 436.

47. TsGAOR, f. 63, 1903, d. 667, vol. 1, p. 73; TsGIA, f. 23, op. 30, d. 13, pp. 406, 417; Rabochee dvizhenie, p. 178.

48. TsGIA, f. 23, op. 30, d. 13, p. 422, 434.

49. Ibid., p. 429. Similar statements can be found ibid., p. 425 and TsGAOR, f. 63, 1903, d. 667, vol. 1, p. 122.

To be sure, there may have been a measure of dissembling in such testimony: what else would one tell the police when questioned about participation in an illegal strike? But the fact remains that many workers, especially compositors in small shops and pressmen, lithographers, and binders even in the large shops, had no knowledge of the intended strike before other workers demanded that they quit work and join the strike. Unaware of the plans for a strike and ignorant of its purposes they may well have felt coerced.

Whether it was to be voluntary or not, ensuring unanimity was a critical concern for workers on strike. As soon as the first enterprises stopped work on September 9, crowds of workers began roaming about their neighborhoods to spread the strike to nearby shops. For example, in the districts around Tver Street between the concentric boulevards and Garden Ring, the location of many fashionable shops, restaurants, and theaters, official buildings, and homes of the wealthy as well as of artisans and workers, a crowd of 500 workers, many of them strikers from the large Levenson and Kushnerev presses, which were also located here, moved from shop to shop to ensure that all of the local printing workers had joined the strike. Most crowds were locally based, but some drew workers from throughout the city, such as the crowd of 2,000 workers that gathered on Red Square on the evening of September 9 hoping to shut down the nearby press of the Holy Synod.[50]

Although these crowds threw rocks at the windows of non-striking shops and sometimes threatened the workers inside with beatings, serious violence was avoided.[51] Crowds always obeyed police orders to disperse (though they would usually gather again a few blocks away). Moreover, crowds themselves were only an occasional feature of the strike. A correspondent for the Social-Democratic paper *Iskra* reported that on the evening of September 9 he found hundreds of striking printing workers lining Tver Street, sitting on stools or benches, strolling, and talking. When the police arrived with an official order that they return home, workers discussed it among themselves and agreed to leave.[52] The local factory inspectors, in their reports on the strike, drew particular attention to the "peaceful and proper" behavior of striking

50. TsGAOR, f. 63, 1903, d. 667, vol. 1, pp. 73–74, 77, 110–11, 220; TsGIA, f. 23, op. 30, d. 13, pp. 404–05, 407, 417, 419, 433.
51. TsGAOR, f. 63, 1903, d. 667, vol. 1, pp. 76–77, 110–11, 220–21; TsGIA, f. 23, op. 30, d. 13, p. 352.
52. *Iskra* 49 (October 1, 1903), pp. 5–6; TsGAOR, f. 63, 1903, d. 667, vol. 1, pp. 77, 91.

printers in comparison to that seen in recent strikes by other workers.[53]

Even a respectable strike such as this one, however, was nonetheless viewed by the police authorities as an illegal and intolerable breach of public order. As police chief Trepov explained to the senior factory inspector at a meeting on September 10, such a large strike, no matter how peaceful, was an inherent threat. Therefore, he ordered on that day the arrest of 300 persons identified as "harmful for public order and peace." By the evening, 412 printing workers were in jail.[54] Officers reported "no resistance or violations of the public order" when they arrested workers,[55] though the senior factory inspector wrote sympathetically that "at every suitable occasion" workers expressed "their surprise that they have been arrested and put in jail."[56]

When these arrests failed to halt the strike, an order signed by Trepov was posted in every printing shop on the morning of September 11, announcing that any worker who did not return to work by noon on the following day would be considered to have quit, and his wages and internal passport would be sent to the authorities at his place of local registration. Unless a worker was registered as a Moscow *meshchanin*, as few were, this action would result in effective expulsion from the city, usually back to a provincial village.[57]

Within a few days of the posting of this order, the strike ended. By the afternoon of September 12, only 947 workers remained on strike, mostly compositors in the larger firms. On the following day, a Saturday, only 612 workers held out. By Monday, work had returned to normal. Many of the workers in police custody were also released on Monday after they agreed to return to work, though 286 were to be sent to their places of legal registration, and 44 "agitators" remained in prison, awaiting further actions against them.[58]

Police repression by itself did not bring the strike to an end. Many workers believed that the police order of September 11 meant that employers had met their demands, and there was good reason for their confidence. Organized employers had initially responded to the outbreak of the strike angrily, viewing it as a conspiracy to "force the own-

---

53. TsGIA, f. 23, op. 30, d. 13, pp. 405, 408, 422, 436.
54. TsGAOR, f. 63, 1903, d. 667, vol. 1, pp. 134–35, 137–41, 221; vol. 4, pp. 7–13, 193–298; TsGIA, f. 23, op. 30, d. 13, pp. 405–07.
55. TsGAOR, f. 63, 1903, d. 667, vol. 1, pp. 80, 92–94, 101, 221; *Rabochee dvizhenie*, pp. 181, 360.
56. TsGIA, f. 23, op. 30, d. 13, p. 408.
57. Ibid., p. 405; *Rabochee dvizhenie*, p. 181.
58. TsGAOR, f. 63, 1903, d. 667, vol. 1, pp. 134–35, 137–41, 221; vol. 4, pp. 193–298; TsGIA, f. 23, op. 30, d. 13, pp. 405–07.

ers of printing firms to agree to the demands presented them by an unknown group of leaders." The Printing Society requested that the
authorities "influence workers to cease their disturbances, resume their
duties peacefully, and await the resolution of the questions that concern
them, which at the present time are already being considered by representatives of typographic, lithographic, and other printing firms in the
Moscow Branch of the Russian Printing Society."[59] In fact, the Moscow branch of the Printing Society had already scheduled a meeting,
for the very day that the strike began, of all printing employers to consider raising wages and shortening the workday. When they met, now
in the face of an unprecedented strike, employers decided in principle to
establish a ten-hour day in all printing firms in Moscow, to raise wages,
and even to request the authorities to allow printing workers to hold a
mass meeting "to consider peacefully the questions that have arisen
among them and to formulate their desires for presentation to the
Council of the Moscow Branch of the Printing Society."[60] Two days
later, on September 11, at a meeting of employers chaired by Vladimir
Borovik, the representatives of sixty-five printing firms, including all of
the large private enterprises, agreed to set a new maximum of ten hours'
work in the daytime and nine at night (the workers had demanded nine
hours in the daytime and eight at night) and to raise most piece rates to
the level requested in workers' demands.[61] Many individual firms, often after the intervention of a local factory inspector, decided to grant
additional economic concessions, particularly to increase the wages of
workers paid by the week or month.[62]

In the opinion of the senior factory inspector, the solidarity of large
employers through the Printing Society, and their willingness to raise
wages and shorten the workday, "greatly facilitated the comparatively
quick conclusion" of the strike.[63] Notwithstanding Trepov's threatening ultimatum of September 11, factory inspectors found that most
workers were not prepared to resume work until they had been assured
that their main demands had been satisfied.[64] In other words, the strike
may be considered a victory for the workers.

59. TsGIAgM, f. 212, op. 2, d. 130, p. 10. See also TsGAOR, f. 63, 1903, d. 667, vol.
1, pp. 61, 79, 98.
60. TsGIAgM, f. 212, op. 2, d. 130, p. 10.
61. TsGAOR, f. 63, 1903, d. 667, vol. 1, pp. 165, 196; TsGIA, f. 23, op. 30, d. 13,
pp. 395, 408.
62. TsGIA, f. 23, op. 30, d. 13, pp. 407, 422, 426.
63. Ibid., p. 406.
64. Ibid., pp. 406–07, 414, 430, 434.

LEADERS AND THEIR VALUES

During the police investigation that followed the strike, interrogators persistently asked arrested workers to identify the members of the intelligentsia who had helped them. As Medvedev recalled, they "could not accept the idea that workers could have organized the strike by themselves."[65] The perplexity of the police is understandable. The workers who organized the strike seem to have appeared out of nowhere. None had been visibly active in the Typographers' Assistance Fund.[66] None was known as a correspondent to *Naborshchik*. Finally, despite the best efforts of the police to prove otherwise, none had evidently been involved in the socialist underground. Even in memoirs written in the 1920s, when ties with the socialist movement were usually emphasized, workers active in the strike mention no contacts before the strike with socialist *intelligenty*.[67] To an important degree, this was a "spontaneously" created leadership. But spontaneous does not mean inexplicable or faceless.

Arrest records and memoirs allow us to identify almost all of the dozen or so printing workers who met together to discuss a collective strategy during the summer and early fall of 1903.[68] With the exception of a single proofreader, who played only a minor role and soon left the leadership, the organizers were all compositors. Three worked at the medium-sized Lissner and Geshel' printing shop (51 workers) where the movement began: Mitrofan Biriukov, Nikita Potashev, and Dmitrii Komkov (who would be elected secretary of the union council). One, Aleksei Medvedev, who became the chairman of the union, was a

65. Medvedev, "Pervaia zabastovka," p. 138. See also TsGAOR, f. 63, 1903, d. 667, vol. 1, p. 217; vol. 2, part 1, p. 229; vol. 1, p. 265 (*Vestnik soiuza tipografskikh rabochikh* 1 [1903]); Reshetov, "Stachka tret'ego goda," pp. 146–47.

66. Whether any were rank-and-file members is more difficult to say. Membership records of the Typographers' fund from 1869 through 1899 show none of the known strike activists among the members. *Sbornik svedenii VKT.* Intercity mobility leaves open the possibility that some may have belonged to funds in other cities. Also, some may have joined after 1899, though neither police arrest records nor later workers' memoirs mention any as members.

67. Even Nikita Potashev, the most politically minded and possibly most politically connected of the strike leaders, was sufficiently distant from the socialist intelligentsia to have remained outside of any political party by the time of his death from tuberculosis in 1917. *Pechatnik* 1917, no. 4 (September 8), p. 14.

68. The following discussion of the backgrounds, occupations, ages, and family situations of these activists is drawn mainly from two kinds of sources. Records of arrests and interrogations are in TsGAOR, f. 63, 1903, d. 667, vol. 1, pp. 1–37, 219–22; vol. 2, part 1, pp. 228–378, and ibid., f. 58, 1904 g., op. 1, d. 357/122, vol. 3, pp. 1–243. Memoirs by Ivanov, Medvedev, Popov, and Reshetov are in TsGAOR, f. 6864, op. 1, d. 216, pp. 1–13, 55–63, and *Moskovskie pechatniki*, pp. 133–51.

senior compositor (*metranpazh*) at the small press of the satirical journal *Budil'nik* (19 workers). The remainder worked in Moscow's largest printing plants—Sergei Reshetov, Sergei Khanskii, and Mikhail Popov from Iakovlev; Aleksei Borisov from Levenson; Sergei Ivanov from Chicherin; Vladimir Kairovich from Kushnerev; and Petr Balashev from Sytin—all enterprises employing at least 250 workers and in some cases many more.[69]

Even among compositors, these activists were distinguished by their skill and experience. The workplaces from which they were drawn are themselves indicative. Larger enterprises generally preferred (and could afford) to employ workers with higher skill, and they paid more to attract them. Medvedev, though employed in a small shop, worked at a periodical press, where the quality of work and hence levels of skill were usually higher than average, and he was himself a skilled *metranpazh* earning a high salary of 50 rubles a month. Similarly, the Lissner and Geshel' shop, though employing only about 50 workers, was known for quality work, and Biriukov found conditions there to be "much better" than the average and found his fellow workers to be "of a higher moral quality."[70]

The age of these activists is also revealing. Of the nine leaders whose birthdates are known, seven were 26 or older (the oldest was 32), and none was younger than 22. Significantly, the most important leaders of the movement in its early and later stages—Biriukov (31), Potashev (29), and Medvedev (29)—were among the oldest members of the group. Although they were hardly old, neither were they raw youths in an industry where the typical compositor began work at 12 to 14 years of age and few survived past 40. This relative maturity of the leadership was reflected in their higher level of skill and better wages. It also meant that many of these activists were not the unencumbered individuals who might be expected to take risks. Many were married and had children. And unlike workers with strong ties to the village, their families generally lived with them in the city. Biriukov was married and lived with his wife and three children. Medvedev was also married with three children. Another activist, 32-year-old Petr Balashev, had five children. Clearly, family responsibilities were not by themselves a deterrent to activism. On the contrary, as will be seen in the arguments

---

69. In addition to these major activists were three individuals about whom I have found no further information: a proofreader named Nikolaev and a compositor named Blinov, both of whom soon left the leadership, and a shop delegate named Kasatkin, who worked at Levenson.

70. TsGAOR, f. 63, 1903, d. 667, vol. 5, p. 434.

workers presented during the strike, the pressures of trying to support a family could be an inducement to demand higher wages and shorter hours.

As important as skill and experience may have been in generating leadership, more essential in distinguishing these activists were less measurable personal qualities. Dmitrii Komkov was said to look and dress like "a young lawyer." A photograph of Medvedev produces much the same impression. And Mikhail Popov maintained such a serious demeanor that he was nicknamed "the Roman Pope."[71] These externals of dress and bearing reflected deeper efforts to become more cultivated and knowledgeable. Popov, for example, was repelled by "uncultured" peasant manners and decided to "seek in books the path to a better life."[72] Medvedev read and probably subscribed to *Naborshchik*, for he occasionally read aloud from it at meetings.[73] Biriukov was fond of poetry—police even found a notebook full of "tendentious verses" when they searched his apartment.[74] Nikita Potashev was "well-read concerning the workers' question."[75]

As these fragments of personal biography suggest, the leaders of the strike were in many ways typical of the "moral vanguard" among workers that I earlier described. The connection is especially evident in the discourse of the strike leaders, in which the values and even vocabulary of *Naborshchik* are pervasive. But the connection should not be made too tightly. *Naborshchik* drew upon broader cultural and intellectual resources, which the activists of 1903 reflected upon as well, whether or not they read *Naborshchik*. Moreover, these activists were pushing beyond the boundaries that men like Andrei Filippov were trying to hold, as was most evident, of course, in their decision to strike. But it was also present in the complex and even contradictory rhetoric of the strike leaders.

Mitrofan Biriukov was certainly the most cautious, opposing the idea of both a strike and a union; he even produced a leaflet arguing

71. Reshetov, "Stachka tret'ego goda," p. 142 (on Komkov); the picture of Medvedev appears with his "Pervaia zabastovka," p. 138 (although the date of the photograph is not indicated, his youth suggests that it was relatively contemporary); TsGAOR, f. 6864, op. 1, d. 216, p. 63 (on Popov).
72. TsGAOR, f. 6864, op. 1, d. 216, p. 52.
73. Ibid., f. 63, 1903, d. 667, vol. 2, part 1, pp. 262–63.
74. Ibid., vol. 1, p. 33; vol. 2, part 1, p. 434.
75. Ibid., vol. 2, part 1, p. 235 (Biriukov's testimony). Forbidden after the strike from living in St. Petersburg or Moscow, Potashev surfaced after 1905 as the head of the Rostov printers' union and an active proponent of an All-Russian printers' union. TsGAOR, f. 102, OO, 1907, op. 8, d. 28, p. 295.

that "compositors are not like other workers, rushing into strikes without warning, making proclamations, damaging machinery, and engaging in fights."[76] Although Biriukov was isolated in his principled opposition to a strike, other members of the leadership shared many of his concerns. When speaking at meetings about the strikes in the south, Vladimir Kairovich always carefully noted the harm caused by those who incited workers to violence and advised his listeners to "avoid this dangerous element."[77] More generally, according to police reports, at meetings the union leaders "instilled the idea of the necessity of conducting oneself quietly, did not allow noise or whistling, [and] did not admit drunks."[78] These leaders even proposed a declaration to all "worker-alcoholics" that they must "reform their lives" and that until they did so they would not be allowed to work in Moscow printing shops and would not be eligible for any grants from the strike fund.[79]

Set in the context of organizing a strike, such declarations suggest the mixture of militance and morality that characterized the entire movement as conceived by these leaders. The motto chosen for the new union suggested precisely this ambiguous mix: "In unity—strength, in thrift—independence." It was also evident in the tactics the union was prepared to use in promoting the workers' economic interests, ranging from "formal requests" (*khodataistva*) to a "general strike."

The relative militance of Medvedev's conception of the union, which was approved by all except Biriukov, deserves emphasis. The very name of the organization—not a "society" or "fund" but a "union" (*soiuz*) —indicated a break with earlier and legal forms of association. And it was to be a union of "struggle." It was also significant that the charter referred to printers as "workers" (*rabochie*), rather than the more traditional *truzheniki*, which had acquired implications exclusive of the less skilled and inclusive of managers and employers. The class identity of the union was made explicit in the decision that this would not be a narrow craft union but an organization uniting all printers.

Militance, however, was closely linked to morality in the design of the union. A member of the union council was expected to "take upon himself the moral obligation not to abandon his activities before the full accomplishment of the [union's] goals." Rank-and-file members were expected to accept "the moral obligation to act in unity with other

76. TsGAOR, f. 63, 1903, d. 667, vol. 2, part 1, p. 229.
77. Ibid., p. 255.
78. Ibid., f. 102, OO, 1898, d. 4, ch. 2, lit. E, p. 7.
79. Ibid., f. 63, 1903, d. 667, vol. 1, p. 18.

union members and with all of their comrades in the profession." Deputies were to be individuals "most dedicated to the cause."[80] These conceptions of moral solidarity and responsibility would have been understood by the activists of the mutual aid funds and *Naborshchik*. But they were put to use to strengthen the workers' hand in a conflict against employers, not to nurture community among them.

The coming struggle was also thought of as both militant and moral. Sometime in August, the leaders produced a leaflet—which was read at meetings, reproduced by hand, and distributed—titled "A Letter to Comrade Compositors."[81] The title of "comrade" introduced a socially combative and exclusive ideal not to be found in *Naborshchik*. But much of the rest of this leaflet sounded more familiar. The "Letter" began with the canonical reference to the "noble but hard labor" of a compositor and described the "impossible" "material and moral" conditions under which he toiled. The author dwelled especially on the physical destructiveness of this labor: "Look around—do you see many old compositors? Where are they? If you do see one, old and decrepit, ask him how old he is. Not more than forty." Was there adequate compensation for this sacrifice of "half of a compositor's life"? "No, and a thousand times no." The "noble labor" of a compositor was also seen as morally destructive. His wages were too low, it was argued, to allow him to care properly for his wife and children, forcing him to work overtime and nights and forcing his wife to seek independent employment. Under these conditions, "What sort of a family can he have? The children are without supervision and the apartment is disordered. . . . One may wish a cozy little corner, a full table, and happy children. But no, this is not for us." The only happiness that a compositor can expect is "at the first available moment to get drunk . . . in order to forget the poverty and need, to forget his back-breaking [*katorzhennaia*] existence." Sobriety and improved family life would result from better material conditions, but these were only facets of the moral transformation that was said to be the real meaning of the struggle for higher wages and a shorter workday. The ultimate aim of the struggle, the

80. The text of the charter, on which the above discussion is based, is in TsGAOR, f. 63, 1903, d. 667, vol. 1, pp. 20, 22.

81. The text of the leaflet is in TsGAOR, f. 102, OO, 1898, d. 4, ch. 2, lit. E, pp. 63, 66. The Okhrana could not determine authorship, other than to conclude that the leaflet came from the same group of compositors who produced the union charter (ibid., p. 54). The police found copies during searches of several apartments on September 6, each copy reproduced in a different hand. (Other leaflets were found during these searches, though I have not been able to locate copies, with the exception of a long hectographed leaflet describing the history of the union, which I discuss below.)

"Letter" made clear, was winning the worker's right "to live as a human being" (*zhit' po-chelovecheski*). A family, a "cozy corner," a full table, were all "our rights as workers and as human beings."

The leaflet concluded by assuring readers that these demands were not "unfair to owners" and also that "our cause is just and God will help us." Such a representation of demands for higher wages and a shorter workday as just, moral, and even sanctified, may have been a calculated effort to persuade cautious and perhaps fearful workers that this struggle was legitimate. More likely, given what is known about the probable authors, these were telling expressions of the moral militance that characterized their outlook. These leaders did not wish to be "unfair" to owners, but neither did they defer to their authority. They may have had faith in God, but they heard from on high not a counsel of patience or forgiveness but a promise of support in their "just cause." Morality tempered their militant purpose; the determination to struggle steeled their morality.

On September 9, another leaflet produced in the name of the union appeared, though it is not clear when or by whom it was written.[82] The lengthy (six-page) leaflet was ostensibly a history of the meetings and difficulties that had led to the union's organization. But it was much more an appeal for a radical social awakening in which the influence of social-democratic thinking was plain. The author sought to convince workers of the necessity of illegal struggle. In great detail, the author described the unsuccessful efforts during the spring and summer to "improve the conditions of their lives by legal means." The "complete bankruptcy" of these efforts gave workers little real choice: either "accept that one has no rights" and return to "the humiliation and the curses, the fines, the poisoning by lead on working days and by the state alcohol monopoly on holidays, the pennies for one's work that force one to take one's children out of school and send them into the same poisonous atmosphere, the unhealthy sleep in filthy rooms, the existence without opportunity to evaluate one's life, and death in a sick bed at the age of thirty," or struggle.

82. The text of the leaflet, titled "The Union of Typographical Workers for the Struggle to Improve the Conditions of Labor (The History of the Emergence of the Union, its Tasks, and its Aims)," is found in TsGAOR, f. 63, 1903, d. 667, vol. 1, pp. 229–30. Although it first appeared on September 9 (ibid., p. 266), the content refers only to events before the September 6 arrests. Since, however, no copy was found during those arrests, it was most likely written by one of the leaders who had not yet been arrested—Balashev, Khanskii, Komkov, Medvedev, Popov, or Reshetov—or by someone from outside this circle.

This leaflet contained little of the moralizing idealism of the earlier "Letter to Comrade Compositors." There was no talk of a "cozy little corner" for one's family, of the "fairness" of workers' demands to owners, or of God's support. Instead, the leaflet bristled with the words and expressions of Marxist political economy: class, proletariat, capitalism, class consciousness, solidarity, cooperatives, collective struggle. The author realized that these words, which mostly retained Latin rather than Slavic linguistic roots, were new to most of his readers, so he carefully and didactically explained the meaning of each. Yet even this leaflet did not lack a moral vision. Like the earlier "Letter," but also like much of the propaganda of Russian populists and later socialists, it presented the fundamental goal of the class struggle as allowing workers to live like human beings, rather than to remain as "working cattle" and "slaves."

Since the authorship of this leaflet is unknown, and its rhetoric so atypical, we must be cautious about claiming its representativeness. On the contrary, later writings by activist workers indicate that a fervent moralism would remain strongly in evidence, giving shape and color to political and social discourse even as activists grew more committed to ideas of socialism and class. In this sense, this leaflet, whatever its source, may have been a herald.

THE AFTERMATH: SOCIALISM AND ZUBATOVISM

During the strike, two representatives of the union council, Dmitrii Komkov and Sergei Reshetov, met with "a representative of the intelligentsia," a correspondent for the Social-Democratic emigré journal *Iskra*, who gave the two compositors money, inquired about the progress of the strike, and advised them in the future to see Sof'ia Germanovna Khrenkova if they wished further support.[83] After the strike, several of the remaining activists in the union contacted Khrenkova. She raised money from sympathizers among the intelligentsia for workers who were still in jail or who had been exiled. She also initiated the instruction of these workers in the socialist world view.[84]

Sof'ia Khrenkova was a natural link between activist printing workers and the radical intelligentsia. Employed at the time as a proofreader in a Moscow printing house, she was a teacher by training, and though politically radical she had yet resisted any strong party affiliation. In the

83. Reshetov, "Stachka tret'ego goda," pp. 146–48.
84. Sher, *Istoriia*, p. 137; Popov, "Sof'ia Germanovna Khrenkova," pp. 161–62.

1890s, while teaching at a village school near Simferopol in the Crimea, she organized free literacy classes for adult peasants. For this activity, the local school authorities transferred her to another village, where she resumed her efforts and was forced to resign. Khrenkova then moved with her two daughters to Tomsk, where her in-laws lived (her husband had died much earlier), and where she again found work as a teacher, again organized free classes for workers, and was again dismissed by the local authorities. In 1903 she moved to Moscow and took a job as a proofreader. She also made contact with local socialists, populists, and liberals. In 1903, she considered herself a "non-party" social democrat, though by 1905 she would become a Socialist Revolutionary.[85]

In late October 1903, under Khrenkova's direction, the printers' union was revived. The union's old council was replaced by a new union "center" (*tsentr*)—a term that still sounded more radical than *sovet*. The center included several workers who had been involved in the union before the strike, notably Sergei Reshetov, Mikhail Popov, and Petr Balashev. Except for Khrenkova and one lithographic drafts-man (*risoval'shchik*), the leaders of the union, as before, were compositors, mainly in their mid-twenties.[86] Rank-and-file support for the union also remained concentrated among compositors. Although the union lacked formal membership, it was able to attract 400 workers, almost all compositors, to a May Day rally in 1904; like the activists in the earlier union, the leaders' average age was twenty-six, and many were married and had children.[87] The workers who were closest to the union lived virtually as a family. Several lived communally at an apartment rented by Reshetov; others lived at Khrenkova's, transforming her apartment, in the words of one of her daughters, "into a workers' boardinghouse."[88]

Unlike the pre-strike union, however, Khrenkova's union was concerned not with organizing workers in defense of their economic interests but with educating them for socialist revolution. A small illegal printing shop was set up, which printed an occasional leaflet and several issues of the union newspaper. A library was organized to lend

85. Ivanova, "S. G. Khrenkova," *Katorga i ssylka* 8 (1924), p. 238; TsGAOR, f. 6864, op. 1, d. 216, pp. 63–64 (memoir by M. Popov).

86. TsGAOR, f. 6864, op. 1, d. 216, pp. 64–65, 68–69; Popov, "Sof'ia Germanovna Khrenkova," p. 162; TsGAOR, f. 58, 1904, op. 1, d. 357/122, vol. 3, pp. 105–06, 114–15 (arrest records).

87. TsGAOR, f. 58, 1904, op. 1, d. 357/122, vol. 3, pp. 1–76.

88. Ivanova, "S. G. Khrenkova," p. 238.

workers both popular and agitational literature. Finally, Khrenkova ran a sort of socialist *salon* for workers. Every evening, ten to fifteen people would gather at her apartment to discuss conditions in the printing plants and articles in the union paper. Students and other *intelligenty* would drop by to talk with printing workers about their lives, read to them, and lead them in song. Politically, these intellectuals were eclectic. Many were socialists like Khrenkova, though from a variety of parties and factions or, like Khrenkova herself, from no particular party or faction. But there were also Tolstoyans, as well as liberals sympathetic to the labor movement.[89]

The ideological contours of the revived union took shape only gradually. The first issue of its newspaper, *Vestnik soiuza tipografskikh rabochikh* (The Herald of the Union of Typographical Workers), which appeared in late September or early October, resembled the early writings by leaders of the union more than it did the socialist leaflet of September 9. It may be that a conscious effort was being made to address workers in more familiar terms. However, in later issues of the paper we see no reluctance to become isolated by taking too radical a stance. For the time being, then, the outlook of the union leaders was still an ethical militance that combined the argumentation and even language of *Naborshchik* with a determination to struggle not beside employers to build a moral community but against them in defense of workers' moral rights.

The first issue of *Vestnik soiuza* looked less like a union newspaper than a lengthy leaflet devoted to assessing the recent strike.[90] The author (or authors) of this essay did not portray the strike as the entry of printing workers into the "proletarian class struggle," as did the leaflet of September 9, but as the opening of a "new epoch" in the lives of printing workers in which both society and workers themselves would recognize workers' human rights:

> In the place of the moribund past, which was distinguished by an unthinking and resigned attitude [*tupoe bezropotnoe otnoshenie*] toward one's fate, there has appeared a consciousness of one's rights to a better life and active struggle for these rights. We greet this movement as the first step toward that great future when a worker will not be a slave without rights, crushed by unbearable toil and need, . . . but a full member of society with all the rights that this entails.[91]

89. TsGAOR, f. 6864, op. 1, d. 216, pp. 63–66 (memoir by M. Popov).
90. A transcript of the text of issue no. 1 of *Vestnik soiuza* is in TsGAOR, f. 63, 1903, d. 667, vol. 1, pp. 264–68. I have not found a copy of the mimeographed original.
91. Ibid., p. 264.

The "consciousness" that led printing workers to strike was seen to have been reflected in the "complete order and calm" of crowds in the streets, despite provocations by the police, and the ability of the workers themselves to "plan, conceive, and carry out the strike . . . without any outside leadership."[92]

The second lesson from the strike was to be learned from the behavior of the authorities, though this was not yet the classic socialist argument concerning the linkage between economic struggle and state repression and thus the necessity for political struggle. The repressive behavior of the authorities was still interpreted primarily in relation to the moral significance of the strike—the workers' struggle for recognition of their natural rights as human beings:

> What guided Mr. Trepov in his thoughtless and brutal tactics? . . . His administrator's brain cannot grasp the idea that one should speak with a worker as with a human being. After all, this would acknowledge that a worker has the right to think independently, and it is precisely such a development that terrifies Mr. Trepov, who believes that one should not speak with a worker at all, but only beat him, and that a worker must not reflect, but only blindly obey.

The unwillingness of the authorities to recognize the workers' "personality" (*lichnost'*), it was argued, was what most deserved the condemnation of conscious printing workers.[93]

Gradually, politics became more and more central to the writings in *Vestnik soiuza*. In the third issue, which appeared in late October or early November, a new program for the union was proposed.[94] The activities of the union were to include economic strikes, mass meetings, active association with other "workers' liberation organizations," and political demonstrations "by tens of thousands of typographic workers carrying banners bearing the slogan 'freedom of assembly, freedom of strikes.' " These militant aims were not to exclude more familiar goals, however. At the top of the list of union aims remained the moral and intellectual cultivation of the individual worker: "the development of self-consciousness, which is achieved by reading good books."[95]

92. Ibid., pp. 265, 266. See also p. 267.

93. Ibid., pp. 267–68.

94. I have not been able to locate original copies of the second or third issues of *Vestnik soiuza*, though V. V. Sher quotes at length from issue number 3 in his *Istoriia*, pp. 141–43. There are also references to the content of this issue in M. A. Popov's memoir in TsGAOR, f. 6864, op. 1, d. 216, pp. 66–67, and in *Iskra 56* (January 1, 1904), p. 7.

95. Sher, *Istoriia*, pp. 141–43.

A number of workers objected to the increasing politicization of *Vestnik soiuza*.[96] But this did not deter members of the union center from moving still further along this path. Arguments about the necessity of political struggle became increasingly explicit:

> If workers had only to deal with employers, then of course we would not be interested in the political conditions under which we live. But . . . everyone knows that in recent times conflicts between workers and employers have brought out troops, who have shot at workers as if they were wild game. These harsh measures were taken not because workers were demanding political reform, but simply because they did not wish to work in unfavorable conditions. Without the least effort, it hits you right in the face that the interests of the capitalist, and in general of every large property owner, are protected by the police and the army.[97]

By December 1903, the members of the union center were prepared to follow the logic of this argument. After a lengthy discussion, it was announced that "the Union of Moscow Typographical Workers for the Struggle to Improve the Conditions of Labor declares itself to be a political union" and that it was adopting as its political platform the complete program of the Russian Social Democratic Workers' Party (RSDRP).[98] Members of the union center still considered formal membership in the RSDRP to be "premature."[99] They hesitated, they explained, because of their doubts about the party's narrow definition of membership, its intolerance for other revolutionary organizations, and its unwillingness to support workers' spontaneous struggles.[100] Later, as they learned of the differences over these questions dividing Bolsheviks and Mensheviks, and as their desire to join the party increased, many would decide to join the Mensheviks, who were more "democratic" in their view.[101]

Their attraction to the democratic ideals of the party, however, was not limited to organizational considerations. The party's radical ideal of democracy was what had appealed to them in the first place—the vision of a "democratic republic" based on broad civil liberties, free elections, and progressive social legislation, though achieved through class

96. *Vestnik soiuza* 4 (December 1903), p. 2.
97. Ibid., pp. 1–2.
98. *Vestnik soiuza* 5 (April 1904), p. 1. See also Sher, *Istoriia*, p. 144; *Iskra* 57 (January 15, 1904), p. 7.
99. *Vestnik soiuza* 5 (April 1904), p. 1; Sher, *Istoriia*, p. 148.
100. *Vestnik soiuza* 5 (April 1904), p. 2.
101. See Chapter 7.

struggle.[102] In turn, this democratic radicalism was not defined strictly in political terms. Or at least politics was defined as an expression equally of both morality and power.

The pages of *Vestnik soiuza* were filled with accounts of the degrading treatment suffered by workers, the consequence of their "lack of rights."[103] The "humiliation and insult of the personality of the worker" (*unizhenie, oskorblenie lichnosti rabochego*) was seen to be the very "foundation of relations between the employer and the worker,"[104] indeed of the entire social and political order. The coming "reign of socialism"[105] was viewed as the current order's moral antithesis. As envisioned by *Vestnik soiuza* in April 1904, under socialism the ruling classes would no longer be able to "corrupt the people" with "debauchery and prostitution"—society would know only "the healthy and moral satisfaction of the sacred instincts of nature." Socialism would also banish the "lower parasitic stratum of society"—the paupers, beggars, and criminals, many of them former workers, whose only happiness was alcohol. Once capitalism was defeated, exploiters and parasites would simply "disappear," and the victorious people would "reforge the cannons into plowshares, and in place of gallows, torture chambers, and prisons," they would build "hospitals and sanatoria—bright and happy buildings where the unfortunate victims of the human-hating [*chelovekonenavistnicheskii*] capitalist system can find rest and treatment."[106]

This humanistic and even utopian vision of emancipation was constructed around a dialectical logic. It was said to be only through the exercise of workers' own might and power that a more humane society could be created. Because "every life is sacred," workers were told, they must "take up arms" against an "enemy that is a murderer of men" (*chelovekoubiitsa*).[107] Much as Marx suggested, the emancipation of all humanity depended for the moment on the particularistic class struggle and revolution. Of course, this mixing of humanistic idealism and class combativeness was not always a matter of logic. It is difficult to ignore the elements of anger, moral outrage, and hopes for revenge. As one writer in *Vestnik soiuza* suggested, one day "all of the oppres-

102. *Vestnik soiuza* 5 (April 1904), p. 1; "Programma rossiiskoi sotsial-demokraticheskoi rabochei partii," pp. 37–43.

103. For example, *Vestnik soiuza* 4 (December 1903), pp. 3, 5; 5 (April 1904), p. 7.

104. Ibid. 4 (December 1903), pp. 4, 5. See also issue no. 5 (April 1904), pp. 4, 12, 21, and the May Day leaflet written by the union, TsGAOR, f. 518, op. 1, d. 55, p. 205.

105. *Vestnik soiuza* 5 (April 1904), pp. 6, 12.

106. Ibid., pp. 13–14.

107. Ibid.

sions, all of the mockery, all of the insults by the fat cats [*sytye indiuki*] against the humiliated personality of the poor man, who is without rights [*prinizhennaia, bespravnaia lichnost' bedniaka*], shall be repaid a hundredfold by the worker conscious of his might."[108]

Of course, most workers were as yet far from accepting the necessity of a social and political revolution. According to these socialist workers, the majority of their fellows were unready to accept even the necessity of sustained class struggle. The typical Russian printing worker, *Vestnik soiuza* observed bitterly at the end of 1903, "resembles a mongrel bitch, who, no matter how many hundreds of times you beat her, will be grateful if you only pet her once and feed her a bit."[109] Unionists sought to convince workers that employer benevolence was a sham. Readers were advised that Otto Herbeck, for example, well known as a " 'humane' employer," was in fact "one of the most vile exploiters," refusing even after the strike to give his workers a ten-hour day.[110] Ol'ga Somova was thought to be "the most liberal of ladies," but in reality she was "only a tightfisted hag" (*kulak-baba*) who feigned "respect" for her workers, even promising them a library, while hiring a brutal foreman, cutting wages, and ignoring workers' complaints.[111]

There is evidence that even after the strike many workers indeed had retained a faith in a paternalistic social ideal. For example, when the management of the large Kushnerev press agreed in late August to satisfy workers' demands to abolish physical searches and to reduce the working day to ten hours, workers took up a collection and organized a thanksgiving service for their employers to express their "gratitude."[112] Similarly, after the owner of the Mamontov press agreed to reduce the working day for press workers to ten hours, workers purchased an icon and presented it to Mamontov to express their appreciation of his "kindness."[113] But for the union leaders, the most disturbing sign of persistently deferential attitudes among printing workers was the success of Zubatovism in the wake of the strike.

In early October, one of Sergei Zubatov's principal working-class disciples in Moscow, Nikifor Krasivskii, recruited the assistance of a compositor and a book gilder to help organize printing workers under official auspices. Several dozen printing workers attended the first meet-

108. Ibid. 4 (December 1903), p. 5.
109. Ibid., p. 6.
110. Ibid.
111. Ibid. 5 (April 1904), pp. 20–21.
112. TsGIA, f. 23, op. 30, d. 13, p. 417.
113. *Vestnik soiuza* 4 (December 1903), p. 6.

ing on October 9 at the Kotov tavern, and perhaps as many as three hundred attended a second meeting held the following week. Speaking at these meetings, Krasivskii denounced strikes as illegal, dangerous, and ineffective, and advised workers that if they would renounce strikes, reject all association with *intelligenty,* and abjure politics, the Okhrana would help them form a legal trade organization that could defend their economic interests.[114] The underground union immediately responded to these meetings with a leaflet warning workers that the Zubatovists really intended not to provide workers with a legal means for economic struggle but only to "trick" the "most conscious comrades among us" into revealing themselves so that the police might identify and arrest them. Besides, "what does a cigarette maker like Krasivskii have to do with printing?"[115] Some workers, however, found the Zubatovist arguments attractive. By mid-October, the Okhrana observed with satisfaction, a "schism" had been created among printing workers.[116]

The new organization was formally approved in 1904 by the government under the name Deliberative Assembly (Soveshatel'noe sobranie) of the Typo-Lithographic and Binding Industry. It met every Thursday evening at a tearoom run by the Temperance Society in the Sukharevskii People's House (Narodnyi dom). From fifty to three hundred printing workers attended each meeting.[117] The Zubatovist society succeeded in attracting a wider range of printing workers than the union or earlier associations. At the first meeting in October 1903, at the Kotov tavern, there were more binders, press workers, and lithographers than compositors.[118] At meetings at the Sukharevskii People's House in 1904, there were also large numbers of press workers and binders, many of them from Kushnerev.[119]

Compositors again played the leading role, however. Ivan Matrosov, a compositor at the Kushnerev press who claimed once to have been a radical populist, was the dominant figure in the society.[120] Also active

114. TsGAOR, f. 63, 1903, d. 667, vol. 1, pp. 259, 273; Sher, *Istoriia,* pp. 128–29. On Krasivskii, see Schneiderman, *Sergei Zubatov,* p. 104.
115. TsGAOR, f. 63, 1903, d. 667, vol. 1, pp. 273–74.
116. Ibid., p. 259.
117. This estimate is from Sher, *Istoriia,* p. 132. The most detailed account of the activities of the assembly is a series of articles written by Ivan Matrosov under the title "A New Society in Moscow," which appeared in *Naborshchik* during the late spring of 1904 and were revised and reprinted in Galaktionov [Shponik], *Lededinaia pesn'* (Moscow, 1904), pp. 17–26.
118. TsGAOR, f. 63, 1903, d. 667, vol. 1, p. 273.
119. *Leninskii zakaz,* p. 34.
120. TsGAOR, f. 63, 1903, d. 667, vol. 1, p. 273.

were several compositors who had been involved in organizing the movement among printers in 1903, including both Biriukov, who had opposed the strike from the first, and Medvedev, who had first proposed it.[121] Their participation, especially that of Medvedev, should remind us of the distance between the ideals of many of the organizers of the September strike and the political class consciousness that developed among the workers who gathered around Khrenkova. But it may also suggest that the goals and values of the Zubatovists may not have been as conservative as they might at first appear.

The message workers heard at meetings of the printers' assembly was much the same as heard by workers in other branches of the Zubatovist movement: avoid politics, devote your efforts to feeding yourself and your family and to your intellectual and moral self-improvement, live your life according to a Christian morality of brotherly love, humility, and duty. For many printers, of course, such ideals were already familiar from Andrei Filippov's *Naborshchik,* a connection that was more than coincidental. Articles from *Naborshchik* were occasionally read at meetings of the assembly, and *Naborshchik* in turn reported the assembly's activities and even reprinted Matrosov's speeches.

Like Filippov, Matrosov considered the commandment to "love one's neighbor as oneself" to be the essential moral foundation for all social activity,[122] and he similarly translated this into an ideal of a paternalistic moral community of workers and employers. There are individuals, Matrosov told his listeners, who "love the people, and wish to become closer to the working people." Workers must offer these caring individuals their "love and trust" and their "simple Russian gratitude."[123] One such person, Matrosov told a meeting of the assembly, was his own employer, the director of the Kushnerev press and until recently the chairman of the Moscow branch of the Printing Society, Vladimir Borovik. When Borovik attended a meeting of the assembly, in May 1904, Matrosov assured the audience, many of them Borovik's own workers, that they should not be embarrassed to speak freely in an employer's presence. After all, Matrosov argued, "such a humane person as Mr. Borovik understands us." In fact, Matrosov continued,

121. Ibid., f. 6864, op. 1, d. 216, pp. 64–65.

122. For example, Matrosov's speech to the assembly on April 22, 1904, in *Naborshchik* 2:28 (June 6, 1904), p. 449.

123. Untitled essay by "Naborshchik-Invalid" (Matrosov) in Galaktionov [Shponik], *Lededinaia pesn'*, p. 22; *Naborshchik* 2:27 (May 30, 1904), p. 429.

many employers "understand us, for among them are many good people who join with us and help us to become more developed."[124]

In contrast to such "good" and "humane" employers, there were workers who, according to Matrosov, were "enemies" of the people—socialists in general and members of the underground printers' union in particular. Claiming to be defending the interests of the workers, they led their fellows down an immoral path of destruction and hatred. If these "destroyers" really loved the workers "in whose name they say that they are fighting," Matrosov told the assembly in a speech in April 1904, they would realize that the people are "undeveloped and materially insecure, and they would concern themselves with this." They would realize that "the Russian people, from the cradle, have imbibed in their mother's milk love for their homeland, for the Church, and for the tsar." They would direct the people toward "the path of becoming men, that is men such as our Great Teacher, Jesus Christ, commanded us to be: to love one's neighbor as oneself."[125]

The printers' assembly would have attracted little interest among workers had its only function been to preach to them about brotherly love. But like the Zubatovist movement generally, the assembly meant much more than this to its members. In general, the Zubatovist strategy of diverting workers from radical politics by encouraging active pursuit of material and cultural needs was a dangerous gamble, as occasional strikes led by Zubatovist unions revealed. And even after 1903, when the authorities were more careful to prevent officially sponsored labor organizations from becoming involved in labor stoppages, organizations like the assembly continued to encourage some workers to feel that the state supported their hopes for improving their lives. Such groups also provided some practical organizational experience.[126]

The printers' assembly played a similarly ambiguous role. When Zubatovists such as Ivan Matrosov praised "loving" employers who deserved workers' gratitude, they implicitly reminded workers of employers who did not. Moreover, in Matrosov's case, "simple Russian gratitude" was not to lead to complacency. At the Kushnerev firm, where many members of the assembly worked, Matrosov became known among his fellow workers not merely for his praise of Borovik's "humanity" but for his readiness to take workers' grievances directly to

124. *Naborshchik* 2:32 (July 4, 1904), p. 514.
125. Ibid. 2:28 (June 6, 1904), p. 449.
126. Bonnell, *Roots of Rebellion*, pp. 80–93; Surh, *1905 in St. Petersburg*, pp. 106–08.

management and to negotiate solutions.[127] The underground printers' union accused the assembly of seeking to "preserve the inviolable position of workers . . . as domesticated animals."[128] But the insistence by Matrosov and other activists on the importance of education, cultivation, personal development, and consciousness—*obrazovanie, samoobrazovanie, razvitie,* and *soznanie*—suggests that, no less than members of the socialist union, the Zubatovists too wished to help workers "live as human beings."

Underlying the differences dividing worker-activists both during and after the strike were common concerns and even common values. They all sought improvement in the material position of printing workers but also envisioned workers learning to live more "conscious" lives, though their definitions varied. They demanded that workers be treated by others with respect for their natural dignity as human beings but also felt that most printing workers themselves lacked this consciousness of self. Perhaps, however, the common masses of printing workers were not as debased as the spokesmen of these new moral vanguards believed, though they were to be found neither drinking tea with Matrosov nor talking politics with Khrenkova, but getting drunk at a local tavern, and reading neither *Naborshchik* nor *Vestnik soiuza,* but the more stimulating news of scandals and tales of adventure in papers like *Moskovskii listok.* Workers who believed themselves to have attained some higher measure of culture and consciousness were not always the fairest judges of the workers who remained behind. The 1903 strike itself, and the many strikes that would follow, should make us skeptical of the dismissive judgments of worker-leaders.

Although most printing workers before 1905 still had no vocabulary for describing their hardships and their hopes other than the familiar moral language taught them at home, in school, and at church, this was yet a critical tradition, able to fuel popular outrage. On the day before the 1903 strike began, an otherwise unknown compositor named Akim Korolev wrote a letter to his parents in his native village to tell them what was about to take place:

Dear Papasha and Mamasha, . . .

The matter about which I write you is a sacred matter, a just matter. Following the example of our brothers in Kiev and Odessa, we want to raise up the book market, we want to raise up the value of our labor to equal that in

127. *Leninskii zakaz,* p. 34.
128. *Vestnik soiuza* 5 (April 1904), p. 4.

St. Petersburg, we want to live, but they tell us to sleep and suck our thumbs, they say that this has been our fate since birth, that we are not the same as others, that we are a different tribe, but we don't believe this. . . . We are asking the government to pay attention to us forgotten workmen of the "living word," for it has become unbearably hard to live, now it is impossible to live like in the 17th century on an "altyn" a week, you need a "ruble," because all the little things you need to live on cost more. We also need free time, not in order to carouse like the sated and overfed rich, but as suits our craft, to go into the light, to have our families be warm and fed. Are we any worse than all the rest? So on Tuesday the 9th we will stop and declare our rights to our employers. . . . Our cause is just, and God is for just causes. . . . Don't be afraid for me, I will be careful, and besides I'm not afraid and I'm not ashamed, for this is no sin.[129]

129. TsGAOR, f. 63, 1903, d. 667, vol. 1, pp. 242–45. This letter fell into the hands of the authorities when Korolov's stepmother turned it over to the local police.

CHAPTER SIX

The Revolution of 1905

In the memory of participants as well as in the accounts of historians, the Russian revolution of 1905 often appears as a moment of social and political illumination. The murderous violence with which police and soldiers met workers marching to the Winter Palace in St. Petersburg on January 9, christened "Bloody Sunday," was for many a kind of moral catalyst, igniting deep feelings of social and political alienation and anger, throwing to the surface conflicts over social and political power. In the words of one of the wounded, spoken to the legal commission charged with investigating the massacre, workers went to the tsar "like children to weep out their sorrows on their father's breast."[1] They returned, according to many observers and participants, as mature adults. As one metal worker recalled, "On that day I was born again—no longer an all-forgiving and all-forgetting child but an embittered man ready to go into battle and win."[2] Even if enlightenment was not always so sudden, by the end of 1905 large numbers of workers were behaving in unfamiliar ways, demanding democratic political change and fighting as a social class. This transformation was as visible among printers as among other workers.

For most printers, as for many others, this was an ambiguous revolution. The permanent end of many years of relative labor peace and the

1. *Nachalo pervoi russkoi revoliutsii*, p. 107.
2. Aleksei Buzinov, *Za Nevskoi zastavoi: zapiski rabochego* (Moscow and Leningrad, 1930), p. 40, quoted in Bonnell, *Roots of Rebellion*, p. 106. See also McDaniel, *Autocracy, Capitalism, and Revolution*, pp. 199–200; Sablinsky, *The Road to Bloody Sunday*, pp. 273–75.

widespread use of a new language of class suggests a radical repudia-
tion of older ways of thinking and acting. But this image exaggerates
both the amity of the past and the enmity of the present. In the past, I
have argued, even among employers and workers most actively seeking
to build a social community in the industry, collaboration was partly
illusory, as workers and employers held different images of what community ought to mean. The events of 1905, in this sense, marked less
the ruin of a conflictless moral community than the continued evolution in the way in which conflict was structured and understood. At the
same time, the increasing explicitness of class in shaping and defining
conflict did not eliminate thoughts of collaboration. The durability of
visions of moral community was as remarkable as the damage done to
them. During 1905 and especially in the years following, both workers
and employers persisted in seeking order and regularity in their mutual
relations and in demanding that these relations conform to common
moral standards. This chapter describes the increasingly open and bit-
ter conflicts between printing workers and employers during 1905.

SKIRMISHES, JANUARY–JULY

On January 7, 1905, striking metal and textile workers began roaming
the streets of St. Petersburg demanding that workers in other industries
join their strike, often emphasizing their appeals with rocks thrown
through windows and shouted threats of violence. The typical first response by printing workers, reportedly, was "bewilderment." The
strike movement had developed largely in discussions among participants of Father Gapon's Assembly of Russian Factory Workers, a
government-sponsored labor organization that, like the related Zubatovist associations, sought to better workers' position through self-
help and cultural self-improvement while drawing workers away from
politics. But few printing workers knew anything about the assembly,
though it had already attracted several thousand workers, mainly from
metal plants and textile mills. Only a small number of lithographers,
bookbinders, and pressmen had attended assembly meetings before
January 7.[3]

Most printing workers, especially compositors, stayed away partly
because the assembly had not made any real effort to attract them,

3. *Istoriia leningradskogo soiuza*, pp. 104–06. See also *Naborshchik i pechatnyi mir*
105 (January 19, 1905), p. 58; Severianin, "Soiuz rabochikh pechatnogo dela," p. 55. On
the assembly and the January strike movement in St. Petersburg, see Surh, *1905 in St. Petersburg*, pp. 106–67.

though also because most printers probably continued to view with condescension the activities of ordinary "workers."[4] It is appropriate, however, that although few printers were involved in the assembly they predominated among its worker leaders: Aleksei Karelin was treasurer and a central figure in the ruling group; Ivan Kharitonov was head of the Kolomensk section of the assembly; and Konstantin Belov and Gerasim Usanov were respectively chairman and secretary of the Vasil'ev Island branch. This was not a typical group of printers: all were lithographic pressmen—a highly skilled and well-paid craft—and had been previously associated with one another in Social Democratic circles.[5]

Once printers were confronted by metal and textile workers demanding that they go on strike, they responded willingly to the opportunity offered them, despite their own very modest history of strikes.[6] Printing workers even began attending meetings of the Gapon assembly, and many joined in the workers' march on January 9 to the Winter Palace to present a petition to the emperor (at which at least fifteen printing workers, mostly compositors and bookbinders, were killed or injured).[7] Thousands of printers joined the strike. By the end of the day on January 7, at least thirty-nine printing firms had stopped work, and by the evening of the eighth, at least another twenty shops had shut down, bringing into the streets 5,700 printing workers, mainly from the larger enterprises. By January 12, when the strike reached its zenith, 6,813, or more than three-fifths of the total number of printing workers in St. Petersburg, were on strike; the fact that they worked in only seventy-two firms, about a quarter of the total number of printing enterprises in the city, suggests their relative concentration in larger enterprises. Workers at the many small presses located near the city center, and thus furthest from the striking factories, generally remained at work.[8]

4. See Chapter 4.
5. Karelin, "Deviatoe ianvaria i Gapon," pp. 106–09; idem, "Soiuz litografskikh rabochikh," p. 13; Surh, 1905 in St. Petersburg, pp. 116–25; Istoriia leningradskogo soiuza, p. 438.
6. See Chapter 5.
7. Istoriia leningradskogo soiuza, pp. 105–07; Kratkii istoricheskii obzor tipografii L.S.P.O., p. 17. Individual memoirs also often describe participation.
8. From a 1905 Strike File, which I have compiled using archival, newspaper, and other sources—especially: TsGIA, f. 23, op. 17, d. 311, pp. 54–185; d. 315, pp. 19–86; f. 150, op. 2, d. 1a, pp. 158–72; LGIA, f. 1229, op. 2, d. 1, pp. 54–138; TsGAOR, f. 63, 1905, d. 773, pp. 11–27; Novaia zhizn' (1905); Simonenko and Kostomarov, Iz istorii

When news of Bloody Sunday reached Moscow, tens of thousands of workers struck, including more than 4,200 printers. The relation between strike propensity and labor concentration is especially evident in Moscow: although more than half of all printing workers in Moscow joined the strike, they worked in only twenty-one firms, only one-tenth of the enterprises in the city. Again, because the largest plants were located nearer the industrial outskirts of the city, the effects of enterprise scale were combined with those of location.[9] Many Moscow printers, of course, had participated in the 1903 strike, so that going on strike was itself less a new behavior than in St. Petersburg. However, they had not before joined with other trades in collective action nor protested conditions that were as much political as economic. This time they walked out without presenting any demands and joined other workers in expressing their outrage over the beating and shooting of workers in St. Petersburg.

In Moscow the illegal printers' union sought to influence the strike soon after it had begun. The handful of radicalized workers and intellectuals who comprised what was left of the union drafted and distributed a list of proposed demands, an amalgam of political and economic demands inspired more by ideology than by the immediate grievances of striking workers. The unionists put at the head of their list demands drawn from the Social-Democratic minimum program: an eight-hour day, civil liberties (freedom of unions, strikes, assembly, speech, and the press), and recognition of May Day as a workers' holiday. Following the example of Western European trade unions, the union also proposed shop-level arbitration boards (*treteiskie sudy*) composed of an equal number of representatives of workers and management together with a third-party arbitrator to "resolve disputes." Unlike the European model, however, these boards were also to control the hiring and firing of both workers and supervisors and to maintain shop discipline. The list of demands concluded with improvements in wages and other economic conditions.[10]

---

revoliutsii 1905 goda v Moskve i Moskovskoi gubernii, pp. 206–11; *Revoliutsiia 1905– 1907 gg. v Rossii.* For Moscow in January, see also the calculations in Surh, "Petersburg Workers in 1905," p. 274.

9. From the 1905 Strike File. See also *Naborshchik i pechatnyi mir* 106 (February 10, 1905), pp. 73–74; Sher, *Istoriia*, p. 153; idem, "Moskovskie pechatniki v revoliutsii 1905 g.," pp. 33–35; *Russkie vedomosti*, January 15, 1905, p. 4.

10. Simonenko and Kostomarov, *Iz istorii revoliutsii 1905 goda v Moskve*, pp. 142– 44; Sher, *Istoriia*, pp. 151–52.

It is impossible to know to what extent rank-and-file workers agreed with or even understood these demands. Many workers may have adopted them at least partly as a symbolic gesture, in order to show that, as in 1903, the force of organization was behind them. When workers did adopt the union list of demands, they often had to add demands covering the sort of everyday matters that the unionists had ignored: providing hot water for tea, paying wages twice monthly, abolishing physical searches and fines, and providing better medical care.[11]

Employers in Moscow were not especially sympathetic to printing workers' demands. The Moscow branch of the Printing Society organized a meeting of the owners of all Moscow printing firms on January 13 to discuss the demands. The employers who attended the meeting concluded, not without justification, that the strikes resulted from the "instigation of agitators and the bad example of other industries" and that the demands presented by workers were made "without serious thought," adding that in view of the 1903 settlement printing workers could have "no particular reasons for dissatisfaction." These employers therefore decided to "maintain the wages and working conditions" that had been established after the 1903 strike.[12]

In St. Petersburg, where the strike was unprecedented, events followed a more elaborate course. Immediately after January 7, employers and workers began meeting to discuss the outbreak of strikes in the industry. Aleksei Suvorin, a major newspaper publisher and printer, invited newspaper editors and publishers and representatives of newspaper compositors to a meeting on January 8; as it turned out, these workers were as yet uncertain of their demands, so employers encouraged them to hold separate discussions on their own. On the same day, at two of the sections of the Gapon assembly, groups of printing workers, mostly compositors, also began to meet to coordinate demands. Finally, at the request of a group of compositors associated with *Naborshchik* together with some members of the Compositors' Assistance Fund, the editor of *Naborshchik*, Andrei Filippov, convened a meeting of elected representatives of all Petersburg compositors on January 12.[13]

11. *Nachalo pervoi russkoi revoliutsii*, p. 282.

12. *Naborshchik i pechatnyi mir* 106 (February 10, 1905), p. 74; Sher, *Istoriia*, pp. 153–54. See also Miretskii, *Pervaia obraztsovaia tipografiia*, pp. 40–41.

13. *Naborshchik i pechatnyi mir* 106 (February 10, 1905), p. 58; Severianin, "Soiuz rabochikh pechatnogo dela," p. 55; *Istoriia leningradskogo soiuza*, p. 106. There is some discrepancy in the sources on the dates of the first meeting of *Naborshchik* correspondents.

Under the chairmanship of Filippov, 150 compositor deputies met at the hall of the Russian Printing Society to discuss the meaning of the strike. Filippov gave an opening speech, followed by August Tens, a compositor and a longtime correspondent for *Naborshchik*. Both spoke of the need to use the opportunity created by the strike to realize the often-discussed goal of a "tariff" (*tarif*) regulating wages and working conditions throughout the printing industry in St. Petersburg. Other speakers agreed and spoke of the many problems that a tariff would correct. The meeting concluded by asking the Printing Society to raise and regulate wages for printing workers in the capital and to enforce the Rules on Apprenticeship it had recently approved.[14]

The employers who headed the Printing Society responded positively and invited owners of all printing firms in St. Petersburg to meet on January 13 to discuss the proposal. In contrast to the printing employers who were meeting in Moscow on the same day, they agreed in principle that wages should be raised and voted to establish a commission to draft a comprehensive tariff to set uniform wage rates and working conditions throughout the city.[15] The commission visibly represented the organizational and social traditions of the past. Almost all its members had been active supporters of the Compositors' Assistance Fund, organizers and patrons of the printing school, participants in the Congress of Printing in 1895, or members or officers of the Printing Society. This background was especially characteristic of the three men chosen to direct the commission's work: Roman Golike, who was elected chairman, and Vladimir Kirshbaum and Andrei Filippov, who were elected respectively vice-chairman and secretary.[16]

Members of the employers' tariff commission invited groups of owners and workers to meet with them over the next several days to discuss conditions in their shops. These discussions had two effects. The first was to convince employers, as Andrei Filippov commented, of "the truly dismal conditions in which Petersburg compositors find themselves"[17] and to lead them to decide unanimously that the compositors' demands for higher wages and better working conditions were just. The second effect, no doubt unintended, was to encourage

14. *Naborshchik i pechatnyi mir* 105 (January 19, 1905), p. 3; *Istoriia leningradskogo soiuza*, p. 107.
15. *Naborshchik i pechatnyi mir* 105 (January 19, 1905), pp. 3–4; 106 (February 10, 1905), p. 58; *Istoriia leningradskogo soiuza*, p. 108.
16. Other members of the commission who had been involved in earlier trade organizations were Alvin Caspary, Heinrich Schröder, Peter Soikin, N. S. Tsetlin, and Alexander Wineke.
17. *Naborshchik i pechatnyi mir* 106 (February 10, 1905), p. 58.

workers' own organization. The commission had asked compositors to elect representatives at their shops, who would then meet and select a smaller group of deputies to meet with the employers' commission. On a smaller scale this arrangement anticipated the government's Shidlovskii Commission, which later that month would authorize factory workers in St. Petersburg, including many printers, to elect deputies who were to gather together to formulate and voice their needs. The effect of the elections among compositors, as among workers involved with the Shidlovskii Commission, was to create a body of elected representatives who would represent workers in more combative ways than had been intended by those who had organized their election.[18]

Had these discussions taken place in an atmosphere less contentious than that of January and February 1905, things might have turned out differently. Surrounded by unprecedented social and political upheaval, a failing war with Japan, and open criticism of the government by diverse groups, printing workers were more likely to feel bold in challenging authority and hopeful for change. Employers, meanwhile, were more likely to feel nervous about threats to their authority. Still, the situation remained unsettled. Direct discussions between representatives of workers and employers continued, but the stubbornness and belligerence of both sides was deepening.

When employers invited the workers' deputies to attend a meeting on February 1 "for mutual consideration" of the first results of their deliberations, a tariff for compositors, they expected ready agreement to their proposals, which seemed to them quite generous. The workday was to be shortened to ten hours, hourly wages were to be raised to 18 kopecks, and piece rates were to be increased by several kopecks, though on the condition of meeting standards of minimum productivity. The commission also proposed to allow news compositors five days of rest each month (staggered for individual workers so as not to interfere with the seven-day production schedule), to apply strictly the rules on apprenticeship drafted by the Printing Society in 1902, and to introduce a number of other improvements in the conditions of labor.[19]

18. Ibid. 105 (January 19, 1905), pp. 3–4; 106 (February 10, 1905), pp. 58–59, 68–69; 107 (March 10, 1905), p. 113; *Istoriia leningradskogo soiuza*, p. 108. On the effects of the Shidlovskii Commission, see Bonnell, *Roots of Rebellion*, pp. 110–16; and Surh, *1905 in St. Petersburg*, pp. 218.

19. "Proekt normal'nogo tarifa dlia pechatnykh zavedenii goroda S.-Peterburga," Part I: "Tarif dlia gg. naborshchikov"; TsGIA, f. 800, op. 1, d. 427, p. 51. The commission announced that work was continuing on a tariff for other crafts, whose representatives would also soon be questioned by the commission. Subsequent events precluded this.

The workers' deputies responded that these proposals were inadequate and on the following day presented their own counter-offer. They insisted on a nine-hour workday, higher wage rates, and lower productivity norms (though they did not oppose the idea of establishing norms). They demanded Sunday rest for all workers and annual two-week vacations. Finally, to employers' stipulation that "in cases of disagreement or dispute between press owners and compositors, these will be considered and settled by the Russian Printing Society," workers added the words "together with deputies of the compositors from that press where the disagreement occurred."[20]

The readiness of these twenty-two workers' deputies to challenge employers must have come as a surprise. They had been elected for the convenience of employers, though they were now calling themselves the *compositors'* tariff commission. Also, the backgrounds of the individuals whom workers had chosen to represent them encouraged expectations that the ideal of social collaboration was intact. Almost all of the worker deputies had been associated with the journal *Naborshchik* or with a workers' assistance fund. The chairman of the deputies' group, Pavel Baskakov, was not even a worker but a former compositor now managing a small shop, who was well known for his essays in *Naborshchik* expressing sympathy for workers' needs. The vice-chairman was Mikhail Kiselevich, a compositor active in the Printers' Burial Society. August Tens, a regular columnist for *Naborshchik* and a strong supporter of the Compositors' Assistance Fund, was elected secretary. Other deputies included Nikolai Vorob'ev, a former compositor who was now managing a government-owned press and was head of the Assistance Fund, and several compositors known for their contributions to *Naborshchik:* A. Tiukhtiaev, a popular worker-poet; Petr Vasil'ev, better known by his nom de plume, Petr Severianin; and Petr Orlov, another regular columnist. Although Andrei Filippov was not elected to the group, he was often asked to preside at its meetings.[21]

That even workers such as these were unwilling to compromise with employers reflected the increasingly defiant mood among those who had elected them. On February 13, the deputies called a meeting of all workshop representatives of compositors. As at earlier meetings Andrei

20. *Naborshchik i pechatnyi mir* 106 (February 10, 1905), pp. 66–70; typographical errors corrected ibid. 107 (March 10, 1905), pp. 109–10. Concerning the participation of workers' deputies in resolving disputes, news compositors referred more generally to involvement by "compositors' representatives."

21. Ibid. 107 (March 10, 1905), pp. 106–08, 113; *Istoriia leningradskogo soiuza*, p. 108.

Filippov presided, and he opened the meeting by reminding workers of the necessity for compromise. But once he had finished, and the shop delegates began to speak, it became clear that most workers were prepared to accept nothing less than the full satisfaction of their demands. The employers' proposed tariff, workers insisted, "does not correspond to those improvements that compositors had come to expect." The meeting resolved, in a vote by closed ballot, to reject the employers' tariff proposal and to resubmit without change the proposals drafted by their deputies.[22] Changes would, in fact, soon be made, but not in the direction of compromise. On February 17 the deputies decided to add additional demands: better workplace sanitation, improved ventilation, free health assistance and medicine, the abolition of searches, "polite address with all workers" (i.e., use of the respectful second-person-plural "vy"), and *paid* summer vacations lasting from one to four weeks, depending on years of work.[23] They also decided to organize a strike in case the demands were refused.[24]

When employers did not indicate any further willingness to compromise, strikes began on Monday, February 28. About 900 workers in a dozen medium-sized enterprises quit work for three days. Employers were not impressed and even members of the compositors' tariff commission recognized that the strike was a failure. Petr Vasil'ev later attributed the meager turnout partly to the fact that many workers had only just recently struck in protest of the government's closing of the Shidlovskii Commission, but mostly to the lack of support by crafts other than compositors and by compositors in small shops. Non-compositors had generally been left out of the tariff discussions, and in the small shops, where conditions were much worse, compositors were likely satisfied with the employers' offers, which raised their wages by as much as 20 percent.[25] The compositors' tariff commission met again on March 3 and agreed for the first time to some minor concessions but remained firm on the major issues of wages, hours, working conditions, and worker participation in the resolution of disputes.[26]

22. *Naborshchik i pechatnyi mir* 107 (March 10, 1905), pp. 106–14.
23. Ibid., p. 110.
24. Severianin, "Soiuz rabochikh pechatnogo dela," p. 56. A year after the strike, Petr Vasil'ev (Severianin) wrote that it had been planned for February 25, though both logic (February 25 was a Friday) and the actual date on which the strike began point to Monday, February 28.
25. Ibid.
26. *Naborshchik i pechatnyi mir* 107 (March 10, 1905), pp. 112–13.

Employers also became more reluctant to compromise, especially in the face of workers' escalating demands. They had made several minor changes in their original offer on February 10, but these were their last.[27] Although the compositors had set March 9 as the final deadline for the employers to respond to their proposals, the employers' commission, symbolically indicating its refusal to be threatened, scheduled a general meeting of all employers for Friday evening, March 11. Roman Golike advised the gathering to reach a decision quickly, explaining that "compositors have waited patiently for a tariff since January 13." But the meeting ended without a decision and was resumed only on March 18. Some seventy employers and managers attended these meetings, representing about one-third of the printing firms in the city.[28]

The choice of leaders at these meetings of employers continued to suggest the influence of traditions of trade community. Count Ivan Tolstoi, head of the Printing Society, was elected chairman, and the ubiquitous Andrei Filippov was chosen as secretary. Both were long-time proponents of collaboration between workers and employers, and neither was an owner of a printing firm. In addition, Pavel Baskakov, a manager and former worker, was invited to participate in the meeting on behalf of the compositors' tariff commission.

However, as among workers, recognition of the leadership role of these traditional proponents of trade community did not exclude growing skepticism about their claims. Not only did employers and managers meeting in March conclude that they had already made enough concessions—even rejecting the demand for a nine-hour day, though a number of printing employers had agreed to it during the January strikes—they also became more openly hostile to workers. Employers complained that so much time was wasted by workers warming up the stoves in the winter, talking among themselves, and failing to show up for work after holidays and paydays that a ten-hour day, which was already standard in many printing firms, was the best they could offer. They rejected any changes in the proposed wage rates, insisting that the proposals of their tariff commission were more than generous. Finally,

27. A copy of their final proposal is in TsGIA, f. 150, op. 1, d. 81, pp. 1–2. It was also printed in *Naborshchik i pechatnyi mir* 106 (February 10, 1905), pp. 64–65; 107 (March 10, 1905), p. 118. Much of this material has been reprinted in *Istoriia leningradskogo soiuza*, pp. 121–31.

28. This estimate is Filippov's. *Naborshchik i pechatnyi mir* 107 (March 10, 1905) [actually printed on a later date], p. 105.

though the employers' commission had proposed that the tariff be in force for five years and workers had accepted this provision, the meeting rejected this in favor of a three-year limit.[29]

The meeting concluded with speeches of self-congratulation at this "first attempt by the interested parties to come to an agreement."[30] To be sure, there was no precedent in the history of Russian labor relations for such collective regulation of conditions, and the readiness of both sides to seek such terms suggests the strength of the idea of agreement among workers and employers. But there was no escaping the "interestedness" of the parties nor the fact that this was only an "attempt" at collective agreement. Ultimately, employers had done no more than affirm proposals that workers had already rejected. And there was no guarantee that the majority of employers would even abide by the agreement, since there were no mechanisms to enforce it. As Count Tolstoi observed at the March 18 meeting, "The tariff has only a moral significance for printing employers."[31] The Printing Society added no more force on April 8, when it approved the tariff as a "useful guide" for employers and workers, though it did offer one significant suggestion: workers and employers should form organizations that could discipline their members to comply with the new rules.[32] There could hardly have been a clearer admission that the model of a community of masters and men was becoming implausible.

During the spring and summer, the most persistent source both of conflict between printing workers and employers and of efforts to resolve problems collaboratively was the question of Sunday and holiday rest for newspaper compositors, who still worked an average of 359 days a year, unusually high even in Russia. In St. Petersburg, representatives of newspaper workers had included Sunday rest in their proposed tariff. As newspaper deputies grew impatient with the failing negotiations, they drafted a direct appeal to publishers and readers. Many publishers and editors expressed sympathy, and on March 22 representatives of nine daily papers met at the Printing Society and passed a resolution supporting the principle of Sunday rest. However, since half of the city's newspapers were not represented at the meeting, they voted to delay any final decision until a larger gathering could be arranged.

29. For protocols of the meetings, ibid. 108 (April 10, 1905), pp. 162–63; 109 (May 10, 1905), pp. 216–17.

30. Ibid., p. 217.

31. Ibid. Tolstoi's words were paraphrased by Andrei Filippov, secretary of the meeting.

32. Ibid. 108 (April 10, 1905), pp. 155–56.

Workers, however, would not wait. They had reason to doubt the result of a larger meeting of publishers and editors, even if it endorsed
Sunday rest, because only a few days earlier a meeting of press owners
had rejected the demand for Sunday rest in the proposed tariff. Perhaps
more importantly, the atmosphere in which these discussions were conducted did not encourage patience. Strikes were breaking out in numerous industries, workers and students were demonstrating in the streets
against the established order, and Social Democratic agitators were
appealing for greater boldness. Also, factory workers were beginning
to experiment with direct imposition of their demands, such as physically expelling despised foremen and instituting an eight-hour workday simply by refusing to work more than eight hours.[33] Perhaps encouraged by these examples, but certainly emboldened by the general
atmosphere of social insubordination, representatives of Petersburg
newspaper compositors decided to introduce Sunday rest by direct action (*iavochnyi poriadok*): beginning April 10, no printer was to work
on Sundays.[34]

This tactic was initially effective: on Monday, April 11, not a single
newspaper appeared in St. Petersburg (and the visibility of its effects
further encouraged the use of direct action by workers in other industries). Employers continued to insist on their sympathy for the principle
of weekly rest, but they argued that in such times of war and political
unrest they had a civic duty to keep the public informed and thus
sought means to resume daily production. The following week a few
publishers managed to issue abbreviated Monday editions by using materials typeset earlier in the week and having apprentices compose the
telegraph-agency reports early Monday morning.[35] As a long-term solution they proposed that all workers be given one day off a week, but
that these be spread throughout the week so as not to disturb production. As during the tariff negotiations, workers rejected the plan and es-
calated their demands. On April 22, a meeting of deputies resolved
unanimously to continue refusing to work on Sundays and to include as
rest days New Year's day, two days each at Christmas and Easter, plus
a dozen additional religious holidays, reducing the number of working

33. Shuster, *Peterburgskie rabochie v 1905–1907 gg.*, pp. 119–27; Surh, *1905 in St.
Petersburg*, pp. 259–67.
34. TsGAOR, f. 6864, op. 1, d. 4, p. 3 (recollections of a deputy of the news compositors); *Knizhnyi vestnik* 1905, no. 13 (March 27), pp. 346–47; *Naborshchik i pechatnyi mir* 108 (April 10, 1905), p. 178; *Istoriia leningradskogo soiuza*, pp. 137–38.
35. Since mechanized press work was less time-consuming than type composition, it
could wait until early in the morning on Monday or after a holiday.

days each year from 359 to 296. In a circular sent to all newspapers, the
deputies announced that any worker who violated this decision would
be publicly shamed by having his name printed in the press.[36] On April
23, all but three of the city's newspaper publishers, meeting at the
Printing Society, agreed to most of these conditions.[37] But they soon
sought to reverse their decision. A few publishers continued to print
Monday editions with the help of apprentices and workers in book
presses—who saw an opportunity to earn some extra income and who,
it was said, resented the better-paid newspaper compositors as "fat and
sated."[38] Other publishers feared losing circulation to these papers and
sought to do the same.

On May 6 the publisher of *Rus'*, A. A. Suvorin, who had consistently
opposed any settlement that would limit publication, organized a meeting between the publishers of twelve newspapers and the representatives of news compositors to reconsider the alternatives. First, the publishers proposed that only one-quarter of the compositors in each shop
work on Sundays and only after five P.M., to enable production of
a Monday edition, and that complete Sunday rest be introduced only
after the 1905 subscription year ended. The compositors insisted that
they had "been authorized" to accept nothing less than their original
demands. In frustration, some publishers offered workers what
amounted to a bribe: if workers accepted these terms, employers would
make a large donation to their union, which was just then forming.
Some employers also made threats: A. A. Suvorin warned that he
would have to replace his workers with typesetting machines if they refused to work Sundays. Finally, the meeting declared that the "temporary" agreement of April 23 was now void.[39] Three weeks later, publishers of six newspapers offered to let their compositors have Sundays
off but maintained their right to hire temporary workers to print Monday editions.[40]

For the whole of the summer and into the fall, workers tried to sustain their position against the determination of employers to print on

36. *Naborshchik i pechatnyi mir* 109 (May 10, 1905), pp. 228–29; *Istoriia leningradskogo soiuza*, p. 139.
37. They resolved that beginning April 24 no work would be allowed on Sundays,
the first day of the Easter celebration, St. Nicholas' day (December 6), and the first two
days of Christmas. *Vecherniaia pochta*, April 24, 1905, p. 2; *Knizhnyi vestnik* 1905, no.
18 (May 1), pp. 452–54.
38. *Pechatnyi vestnik* 1905, no. 3 (June 23), pp. 26–27.
39. Ibid. 1905, no. 1 (May 15), pp. 9–10; TsGAOR, f. 6864, op. 1, d. 4, p. 5; *Istoriia
leningradskogo soiuza*, pp. 147–49.
40. *Naborshchik i pechatnyi mir* 110 (June 10, 1905), p. 284.

Sundays, against book compositors who were willing to work in place of regular newspaper workers on Sundays, and against some of their own coworkers. Although workers' leaders appealed to renegade workers and shamed them in the press, and on occasion compositors even ceremoniously put strikebreakers into trash cans and carried them out to the street,[41] they could not enforce full Sunday rest.

In Moscow, the campaign for Sunday rest proceeded much the same, except that the underground union played the part that the workers' tariff commission played in St. Petersburg. On April 22, in the city's main evening newspaper, the union printed an appeal to all newspaper compositors, as the "motive force of enlightenment," to join with their "Petersburg comrades" in introducing Sunday rest in Moscow, to begin on May 1.[42] In the week preceding May 1, representatives elected by newspaper compositors met and voted to support this suggestion. Meanwhile, publishers expressed their sympathy for workers' desire for rest but insisted that general Sunday rest would harm the "public interest" by depriving readers of Monday-morning newspapers. As in St. Petersburg, they offered to find some means to allow individual workers a day of rest each week without disturbing production. As an extra incentive to accept this compromise, employers also agreed to recognize May 1 (on the Russian calendar) as a "workers' holiday."

The recognition of May 1 effectively delayed the confrontation. But employers' proposals were not enough to prevent it. On Friday, May 6, workers' representatives and newspaper publishers each met again and reaffirmed their respective positions. On Sunday, May 8, workers at several major newspapers refused to work. Employers repeated their offer to satisfy workers' desire for rest on an individual basis only and threatened to fire workers who independently refused to work on Sundays. As in St. Petersburg, workers were unable to press their claims any further. The divisions among printing workers and the lack of effective organization limited the ability of newspaper compositors to enforce their will. As in St. Petersburg, book workers were willing to work in the place of newspaper compositors, piece-workers were willing to work in the place of salaried workers, and unemployed workers were willing to work in the place of anyone.[43]

41. *Pechatnyi vestnik* 1905, no. 5 (July 31), p. 7.
42. *Vecherniaia pochta*, April 22, 1905, p. 3.
43. *Naborshchik i pechatnyi mir* 109 (May 10, 1905), p. 221; 110 (June 10, 1905), p. 272; *Pechatnyi vestnik* 1905, no. 2 (June 12), pp. 18–19; TsGAOR, f. 6864, op. 1, d. 25, p. 8.

CONFRONTATIONS OVER AUTHORITY,
AUGUST–OCTOBER

Challenges to authority in Russia continued to grow more varied and threatening during the summer, though strikes subsided. The liberal and democratic opposition blossomed with a profusion of meetings, congresses, publications, and organizations, especially in the wake of the humiliating defeat of the Russian navy by Japan in the Straits of Tsushima on May 14. Socialists and even anarchists found a growing audience for their messages. Students, sailors, peasants, and national minorities joined workers in defying authority.[44]

Although printing workers were affected by this atmosphere of revolution in the early fall of 1905, they also responded to more immediate experiences. In Moscow, printers had still achieved virtually nothing since the start of the year. So as the traditionally busy fall printing season approached, workers in the shops began to discuss renewing their efforts to improve wages and working conditions. In a few cases, such as at the large Kushnerev and Sytin plants in early August, workers elected representatives and presented management with lists of demands.[45] The underground printers' union responded, as in January, by appealing for common demands in all firms and distributing a printed list of suggested demands. This time, however, explicitly political demands were omitted. Most demands focused on higher wages and better working conditions: an eight-hour day, annual paid vacations, illness and maternity leave, improved sanitary conditions, limitations on the number of apprentices and improvements in their working conditions, and the abolition of subcontracting, overtime, fines, and physical searches. At the head of the list was a demand, increasingly heard among Russian workers in 1905 and already proposed by the Moscow printers' union in January, that sought to link better working conditions to workers' own power at the workplace: the recognition of elected worker deputies, who would serve not only as permanent representatives of workers' interests before management but also as direct agents of these interests by controlling shop discipline and the hiring and firing of workers and apprentices. The union advised workers to discuss these demands and propose corrections and modifications but to avoid taking any action until all workers understood and accepted the common demands and a general strike could be organized.[46]

44. Ascher, *The Revolution of 1905*, pp. 152–207.
45. *Vestnik soiuza tipografskikh rabochikh* 9 (August 1905), p. 7; TsGAOR, f. 63, 1905, d. 773, p. 27.
46. TsGAOR, f. 518, op. 1, d. 55, p. 208.

As it turned out, the union lacked the authority to enforce such discipline. On August 11 workers from all of the shops of the Sytin plant met and presented management with a list of demands, which included a nine-hour workday (eight on Saturdays and before holidays), graduated pay raises that would decrease pay differentials among workers, sick pay, maternity leave (of interest to female binding workers), and no retribution against workers who participated in negotiations. Although Sytin workers asked for an answer in two days, they were not in fact especially impatient. After managers explained that some of the directors were out of town and that their answer to workers would in any case depend on the results of sales at the Nizhnii Novgorod fair, workers agreed to wait an entire month for an answer to their demands. When Sytin and his fellow directors responded on September 13, they offered only a nine-hour day and sick pay for two weeks a year. For compositors and binders, who were paid by the piece, such a reduction in the workday without any increase in wages meant a serious loss in earnings. They refused to accept management's answer, waited until after they collected their next paychecks on September 19, and went on strike. They were immediately joined by most other workers in the plant.[47]

Union leaders were visibly annoyed: "The Sytintsy have started," they proclaimed in a leaflet, "without waiting for the Union to declare a general printers' strike when fully certain of success."[48] The unionists tried nonetheless to influence events that had started without them, organizing a meeting on September 20 in the yard of the Sytin plant, at which workers elected shop deputies and adopted most of the union's twenty-four demands, with a couple of significant exceptions: they replaced the symbolic demand for an eight-hour day with the more realistic demand for nine hours, and they added the demand that men and women doing the same work be paid equally (presumably reflecting the involvement of female bindery workers).[49] Over the next few days, workers at other presses joined the strike, often presenting the union's list of demands.[50] By the end of the week, almost

47. TsGAOR, f. 63, 1905, d. 773, p. 27; Sher, *Istoriia,* 164–65; *Vserossiiskaia politicheskaia stachka,* pp. 55–56.

48. TsGAOR, f. 518, op. 1, d. 55, p. 214. See also *Vserossiiskaia politicheskaia stachka,* p. 48.

49. Sytin workers also dropped a few demands that did not apply to them (such as the abolition of subcontracting and of requirements that workers live and eat with the employer). TsGAOR, f. 63, 1905, d. 773, pp. 13–14. See also *Vserossiiskaia politicheskaia stachka,* pp. 49–50.

50. TsGAOR, f. 63, 1905, d. 773, pp. 19, 52, 115–16, 141–43; f. 518, op. 1, d. 55, p. 215.

all of the large printing firms in Moscow and many smaller firms had
been closed down.[51]

Unanimity among workers was far from complete, however. Some
workers joined the strike only after being threatened by crowds of
strikers in the streets.[52] Many newspaper compositors, whose wages
were higher than those of book workers and who probably resented the
lack of support by book workers in their efforts to win Sunday rest,
were now reluctant to strike until crowds of strikers descended on
newspaper offices, breaking windows and shouting threats at the workers inside. Union leaflets admonished newspaper compositors for their
lack of support for "the common cause" and admitted that most newspaper workers who did strike did so "only because they were asked to
in a manner that was not especially polite."[53] Still, once newspaper
compositors joined the strike they met together and drafted their own
list of demands.[54] In order to make the strike more effective, the union
organized a Council of Deputies (Sovet deputatov), which first met on
September 25 and soon included representatives from most printing enterprises in the city.[55] Its first task was to revise and promote the demands that had been proposed by the union. The new list was approved
on September 26, with the addition of two demands reflecting the
greater role of workers other than compositors: free nurseries for the
children of working women (there were still very few women compositors, though many worked in bookbinding) and polite address to all
workers (this was especially a problem for workers other than
compositors).[56]

Employers in Moscow also sought to coordinate their activities and,
as in January, turned to the Printing Society. On September 22, meeting at the offices of the society, employers declared their refusal to negotiate. But as the strike continued, and especially as it was reinforced
by a mass upsurge of labor protest throughout the city, employers
backed down. On September 26 the chairman of the Moscow branch

51. The senior factory inspector reported that between September 19 and September
24 all 89 printing firms under his supervision took part in the strike. TsGAOR, f. 63,
1905, d. 773, p. 257. Laura Engelstein has calculated that one-half of the work force in
larger plants (of more than 100 workers) and one-third of the workers in smaller plants
participated in the strike. Engelstein, Moscow, 1905, pp. 76–77. The Moscow printers'
union announced in a leaflet on September 23 that "all large firms and a large number of
smaller ones" had struck. TsGAOR, f. 518, op. 1, d. 55, p. 215.
52. Pravo, September 25, 1905.
53. TsGAOR, f. 518, op. 1, d. 55, p. 215.
54. Russkoe slovo, October 5, 1905, p. 2.
55. The genesis and structure of the council is discussed below.
56. TsGAOR, f. 518, op. 1, d. 55, pp. 215–16. See also Sher, Istoriia, pp. 171–74.

of the Printing Society invited workers' representatives to a meeting with employers, to which the Council of Deputies sent members of its executive committee. Discussions continued for several days, though both sides refused to make any significant concessions. By early October, the leadership of the council was forced to recognize that after two weeks on strike workers were "worn out" and would not be able to hold out much longer. According to one member, the council began to look for "any sort of an acceptable compromise that would allow them to end the struggle in a way that was honorable for the workers."[57] Employers also began to seek a solution, though as individuals rather than as a group. Although the Printing Society continued to endorse resolutions opposing concessions and even, on October 13, resolved to lock out workers if they did not end the strike,[58] individual employers had already begun offering concessions to get their workers back to work.

On October 4, the management of the Sytin plant, which soon after the strike began had sought to end it by offering some additional concessions,[59] announced that it was now ready to agree to a nine-hour day, a raise in pay of from 7 to 10 percent, and half-pay for time spent on strike. At the same time, newspaper publishers met separately from the Printing Society and agreed to many of the workers' demands. Seeing its opportunity for an "honorable" way out, the printers' council advised workers to return to work if they could attain conditions similar to those won at Sytin and authorized newspaper workers to return to work immediately and use their wages to give material support to those who remained on strike. Many employers also grasped this opportunity to end the strike and thus ignored the Printing Society's resolution and accepted the Sytin compromise. Small employers, for whom the cost of the settlement was less sustainable, were typically more stubborn and often forced their workers back to work without making concessions. At least one large enterprise also refused to compromise, the Kushnerev plant, which was under the directorship of Vladimir Borovik, formerly chairman of the Printing Society. Workers at the plant, once a stronghold of Zubatovism, continued their strike until October 19, when Borovik

57. Sher, *Istoriia*, pp. 177–80; idem, "Moskovskie pechatniki," pp. 56–58; *Naborshchik i pechatnyi mir* 114 (October 10, 1905), p. 455.

58. *Russkoe slovo*, October 14, 1905, p. 3.

59. TsGAOR, f. 63, op. 1905, d. 773, pp. 67–69 (declaration by management dated September 21).

finally agreed to limited concessions.[60] In this first open confrontation in the industry between organized workers and organized employers, though both sides ultimately compromised, only employers retreated in organizational disarray.

On October 2, three thousand printing workers met in St. Petersburg to hear a delegate from the Moscow Council of Deputies. The meeting agreed to raise money to support the Moscow strikers and to declare a three-day sympathy strike. However, as in previous efforts at collective action, workers were divided. Within individual enterprises, compositors usually struck first and then, with varying degrees of success, persuaded workers in other crafts to join them. Some firms were struck only after threats from crowds of workers in the streets. In the end, at least fifty-nine printing enterprises and almost six thousand workers are known to have gone on strike, representing about one-third of the printing workers in the city. Virtually every daily newspaper in the capital was shut down, which increased the public impact of the strike,[61] an impact reinforced by the spread of strikes to other industries.

When Leon Trotsky later described the September 1905 strike among Sytin printers as "the strike that started over punctuation marks [and] ended by felling absolutism,"[62] he emphasized that printers quit work with the intent only of forcing changes in their own working environment. However, as in other industries, the momentum of protest soon led printing workers to look beyond "punctuation marks" to view their actions as part of a wider challenge to social and civic authority.

CHALLENGING THE STATE

During the early months of 1905, most printing workers were generally silent about political matters and sometimes even hostile to radicals who were viewed as endangering the economic struggle by introducing politics. At the large Iablonskii press, workers even threatened to throw their elected representative to the Shidlovskii Commission out

60. Sher, Istoriia, pp. 180–81; Engelstein, Moscow, 1905, pp. 91–92; Vserossiiskaia politicheskaia stachka, pp. 413, 417–19, 420–21; Vecherniaia pochta, October 7, 1905, p. 2.

61. Data on the number of enterprises and workers involved in the strike are from my 1905 Strike File. See also Istoriia leningradskogo soiuza, p. 186; Torgovo-promyshlennaia gazeta, October 8 (21), 1905, p. 3.

62. Trotsky, 1905, p. 102.

of a fourth-floor window when they learned that he had supported the inclusion of demands for political rights.[63] There is evidence that some workers retained feelings of loyalty to the imperial family. In Moscow, after Grand Duke Sergei Aleksandrovich, the governor-general of the city and Nicholas II's uncle, was assassinated by Socialist Revolutionaries on February 4, a large crowd of printing workers attended a Mass sponsored in his memory by the Typographers' Assistance Fund.[64] In St. Petersburg, some printing workers still sang "God Save the Tsar" at cultural gatherings, and many contributed money to "patriotic collections" to aid the families of the wounded and killed and to "strengthen the navy" in the war against Japan.[65] On the other hand, nearly two thousand Petersburg printing workers (though working in only fifteen enterprises) joined protest strikes in mid-February over the government's refusal to alter conditions limiting the free action of worker deputies to the Shidlovskii Commission.[66] Although many workers remained hesitant to compromise their economic struggles by including political demands, many were prepared to challenge political repression and the lack of civil rights when these compromised their ability to express their needs. This nascent political awareness grew rapidly during the last months of 1905.

Although membership in the underground socialist union in Moscow gradually increased after January 9, and small groups of workers began meeting in the capital to discuss political issues,[67] workers' hesitation to become involved in open political struggles persisted until the fall. In St. Petersburg, the leaders of the printers' union encouraged this political caution. Although civic concerns were certainly implied by statements about the need to defend the "legal rights" (*pravovye prava*) of members, one of the stated goals of the union, and despite occasional expressions in *Pechatnyi vestnik* of thinly veiled hopes for political reform,[68] until October the union leaders did all they could to avoid political issues. The workers who led the union wished to create a legal and open professional organization and feared the divisive effects, and risks, of direct political involvement.[69]

63. *Kratkii istoricheskii obzor tipografii L.S.P.O.*, p. 18.
64. *Naborshchik i pechatnyi mir* 106 (February 10, 1905), p. 73.
65. Ibid. 107 (March 10, 1905), p. 144; collections were regularly reported in *Naborshchik i pechatnyi mir* during the first months of 1905.
66. From the 1905 Strike File.
67. Sher, *Istoriia*, pp. 154–55; *Tipografiia Lenizdata*, pp. 30–31.
68. For example, *Pechatnyi vestnik* 1905, no. 7 (August 7), pp. 2–3; no. 9 (August 28), p. 1.
69. Ibid., no. 15 (October 15), pp. 2–3.

This reluctance was appropriate to the mood of most workers. In Moscow, where the union was already illegal and politicized, efforts to convince workers of the linkage between economic and political struggle had little impact before October. Most workers, unionists admitted, would "run away" when they tried to speak to them about politics.[70] Even as late as September, most of the workers elected to the Council of Deputies were said to be "absolutely against any sort of 'politics.' "[71] The first meeting of the council almost collapsed in a riot, the chairman recalled, when a socialist declared that "before we pull the hats off the heads of our bosses, it is necessary to pull the hat off the big boss sitting in St. Petersburg."[72]

The behavior of the political authorities helped to erode this political reluctance quite rapidly in the early fall. As in 1903, printers in Moscow spread their strike by means of crowds moving from shop to shop. In the more threatening atmosphere of 1905, however, the police were not so tolerant. The first clash occurred on September 22. After police dispersed a crowd of workers that had broken windows and threatened non-strikers at several presses, the crowd formed again around the Pushkin monument on Tver Street, surrounded by police, cossacks, and soldiers. A witness described the scene in a letter:

> Cossacks with their swords unsheathed and infantry with their guns cocked formed a tight circle around the crowd. The cossacks closed in, tightening the circle. . . . Shots suddenly rang out from the crowd, and a gendarme tottered on his horse and fell. The crowd, frightened by the shots, turned and ran. Mounted cossacks set out after them. What followed cannot be described; even now recalling this terrible scene makes my blood run cold.[73]

The following day, printing workers returned to the streets, stoning presses and breaking down gates but also, in at least one case involving one thousand workers on Tver Street, confronting gendarmes and cossacks with bricks, cobblestones, and even a few guns.[74] Over the coming days, as the printers' strike grew into a citywide general strike, there were more clashes, in which dozens of workers were killed or injured.[75] The boldness of printing workers and their outrage at police violence

---

70. *Vestnik soiuza tipografskikh rabochikh* 9 (August 1905), p. 6.

71. Sher, *Istoriia*, p. 169.

72. N. Chistov, "Moskovskie pechatniki," p. 138. This incident is also described in TsGAOR, f. 6864, op. 1, d. 48, p. 27; *Moskovskie pechatniki v 1905 godu*, p. 130.

73. Sher, "Moskovskie pechatniki," p. 51.

74. Ibid., p. 50; Sher, *Istoriia*, pp. 166–67; TsGAOR, f. 63, op. 1905, d. 773, pp. 151, 157, 206.

75. Engelstein, *Moscow, 1905*, pp. 87–90.

were encouraged by the sight of much of urban society challenging the political status quo.

The growing willingness of Moscow printers to become involved in matters reaching beyond their own immediate professional interests was visible at a meeting of the Moscow Council of Deputies on October 2. Printers at this meeting discussed their own recent experiences but also heard a report by a representative of strikers from the Filippov bakery who were severely beaten while in police custody on the night of September 24. Deputies who had only a week earlier shouted down political speakers now not only listened to militant political speeches but themselves declaimed against the brutality of the autocratic order. The meeting concluded by approving a resolution, with only four dissenting votes, proclaiming that "only when the entire people govern the country through its representatives, elected by universal, equal, direct, and secret suffrage, will we be protected from police tyranny [proizvol] in our struggles with employers." Even former Zubatovists, it was said, "made revolutionary speeches."[76]

By October 19, at a meeting of several thousand printing workers at the Moscow Conservatory, every political statement made by representatives of the various left-wing parties was greeted with sympathy. Resolutions passed at the meeting demanded amnesty for all political and religious prisoners and the end of the use of troops to maintain civil order and called on workers to join the Russian Social-Democratic Workers' Party and to prepare for an armed struggle to realize a "new state order" based on universal, equal, and secret suffrage.[77]

In St. Petersburg, we see the same emergent sense among workers of being part of a larger confrontation than between themselves and their employers. Although the October strike in support of Moscow printers did not address larger social or political matters, the boundary between professional and civic concerns quickly disappeared. On October 14, at a meeting at the university, several thousand printing workers approved a resolution, introduced by Social Democrats (possibly Bolsheviks),[78] that openly called on workers to arm themselves—"including by breaking into gun shops and seizing arms from police and soldiers where

76. Chistov, "Moskovskie pechatniki," p. 138; Sher, Istoriia, p. 179; Vserossiiskaia politicheskaia stachka, p. 404.
77. Russkie vedomosti, October 20, 1905, p. 3; Sher, "Moskovskie pechatniki," pp. 63–64; Sher, Istoriia, pp. 185–86; Pechatnik 1906, no. 1 (April 23), pp. 8–9.
78. This was the claim of the authors of Istoriia leningradskogo soiuza, p. 198. The call for armed struggle in the resolution suggests that Bolsheviks may indeed have been the sponsors of the resolution.

this is possible"—in order to "turn the army of the striking working class into a revolutionary army." The resolution defined the workers' aim as overthrowing the autocracy and establishing a "democratic republic."[79] On October 15, many printers in St. Petersburg again quit work in support of the growing national political strike. The union paper *Pechatnyi vestnik,* which had been studiedly non-political, reflected these changing concerns, especially after the tsar's promise of political reform on October 17. For the first time, articles began to call for elections to a constituent assembly; freedom of assembly, speech, and the press; and support for the Russian Social-Democratic Workers' Party. For the first time, the union paper also welcomed contributions from non-workers.[80] By early November, politics had become part of the daily life of organized printers. At a meeting of seven thousand printing workers on November 4, workers who sought to limit the discussion to economic issues were not even allowed to speak.[81]

Workers' growing attention to politics in the fall of 1905 partly distracted them from workplace issues. But politics had not become abstracted from social relations. It became conventional for printing workers at mass meetings, repeating the arguments of the socialists, to criticize other classes for political vacillation. As a resolution adopted by Moscow printers on October 19 stated: "The Manifesto was not given voluntarily. It was seized by force. Everyone must recognize that this victory belongs to the working class, which carries on its shoulders the entire weight of the struggle for political freedom."[82]

This perceived connection between class and politics was also expressed in efforts by organized printers to build alliances with other labor organizations. The Moscow Council of Deputies sent representatives to a meeting on October 2 through 4 to plan a citywide workers' council, to the First All-Russian Conference of Trade Unions in Moscow on October 6 and 7, and to the Moscow Soviet of Workers' Deputies in November. In St. Petersburg, the printers' union sent representatives to the Conference of Trade Unions, joined other unions in organizing a Central Bureau of Trade Unions, and participated actively in the soviet. In both cities, activist printers produced the newspapers of the soviets at presses specially "seized" at night for this purpose.

79. Kiselevich, "Soiuz rabochikh pechatnogo dela," p. 297.
80. See, for example, *Pechatnyi vestnik* 1905, no. 16–17 (October 30), pp. 2–9; no. 18 (November 27), pp. 1–6; no. 19 (December 4), pp. 1–5.
81. *Vysshii pod"em revoliutsii,* pp. 366–67.
82. *Russkie vedomosti,* October 20, 1905, p. 3.

Printing workers also joined the political strikes that were organized by these class organizations. In St. Petersburg in early November, more than five thousand printing workers (from fifty-seven firms) responded to an appeal by the soviet to strike in protest against the declaration of martial law in Poland and the threat to execute rebellious soldiers and sailors of the Kronstadt garrison. Many would again strike in December in support of the Moscow uprising.[83] In Moscow itself, nearly six thousand printing workers quit work in support of the uprising, and many took up arms.[84]

The intermingling of politics and class was especially evident in the political issue that most preoccupied printing workers in the last months of 1905—censorship. The owners of printing firms, especially those also involved in publishing books and periodicals, had long been critical of censorship, a government practice that offended them both politically and professionally. After the government established the Kobeko Commission on censorship reform in January 1905, publishers tried to push forward its slow-moving efforts. Frustrated, and encouraged by the promises of the October Manifesto, publishers of most of the journals and newspapers in St. Petersburg met on October 17 to establish a Union for the Defense of Press Freedom; they also agreed to cease submitting materials to the censor as of October 22.[85]

In Moscow, nine periodical publishers and six book publishers met on October 19 and similarly resolved to stop submitting materials to the censor. They also called on press owners, the Russian Printing Society, and the union of printing workers to support them in their campaign.[86] Moscow press owners proved less bold than the publishers (some of whom, however, were also press owners): a meeting of owners of printing enterprises on October 28 concluded that direct action was "too risky" and resolved to wait for the government to offer its new censorship law.[87]

On October 19, the St. Petersburg Soviet of Workers' Deputies, as part of its efforts to continue and expand the political struggle after the October Manifesto, adopted a resolution proposed by the leadership of the printers' union announcing its own campaign to introduce freedom

---

83. Calculated from the 1905 Strike File. This number does not include the workers at the massive Office for the Manufacture of Government Paper, who had been on strike for nonpolitical reasons since October 26.

84. Engelstein, *Moscow, 1905*, p. 229.

85. *Knizhnyi vestnik* 1905, no. 13 (March 27), pp. 327–28; no. 44 (October 30), pp. 1255–1257, 1267–68.

86. Ibid., p. 1269; *Russkie vedomosti*, October 20, 1905, p. 3.

87. *Russkoe slovo*, October 29, 1905, p. 3.

of the press. Like the publishers' union, the soviet proposed to end preliminary censorship of periodicals by refusing to submit materials in advance of publication. The soviet resolution added that "freedom of the press must be won by the workers" and threatened strikes and even sabotage against employers who continued to submit to the censors. On October 30, a mass meeting of printing workers approved this plan to create an uncensored press by direct action.[88] In Moscow, also on October 30, a mass meeting of printing workers approved the publishers' proposal to print without censorship and berated press owners who hesitated. On November 7, a mass meeting resolved to "boycott" firms that continued to submit materials to the censor.[89]

Despite the shared goal of a free press, it was evident that workers did not feel a sense of common cause with their employers. Organized workers treated employers as unwilling allies at best. At mass meetings in St. Petersburg on October 30 and in Moscow on November 7, workers authorized the leaders of their unions to "discuss" their decisions with publishers and press owners, but not to negotiate—employers were either immediately to stop submitting to censorship or be "boycotted," that is, workers would refuse to work in their shops.[90] Even amidst a struggle that might so well have served to unite workers and employers in the spirit of common interest and moral conviction, the old dream of trade community seemed increasingly unreal and distant.

88. *Pechatnyi vestnik* 1905, no. 16–17 (October 30), p. 2; *Istoriia leningradskogo soiuza*, pp. 204–05; *Novaia zhizn'*, November 2, 1905, p. 3; *Vysshii pod"em revoliutsii*, p. 345.

89. *Russkie vedomosti*, October 31, 1905, p. 3; *Vecherniaia pochta*, November 9, 1905, p. 3. See also Sher, *Istoriia*, p. 213.

90. *Novaia zhizn'*, November 2, 1905, p. 3; *Vysshii pod"em revoliutsii*, p. 345; *Vecherniaia pochta*, November 9, 1905, p. 3; *Moskovskaia gazeta*, November 12, 1905, p. 3; Sher, *Istoriia*, p. 213.

CHAPTER SEVEN

Organizing Class Relations, 1905–1907

The growing enmity between workers and employers in 1905 was expressed in their segregation into class organizations. This process, already under way by the summer of 1905, was accelerated by Nicholas II's proclamation on October 17 that it was his "inflexible will . . . to grant the population the unshakable foundations of civic freedom"[1] and, after a period of repression provoked by armed uprisings in Moscow and other cities, by the legalization of trade unions on March 4, 1906. This legislation was designed, in the hopeful words of the State Council, to signify the transition to a system of labor relations in which both employers and workers could "conduct autonomous and, at the same time, legal activity within the framework of professional organizations" in order to "coordinate and reconcile *conflicting* interests."[2]

There is little doubt that workers and employers had come to see their interests in conflict. Developments in the printing industry exemplify this social breakdown, as workers and employers organized their own unions and made frequent and often innovative use of such weapons of class combat as coordinated strikes and lockouts, boycotts and blacklists, and coercively enforced solidarity. But the example of printers also illustrates the continuing efforts to "coordinate and reconcile" conflicting interests. Notwithstanding the resistance by large employers' associations such as the Petersburg and Moscow Societies of Factory Owners to recognize trade unions, many individual employers and

1. Ascher, *The Revolution of 1905*, p. 229.
2. Quoted in Bonnell, *Roots of Rebellion*, p. 200. Emphasis in original.

single-industry owners' groups, including those organized by press owners, engaged in collective bargaining with workers and accepted mediation of disputes. The leaders of workers' unions similarly, and often more vigorously, sought to establish collective agreements, arbitration, and institutional procedures for expressing grievances.[3]

Dualistic strategies characterized the practice of many groups of workers and employers in Russia during 1905 and especially in 1906 and 1907, as both sides confronted one another over questions of interest and authority and at the same time pursued regulative reform of their relations.[4] In the printing industry in particular, we see struggles over class autonomy and power intermingling with efforts to preserve and retain traditional social bonds or establish new forms of social order and cooperation. In part, we may speak of a recalculation of self-interest. The effective organization of workers and employers demanded that both seek more effective means of defending and promoting their interests than brute confrontation. But employers and workers also brought into their restructured relations older values of regulation, professional improvement, and morality.

WORKERS' UNIONS: FORMATION AND STRUCTURE

At the end of March 1905, several members of the compositors' tariff commission in St. Petersburg discussed among themselves the possibility of establishing an independent professional organization for printing workers. Although some of these proponents of unionization were members of existing assistance funds, they sought to create an organization that would be different from the funds in both structure and function. The behavior of officials of the Compositors' Assistance Fund during the tariff negotiations reinforced their desire to create a new organization. The leaders of the fund, mainly employers and managers, openly criticized the tariff proposals drafted by compositors and refused even to assist the compositors' deputies in their work (even though one of these deputies, Nikolai Vorob'ev, headed the fund). It seemed clear to many of these deputies that the interests of the employers and managers who controlled the fund were "completely opposed to the interests of rank-and-file workmen."[5]

3. Ibid., ch. 7.
4. For a similar argument focusing on trade union strategy, see ibid., esp. pp. 265, 316, 455.
5. *Pechatnyi vestnik* 1905, no. 1 (May 15), pp. 8–9.

In order to establish an organization to defend workers' separate interests, members of the tariff commission arranged a meeting of shop representatives to hear a report on the history and function of trade unions in Western Europe and the United States. The report was presented by August Tens, a member of the deputies group who had participated in trade unions while working in Western Europe, at a meeting held at the Printing Society on April 3. Tens described the history of unionism in the West and the ongoing dispute between those who advocated purely economic trade unions and those who insisted on broader social and political goals as an expression of the position of workers as "a special social class." He offered no opinion of his own but noted in conclusion that printing workers everywhere were in the front ranks of the labor movement.[6] After a discussion, the meeting endorsed the proposal to form a trade union and elected an organizational bureau to draft a charter.[7]

The membership of this bureau suggests the strength both of past organizational traditions and of recent innovations. Not surprisingly, most of the members were compositors: Mikhail Kiselevich, Ivan Liubimtsev, August Tens, Stepan Tsorn, and Petr Vasil'ev (Severianin). The only non-compositor elected to the organizational bureau was Zoia Voronova, a proofreader and the coeditor of *Naborshchik*, who was elected on the recommendation of Tens and others. Perhaps feeling out of place—in her views, occupation, and sex—she quickly resigned.

The five compositors who comprised the union's organizational bureau had all been involved in earlier organizations. Tens, Tsorn, and Vasil'ev were well known as columnists for *Naborshchik*. Two members of the bureau had been active in mutual aid funds (though not in the Compositors' Assistance Fund): Kiselevich with the Printers' Burial Society and Tsorn as the chief organizer of an assistance fund in Ekaterinoslav in 1902. Finally, Kiselevich, Tens, and Vasil'ev had been members of the compositors' tariff commission.

The background of the fifth member, Ivan Liubimtsev, who had arrived in St. Petersburg only a few months before, was quite different. Liubimtsev was the only member of the organizational bureau not previously associated with *Naborshchik* or a mutual aid fund. His earlier organizational experiences had been in the Social-Democratic underground, with which he had become involved as a young compositor in

6. Ibid., pp. 4–8.
7. *Naborshchik i pechatnyi mir* 108 (April 10, 1905), pp. 178–79; *Pechatnyi vestnik* 1905, no. 1 (May 15), p. 2; *Istoriia leningradskogo soiuza*, pp. 134–35.

Nizhnii Novgorod in the 1890s. By the time he arrived in St. Petersburg in January 1905 he had already been arrested twice for his activities and had spent two years in prison and three years in exile. Considering this past, it was remarkable that Liubimtsev was not only elected to join recent partisans of *Naborshchik* and the assistance funds in founding a new organization but was even chosen by these others to be their chairman. Even if his affiliations and history were unknown to most of his fellow workers and activists, as is likely, his outspokenness and militance were not.[8]

Over the next three weeks, the members of the organizational bureau prepared the foundation for the Petersburg Union of Printing Workers. They discussed the principles that should guide the new union, the differences between trade unions and mutual aid societies, the appropriate social and craft composition of the union, the possibility of national organization, methods of struggle, and the relationship of the union to the political parties. Their conclusions were embodied in the charter they drafted, which they presented to a meeting of shop representatives on April 24.

Liubimtsev, who read the opening report on behalf of the organizational bureau, pointedly explained that the bureau conceived of the union as a class organization, excluding employers and managers from membership while including all printing workers irrespective of craft. The bureau was convinced, he explained, that a "narrowly professional, egoistic organization for the defense of the interests of only one craft, such as compositors," would be too weak to achieve its goals. The union would also welcome workers of all nationalities and religions—unlike the assistance funds, which were still divided into German and Russian organizations—since "all workers feel the yoke of exploitation in the same way, independently of which religion they profess."[9]

Although several craft unions were eventually established as sections of the printers' union—or, in the case of proofreaders, organized separately and then joined with the main union—only the union of lithographers may be considered a deviation from the early tendency to-

8. Tens, Tsorn, and Vasil'ev are discussed in Chapter 4. On Kiselevich, *Naborshchik i pechatnyi mir* 114 (October 10, 1905), p. 460. On Liubimtsev, *Istoriia leningradskogo soiuza*, p. 438.

9. *Naborshchik i pechatnyi mir* 109 (May 10, 1905), pp. 202–06; *Pechatnyi vestnik* 1905, no. 1 (May 15), p. 2. The text of Liubimtsev's speech and the first draft of the union's charter were reprinted separately by *Naborshchik* as Liubimtsev, *Ob osnovnykh printsipakh organizatsii Soiuza rabochikh pechatnogo dela*. See also *Istoriia leningradskogo soiuza*, pp. 141–47.

ward industrywide unity. This is explained by the unique existence of a group of lithographers with an older organizational tradition—the handful of lithographers who had been among the leaders of Father Gapon's Assembly of Russian Factory Workers.[10] At the end of 1904, these lithographers had begun to establish a separate organization for their craft, though it had made little progress when they were arrested in the wake of Bloody Sunday. Once freed from prison, they immediately began to organize a craft union for lithographers, for which a founding meeting was held in early October 1905. The directing board of the union included most of the former activists in the Gaponist Assembly, Aleksei Karelin, Ivan Kharitonov, Konstantin Belov, and Gerasim Usanov. Lithographers also elected Karelin to represent them in the Soviet of Workers' Deputies. Although the lithographers' union often cooperated with the larger printers' union and even formally agreed at the end of 1906 to merge with the main printers' union (against Karelin's opposition), it maintained its independent existence until it was closed in 1907.[11]

During the spring and summer of 1905, the printers' union was mainly preoccupied with strengthening its organizational structure. On April 24 a larger organizational bureau was elected to manage the affairs of the union and to finish drafting the charter, which was approved at a meeting of shop representatives in late June and submitted to the government for approval, though trade unions were still illegal. The nine men elected to the new bureau were all compositors; the absence of other crafts was blamed on their passivity.[12] Four of the nine— Mikhail Kiselevich, Ivan Liubimtsev, August Tens, and Petr Vasil'ev— were members of the original organizational bureau. Of the five new members, two were members of the compositors' tariff commission, but little else is known about them and nothing is known about the others. Although the continuity of leadership was significant and would persist throughout the year, the sources of leadership were expanding.

Membership grew rapidly. By July, more than 2,000 workers had been signed up,[13] though the growth of the number of dues-paying members was less impressive; only 616 workers had paid dues by the end of September. The outbreak of mass strikes in October and November, however, encouraged more workers to seek formal membership,

10. See Chapter 6.
11. Karelin, "Soiuz litografskikh rabochikh," p. 13; *Istoriia leningradskogo soiuza*, pp. 252–53, 438.
12. *Pechatnyi vestnik* 1905, no. 1 (May 15), p. 2.
13. Ibid. 1905, no. 4 (July 24), p. 9.

and in the two weeks between the sympathy strike and the general political strike, membership in the union nearly tripled. By the end of November, the union had more than 3,000 paying members.[14] Union-sponsored meetings attracted even larger numbers: meetings held between October 2 and December 6 were attended by between 2,000 and 7,000 workers.[15] In 1906 and 1907, despite being repeatedly closed down by the government and having to function illegally for several months at a time, the Petersburg printers' union continued to grow; by the beginning of 1907 the union claimed 11,000 members. Including the 600 members of the lithographers' union, most typographic and lithographic workers in St. Petersburg were organized, though less than one-third of these actually paid dues and many paid only part of the required sum.[16]

As the union expanded, the influence of older organizational traditions among printing workers grew increasingly attenuated. To be sure, familiar individuals remained active. Petr Orlov, a senior compositor who had contributed articles to *Naborshchik* since 1903 and then helped to establish the trade union paper *Pechatnyi vestnik* in 1905, continued to edit the journal in 1906 and was elected chair of the union in 1907 and again in 1908. Petr Vasil'ev (Severianin) also remained a regular writer for the union press, as did August Tens, who became a leading officer in the union again in 1907. However, the majority of the union's most active worker leaders in 1906 and 1907 were self-defined socialists with no known connections to *Naborshchik* or to other pre-1905 professional associations. The secretary of the union during 1906 (winning the largest number of votes in the spring elections) was Aleksandr Sharek, a leading militant voice in the union press who, though a metalworker by profession, impressed printers by his "love and energy for the cause of printing workers."[17] Another union officer and regular columnist in the union press was the bookbinder Pavel Bogushevich, a member of the Socialist-Revolutionary Party, who had arrived in St. Petersburg from the Baltic provinces only in 1906.[18] The

14. Ibid. 1906, no. 5 (March 19), p. 13; Severianin, "Soiuz rabochikh pechatnogo dela," p. 30.
15. *Istoriia leningradskogo soiuza*, pp. 59, 197, 206, 238; *Naborshchik i pechatnyi mir* 114 (October 21, 1905), p. 460; 116 (December 20, 1905), pp. 543–44; *Novaia zhizn'*, November 2, 1905, p. 3; *Vysshii pod"em revoliutsii 1905–1907 gg.*, pp. 366–67.
16. *Protokoly pervogo vserossiiskoi konferentsii soiuzov rabochikh pechatnogo dela*, p. 19, *Istoriia leningradskogo soiuza*, p. 283.
17. *Vestnik pechatnikov* 1906 (April 21), pp. 3–4; *Pechatnyi vestnik* 1906, no. 4 (March 8), p. 12 (union board election results).
18. *Istoriia leningradskogo soiuza*, p. 436.

compositor Sergei Khanskii, also a union officer, was another recent arrival to St. Petersburg, in his case from Moscow, where he had helped to organize the 1903 strike.[19]

The background of one of the most popular leaders after 1905 exemplifies both the continued influence and the growing distance from past traditions. The second largest number of votes for a candidate for the union directing board (*pravlenie*) in 1906 went to a female Jewish proofreader (and, according to the police, also a midwife) named Tauba Abramovna Rubinchik. By 1907, she would be elected to head the union and become editor of the union paper. Active in the union since 1905, she had also been involved in the Typographers' Music and Drama Circle since 1904, was a member of the Burial Society, and had at least on one occasion, in 1902, written on cultural matters for *Naborshchik*.[20]

As in most Russian unions, Social Democrats had a growing role to play in the Petersburg union. The prominant Menshevik P. N. Kolokol'-nikov had been directed by the Petersburg party group to work among printers,[21] and many articles in the union journal appear to have been written by party *intelligenty*. Many union members also considered themselves socialists, though only a minority were party members: the leaders of the union reported in 1906 that out of several thousand members, only two hundred belonged to the Russian Social Democratic Workers' Party.[22]

Factional affiliation was even less determinate. Petr Vasil'ev (Severianin) would later insist—perhaps disingenuously, since he was writing in 1928—that "the widespread view that Petersburg printers were always under the influence of Mensheviks" was too simple.[23] Certainly, as we have seen, one of the organizers of the union in 1905, Ivan Liubimtsev, was a Bolshevik, and Vasil'ev and other printers active at the time have identified other Bolshevik as well as Menshevik workers among the union's activists. Most socialist workers probably distinguished very little among the different socialist tendencies. The portraits of Marx, Lassalle, and Bebel hanging on the walls of the union offices in St. Petersburg suggest the rather catholic socialism that inspired them.

19. TsGAOR, f. 63, 1903, d. 667, vol. 1, p. 1; f. 6864, op. 1, d. 216, p. 55.

20. *Pechatnyi vestnik* 1906, no. 4 (March 8), p. 12; 1905, no. 4 (July 24), p. 9; *Naborshchik* 1:8 (December 22, 1902), pp. 142–43; *Naborshchik i pechatnyi mir* 114 (October 10, 1905), p. 460; TsGAOR, f. 102, OO, 1907 g., op. 8, d. 28, p. 18; Shalyt, "Revoliutsionnoe gnezdo," p. 12.

21. Bonnell, *Roots of Rebellion*, p. 255.

22. Ibid., citing *Ekho*, June 29, 1906, p. 3.

23. *Pechatnik* 1928, no. 3 (January 22), p. 5.

Unionization in Moscow proceeded somewhat differently, as several organizations already claimed to represent the interests of printing workers in the early months of 1905, each in some way a product of the 1903 strike. Unlike in St. Petersburg, where the mutual aid society opposed workers' organizing efforts,[24] the Typographers' Assistance Fund (Vspomogatel'naia kassa tipografov) served as a basis for unionization. Although the 1903 strike did not alter the structure or purposes of the fund—it remained an organization based on the principle of collaboration between workers, managers, and employers—many members were affected by the new mood in 1905. Earlier, near the end of 1904, the fund had decided to establish a special fund to aid the growing number of unemployed printers in Moscow, and volunteers were solicited for a commission to draft a charter. A number of workers signed up, mostly compositors but a few lithographers and bookbinders as well. As the commission's work continued into 1905, its purposes began to change. When the group finally announced the completion of a charter, in July 1905, it was clear that they had altered their mandate and proposed not an assistance fund to help the unemployed but a full-fledged labor union.[25]

The new organization was still to be called a "fund" (though now using the word *fond* rather than the more traditional *kassa*): the Fund for the Improvement of the Conditions of Labor of Working Men (*truzheniki*) in Typo-Lithographical Enterprises. And it was to remain a constituent part of the Typographers' Assistance Fund, which gave it legality. But it differed from the usual assistance fund in both structure and aims. First, employers and "individuals occupying important administrative positions" were excluded from membership. Second, the stated goals of the fund were almost literally reproduced from the charter of the Petersburg Union of Printing Workers: "(a) To defend the legal and professional interests of its members; (b) to aid the improvement of the conditions of labor and life of its members, and to seek a path for their moral and intellectual development; (c) to assist members materially during strikes and unemployment."[26] There were

24. *Zhizn' pechatnika* 1907, no. 9 (August 11), p. 6.
25. *Naborshchik* 2:45 (October 3, 1904), p. 706; *Naborshchik i pechatnyi mir* 105 (January 19, 1905), p. 23; 112 (August 10, 1905), p. 357; *Pechatnyi vestnik* 1905, no. 8 (August 21), p. 11.
26. *Naborshchik i pechatnyi mir* 112 (August 10, 1905), pp. 345–46. The full text of the charter was printed as a pamphlet at the end of July and appeared in both *Naborshchik i pechatnyi mir* and *Pechatnyi vestnik* in August. A preliminary draft appeared in *Vecherniaia pochta*, July 15, 1905, p. 3.

even considerations that the new fund ought to become a branch of the Petersburg union, as was strongly advocated by I. Zheludkov, a compositor sent by the Petersburg union, and by P. Nechaev, a Moscow compositor who helped organize the fund and had earlier been involved in the 1903 strike and contributed essays to *Naborshchik*.[27] In practice, the fund seems to have existed mainly on paper, though as late as October, Zheludkov and Nechaev represented it at the First All-Russian Conference of Trade Unions in Moscow.[28]

A second claimant to the role of workers' advocate among Moscow printers in 1905 was the Zubatovist Assembly of the Typo-Lithographical and Binding Industry. As before 1905, the assembly remained influential especially among non-compositors and generally among workers at the Kushnerev press. After Bloody Sunday, according to one member, the assembly began to attract new members and become more active, though its leaders continued to promote political loyalty to the regime. Indeed, members of the assembly participated in the best-known—and for many the most notorious—manifestation of worker devotion to the emperor in 1905. Shortly after Bloody Sunday, on January 19, Nicholas II received a delegation of thirty-four workers, most of them selected by factory managers and police officials, to hear a brief address directed especially at workers.[29] Ivan Matrosov, a compositor at the Kushnerev press and the most visible leader of the printers' assembly, was among the delegates to go to the tsar.[30]

Political loyalism did not prevent the assembly from acting as an advocate of workers' economic and social interests. On February 17 members unanimously approved a petition to the Minister of Finance listing workers' main demands, most of which were the same as had been refused during the January strikes: minimum wages "that would assure workers a healthy and human existence;" abolition of work on Sundays, holidays, and nights; free medical care, maternity leave, and sick leave; abolition of fines; state insurance; limitation on the "arbitrary authority" (*proizvol*) of foremen; and enterprise commissions

27. *Pechatnyi vestnik* 1905, no. 4 (July 24), p. 9; *Naborshchik i pechatnyi mir* 112 (August 10, 1905), pp. 344–45, 357–58; Sher, "Moskovskie pechatniki v revoliutsii 1905 g.," p. 47. According to one historian, Zheludkov was a Social Democrat converted in 1905 to the liberalism of the Union of Liberation. Milonov, *Kak voznikli professional'nye soiuzy v Rossii*, p. 117.

28. Kolokol'nikov and Rapoport, *1905–1907 gg. v professional'nom dvizhenii*, pp. 147, 162–63.

29. Ascher, *The Revolution of 1905*, p. 97.

30. TsGAOR, f. 6864, op. 1, d. 48, p. 20 (reprinted in part in *Moskovskie pechatniki*, p. 122).

composed of representatives of workers and management that would settle disputes and oversee work.

This appeal to the government for support of their demands was, of course, a tentative expression of class militance. Similarly ambiguous was a conflict at the Kushnerev plant in which members of the assembly were also almost certainly involved. On August 5, representatives of the various shops presented management with a request for a nine-hour workday on Saturdays (to remain ten hours during the week) and the abolition of fines. When the director, Vladimir Borovik, agreed to reduce Saturday hours and to allow a worker to be late for work twice a month without fine, the deputies warmly thanked him for his kindness.[31] That the mood of members of the assembly was changing during 1905 was evident from a report in March that several leaders of the society had been "locked out" because their activities were "opposed to the views of the majority."[32] By the end of the summer, membership in the assembly began to decline, and after the fall strikes the assembly simply vanished, many of its members appearing among the leading activists of the trade union.[33]

The illegal Union of Typo-Lithographical Workers for the Struggle to Improve the Conditions of Labor also sought to represent printing workers in Moscow. Although the union had been created in 1903 as a strike organization, "little by little," as one of its members recognized, it had lost its "physiognomy as a distinctive workers' group" and begun to "remind one of the usual type of Social-Democratic committee."[34] In 1904 the union was decimated by arrests for its involvement in a May Day demonstration, but it was reestablished later in the year with the help of the student Konstantin Moldavskii, a Social Democrat who viewed the union primarily as a means of getting socialist ideas to the working class. He organized discussions for printing workers at his apartment and invited other students to participate. Among them was Vasilii Sher, soon to become a leader of the union.[35]

During the early months of 1905, the union maintained its political orientation. Its newspaper, *Vestnik soiuza,* was composed largely of articles on political subjects, often written by *intelligenty.* Because illegal-

31. *Vestnik soiuza tipografskikh rabochikh* 9 (August 1905), p. 7.

32. *Naborshchik i pechatnyi mir* 107 (March 10, 1905), pp. 129–30.

33. TsGAOR, f. 6864, op. 1, d. 48, p. 20; *Moskovskie pechatniki,* p. 122; *Vospominaniia rabochikh 16-i tipo-litografii Mospoligraf (b. Levenson),* pp. 91–92; Sher, "Moskovskie pechatniki," pp. 54, 86.

34. Sher, *Istoriia,* pp. 150–51.

35. Ibid.; TsGAOR, f. 6864, op. 1, d. 216, pp. 70–73 (recollections of a worker member of the union).

ity was viewed as a matter of principle, when an opportunity arose to become a legal section of the Petersburg union the Moscow unionists refused.[36] To be sure, they recognized that the union's identity as an underground socialist organization discouraged workers from joining the union,[37] which as late as the end of the summer of 1905 could claim no more than three hundred members.[38] But far from discouraged by their limited appeal, they decided to reinforce their illegality and politicization by joining the Social-Democratic Party as a political union of workers. Union activists had been prepared to join the party earlier but were put off by the split between Bolsheviks and Mensheviks, which they had hoped would be overcome. As the differences between the two factions became clearer, and thus the possibility of reconciliation more remote, the Moscow unionists were able to choose, and they chose the Mensheviks. They were attracted, they explained, by the greater "democratization" in the Menshevik faction, which was itself the consequence, in their view, of greater "trust in the broad proletarian masses."[39] However, for the moment, their decision to become a party organization further discouraged the "broad masses" from joining the union.

Involvement in the fall strikes helped overcome the union's isolation but also altered its structure and function. When the September strikes began, the union abandoned its principled illegality and turned to the police authorities with a request for permission to hold a meeting of worker deputies, who were already being elected in most large plants. The local authorities, perhaps recalling the peaceable and non-political behavior of striking printers in 1903, agreed. The city government even provided a place for them to meet. On September 25, 87 deputies from 34 different firms, including all of the largest printing plants in the city, and representing nearly half the workers in the industry, attended the first meeting of what was called the Council of Deputies (*Sovet deputatov*).[40] Over the course of ten meetings, held between September 25 and October 4, the membership of the council grew to 264 deputies representing 110 enterprises.[41]

36. Sher, *Istoriia*, pp. 158–59; Sher, "Moskovskie pechatniki," p. 47.

37. *Vestnik soiuza tipografskikh rabochikh* 9 (August 1905), p. 6.

38. Sher, *Istoriia*, pp. 154–55; Sher, "Moskovskie pechatniki," pp. 40–43.

39. See Sher, *Istoriia*, pp. 155–56; Sher, "Moskovskie pechatniki," pp. 40–42; open letter to *Iskra* (no. 98) in TsGAOR, f. 518, op. 1, d. 55, p. 207.

40. All six printing firms employing over 300 workers were represented at the first meeting of the council, as were all four firms employing between 200 and 300 workers. *Vserossiiskaia politicheskaia stachka*, p. 63n.

41. Sher, *Istoriia*, p. 168; *Biulleten' muzeiia sodeistviia trudu* 1 (November 16, 1905).

Activists from the illegal union—both workers and *intelligenty*—
were clearly in command of the council: they drafted the resolutions
that were discussed at meetings, were the main orators, were elected to
the council's executive committee, and represented the council in relations with other organizations and with employers.[42] The chairman of
the council was Nikolai Chistov, a compositor, member of the underground union, and a Menshevik. Chistov also represented the council
at the meeting of "deputies from various professions" (October 2–4),
which planned the organization of the Moscow soviet, at the First All-
Russian Conference of Trade Unions (October 6–7), and later in the
Moscow soviet itself, which would elect him as its first chairman. Another member of the executive committee, the compositor Vladimir
Kairovich, had helped organize the 1903 strike, had been a union member, and had represented printers in the soviet. Two intelligentsia activists, involved with the printers' union since 1904, were elected to the
executive committee of the printers' council in September—Vasilii Sher
(known as Uncle Vasia and Petr Petrovich) and Aleksandr Orlov (calling himself I. Kruglov), both Mensheviks. Orlov, who would succeed
Chistov as chairman of the Moscow soviet, was also sent to St. Petersburg to win support for the September strike. Sher, who also represented printers in the soviet, was elected to its executive committee.

As the printers' strike was ending in early October, the Council of
Deputies met to decide its own future. At an illegal meeting at the university—the police had forbidden further legal meetings on October
2—the council voted to disband but to form a new union and authorized the executive committee to prepare a charter. Once the October
general strike began, it became possible to hold a general meeting of all
printing workers, which was held at the Moscow Conservatory, where
it was reported that as many as 8,000 printing workers attended and
supported the idea of establishing a union. At a second mass meeting,
on October 30, a charter was approved and officers elected. By the end
of November the Moscow union reported having 3,500 paying members and attracting an even larger number at meetings held under its
auspices.[43] Although most workers viewed the union as the successor
to the elected Council of Deputies,[44] it was clear that it also inherited

42. Sher, *Istoriia*, pp. 168–69; Chistov, "Moskovskie pechatniki," pp. 138–39;
I. Nechaev, "K sobytiiam 1905 goda," in *Moskovskie pechatniki*, p. 156; *Biulleten'
muzeiia sodeistviia trudu* 1 (November 16, 1905).
43. *Russkie vedomosti*, October 20, 1905, p. 3; October 31, 1905, p. 3; November
17, 1905, pp. 3–4; Sher, *Istoriia*, pp. 184–87; Sher, "Moskovskie pechatniki," p. 66.
44. According to Sher, "Moskovskie pechatniki," p. 66.

the membership and leadership of the underground socialist union. Among the leaders of the new union were many of the leaders of the old, especially the compositors Vladimir Kairovich and Nikolai Chistov (who was elected secretary, the only full-time paid official), and the Menshevik *intelligenty* Vasilii Sher and Aleksandr Orlov.

Like other Moscow unions, the printers' union suffered in the first months of 1905 from the effects of repression in the wake of the armed uprising in Moscow in December, in which many printers were involved, and from growing unemployment (made especially bad by the near-destruction by fire of the large Sytin plant during the fighting in December). By early May 1906, soon after registering under the new law, the union had 3,658 members, though nearly 5,000 came to a union meeting that month.[45] By the end of the year, even though the union was briefly closed by the government in August, the printers' union had 5,260 paid members, approximately 70 percent of all typographic and lithographic workers.[46]

As in St. Petersburg and in many other Russian trade unions at the time, the formal political stance of the union was that of "party neutrality."[47] But as the lead editorial in the first issue of the union paper in 1906 made apparent, with its insistence on the need to develop the workers' "class consciousness" and to fight against the autocracy through "independent class organizations,"[48] the Social Democratic orientation of the leadership remained strong. Although Sher, Orlov, and Chistov were exiled from Moscow by early 1906, another Menshevik, S. Ia. Kibrik (calling himself S. Iakovlev), was sent by the Moscow party group to work among printers[49] and quickly became a leading figure in the union (and, in 1907, secretary of the nationwide Central Council of printers' unions). Many of the lead articles in the union press also continued to reflect the influence of socialists. The Moscow Okhrana, at least, considered their influence to be considerable, succinctly concluding in 1907 that "printers on the whole are Mensheviks."[50]

The leaders of the printers' unions in both Moscow and St. Petersburg considered rank-and-file participation in the affairs of the union, including participation by non-members, to be essential to

45. *Pechatnik* 1906, no. 3 (May 14), pp. 8–9; no. 4 (May 21), p. 4.
46. Sher, *Istoriia*, p. 291.
47. *Pechatnik* 1906, no. 1 (April 23), p. 1.
48. Ibid.
49. Bonnell, *Roots of Rebellion*, p. 255, n. 61.
50. TsGAOR, f. 102, OO, 1907, op. 8, d. 28, p. 258. See also Sher, *Istoriia*, pp. 279–84.

an effective organization. To keep workers informed of union activities and give them a forum in which to express their views and needs, both unions established regular journals, which published legally. In May 1905, several leaders of the Petersburg union who in the past had been correspondents for *Naborshchik*—most notably August Tens and Petr Orlov—received government permission to publish a new paper, to be called *Pechatnyi vestnik* (The Printing Herald), with a more exclusive worker orientation. Tens became the publisher and Orlov the editor. In June, when the paper declared itself the official organ of the Petersburg printers' union, Orlov became both editor and publisher. The establishment of *Pechatnyi vestnik* provoked a mass defection of worker-writers from *Naborshchik*, including even Filippov's coeditor, Zoia Voronova.[51]

During 1906 and 1907, in both St. Petersburg and Moscow, despite harassment and repeated closures by the government, the printers' unions continued publishing journals. Although the links to the union were often not explicit, the editors and publishers were almost always union officers. These papers regularly reported on union finances, dealings with employers, workplace conflicts, and meetings of the union, including of its directing boards. They also included critical essays on social or political themes, short literary works with professional or political messages, news on the Russian and European labor movement, letters from readers, job advertisements, and book reviews. During 1907, members of the Petersburg union even produced a small journal—quickly closed by the government, reestablished, and then banned again—devoted entirely to satirical humor.[52]

Union organizers also sought to strengthen the connections between leaders and rank-and-file workers in the structure of the unions themselves. In St. Petersburg, union leaders incorporated into the union structure the shop representatives who had been elected during the 1905 tariff campaign and continued to represent workers at many workplaces.[53] The organizational meetings on April 3 and 24 were gatherings of shop deputies, and during the summer of 1905 the union held regular Sunday meetings of shop representatives from each dis-

51. *Pechatnyi vestnik* 1905, no. 10 (September 4), p. 7.
52. Three issues of *Balda* appeared between January 7 and 16, followed by two issues of *Topor* between February 3 and 18.
53. Filippov, "Avtonomiia pechatnikov v 1905 godu;" *Pechatnyi vestnik* 1905, no. 14 (October 14), p. 11; *Novaia zhizn'*, November 1, 1905, p. 5, and November 2, 1905, p. 3; Gordon, *Ocherk ekonomicheskoi bor'by rabochikh Rossii*, p. 142. Other functions of these representatives will be discussed below.

trict, district-level meetings being necessary because the rooms of the Printing Society were not large enough to accommodate a general meeting of all shop representatives. In reality, the workers who came to these meetings were those who wished to, whether or not they were properly elected deputies, which made the Sunday assemblies into local gatherings of worker activists more than properly representative councils of shop stewards. Therefore in September 1905 the union leadership established a more formal system of shop representation, announcing that workers in every firm employing fewer than thirty workers were to elect one deputy, and workers employed in larger workplaces were to choose representatives from each shop (typesetting, presswork, binding, and so forth) who were then to select a single deputy to the union. These deputies were then to unite into a single Institute of Delegates (*Institut vybornykh-upolnomochennykh*).[54]

In practice, the union's delegate council (*sovet vybornykh*), as it became generally known, and especially the local district councils, played an increasingly important role in the life of the union during 1906 and 1907, especially during the recurring periods of illegality. Meetings of shop representatives made decisions about strikes and other union actions, supervised the activities of delegates in the shops, and handled a wide range of worker complaints. Within the shops, delegates promoted union membership, collected dues, distributed the union paper, and represented the union in negotiations with employers.[55]

The Moscow union had been established by an organization of shop delegates and similarly sought to incorporate shop representation into its structure. During the September strike in 1905, the stated function of the printers' Council of Deputies—according to a resolution drafted by the leaders of the underground union and approved by the council on September 25—was to act only as an executive committee of a general meeting of all printing workers. The council was authorized only to convene general meetings, prepare questions for consideration, carry out approved decisions, disburse funds donated in support of the strike, and conduct negotiations with the owners.[56] In practice, since permission to hold a general meeting was repeatedly refused by the police, the

54. *Pechatnyi vestnik* 1905, no. 13 (September 25), p. 4; *Istoriia leningradskogo soiuza*, pp. 171–73.
55. There were frequent reports on meetings of delegate councils in the union press. See also *Zhizn' pechatnika* 1907, no. 8 (July 20), p. 11, and *Istoriia leningradskogo soiuza*, pp. 250, 348, 351–63.
56. This decision was described in a leaflet issued by the union on September 27. TsGAOR, f. 518, op. 1, d. 55, p. 211.

council remained the only source of authority, though its mandate to itself still insisted that even if a general meeting could not be held delegates must be "responsible before their electors."[57]

When the strike council dissolved itself to establish a trade union, shop representation remained part of the structure of the union. In October 1905, the union leadership drafted a "Statute on Factory Deputies" (*Polozhenie o fabrichnykh deputatov*), which recognized "councils of deputies" within each plant that would not only represent workers in their conflicts with management[58] but also serve as intermediaries between the union and individual shops. According to the "Guide" or "Handbook" (*Rukovodstvo*) for deputies that accompanied the statute, deputies were to be members of the trade union (though they were elected by both members and non-members), to represent the union at their enterprise, and to represent the workers of their shop before the union.[59]

During 1906 and 1907, these elected delegates collected membership dues, recruited new members, and informed the union about layoffs and vacancies. Delegates were also automatically made members of the union's Assembly of Deputies (*sobranie upolnomochennykh*). During most of 1906, when the Moscow union was allowed to function fairly freely, the assembly debated and in reality decided the main questions of union policy. Although decisions formally had to be approved by a general meeting, because such meetings were usually attended by five to six thousand workers they could only really have what union leader Vasilii Sher called an "agitational" function. Real power lay with the assembly and in the executive board (*pravlenie*), which proposed and carried out policies. When the government refused to allow general meetings, as during most of the winter of 1906–07, the Assembly of Deputies functioned in its place, deciding major questions about relations with employers and even electing new officers.[60] In one important sense, the growing authority of the Assembly of Deputies was a democratizing trend. As Sher observed, "the executive board, which was elected by union members, was subordinated to the assembly of deputies, which was elected by all workers, both members and non-members."[61]

57. *Vserossiiskaia politicheskaia stachka*, pp. 61–63.
58. The workplace functions of these deputies are discussed in more detail below.
59. Sher, *Istoriia*, pp. 206–07.
60. *Pechatnoe delo* 13 (January 26, 1907), pp. 5–6; Sher, *Istoriia*, pp. 272–73, 374–77.
61. Sher, *Istoriia*, pp. 376–77.

Efforts to involve as many workers as possible in union life through delegate councils, journals, and other structures were visible in many Russian unions during this period,[62] though printing workers appear to have responded more readily than most workers. In this, they resembled printers in other countries. And like other printers, the relatively high degree of "democratic" organization among Russian printing workers may also be explained by the high levels of craft pride, literacy, and job mobility, together with the existence prior to unionization of an "occupational community" expressed in traditions of mutual association and action.[63]

Practical considerations motivated union leaders to widen and deepen rank-and-file participation in union life. In this way, it was felt, the union could most effectively mobilize workers for collective action. But not only tactical concerns were evident. The political values and strategies of the socialist leaders of most unions, especially of the Mensheviks who predominated among printers, were also an influence. As the Menshevik organizer S. I. Somov wrote, Social Democrats approached the labor movement with a "strong pedagogical tendency," a desire to create opportunities for workers to improve their "fighting capacity and consciousness,"[64] to develop through experience, as an activist in the Moscow printers' union argued, the "solidarity and discipline" necessary to make real the Marxist ideal that the "workers' cause is the cause of the workers themselves."[65]

For many individual workers, participation in union affairs had precisely this educational effect. A member of a neighborhood delegate council of the Petersburg union described the organizational skills and self-confidence that often resulted from regular involvement in these meetings, which were usually attended by only fifteen to twenty people and generally without the presence of the *intelligenty* who often dominated general meetings:

> Everyone knows how difficult it is for a working person to begin to write or make a speech. In your head you have some useful idea, but you start laying it out and all you get are scraps of phrases. You are embarrassed to put yourself before the gaze of a huge meeting; your clumsiness provokes embarrassed laughing. And then some lawyer cuts in with a biting remark or the

62. Bonnell, *Roots of Rebellion*, pp. 240–41.
63. Lipset, Trow, and Coleman, *Union Democracy*, esp. pp. 3–32, 69–73, 102–97, 393–400.
64. Somov, "Iz istorii sotsialdemokraticheskogo dvizheniia v Peterburge v 1905 gody," p. 162.
65. *Pechatnoe delo* 13 (January 26, 1907), p. 6.

chairman offers words of wisdom, "comrade, you are not speaking to the point." Finally impatient comrades shout "enough, finish!" In district meetings things are completely different. Here . . . everyone feels free and is not afraid to speak up. If you say something wrong, your comrades will correct you, without mocking you. It will happen that a comrade who could at first not make a speech of more than 10–15 words will in time be able to deliver a clear and solid report.[66]

The effects of these democratic structures were not always so beneficial, of course. Delegates complained that some shop representatives showed up drunk at meetings and even stole part of workers' dues.[67]

EMPLOYERS' ASSOCIATIONS

Employers, like workers, first made use of existing organizations, especially the Russian Printing Society, to represent their needs and interests. During the January strikes in 1905, meetings of press owners to discuss workers' demands, in both St. Petersburg and Moscow, were organized by the local printing societies. During the tariff campaign in St. Petersburg, most of the members of the employers' tariff commission were members of the Printing Society, and they included in their proposals the stipulation that future disputes between workers and employers be resolved through the society. During the September and October strikes in Moscow the Printing Society similarly represented employers in responding to workers' demands.

The effectiveness of the Printing Society in representing and uniting employers was limited, however. In Moscow, its inability during the strikes of September and October to enforce even among its own members its decision against concessions to workers led a number of employers to establish an organization with more effective means of ensuring collective discipline. On October 23, a group of press owners attending a meeting of the Union of Publishers—which had recently been established for the purpose of promoting a free press—proposed organizing an owners' association. By November, members were being enrolled in the Moscow Society of Typo-Lithographers. Like the Printing Society, this new organization was established and dominated by the owners of the largest printing houses. Representatives of only eleven firms attended the founding meeting, but their enterprises employed over thirty-five hundred workers, nearly half of the labor force. To en-

66. *Istoriia leningradskogo soiuza,* pp. 360–61.
67. *Zhizn' pechatnika* 1907, no. 8 (July 20), pp. 11–12.

sure their continuing control, especially as owners of smaller enterprises joined, the organizers stipulated in the society's charter that the
number of votes each employer possessed was proportional to the number of workers he employed.[68]

Petersburg printing employers had an even more compelling reason
to organize separately from the Printing Society, for the Petersburg society had always been a reluctant advocate of employers' interests.
During the tariff negotiations many of the non-employer leaders of the
society openly positioned themselves as mediators between workers
and employers. The chairman, Ivan Tolstoi, agreed to preside over the
meetings of both employers and workers, which were held in rooms
provided by the society, and he made a point of sending a message of
sympathy to workers.[69] On October 5, at a meeting at the Printing Society, press owners decided to form a new organization, the Union of
Press Owners (Soiuz vladeltsev pechatnykh stankov). The leaders of the
Printing Society refused to sponsor the founding meeting to avoid vio-
lating the society's "neutrality" in relations between workers and employers. The meeting was held, nonetheless, on October 23 and was
attended by the owners of 140 printing and binding firms. Roman Golike, an active participant and leader in the Printing Society, as in virtually every other printers' organization since the 1890s, was elected
chairman of the union.[70]

If printing employers often seemed bewildered during much of
1905 as they tried to respond to workers' unprecedented protests,
they acted more confidently in defending their interests by the end
of the year and especially in the years following. In Moscow, the Society of Typo-Lithographers, headed by A. A. Levenson, united employers around a program that promised financial support to any member
who resisted workers' "unjust demands" and specifically forbade employers to pay workers for time on strike (unless specifically authorized by the employers' association) or to allow workers' deputies to
"interfere" in hiring or firing. The association also drafted workplace
regulations that strictly defined acceptable rules for worker conduct.

68. *Russkoe slovo,* October 25, 1905, p. 3; October 29, 1905, p. 3; Sher, *Istoriia,* pp.
200–201.

69. On February 25, Tolstoi sent compositors a letter expressing the "very pleasant
impression" that their meetings had made on him, wishing them "success and fruitful
work," and advising them "to concede all that they may concede without harming themselves and their profession." *Naborshchik i pechatnyi mir* 107 (March 10, 1905), p. 109.

70. *Naborshchik i pechatnyi mir* 114 (October 10, 1905), p. 459; TsGAOR, f. 6864,
op. 1, d. 8, p. 35; *Torgovo-promyshlennaia gazeta,* June 8 (21), 1906, p. 2; *Istoriia leningradskogo soiuza,* pp. 188, 219.

Any member who violated a decision of the employers' union was required to pay a fine.[71]

Above all, the Moscow employers' association was determined to hold the line on workers' demands. In May 1906, for example, the society staged a lockout to force workers to drop preconditions for contract negotiations, especially the demand for recognition of permanent shop representatives. The lockout failed, largely because of public criticism and the lack of support, especially from the owners of smaller firms who were less able to afford the inevitable loss of customers to shops not represented in the employers' union.[72] Nevertheless, in February 1907, the owners' association again threatened a lockout, this time because workers throughout the city were refusing to take work from the Iakovlev press, where workers were striking against an effort to increase the length of the night shift from eight to nine hours. Individual employers shut out their workers, and the owners' association threatened a mass lockout in two weeks if striking workers failed to return to work. The lockout did not occur only because workers accepted the employers' proposal for binding arbitration, which ultimately decided against the employers.[73]

Press owners in St. Petersburg were also increasingly prepared to defend their interests and authority. By early 1906, some employers felt that the Union of Press Owners was insufficiently aggressive, and in June 1906 they announced the formation of a second owners' union aimed explicitly at "struggle with the workers' union."[74] Both employers' associations registered in 1906, though the newer Society of Owners of Printing Enterprises (Obshchestvo vladeltsev pechatnykh zavedeniiakh) became predominant; the Union of Press Owners was closed in 1908 for inactivity.[75]

Although the Petersburg Society of Owners remained willing to negotiate collective agreements with representatives of the workers' union, members of the society wished to ensure that individual employers did not agree to any additional concessions. Rules for members adopted in May 1907 insisted that once a tariff had been accepted by both sides any additional demands from workers would not be toler-

---

71. *Ustav Moskovskogo obshchestva tipo-litografov*, pp. 3–15; Moskovskoe obshchestvo tipo-litografov [MOT-L], *Ustav i pravila*, pp. 13–55.
72. *Pechatnik* 1906, no. 5 (May 28), p. 3; no. 7 (July 9), p. 2; Sher, *Istoriia*, pp. 264–67.
73. *Novoe vremia*, 1907: February 19, 24, 26, 27, March 6, 9, 11, 13, 24; Sher, *Istoriia*, pp. 316–38.
74. *Torgovo-promyshlennaia gazeta*, June 8 (21), 1906, p. 2.
75. Markson, *Tipografskii karmannyi kalendar' na 1914 god*, p. 119.

ated. Members who violated any association rules or decisions would be fined. Among these rules was a prohibition against allowing any workers to influence hiring and firing or the work process. The society also established standards for workers' conduct, which prohibited workers from "gathering in a crowd" or "disturbing the peace with noise, shouting, singing, swearing, arguing, or fighting, or in general conducting themselves improperly, scandalously, or in a disorderly manner."[76]

An even more antagonistic stance toward labor was taken by the owners of large binding and lithographic printing firms, who in 1907 organized as sections within the Petersburg Society of Factory Owners (Obshchestvo zavodchikov i fabrikantov), an association known for its particular hostility to workers' demands for representation and collective bargaining. In the general spirit of the organization, the binding and lithographic sections adopted instructions for members that forbade dealing with any "outside individuals" in resolving conflicts with their workers, identified "lockouts" as a possible means of action, promised financial support to any employer involved in a conflict with his workers, and set steep fines for members who violated its rules or decisions. These employers were most adamantly opposed to workers' demands for control over hiring and firing, and expressly prohibited members from agreeing to such a demand, since this would "create an undesirable precedent for the whole industry."[77]

REGULATING THE CLASS STRUGGLE

Although employers and workers had withdrawn into hostile class organizations, the battle lines were yet not as clear as they might seem. Familiar voices were still to be heard and still attracted an audience. The assistance funds and the Petersburg printing school and sanatorium retained supporters and members long after 1905.[78] Andrei Filippov's *Naborshchik*—renamed *Naborshchik i pechatnyi mir* (The Compositor and the Printing World)—continued to attract readers and subscribers among workers and employers, though especially among supervisors, with its message of uniting employers and workers in recognition of their common interests. Filippov himself, in April 1905, announced that he had resigned his membership in the Russian Printing Society,

76. TsGIA, f. 150, op. 1, d. 78, pp. 1–2; d. 79, pp. 37–44.
77. Ibid., d. 79, pp. 70–71, 78.
78. Markson, *Tipografskii karmannyi kalendar' na 1914 god*, pp. 118–42; *Otchet po shkole pechatnogo dela Imperatorskogo Russkogo tekhnicheskogo obshchestva;* and frequent reports in *Naborshchik i pechatnyi mir.*

which he had helped to establish in the 1890s, since it had failed, in his view, to realize its mission "to coordinate and reconcile the interests" of workers and employers.[79] He focused his hopes instead on the new workers' union. Over the next several months, Filippov and others associated with him would appeal to workers to include foremen and managers in the new union and to orient the union toward the traditional collaborative goals of "regulating" relations in the industry.[80]

By the end of 1905, production managers and foremen recognized that they were unwelcome among both workers and employers and so began to establish their own separate professional organizations. In Moscow, a Union of Employees (*sluzhashchie*) in Printing Firms and Editorial Offices was organized in November.[81] In St. Petersburg, in October 1905, a group of managers and supervisors established the Union of Plant Directors, Production Managers, Senior Compositors, and Press Masters (Soiuz upravliaiushchikh, faktorov, metranpazhei i masterov), which was soon renamed the Russian Professional Union of Printing (Rossiiskii professional'nyi soiuz pechatnogo dela) and in 1906 again renamed the Union of Employees in Printing Enterprises. Despite their separate organization, some supervisors clearly held out hope for social reconciliation. In 1906, the head of the Petersburg union, Gerasim Grents, proposed that the Union of Employees seek to become a section of the union of printing workers.[82]

The frustrated isolation of supervisory employees reflected the atmosphere of class hostility and solidarity in 1905 and after, but even the new class organizations did not abandon all efforts toward collaborative regulation of social relations. Even during the contentious "days of liberty" after the October Manifesto in 1905, printing employers' associations in both Moscow and St. Petersburg continued to appeal to workers to join them in "regulating relations between owners and workers."[83] And despite the failure during 1905 of contract negotiations in St. Petersburg and of the efforts by Moscow workers to revise

79. *Naborshchik i pechatnyi mir* 108 (April 10, 1905), pp. 152–53. He also seems to have felt, though this is less explicit, that as a manager who had risen from the ranks of compositors he was treated arrogantly by the intellectuals, publishers, and wealthy entrepreneurs who led the Printing Society.

80. For example, ibid. 110 (June 10, 1905), pp. 244–47. These views are discussed in more detail in Chapter 8.

81. *Vecherniaia pochta*, November 6, 1905, p. 1; November 14, 1905, p. 3; December 1, 1905, p. 3.

82. Galaktionov, *Obshchestvo sluzhashchikh v pechatnykh zavedeniiakh*, pp. 2–22; *Novaia zhizn'*, November 18, 1905, p. 4; *Naborshchik i pechatnyi mir* 122 (June 1906), pp. 751–54, and 123 (July 1906), pp. 801, 807.

83. Sher, *Istoriia*, p. 210; *Naborshchik i pechatnyi mir* 115 (November 20, 1905), p. 484. See also Chapter 8.

the terms of the 1903 agreement, organized printing workers remained prepared to negotiate labor conditions and settle disputes by means other than coercive strikes. Throughout these years, organized employers and workers would continue to place their hopes in regulating social relations.

Efforts to negotiate comprehensive citywide labor contracts, or tariffs (*tarify*), were the touchstone of these efforts. The idea of a tariff not only was in accord with the regulative traditions of the trade community but echoed specific discussions about regulating labor-management relations since at least the 1880s. Suggestions about the need for a wage "tariff" had been discussed in the printers' trade press as early as 1884,[84] and employers at the 1895 Congress of Printing had endorsed German and French wage tariffs as useful models.[85]

Although proposals for a tariff in St. Petersburg in 1905 were made amidst an unprecedented strike, older relationships retained their influence. As we have seen, soon after the January strikes began, employers associated with the Russian Printing Society offered workers a place to meet and formulate their demands, and when workers responded by appealing to the Printing Society to draft a tariff to improve and regulate wages and working conditions in the industry, employers invited workers to elect representatives to discuss the details. In turn, when compositors met on February 13, they nearly unanimously elected Andrei Filippov, who was also a member of the employers' tariff commission, to chair their first meeting, and when Count Ivan Tolstoi, head of the Printing Society, entered the hall, they invited him to chair the meeting in recognition of his "sympathy" for workers.[86] At a second meeting on February 25, workers asked Petr Mikhailov, co-owner of the Lehmann typefoundry and a longtime activist in the Compositors' Assistance Fund and the Printing Society, to lead their meeting. And they greeted Roman Golike, the chairman of the employers' tariff commission, with loud applause after a lengthy speech in which he asked workers for "peace and patience."[87]

Notwithstanding the conflicts that filled the next several months, indeed encouraged by the fact that both sides were effectively poised for battle, collaborative efforts continued after 1905. In Moscow, after

84. *Obzor graficheskikh iskusstv* 1884, no. 2 (January 15), p. 14. This reprinted an essay in *Ekho* by a compositor who suggested that a wage tariff would end the "arbitrariness" governing wage payments. *Ekho*, January 2, 1884, pp. 2–3.

85. *Trudy pervogo s"ezda*, p. 107.

86. Similar sentiments were expressed in a letter sent by the workers' deputies to Tolstoi. *Naborshchik i pechatnyi mir* 106 (February 10, 1905), p. 59.

87. Ibid. 107 (March 10), pp. 106–14.

employers' initial attempt during the summer of 1906 to establish workplace conditions by the force of a lockout, representatives of the Moscow Society of Typo-Lithographers and of the printers' trade union began working out the outlines of a citywide tariff agreement that would establish new wage norms, rules of internal order, standard hours of work, and other conditions. While the negotiations were under way, both sides agreed to refrain from making any demands or changing existing conditions and to submit all disagreements to a conciliation board established by the two organizations. As a preliminary condition to negotiations, employers even agreed to recognize workers' representatives at the shop level. These discussions ended when the union was temporarily closed in August 1906. However, during the spring of 1907, tariff negotiations resumed after employers lost in arbitration their case against workers who had struck when employers tried to alter working conditions in the industry, a move perceived by workers as a violation of the 1906 preliminary agreement. Again, negotiations were curtailed only by the government's closing of the union in June 1907.[88]

The leaders of the Petersburg printers' union were especially attracted to the idea of "regulating relations between labor and capital."[89] Even though members of the union's tariff commission were arrested in July 1906 and the union was shut down twice during the year, leaders of the union continued promoting the idea of a tariff and compiling information needed to produce a draft proposal. In May 1907, after the union regained its legal status, the Society of Owners of Printing Enterprises agreed to begin negotiating a tariff with union representatives. As a condition to negotiations, as in Moscow, both sides agreed to refrain from seeking or making any changes in conditions in individual shops and to submit any disagreements to a conciliation board. Negotiations progressed so well that an agreement, which would have been the first citywide collective labor contract in Russia, was very near completion when the government declared the trade union illegal in October 1907, effectively halting the negotiations.[90]

Organized employers and workers also sought to regulate conflicts after they had already broken out. In November 1905 in St. Petersburg,

---

88. Sher, *Istoriia*, pp. 262–67, 314–38; Bonnell, *Roots of Rebellion*, pp. 294–98.
89. *Protokoly pervoi vserossiiskoi konferentsii*, p. 75.
90. *Istoriia leningradskogo soiuza*, pp. 322, 372–75, 395–97; Vasil'ev-Severianin, "Tarifnaia bor'ba soiuza rabochikh pechatnogo dela v 1905–7 godakh," pp. 157–71; *Protokoly pervoi vserossiiskoi konferentsii*, pp. 75–82; Bonnell, *Roots of Rebellion*, pp. 298–304.

the newly formed printing employers' association and the union of printing workers jointly established a conciliation board (*primiritel'-naia kamera*), composed of four representatives from each organization. Even before the end of 1905 the board successfully settled several disputes between workers and managers or employers.[91] During 1906 and 1907, as tariffs were under negotiation, organized employers and workers in both St. Petersburg and Moscow agreed to resolve individual disputes through conciliation boards, composed of equal numbers of representatives of workers and employers, or through tripartite arbitration courts, which added an outside arbiter.

Formalized conflict resolution was sanctioned by organized workers and employers not only in lieu of a contract but also as a permanent mechanism for resolving disputes. During 1906 and 1907 the printing employers' associations in both cities agreed to workers' demands to include conciliation and arbitration in the tariffs themselves, voiced their support for conciliation as a matter of principle,[92] and in practice joined workers in submitting a number of disputes to conciliation boards or to arbitration, even though the decisions often went against employers.[93]

As these efforts suggest, many printing employers—possibly more than in other Russian industries—were willing to accept the idea of organized worker representation as a means of restoring normalcy and order to relations at the workplace. This meant implicitly recognizing trade unions by negotiating with union representatives. At least in St. Petersburg, this recognition went so far as to have employers representing the Petersburg owners' association in tariff negotiations in 1907 agree to closed shops in which only union workers could be hired.[94] Equally important, a significant number of printing employers were willing to recognize direct worker representation at the workplace. In

91. *Pechatnyi vestnik* 1905, no. 18 (November 27), p. 8; no. 19 (December 4), p. 12; *Istoriia leningradskogo soiuza*, pp. 220–21.

92. *Torgovo-promyshlennaia gazeta*, June 8 (21), 1906, p. 2; *Ustav MOT-L*, p. 4; TsGIAgM, f. 2069, op. 1, d. 8, pp. 170–71; TsGAOR, f. 6864, op. 1, d. 207, pp. 202, 229 (MOT-L Bulletins for 1907).

93. Moscow: *Pechatnik* 1906, no. 5 (May 28), p. 3; no. 7 (July 9, 1906), p. 14; no. 8 (July 23), pp. 10–11, 17–18; TsGAOR, f. 518, op. 1, d. 85a, p. 63 (protocols of December 1906 meetings of directing board of workers' union); TsGIAgM, f. 2069, op. 1, d. 8, pp. 170–267; reports on arbitration of Iakovlev dispute in *Pechatnoe delo* 16–21 (February 17, 1906–March 30, 1907); Sher, *Istoriia*, pp. 316–22.

St. Petersburg: *Zhizn' pechatnika* 4 (June 9, 1907), p. 11; *Knizhnyi vestnik* 1907, no. 24 (June 17), pp. 728–29; no. 30 (July 29), pp. 915, 916; *Dvadtsatyi vek*, May 23 (June 5), 1906, p. 2.

94. *Zhizn' pechatnika* 12 (September 14, 1907), addendum.

1905, many employers agreed to meet with workers' elected representatives, to recognize shop deputies as "intermediaries," and even to allow workers to enforce workplace discipline (especially since, as will be
seen, workers enforced a quite strict regime), though they refused to
yield control over such fundamental employer prerogatives as hiring
and firing.[95] Similarly, employers' associations found the idea of organized worker representation appealing as a means of bringing order to
labor-management relations. Thus, in June 1906, even the relatively
belligerent Moscow Society of Typo-Lithographers endorsed the idea of
permanent worker representation at the workplace, reaffirming this decision in February 1907, recognizing deputies as needed "guardians of
workers' interests" and representatives of organized labor.[96] Representatives of Petersburg press owners chosen to negotiate a tariff in the
summer of 1907 similarly agreed to allow elected worker representatives a permanent role in workplace relations: not to control hiring, firing, or discipline, but to "represent workers' interests" in overseeing
the rules of internal order as agreed upon in the tariff (which included
rules regulating conditions of hire and discipline).[97] Employers accepted worker representation and even limited participation in workplace relations as a means of introducing the same regularity and order
that they were seeking in the industry as a whole through labor contracts, conciliation boards, and arbitration. These measures were
clearly meant as an alternative to a dangerous clash of class interests
and thus to strengthen and not undermine their own material interests
and authority.

Workers, however, persisted in demanding the autonomous control
at the workplace that employers could not accept. In Moscow in September 1905, the demand for direct workers' control over hiring and
firing and other workplace conditions stood at the head of the list of
strike demands circulated by the printers' union and approved by the
Council of Deputies:

> Every shop shall have permanent workers' deputies. . . . The employer does
> not have the right to fire [a deputy] nor the police to arrest him. . . . [O]ver-
> time work may be assigned only with the consent of the deputies. . . . Dep-
> uties shall examine all cases of deviation from the factory order. . . . The

95. *Russkoe slovo*, December 1, 1905, p. 3; Sher, *Istoriia*, pp. 208–09; *Obshcheprofessional'nye organy*, p. 129.
96. TsGAOR, f. 6864, op. 1, d. 207, p. 202; Sher, *Istoriia*, pp. 265–78; *Pechatnik*
1906, no. 8 (July 23), pp. 7–8.
97. *Zhizn' pechatnika* 12 (September 14, 1907), addendum.

hiring and firing of workers shall take place only with the consent of the
deputies. Workers may demand the firing of members of the administration.
The final decision belongs to the deputies.[98]

In October the union drafted a "Statute [*Polozhenie*] on Factory Deputies"—approved on November 15 at a mass meeting so large as to have
to be held simultaneously in two separate theaters—which standard-
ized the variations on these demands that workers had been presenting
during individual strikes in 1905: deputies' committees in each workplace were to be given sole authority to hire and fire workers, to determine the number of apprentices, and to enforce shop regulations.[99] In
St. Petersburg in 1905, shop-level committees of deputies demanded
control of discipline and the hiring and firing of workers in their
shops.[100] During 1906 and 1907, committees of shop deputies, known
generally as "autonomy commissions" (*komissii avtonomii*) in St.
Petersburg and as deputy "councils" or "institutes" in Moscow, continued to seek worker control over hiring, firing, and discipline.[101] The Petersburg union leaders, in negotiations with employers, continued to
demand the same.[102]

The class militance of these demands should not be overstated. Like
efforts to negotiate collective contracts and organize conciliation
boards, demands for autonomy also represented efforts to normalize
and institutionalize social relations, even as the extent of each group's
authority at the workplace remained in dispute. In Moscow, although
the 1905 statute gave to deputies considerable shop authority, the regulations they were to enforce were to be established only by agreement
with employers. In addition, the statute restricted the main activity of
deputies to representing workers' grievances before employers, thus
channeling discontent. The inclusion of the demand for worker control
in tariff negotiations after 1905 further diluted its force. To attain an

98. TsGAOR, f. 518, op. 1, d. 55, pp. 208, 216; f. 63, 1905, d. 773, pp. 13–14, 52;
Vserossiiskaia politicheskaia stachka, pp. 49–50.

99. The text of the statute appears in *Professional'nyi soiuz* 1906, no. 16–17, pp. 74–
76, and in *Materialy po professional'nomu dvizheniiu rabochikh* (Moscow) 1 (February
1906), reprinted in *Obshcheprofessional'nye organy*, pp. 83–84. See also Sher, *Istoriia*,
pp. 204–06.

100. Filippov, "Avtonomiia pechatnikov v 1905 godu"; *Pechatnyi vestnik* 1905, no.
14 (October 14), p. 11; *Novaia zhizn'*, November 1, 1905, p. 5, and November 2, 1905,
p. 3; Gordon, *Ocherk ekonomicheskoi bor'by rabochikh Rossii*, p. 142.

101. *Vestnik pechatnikov* 1906, no. 1 (April 21), p. 8; TsGIA, f. 150, op. 1, d. 79,
p. 159 (December 1907). For additional sources and details, see the discussion of worker-
generated rules of discipline in Chapter 8.

102. *Protokoly pervoi vserossiiskoi konferentsii*, pp. 10–11 (St. Petersburg tariff proposal, 1907).

agreement, workers generally agreed to accept a more restricted authority for deputies as empowered mainly to ensure that employers obeyed the terms of the agreement. Of course, the fact that the tariffs themselves were to stipulate rules of discipline and the specific conditions under which a worker could be hired and fired was an important limitation of the power of employers, and reflected workers' strength in winning this demand. Still, it was a limitation imposed by rules agreed upon by both sides rather than imposed directly by the workers themselves.[103]

Finally, even as workers sought to extend their authority at the workplace, they also agreed to maintain order. In many shops workers drew up their own rules of conduct, which strictly forbade such disorderly behavior as loud talking, swearing, fighting, or other disruptions of "peace and quiet," drinking or drunkenness on the job, and "impolite address" with other workers or management.[104] In 1907, the Petersburg union's proposed tariff included work rules prohibiting shouting, noise, singing, loud conversation, arguing, swearing, drinking, or playing games.[105]

Like tariffs and conciliation procedures, autonomy rules were simultaneously assertions of workers' separate class authority and of their desire to create what amounted to a constitutional order in industry.[106] Like political constitutions, autonomy rules proposed to normalize power relations under the equivalent of the rule of law and participatory consent, though in a polity made more democratic and inclusive. Like much else in the restructuring of social relations after 1905, organized workers and employers sought both to assert their own interests and power and to stabilize the terms of their interdependence.

103. Sher, *Istoriia*, pp. 265–78; TsGIAgM, f. 2069, op. 1, d. 8, pp. 171–73; *Pechatnik* 1906, no. 8 (July 23), pp. 7–8; *Zhizn' pechatnika* 12 (September 14, 1907), addendum.

104. *Vestnik pechatnikov* 1906, no. 1 (April 21), p. 8; 1907, no. 1 (February 2), pp. 17–18; *Pechatnik* 1906, no. 3 (May 14), p. 14; no. 6 (June 4), p. 16; *Knizhnyi vestnik* 1907, no. 41 (October 14), p. 1274; *Torgovo-promyshlennaia gazeta*, December 12, 1907; TsGAOR, f. 518, op. 1, d. 85a, pp. 142–43; *Istoriia leningradskogo soiuza*, pp. 273–75, 279.

105. *Protokoly pervoi vserossiiskoi konferentsii*, p. 11; *Zhizn' pechatnika* 12 (September 14, 1907), addendum.

106. On autonomy rules as "factory constitutions," see Sher, *Istoriia*, p. 204; Pankratova, *Fabzavkomy Rossii v bor'be za sotsialisticheskuiu fabriku*, pp. 113–15.

CHAPTER EIGHT

The Language of Revolution

As government control of public life faltered in the face of the protests evoked by Bloody Sunday, and as individuals were swept up by the momentum of events, talking and writing became among the most pervasive revolutionary acts. Countless meetings were held in theaters, schools, organizational offices, factory yards, workshops, and apartments. Newspapers and journals defied what had been the limits of tolerated speech. The result was an unprecedented torrent of words in which people thought out loud about the meaning of their actions and experiences. As it was said, people's "tongues were freed."[1] The government's promise of "civic freedom" in the Manifesto of October 17, followed by reform of the press laws in November 1905 and April 1906, the legalization of trade unions in March 1906, and the creation of an elected legislature, the State Duma, helped keep this discursive revolution alive, albeit harassed, until Prime Minister Stolypin's repressive "coup d'état" in June 1907.

One cannot be too precise about who was represented by the words that were spoken and written during these years. In certain respects the voices of the most outspoken individuals were part of a collective practice. At meetings, especially, speakers tried to articulate a sense of the collectivity with which they identified and whose experiences they shared; the approving shouts or derisions of the crowd helped to shape what was said; and formal votes endorsed or rejected statements. But

1. *Pechatnyi vestnik* 1905, no. 18 (November 27), p. 5.

oral and written expression remained essentially an individual act and thus reflected ideas shaped also in ways that cannot be easily generalized. Indeed, many of the people whose words I examine stood consciously out in front of their fellow workers or employers, seeing themselves not as mere mouthpieces for the collective but as leaders and guides. The terrain that this chapter explores, therefore, though at the center of social and political life in these years, also lay on the boundary between the personal and the collective.

The structure of social relations in the printing industry during the years 1905 through 1907, as we have seen, revealed a mixture of combativeness, negotiation, and conciliation: workers and employers drew apart into new class organizations but repeatedly came together to create institutions for resolving conflicts and regulating conditions; the readiness of workers and employers to negotiate with one another was matched by their stubbornness while negotiating. This ambivalence was especially evident as they sought to explain the meanings of their actions. The new rhetoric of class was not free of ideas about more embracing communities of interest and values, while notions of community and morality remained enmeshed with perceptions of class interest and assertions of power.

CLASS

Individuals who continued to speak during 1905 of the community of workers and employers admitted that they were increasingly likely to provoke "suspicious smiles," especially among workers.[2] As one press manager complained in June, instead of sharing with employers and managers a common identity as "free artists of the printed word," compositors and other printers were trying as hard as they could "to be considered 'workers' [*rabochie*], since this is fashionable and up to date."[3] The language of class identity and interest had become a new norm. To the extent that the metaphor of social family was still used by workers in 1905 and after, the reference was more likely to be to the "proletarian family."[4]

Many workers, especially worker leaders, openly derided ideals of trade community. In the opening speech at the organizational meeting

2. *Naborshchik i pechatnyi mir* 115 (November 20, 1905), p. 478. See also 114 (October 10, 1905), p. 439.
3. Ibid. 110 (June 10, 1905), pp. 245–46.
4. *Pechatnik* 1906, no. 3 (May 14), p. 12; *Vestnik pechatnikov* 1907, no. 1 (February 2), p. 6.

for the Petersburg printers' union on April 3, August Tens, once a regular correspondent to *Naborshchik*, stated bluntly, "The unity of all printers, from employers to the lowest press helper, about which some dreamers fantasize, is dangerous for the workers. This would be a union of the wolf, the goat, and the cabbage. The goat would eat the cabbage and the wolf devour the goat."[5] The "dreamer" whom Tens most likely had in mind was Andrei Filippov, who remained the editor of *Naborshchik*. Another speaker attacked Filippov personally, arguing that his devotion to the interests of both employers and workers was like trying to "sit between two chairs."[6] At a meeting later in April, on behalf of the union's organizational committee, Ivan Liubimtsev argued that the "failure" of the old assistance funds "to improve fundamentally" the conditions of labor could be explained by their inclusion of employers and managers. "The cause of the liberation of the workers," he insisted, "is the cause of the workers themselves."[7]

Many workers evidently agreed. By the fall, workers ceased to cheer sympathetic employers and managers at their meetings, much less invite them to preside or even speak. On the contrary, when a worker at a meeting of two thousand printing workers in early October announced the presence of a handful of employers and managers seated in the crowd, the entire audience began hooting, whistling, and chanting "Throw them out, throw them out."[8] Even workers' dress became an expression of class identity. In meetings with employers in Moscow in late September, worker deputies who had normally worn jackets, white shirts, and ties on formal occasions made a point of wearing ordinary workers' clothing.[9] Most important, class struggle was seen as the only possible means for improving workers' lives. Meeting in November, several thousand printing workers in Moscow resolved that "the means for achieving our demands cannot be words or persuasion, but only employers' fear of our strength and of the new losses that we can inflict on the employers' pockets through our strikes."[10]

Even some members of the traditionally collaborative assistance funds began to speak of the separate class identity and interests of

5. *Pechatnyi vestnik* 1905, no. 2 (June 12), p. 15.
6. *Naborshchik i pechatnyi mir* 108 (April 10, 1905), p. 154.
7. Ibid. 109 (May 10, 1905), pp. 202–06; Liubimtsev, *Ob osnovnykh printsipakh organizatsii Soiuza rabochikh pechatnogo dela; Istoriia leningradskogo soiuza*, pp. 141–47.
8. *Naborshchik i pechatnyi mir* 114 (October 10, 1905), p. 460; *Pechatnyi vestnik: iubileinyi vypusk*, p. 26 (recollections of A. Sevast'ianov).
9. *Pechatnik* 1906, no. 1 (April 23), p. 7.
10. *Vysshii pod"em revoliutsii 1905–1907 gg.*, p. 595; *Bor'ba* 1905, no. 7 (December 4 [17]), p. 3.

workers. When members of the Typographers' Assistance Fund founded a new workers' organization in the summer of 1905, they refused to allow employers and managers to become members and stated their goals as being to "defend" workers' "legal and professional interests," even with strikes.[11] Not surprisingly, more conservative members of the fund were appalled by what they considered a "mutinous" (*buntovskii*) organization.[12] Supporters of the new union tried to calm their critics by insisting that they were not led by "revolutionaries" but inspired "by the interests of the working class."[13] Such language could hardly have been reassuring to men who understood workers' "interests" as bound together with those of employers. The traditionalists of mutual aid were discovering what the conservative leaders of the Zubatovist printers' assembly in Moscow were also finding: "New people have appeared who speak in different ways than the old ones."[14] It would have been more accurate in many cases to say that many of the "old" people were beginning to talk in new ways.

Employers were initially more reluctant to speak so bluntly of class interests, perhaps partly since notions of common interest had served their own interests rather well. But workers' "assault" on authority, as many viewed it, encouraged them to respond in kind. When employer associations were established in 1905 and 1906, their charters and other statements of purpose spoke openly of the "interests" of employers.[15] The same recognition motivated A. I. Shutov to establish a journal for printing employers, *Vestnik pechatnogo dela* (The Printing Herald), in 1908. Shutov—the director of a large printing house in St. Petersburg, a former secretary of the Russian Printing Society, and since 1905 a leader of the press owners' association—made it clear from the outset that unlike the printing trade journals that existed before 1905, which pursued "extremely broad tasks," his journal would "serve the interests of owners of printing firms."[16]

11. *Naborshchik i pechatnyi mir* 112 (August 10, 1905), pp. 345–46.
12. Ibid., p. 357; *Pechatnyi vestnik* 1905, no. 8 (August 21), pp. 7, 12; no. 9 (August 28), pp. 5–7; no. 11 (September 11), pp. 6–8.
13. *Pechatnyi vestnik* 1905, no. 9 (August 28), p. 6.
14. *Naborshchik i pechatnyi mir* 107 (March 10, 1905), p. 129.
15. *Torgovo-promyshlennaia gazeta*, June 8 (21), 1906, p. 2; TsGIA, f. 150, op. 1, d. 79, p. 41 (1907 charter of Petersburg Obshchestvo vladel'tsev pechatnykh zavedeni-iakh); TsGIA, f. 150, op. 1, d. 79, p. 65 (lithographic section of Obshchestvo zavodchikov i fabrikantov, St. Petersburg, 1907); *Ustav MOT-L* p. 3 (1906 charter); MOT-L *Ustav i pravila*, pp. 3–4.
16. *Vestnik pechatnogo dela* 1:1 (December 15, 1908), p. 1. In 1917, Shutov headed the typographic press owners' section of the Petersburg Society of Factory Owners.

Even when workers and employers appeared to agree, mutual understanding was often tenuous at best. Although employers and workers in 1905 repeatedly voiced their agreement over the principle of Sunday and holiday rest for newspaper compositors, workers' representatives in both St. Petersburg and Moscow turned down every proposal that employers offered and even increased their demands to encompass additional holidays. Workers in both cities, as employers saw it, took the "unreasonable" stance of insisting on nothing less than complete capitulation by employers to their demands. For workers, of course, more was at issue than the physical need for rest, since employers' repeated offer of staggered holidays would have satisfied this. Workers themselves explained that a common day free from work was necessary to facilitate collective association. But one also senses an intransigence for its own sake—as an expression of class resentment, of a wish to see employers humbled, of a desire to decide their own fate.

Like the principle of Sunday rest, opposition to state censorship and other restrictions on speech, assembly, and belief, was a shared goal over which printing workers and employers repeatedly clashed. At meetings and in the press at the end of 1905, workers and their leaders argued that employers could not be relied upon to end censorship and insisted on the need for direct worker action. Distrust of employers seemed at times almost visceral. At a meeting of printing workers in Moscow on October 30, speakers bitterly derided press owners for their decision to wait until a new law was passed, and the final resolution expressed workers' "contempt and indignation at employers who refused out of cowardice to introduce freedom of the press immediately."[17]

Class distrust not only affected the strategies that workers brought to the struggle for a free press but also generated different ways of understanding this common goal, as was illustrated by workers' introduction of what amounted to class censorship. In early November, compositors in both St. Petersburg and Moscow began refusing to set into type materials that they considered politically reactionary, sometimes even including statements such as the proclamation announcing the formation of the moderate-conservative Octobrist party, which compositors at the Kushnerev press refused to typeset on November 7, not only because it opposed a constituent assembly but especially because it was

17. *Russkie vedomosti*, October 31, 1905, p. 3.

written in "a clever and sly manner."[18] More common were refusals to print materials submitted by more blatantly reactionary groups such as the Union of Russian People and the Brotherhood of Freedom and Order.[19] As workers at the Sytin press explained, when they refused to print an entire issue of the journal *Kreml'*, "Even freedom of the press can hardly require the printing of obviously Black-Hundred works that, though in a disguised manner, call for violence and beatings against those who are fighting for a new order."[20]

The initiative for this redefinition of freedom of the press came from the shops. The printers' unions in both cities initially criticized this tactic, the leaders of the Moscow union arguing that "one must not use force against the free word" but oppose reactionary literature only "with the same free word." However, the leaders of both unions soon sanctioned this "partisan struggle" against perceived reaction.[21] The office of the Moscow union even became a kind of censorship board, deciding whether workers should print particular materials about which they reported political misgivings.[22] Vasilii Sher, a Menshevik who participated in these activities, later considered these actions to have been a dangerous foreshadowing of the "class censorship" of the Soviet regime.[23] Although the political context and especially the source of initiative would be quite different after 1917, the comparison points to the similar refraction of democratic goals through the perceived needs of a single class.

The linkage of inclusive democratic politics and exclusive class means was often explicit in speeches at workers' meetings in the fall of 1905. Responding to the suggestions of socialists, workers began to refer to their own special role in the political struggle. The October Manifesto was spoken of as a victory that "belongs to the working class, which carries on its shoulders the entire weight of the struggle for political freedom." In the struggle against censorship it was said that "on us workers lies the sacred duty of tearing loose that which our government so stubbornly hangs on to." More generally, it was felt that "only one class, the proletariat, is the enemy of all forms of coercion

18. *Moskovskaia gazeta*, November 15, 1905, p. 4.
19. For examples from St. Petersburg, *Pechatnyi vestnik* 1905, no. 19 (December 4), pp. 12–13; *Istoriia leningradskogo soiuza*, p. 214. For Moscow, *Moskovskaia gazeta*, November 15, 1905, p. 4; November 20, 1905, p. 2; Sher, *Istoriia*, pp. 216–20.
20. *Moskovskaia gazeta*, November 15, 1905, p. 4.
21. Ibid.; Sher, "Moskovskie pechatniki," p. 69; *Istoriia leningradskogo soiuza*, p. 214.
22. Sher, "Moskovskie pechatniki," p. 69.
23. Ibid., p. 67.

[*nasilie*]."[24] Such expressions suggest an implicit theory of worker leadership in the democratic revolution but also a plain distrust of other classes.

During the last months of 1905 and throughout 1906 and 1907, the issue that most sharply divided workers and employers was everyday workplace authority. Although some employers were ready to recognize shop deputies as "intermediaries" and even to yield enforcement of discipline to workers, for they saw here the promise of regulating social relations according to established rules, they refused to surrender control over such fundamental employer prerogatives as hiring and firing. But workers often refused to compromise on precisely this demand. In some shops in St. Petersburg in 1905, "autonomy" was simply introduced by workers' direct action. Similarly, when the Statute on Factory Deputies was approved at huge mass meetings in Moscow in November 1905, workers agreed that in the event that employers rejected the statute it would be introduced by "revolutionary means," that is, by direct worker action, as Sytin workers had already done in September.[25] Many workers viewed workplace control as a clear expression of independent class power, defining "autonomy," as one worker put it in 1906, "as a situation in which members of a single corporation manage their own local affairs."[26]

As employers felt their authority become more threatened they naturally grew more defensive. In Moscow, in early October 1905, a meeting of employers threatened a lockout "until such time as it appears possible to conduct work in these establishments peacefully under normal conditions."[27] For employers, "normal conditions" presumably implied the preservation of employer authority. That this was at issue was suggested even more clearly by an incident in St. Petersburg in the fall, in a scene resembling occurrences in many industries in 1905 and after. In early November, Roman Golike, then head of the Petersburg union of press owners, fired six workers, all members of the printers' union. The workers' union and Golike both understood that the issue was not the fate of these six individuals but the question of authority at

24. *Russkie vedomosti*, October 20, 1905, p. 3; *Moskovskaia gazeta*, November 12, 1905, p. 3; *Novaia zhizn'*, November 2, 1905, p. 3.
25. *Russkie vedomosti*, November 17, 1905, pp. 3–4; *Moskovskaia gazeta*, November 18, 1905, p. 3; Sher, *Istoriia*, p. 208.
26. *Vestnik pechatnikov* 1906, no. 8 (June 11), pp. 2–3. "Autonomy" was defined in the leading encyclopedia of the day as "the right granted to a body, estate, or corporation to be guided by its own norms and rules within defined limits." *Entsiklopedicheskii slovar'*, vol. 1, p. 126.
27. *Russkoe slovo*, October 14 (27), 1905, p. 3.

the workplace and by extension throughout the industry. The trade union leaders insisted that the firing was an example of the "arbitrary authority" (*proizvol*) that employers could wield in their own firms, of workers' complete lack of "rights." Golike agreed, viewing the activities of the union and its representatives as a threat to his legitimate authority as an employer. He wished to be generous, offering to pay the fired workers a full month's wages instead of the two weeks' pay required by law, but he refused to rehire them. "I cannot work with them," he explained to union negotiators, "I am the master [*ia zhe khoziain*], and I can dismiss workers from my shop if I don't like them."[28]

This blunt statement, spoken by one of the leading figures in efforts to build a trade community before 1905, indicates how dramatically relations between workers and employers had deteriorated. It also points to the boundaries that had always delimited the purpose of community, at least as it was viewed by employers. The ideal of a moral community uniting masters and men was never meant to efface differences in power and position, only to inspire employers and workers to recognize the mutual dependence and moral duties that would insure the stability and legitimacy of these differences. By the end of 1905, workers' demands for workplace control often threatened to subvert power relations more than they promised to normalize them.

During 1906 and 1907 the question of entrepreneurial authority remained central to employers' behavior and language. Leaders of the Moscow Society of Typo-Lithographers stated that it was their purpose to defend the "freedom of industry,"[29] which meant, as their actions demonstrated, freedom from interference by workers. "Until now," an agitational leaflet addressed to employers in the name of the Moscow Society of Typo-Lithographers warned in 1906, "workers have considered themselves slaves of the entrepreneurs, but now you are the slaves of your workers."[30] The symbol of this reversal was workers' demand to control hiring and firing. For employers there could be no compromise with a demand that threatened to overturn the normal order of things, to "turn the employer," as a columnist for *Vestnik pechatnogo*

28. *Novaia zhizn'*, November 11, 1905, p. 3. See also *Naborshchik i pechatnyi mir* 115 (November 20, 1905), p. 483; and *Pechatnyi vestnik* 1905, no. 18 (November 27), pp. 7–8.

29. *Ustav MOT-L*, pp. 3–4.

30. According to a report from one employer to the workers' union, the author of this leaflet was A. A. Levenson, chairman of the Society. *Pechatnik* 1906, no. 5 (May 28), pp. 2–3; no. 6 (June 4), p. 6.

dela would argue in 1909, "into a worker for his own workers."[31] Employers were not far wrong, of course, in thinking, as one printing employer would later put it, that "autonomy smells of socialism."[32]

Employers had reason to be suspicious even of workers' efforts to regulate labor-management relations through tariffs, conciliation boards, and arbitration. Many rank-and-file workers, union leaders complained, felt that suggestions that conflicts be resolved "peacefully" were too "dull" a course of action and complained that they felt deprived of a chance "to show [their] toughness."[33] Some union leaders themselves were uncomfortable with bargaining and conciliation. The Menshevik S. Ia. Kibrik (S. Iakovlev), a leader of the Moscow union and one of the organizers of the 1907 national conference of printers' unions, was probably not alone in finding "the subjective experience" of participating in collaborative meetings with employers to be "unpleasant."[34]

Even when workers embraced collective agreements and conciliatory arrangements with employers, they often portrayed these as expressions of class struggle. At the 1907 conference speakers described the collective contract as a "temporary truce" allowing workers to prepare themselves for future struggles, "a protocol that takes account of the strength of the two sides, and is therefore . . . not a cessation of struggle, but its continuation" and even a step toward the "final goal of socialism."[35] Identical arguments were made in defense of arbitration and conciliation. Although "on the surface," speakers admitted, "it would seem as if direct and unmediated struggle has been replaced by trade,"[36] this was only the appearance of things. Behind superficial conciliation, it was said, lay the class power of employers and workers, the recognition by employers of the workers' union, the husbanding of organizational resources and energy for larger questions and bigger battles,[37] and even, as leaders of the Moscow union would argue in later years, a "school of class struggle."[38] Of course, the repeated

31. *Vestnik pechatnogo dela* 1: 5–6 (April–May 1909), pp. 4–6 (quotation on p. 4). See also TsGIA, f. 150, op. 1, d. 79, p. 306; d. 81, p. 68.
32. "Tarifnoe dvizhenie v Petrograde za 1917–1918 gg.," p. 20.
33. *Pechatnik* 1906, no. 7 (July 9) p. 6.
34. *Protokoly pervogo vserossiiskoi konferentsii,* p. 104.
35. Ibid., pp. 76, 104, 109.
36. Ibid., p. 104.
37. Ibid.; *Pechatnik* 1906, no. 3 (May 14), p. 11 (by Vladimir Kairovich); no. 6 (June 4), pp. 12–13; no. 7 (July 9), pp. 6–7.
38. *Pechatnik* 1917, no. 5 (October 8), p. 6.

insistence by activists that conciliation or arbitration was not an aban-
donment of class struggle may also suggest their uneasy feeling that
it was.

COMMUNITY

Many people were saddened and distressed that the main effect of 1905
on social relations had been to "create hatred, sow enmity, and instill
distrust" between employers and workers, as the former compositor
Gerasim Grents sadly observed in the fall of 1905.[39] It is not surprising,
of course, that supervisors and production managers, especially if
former workers, should have remained the most stubborn proponents
of social community, of the idea that workers and employers shared
common interests. As was said of Andrei Filippov, they were socially as
well as philosophically "sitting between two chairs."[40] Filippov's journal *Naborshchik*—retitled in 1905 *Naborshchik i pechatnyi mir* (The
Compositor and the Printing World) to better express the view that
compositors belonged to a larger community—remained the most important forum for these advocates of social community.

Throughout 1905 and after, Andrei Filippov and his allies continued
to insist that "the worker's welfare is inseparably linked to the welfare
of the owner."[41] As in the past, Filippov and his associates considered
themselves advocates of workers' needs, but they defined these needs in
a particular way. Leading a meeting of elected worker representatives
on February 13 to discuss employers' proposals for a tariff, Filippov appealed to workers for conciliation and advised them that employers
had increased wages as much as possible given the current economic
conditions. It was the "duty" of both sides to compromise, he argued.
Drawing at length on the history of labor conflicts in Western Europe,
he advised workers that "the struggle of labor against capitalism" was
futile since it "served only to strengthen the latter."[42]

During the spring, *Naborshchik* initially welcomed workers' plans
to organize a trade union, regularly reported union activities, and even
reprinted speeches by union leaders. But Filippov and his colleagues

39. *Naborshchik i pechatnyi mir* 114 (October 10, 1905), p. 439.
40. Ibid. 108 (April 10, 1905), p. 154.
41. Ibid. 115 (November 20, 1905), p. 478. There was some difference of emphasis as
to whether there was "complete unity of interests of owners and workers," or the interests of workers and owners only "partly coincided." Ibid. 116 (December 20, 1905),
p. 519; 107 (March 10, 1905), p. 117.
42. Ibid. 107 (March 10, 1905), pp. 106–08.

had their own idea of what unionization ought to mean. To their mind, a union ought to serve the interests of both workers and employers, its purpose ought to be to "regulate" and "uplift" the entire "corporation" of printers out of a common interest in improving the "art."[43] Although they did not insist that this corporative ideal require including employers as members of the union, they saw no reason to exclude supervisors and managers. Workers and managers, they insisted, were all part of "one working family," all "workers" and "brothers," whose "interests completely coincide."[44] Besides, Filippov argued, managers and supervisors "more than anyone else have labored for their younger brothers."[45] In fact, many of these former workers were "offended," as Pavel Baskakov was, when the union announced that they could not be members. Still, they hoped that the decision was not final and that "the word worker [would] be understood in its widest sense," just as the word soldier was understood to "include generals."[46]

Even as these former workers accepted their exclusion from both workers' and employers' organizations and established their own union of supervisors or managers, they resisted the logic of their own actions. Although the stated purpose of the new union was "defending the legal and professional interests" of supervisors and managers and improving their "material conditions of life and labor," they refused to limit their tasks to these aims. At the founding meeting in November 1905, one of the organizers, Gerasim Grents, defined the purpose of the supervisors' union as also serving as an "intermediary between owners and workers." Even their chosen name, the Russian Professional Union of Printing, indicated a hesitation to define themselves apart from the general interests of the whole trade.[47]

Although these advocates of trade community often complained of the deterioration of social relations in the industry, they were not entirely voices in the wilderness. In St. Petersburg, as we have seen, despite the unprecedented strikes by printing workers in January 1905, employers and workers often continued to address one another in the collaborative language of the past. At a meeting of elected worker representatives on February 13, the compositor Petr Orlov, a member of

43. Ibid. 108 (April 10, 1905), p. 153; 110 (June 10, 1905), pp. 244–46, 262; 111 (July 10, 1905), pp. 295–96.
44. Ibid. 109 (May 10, 1905), p. 197; 112 (August 10, 1905), pp. 340, 346. Following the same logic, Filippov initially opposed suggestions to establish a separate union of managers, supervisors, and correctors. Ibid. 109 (May 10, 1905), p. 229.
45. Ibid. 109 (May 10, 1905), pp. 197, 229.
46. Ibid. 110 (June 10, 1905), p. 247.
47. Ibid. 115 (November 20, 1905), pp. 485–86.

the workers' tariff commission, spoke of the "deep gratitude" workers felt toward employers for their "labors on our behalf."[48] Similarly, Roman Golike, the chairman of the employers' tariff commission, spoke at length before a meeting of workers on February 25 asking workers to join with employers to "regulate together our common profession,"[49] to which workers responded sympathetically. They also unanimously resolved to thank Count Tolstoi, the leader of the Russian Printing Society, for his "attentions to the needs of printing workers."[50]

During the conflict over Sunday and holiday rest for newspaper compositors in the spring and early summer of 1905, employers and workers, especially in St. Petersburg, kept alive the rhetorical traditions of moral community. Sunday rest was a goal long shared by employers and workers. When a seven-day work week for newspaper compositors was introduced in the middle of the nineteenth century, workers did not initially protest this degradation of conditions (possibly because it also resulted in higher earnings for them as piece-rate workers), but many press owners and publishers did speak against it as an example of the ill effects of unregulated competition. At the 1895 Congress of Printing, speakers noted the moral and physical harm that the seven-day work week caused compositors and the Congress voted in principle to end Sunday work.[51] Since employers felt that competition for readers made it difficult for any individual employer to act on this goal until he could be sure that others would do the same, the Printing Society in 1900 requested the Ministry of the Interior to introduce legislation requiring presses to be closed on Sundays and major holidays.[52] When workers themselves began to voice a desire for Sunday rest, their tone and language remained within the boundaries of the collaborative ideal of trade community. In 1904, for example, compositors working on the St. Petersburg newspaper *Slovo* sent a letter to the editor when the owner of the press reversed his earlier promise to end Sunday work. The title of their piece, "Cry of the Compositors" (*Vopl' naborshchikov*), suggests their manner. Workers did not *demand* Sunday rest or threaten to strike to regain it but appealed to the "humanity" of employers and the sympathy of readers.[53]

48. Ibid. 107 (March 10, 1905), pp. 106–08.
49. Ibid., p. 110.
50. Ibid., p. 109.
51. *Trudy pervogo s"ezda*, pp. 40, 117; *Obzor pervoi vserossiiskoi vystavki* 15 (April 10, 1895), pp. 3–4.
52. Grents and Galaktionov, *Obzor*, p. 20.
53. *Slovo*, March 3, 1904, p. 2. For other examples, *Pechatnoe iskusstvo* 2:7 (April 1903), pp. 242–43; *Naborshchik* 1:9 (December 29, 1902), pp. 156–57; 1:17 (February 25, 1903), p. 278; 1:52 (October 26, 1903), pp. 782–84.

This rhetorical tradition persisted into 1905. Employers continued to express "concern" and "sympathy" with workers' demands for Sunday and holiday rest and to propose various means of achieving it. Workers also expressed hope that the problem could be resolved amicably. Even after organized printing workers in St. Petersburg decided to introduce Sunday rest by direct action, they celebrated their first success, on Sunday, April 10, by attending a special church service to which publishers, editors, managers, and their families were also invited and willingly came. Here was a fitting symbol of the ambiguities of class conflict in the early months of 1905: a ritual for the "family" of all printers, reminiscent of the trade festivals of the nineteenth century, celebrating what amounted to a mass strike.[54]

Even in Moscow, notwithstanding the earlier strike in 1903, some workers continued in the early months of 1905 to view relations with authority in collaborative terms. When members of the Typographers' Assistance Fund announced plans in the middle of 1905 to establish an independent labor union, they rejected much of the tradition of mutual aid by refusing to allow employers and managers to become members but also distanced themselves from the class combativeness of the underground union. In direct contrast to the illegal Union of Typo-Lithographical Workers (*rabochie*) for the Struggle to Improve the Conditions of Labor, they called their union the Fund (*Fond*) for the Improvement of the Conditions of Labor of Working Men (*truzheniki*) in Typo-Lithographical Enterprises. And although they spoke of defending "working-class interests," they insisted that this did not mean that they sought "to radically remake the life of the printing worker," but only to "regulate relations between labor and capital."[55]

As late as the final months of 1905, when it seemed that the old trade community had disintegrated in the face of class struggle, some employers and managers resisted such an outcome. According to Georgii Nosar', the legal adviser to the Petersburg printers' union, even in October there was "a whole category of employers who dream of establishing harmony between labor and capital," whose incomprehension of the changes around them was so great that they even asked

54. TsGAOR, f. 6864, op. 1, d. 4, p. 3. This account by A. Sevast'ianov, a newspaper compositor elected to the workers' tariff commission, also appears in part in *Istoriia leningradskogo soiuza*, p. 138. When writing this memoir in the 1920s, Sevast'ianov claimed that this service and the presence of employers and managers were a "guise" to camouflage the fact that "Sunday rest had been seized by revolutionary means." There is no other evidence, however, that this was the intent or the perception at the time.

55. *Pechatnyi vestnik* 1905, no. 7 (August 14), p. 11; *Naborshchik i pechatnyi mir* 112 (August 10, 1905), pp. 345–46.

to become members of the union.[56] Even as owners organized to defend employer interests and to resist workers' "excessive" demands, they often continued to refer to the collaborative and regulative traditions of the past. At the founding meeting of the Petersburg press-owners' union, Anton Lesman, one of the organizers, who was also a member of the Printing Society, represented the goal of the new union as giving press owners "the possibility to properly organize assistance to workers (wages, education of their children, medical treatment, pensions, etc.)" and to "struggle" against "competition."[57] The chairman of the union, Roman Golike, argued similarly in December that the creation of unions of workers and employers made it possible "to establish correct and just relations between employers and workers, by which all conflicts might be resolved by conciliatory means."[58] In Moscow, too, employers advocated measures that might reconcile workers and employers, even that shop deputies elected by workers might serve as useful "intermediaries between employers and workers."[59] In both Moscow and St. Petersburg, as late as November 1905, the employers' unions continued to speak of the need for "mutual regulation of relations" between owners and workers.[60]

Within their own plants, many employers also persisted in efforts to preserve bonds of loyalty uniting workers to themselves. In Moscow, Ivan Sytin, like many other large employers, spent tens of thousands of rubles during 1905 on what he called "charitable" benefits for his workers.[61] Even when his workers struck in September, the company issued a statement reminding workers of their higher than average wages and of the many additional benefits that employment at Sytin brought them: "At the present time there has already been established a kitchen and a library, medicine is given out without charge, and a school has been organized. One should also keep in mind that in the future grants will be given out during times of sickness. All of this is at great expense to the Company."[62] Such tangible expressions of paternal benevolence—and Sytin was considered relatively belated and backward in these efforts—were reinforced, as in the past, by company

56. *Novaia zhizn'*, October 30, 1905, p. 3.
57. TsGAOR, f. 6864, op. 1, d. 8, p. 35.
58. LGIA, f. 1513, op. 1, d. 12, p. 8.
59. *Naborshchik i pechatnyi mir* 108 (April 10, 1905), p. 167.
60. Sher, *Istoriia*, p. 210; *Naborshchik i pechatnyi mir* 115 (November 20, 1905), p. 484.
61. TsGIAgM, f. 2316, op. 1, d. 2, pp. 102, 104, 106, 115, 121, 125.
62. TsGAOR, f. 63, 1905, d. 773, pp. 67–69.

jubilees and celebrations of career anniversaries of employers or managers at which workers and employers joined together in rituals of workplace community.[63]

During 1906 and 1907, the ideal of a regulated trade community continued to be invoked. Partly, as in the past, concerns focused on the effects of unbridled business competition.[64] But the problems of competition were viewed as inseparable from larger social issues, specifically the need to "regulate relations between entrepreneurs and workers" through labor contracts (tariffs) and institutionalized means of resolving disputes.[65] As in the past, behind the ideal of regulation (*uregulirovanie*) lay the claim that employers and workers had interests in common. In late 1906 the Bulletin of the Moscow Society of Typo-Lithographers printed a letter from a member suggesting that especially now, after the government had closed the workers' union, it was necessary to make workers "understand that their interests are in solidarity with the interests of owners."[66] Similarly, an article in *Vestnik pechatnogo dela* argued that at least in certain areas—such as the regulation of competition—"the interests of reasonable employers and of conscious workers undoubtedly coincide."[67] Such claims were sufficiently common in these years to cause union activists to warn workers against being tempted by ideas of the solidarity of their interests and those of employers. Such an alliance, one Petersburg union leader cautioned in 1906, would be as unnatural as marrying a man to a monkey.[68]

Employers' appeals to common interest and community were not meant to contradict their own interests or authority. As before 1905,

63. For example, *Naborshchik i pechatnyi mir* 107 (March 10, 1905), pp. 141–42 (anniversary of the Wineke press; also a career anniversary of a printing master); 108 (April 10, 1905), p. 178 (Artur Wilborg's retirement from the firm of Golike and Wilborg); 109 (May 10, 1905), p. 231 (for the manager of Weisberg); 110 (June 10, 1905), p. 283 (annual celebration at the State press); 112 (August 10, 1905), pp. 356–57 (for Borovik, director of Kushnerev); 113 (September 10, 1905), p. 420 (for Grents, manager of Tile).

64. *Torgovo-promyshlennaia gazeta*, June 8 (21), 1906, p. 2; MOT-L, *Ustav i pravila*, pp. 4, 10; MOT-L Bulletins in TsGAOR, f. 6864, op. 1, d. 207, pp. 197–98, 229; *Vestnik pechatnogo dela* 1:1 (December 15, 1908), p. 2; 1:5–6 (April–May 1909), p. 2.

65. *Ustav MOT-L*, p. 4. See also TsGIAgM, f. 2069, op. 1, d. 8, pp. 170–71 (Moscow, 1906); TsGAOR, f. 6864, op. 1, d. 207, pp. 202, 229 (MOT-L Bulletins for 1907); *Vestnik pechatnogo dela* 1:1 (December 15, 1908), p. 2; 1:5–6 (April–May 1909), pp. 4–6; 1:7 (June 1909), pp. 2–4; *Knizhnyi vestnik* 1909, no. 32 (August 9), p. 375 (proposals for a congress of printing employers).

66. TsGAOR, f. 6864, op. 1, d. 207, p. 129.

67. *Vestnik pechatnogo dela* 1:7 (June 1909), pp. 2–3.

68. *Vestnik pechatnikov* 1906, no. 1 (April 21), p. 3; *Pechatnik* 1906, no. 1 (April 23), pp. 11–12, 15.

social collaboration was aimed at preserving the hierarchy of authority by making it more responsive and fair and at advancing employers' interests by attending to the interests of all. In 1905 and after, though the notion of class interest had become far more explicit and pervasive than before, even the most benevolent employers apparently saw no contradiction between the interests of the industry as a whole and their own interest in preserving their authority and ensuring their profits.

As the complaints of trade union militants make clear, many workers, too, were still attracted by arguments about the common interests of workers and employers. "Despite the events of the past year," the leaders of the Petersburg printers' union observed in September 1905, "very very few among the working class truly understand their position."[69] Too many printing workers, another unionist observed at about the same time, "still uphold old slavish habits, which are rooted in their flesh and blood, and want to hear nothing about the new."[70] The most distressing sign of the persistence of traditional conceptions among workers was the deferential gratitude that many continued to offer employers and managers. In 1905, following successful strikes or positive responses to demands, workers sometimes thanked their employers in the same grateful terms used at earlier celebrations of trade community.[71] And when employers organized company jubilees or career anniversaries, many workers not only took part but offered "laudatory and grateful addresses" to managers or employers.[72] For example, at a retirement party for Artur Wilborg in April 1905, a representative chosen by the workers praised Wilborg as "a friend of the workers" who had always been "good and loving" and had done "much for his younger brother-workers . . . sometimes even at a loss to himself."[73] Such behavior was less common by the end of 1905, but it was far from eradicated, as may be judged from the continued complaints by unionists after 1905 about the "shameful" persistence of a "slave mentality" among workers who could not see that by participating in such affairs they were celebrating "years of blood sucking."[74]

69. *Pechatnyi vestnik* 1905, no. 12 (September 18), p. 3.
70. Ibid. no. 9 (August 28), p. 12.
71. For example, *Vestnik soiuza tipografskikh rabochikh* 9 (August 1905), p. 7; *Naborshchik i pechatnyi mir* 112 (August 10, 1905), pp. 356–57; TsGIA, f. 800, op. 1, d. 427, p. 34.
72. TsGAOR, f. 6864, op. 1, d. 60, p. 11 (from recollections by a Petersburg compositor).
73. *Naborshchik i pechatnyi mir* 108 (April 10, 1905), p. 178.
74. *Pechatnyi vestnik* 1906, no. 2 (February 19), p. 8.

MORALITY

Individuals who openly condemned the spread of class conflict in the printing industry insisted that their path was the moral high road. When Andrei Filippov was accused of trying to "sit between two chairs" he answered that he was "not offended."[75] To his mind this was the more virtuous position. At issue, as Filippov and other proponents of social community maintained in essays, poems, and other writings in *Naborshchik*, in 1905 and after, were such "eternal" values as goodness, honor, reason, trust, kindness, and especially "love of one's neighbor."[76] In 1905, shortly after Bloody Sunday and the mass strikes of January, Filippov expressed his hope that the Russian printing trade, now a "ship without rudder or sail," would be seized by "powerful waves" and brought into "that safe harbor, where there is concern, love, and kindness."[77] He continued to cherish this hope even in the midst of the October general strike, when he called upon "everyone, from the employer to the least worker" to remember that "the finest feeling of the human spirit is sympathy for one's neighbor."[78]

Even as Filippov and his supporters withdrew into their own separate organization, the Russian Professional Union of Printing, they persisted in seeing their purpose as moral advocacy. Although they recognized that the union must defend the "interests" of supervisors, they also wished it to serve as an "intermediary between owners and workers" and specifically as a mediating moral force. The Professional Union, Gerasim Grents told the founding meeting in November 1905, was to be "a stronghold of humane principles" whose members "manifest virtuous feelings" (*chuvstva dobrodeteli*) in all their actions and travel "the path of true brotherhood, freedom, and love."[79]

As before 1905 this vision of employers and workers united by moral bonds had a sharp, challenging edge. Contributors to *Naborshchik* did not pretend that the benevolent employers whom they admired were the norm. "Many printing workmen are envious that they do not have

75. *Naborshchik i pechatnyi mir* 108 (April 10, 1905), p. 154.

76. For a few of many examples, ibid. 105 (January 19, 1905), pp. 5–7; 107 (March 10, 1905), p. 141; 108 (April 10, 1905), p. 160; 111 (July 10, 1905), pp. 295–96; 114 (October 10, 1905), pp. 433–37, 449; 115 (November 20, 1905), p. 485; 116 (December 20, 1905), pp. 519–20.

77. Ibid. 105 (January 19, 1905), pp. 5–7.

78. Ibid. 114 (October 10, 1905 [*sic*; written and printed after October 17]), pp. 436–37.

79. Ibid. 115 (November 20, 1905), pp. 485–86.

such a warm, humane, and at the same time modest employer . . . as
V. I. Markevich," Filippov wrote in September.[80] Nor were they forgiv-
ing of the less benevolent: it was one thing, they admitted, to "preach
about unity" with employers "who are attentive to the interests of
workers, and pay them honestly for their labor," but with the rest it is
"impossible to live together."[81]

Employers also often continued to cast social relations in an ethical
mold. Although they were well aware of the material costs of strikes
and other labor conflicts,[82] many employers continued to insist that
preserving bonds between workers and employers was also a matter of
morality. During the tariff negotiations in St. Petersburg in 1905, S. M.
Propper, the publisher and printer of the Petersburg stock-exchange
newspaper *Birzhevye vedomosti* and a longtime activist in the Printing
Society, told a meeting of printing employers that they should agree to
raise wages, not as a concession to workers' demands but as a voluntary expression of employers' sympathy: "It is essential to treat people
with trust and not to look upon compositors as if they were machines."
He denounced employers who might disagree with him, in the ethical
tradition of the trade community, as common "exploiters."[83]

As employers found themselves increasingly on the defensive during
the course of 1905, the tone of their moral advocacy changed. Some,
like Golike, first pleaded with workers for understanding and "patience" and then, when this failed to bring workers to their senses, reminded workers of employers' "rights." Many viewed labor unrest as a
sign of workers' moral deficiency. In March an employer wrote to *Naborshchik* that he considered it pointless to negotiate a wage tariff with
workers, since so many compositors were "alcoholics" who would
work for any wage.[84] At meetings in St. Petersburg later in the spring,
some employers argued that higher wages would only encourage workers' bad habits.[85] One press owner even declared at a meeting of
employers that "there are no longer any real compositors—only hoo-
ligans."[86] Faced with insubordination, employers often saw moral
degeneration. Social morality was meant to strengthen order and authority not undermine it.

80. Ibid. 113 (September 10, 1905), p. 383. See also 108 (April 10, 1905), p. 154.
81. Ibid. 116 (December 20, 1905), p. 520.
82. Ibid. 108 (April 10, 1905), p. 163.
83. Ibid.
84. Ibid. 107 (March 10, 1905), p. 146.
85. Ibid. 108 (April 10, 1905), p. 163.
86. Ibid. 109 (May 10, 1905), p. 217. See also 108 (April 10, 1905), pp. 159–60.

Nonetheless, once the revolutionary fires of 1905 died down and workers became, as it was said, more "careful" and "sane,"[87] employers revived the language of moral authority. Some of the richest employers began again to distance themselves from suggestions that they were motivated by mere material interest. At the twenty-fifth anniversary celebration of the Moscow printing house of A. A. Levenson in December 1906, a guest argued—and this was quoted in an account Levenson published—that profit was not a "golden calf" for Levenson, that in him the "egoistical goals" of a "capitalist-entrepreneur" were properly combined with a dedication to "social service."[88] During the 1906 tariff negotiations, Levenson himself, as head of the Moscow press-owners' association, appealed to workers to "be friends."[89] Similarly, during the February 1907 lockout, Ivan Sytin assured his workers that he opposed the lockout, that he was consulting with his lawyers about quitting the owners' union, and that he personally considered himself to be "a friend of the workers."[90] Years later, when Sytin celebrated his fiftieth jubilee, speakers noted that although Sytin's company was one of the largest printing firms in Russia, he "completely lacked the defining characteristic of the merchant—thought of personal gain, of his own enrichment."[91] Accounts of Sytin's life make it clear that this was a myth, and contemporary critics more than once accused Sytin of unprincipled profiteering.[92] But that this was the myth with which many employers continued to present themselves in public suggests not only a continued concern with social esteem but also continued moral ambivalence about capitalist entrepreneurship.

Employers also continued to insist on their sympathy for workers' interests, "love" for their workers, respect for workers' "rights," and willingness to satisfy "just" demands.[93] The advantages of collective contracts and grievance procedures were described in this light: according to the official Bulletin of the Moscow Society of Typo-Lithographers in 1906, "concord" (*soglashenie*) was necessary not only

87. *Pechatnik* 1906, no. 8 (July 23), p. 4 (quoting from the liberal newspaper *Put'*).
88. *Dvadstatipiatiletie skoropechatni tovarishchestva A. A. Levenson, Moskva 1881–1906*, no pagination (the speaker was P. V. Bel'skii).
89. *Pechatnik* 1906, no. 6 (June 4), p. 5.
90. TsGAOR, f. 518, op. 1, d. 85a, pp. 227, 234.
91. *Polveka dlia kniga, 1866–1916*, pp. 59, 61. Sytin was described in 1917 in an essay in his own newspaper, *Russkoe slovo*, as a man whose business achievements brought him into the ranks of the Russian bourgeoisie, but who "did not himself become a 'bourgeois.' " *Russkoe slovo*, February 19 (March 4), 1917, p. 2.
92. Ruud, *Russian Entrepreneur*.
93. See, for example, discussion in *Pechatnik* 1906, no. 7 (July 9), p. 15.

to the shared material interests of workers and employers but also to "establish just and humane relations" between them.[94] Employers also measured one another against this moral standard. In 1906, one Moscow employer derided many of his fellows as men with "predatory jaws" motivated by "mercantile greed."[95] Echoing a tradition of employer discourse in printing that went back to the 1860s, a contributor to the printing employers' journal *Vestnik pechatnogo dela* distinguished between "honorable" employers and those who "exploit" their workers.[96]

To symbolize and demonstrate these claims, employers made use of many of the same forms as in the past. Large employers, especially, continued to offer workers free medical care, paid vacations, sick pay, low-price meals, educational stipends for their children, subsidized assistance funds, and even unemployment aid.[97] Organized employers also continued the tradition of direct paternal assistance to workers. The Moscow employers' union in May 1906 established a subsidized burial fund for workers and in 1907 offered job placement and considered giving financial help to the unemployed.[98] The Petersburg owners' union made plans in 1907 to establish free medical clinics around the city for printing workers whose employers could not afford to give free care.[99] As in the past, the message that these benefits sought to convey was sometimes reinforced with customary speeches, gift-giving, and toasts at workplace festivals on holidays and anniversary celebrations.[100]

Worker activists, including many who had once been associated with *Naborshchik*, mocked employers' efforts to convince workers of the viability of the old ideal of a unifying social community. They sought to unmask "father-benefactors" (*otsy-blagodeteli*) who shed

94. TsGAOR, f. 6864, op. 1, d. 207, p. 127. In 1916, even the typographic printers' section of Petrograd Society of Factory Owners would argue that it was necessary to regulate economic competition between enterprises in the interests of both employers and workers and in order to protect professional "honor," "conscience," and "correctness." TsGIA, f. 150, op. 1, d. 78, pp. 160, 218.

95. *Pechatnik* 1906, no. 1 (April 23), p. 7.

96. *Vestnik pechatnogo dela* 1:7 (June 1909), p. 2.

97. TsGIAgM, f. 2069, op. 1, d. 4, p. 44 (Levenson, 1907); TsGIA, f. 800, op. 1, d. 490, p. 1 (St. Petersburg Synod press, 1908–1909); LGIA, f. 1458, op. 2, d. 888, p. 413 (Office for the Manufacture of Government Paper, 1910); TsGIA, f. 150, op. 1, d. 79, p. 182 (on several Petersburg lithographic shops, 1910); *Otchet pravleniia Obshchestva vzaimopomoshchi sluzhashchikh i rabotaiushchikh v Senatskoi tipografii.*

98. *Pechatnik* 1906, no. 3 (May 14), p. 10; TsGAOR, f. 6864, op. 1, d. 207, pp. 167–69, 175–76, 200, 221 (reports on burial fund, 1906–1907), 237, 243; MOT-L, *Ustav i pravila*, p. 14.

99. TsGIA, f. 150, op. 1, d. 79, p. 37.

100. *Pechatnyi vestnik* 1906, no. 2 (February 19), p. 8; *Vestnik pechatnogo dela* 1:3 (February 1909), p. 15.

"crocodile tears" of sympathy for the worker.[101] And they condemned not only hypocrisy but paternalistic benevolence itself. "Charity," though once praised, was now repudiated as "degrading" to the worker, undermining his necessary "freedom and independence," and interfering with his "self-reliance."[102]

Although this critique was often cast in the vocabulary of class identity and struggle, it was as much a moral challenge as a social one. This moral content was partly a matter of tone. Expressions of class protest were often imbued with a moral ethos, an emotional faith in the righteousness of the cause. When Nikolai Chistov, the Social Democratic worker-leader of both the Moscow printers' union and the Moscow Soviet of Workers' Deputies, was arrested in December 1905, his reaction to his imprisonment reflected a view—influenced, he admitted, by Populists, Tolstoyans, and the church, as well as by Marxists—of the moral significance of his acts and his suffering.

> When they put me in an isolated cell in the Taganka, I looked around and in my mind arose the idea that in just such a cell as this have been held holy people who struggle for the workers' cause. In order to fortify myself for the struggle, I pulled off the prison mattress and for two or three nights tried to sleep on the bare iron grate, to temper myself for the future struggle for the workers' cause. Whenever I became depressed, I fell on my knees and prayed to God, turning my gaze to the corner, though no icon was there.[103]

Chistov's prayer may have been, as he says, a desperate response to his suffering, but it may also have expressed an elevated moral sensibility, a self-identity as a holy martyr, an image shaped, it would seem, equally by the Lives of Saints as by the legends of revolutionaries.

The involvement of thousands of workers for the first time in social and political struggle in 1905 was often viewed by activists as a moral awakening. The masses of workers were said to have "woken up from a long and heavy sleep" so that "every individual is aware that to live as they lived before is impossible."[104] Political awareness, especially, was often described as sudden enlightenment. One worker recalled the experience of many when several thousand printing workers met on October 19 in the main hall of the Moscow Conservatory, applauding

101. *Pechatnyi vestnik* 1905, no. 4 (July 24), p. 4; no. 7 (August 14), pp. 9–10; no. 14 (October 2), pp. 5–7; no. 15 (October 10), p. 3.

102. Ibid. 1905, no. 14 (October 2), p. 3; no. 9 (August 28), p. 8; no. 4 (July 24), p. 4.

103. TsGAOR, f. 6864, op. 1, d. 248, pp. 28–29. This is from an "evening of reminiscences" in which Chistov participated in the early 1920s. Most of Chistov's contribution, though not his mention of prayer, was reprinted in *Moskovskie pechatniki v 1905 godu*, p. 132.

104. *Pechatnyi vestnik* 1905, no. 7 (August 14), p. 3.

and cheering every political statement made by representatives of the various left-wing parties. After electrical power was cut off toward the end of the meeting—an effect of the general strike—the gathering concluded, near one o'clock in the morning, with workers standing and holding candles, as in church on Easter, singing the Funeral March in memory of those who had fallen in the struggle. "Leaving the gates of the conservatory," this worker recalled, a worker felt "that a great change had occurred in his soul, in his life."[105] Socialist *intelligenty* active among printers agreed that "political consciousness arose literally before one's eyes."[106] This was a moral conversion as much as a rational one.

The fact that official violence was most often responsible for provoking workers into political protest further suggests the centrality of moral judgment. Radical propagandists, of course, often pointed to state violence as evidence that success in the economic struggle depended on political freedom.[107] But it is not clear that this was the rationale that propelled most workers to join in political protest. As a socialist activist in St. Petersburg recognized, "more than 50 percent of all printing workers joined the [October] political strike purely instinctively, feeling that here is truth and justice [*pravda*], but not understanding the connection between politics and economics."[108] The very language and imagery workers often used when they spoke about political emancipation suggests this essential moralism: freedom of speech and the press, for example, were likened to "the sun's rays," which will "dispel the darkness that shrouds the old and rotten state organism."[109]

Activist workers did not merely infuse their struggles with a moral ethos; they often treated collective struggle itself as a moral principle, as is evident in workers' insistence on unity of action. Of course, the practical need to extend and deepen the solidarity of workers during strikes or other collective actions was obvious. But so appears to have been its moral necessity. Voting at mass meetings, especially during 1905,

105. *Pechatnik* 1906, no. 1 (April 23), pp. 8–9. Some of the details of this meeting are taken from *Russkie vedomosti*, October 20, 1905, p. 3; Sher, "Moskovskie pechatniki," pp. 63–64; Sher, *Istoriia*, pp. 185–86.

106. Sher, "Moskovskie pechatniki," p. 55; *Pechatnyi vestnik* 1905, no. 16–17 (October 30), p. 6.

107. For example, TsGAOR, f. 518, op. 1, d. 55, p. 211; *Vserossiiskaia politicheskaia stachka*, pp. 72–73.

108. *Pechatnyi vestnik* 1905, no. 16–17 (October 30), p. 6.

109. A reporter's paraphrase of a speech. *Moskovskaia gazeta*, November 12, 1905, p. 3.

among printers as among other workers, was almost invariably unanimous. In addition to the "coercion of mass enthusiasm"[110] that often produced such unanimity, militant workers also employed more direct means to ensure solidarity. In 1905, as we have seen, crowds of striking workers stoned the windows of non-striking shops and threatened to beat workers who refused to strike. Threatened and actual beatings were used in later years to compel conformity, especially for strikebreakers but also for workers considered to be politically reactionary.[111]

Symbolic moral sanctions were also often used against individuals who refused to conform to collective decisions. A resolution adopted by printing workers in Moscow in early November 1905 warned workers who continued even to work for employers who still submitted to the censorship that they would be subject to "contempt, boycott, and ostracism."[112] In 1906 and 1907, individuals who worked during strikes or agreed to work overtime might be treated to a ceremonial expulsion from the shop in a cart or a trash can.[113] A strikebreaker might also be treated to the mockery of "rough music" (*shumnaia musika*), followed by carting out and then ostracism, known as personal "boycott."[114] To facilitate personal boycott, the names of strikebreakers were published in local union papers.

Such public shaming, found among many Russian workers,[115] was reminiscent of peasant rituals of popular justice in which offenders of community moral norms were led out of the community in carts, verbally and symbolically mocked, and sometimes forced to beg the community's forgiveness.[116] But it also reflected traditions rooted in the history of urban crafts like printing. Among the skilled crafts especially, the print shop had traditionally been a moral community in which a worker was under a strong conformist pressure to be a "comrade." As workers had long been ostracized for refusing to drink with their shop comrades or to join in shop rituals, so were they now expected to conform to a new definition of comradeship. The class community, too, was expected to be a moral community.

110. McDaniel, *Autocracy, Capitalism, and Revolution in Russia*, p. 262.
111. *Kur'er*, June 3, 1906, p. 3; June 9, 1906, pp. 3–4; *Golos truda*, June 27 (July 9), 1906, p. 3.
112. *Vecherniaia pochta*, November 9, 1905, p. 3.
113. *Golos truda*, June 27 (July 9), 1906, p. 4; TsGAOR, f. 6864, op. 1, d. 207, p. 174; TsGAOR, f. 102, 4 d-vo, 1907, d. 42, ch. 2, p. 119.
114. Iuferovyi and Sokolovskii, *Akademicheskaia tipografiia*, p. 96.
115. See McDaniel, *Autocracy, Capitalism, and Revolution*, pp. 262–63.
116. Frank, "Popular Justice, Community, and Culture among the Russian Peasantry," pp. 239–66.

The vocabulary with which workers condemned strikebreaking and other violations of collective discipline further suggests this definition of class as a moral community. Strikebreakers, who betrayed that community and violated its norms, were branded as "demons from hell" (*ischadie ada*), "traitors," "turncoats," "Judases prepared to sell out their comrades for a farthing."[117] The idealized moral community of the working class was even seen to have international reach. In 1907, a year after a former officer of the Petersburg printers' union absconded with the union treasury and fled to America, he was found by the New York branch of the International Typographical Union, which he had joined but whose officers had been warned about his crime. On receiving the news from New York that he had been persuaded to return the money, the journal of the Petersburg printers' union proclaimed that the "proletarian family is so close and united that any who violate its interests will everywhere and anywhere be punished for their crimes, everywhere and anywhere be banished, everywhere and anywhere be boycotted."[118]

In addition to imbuing their struggles with a moral sensibility, workers also often viewed class struggle as having a moral logic. In challenging inequality and exploitation, rarely did workers make use of the abstract and analytical class vocabulary of Marxism, though they were increasingly exposed to it.[119] More commonly, workers used a language of class that was both more concrete and more ethical. Class opponents were typically represented not as "capitalists" definable by their relations to the means of production but as "tyrants" and "bloodsuckers" definable by their moral relations to people.[120] Although workers often accepted the notion of irreconcilable conflict between labor and capital, they viewed it less as a structural conflict of interest between classes than as a moral battle between, to use their own vocabulary, good and evil, light and darkness, honor and insult.[121]

Unlike earlier critical writings in *Naborshchik*, sometimes by the same individuals, the most outspoken workers in 1905 and after tended to view employer tyranny as a collective rather than merely individual sin. Evil was now viewed as embedded in the social structure. However,

117. *Pechatnik* 1906, no. 3 (May 14), p. 7; no. 4 (May 21), p. 4.
118. *Vestnik pechatnikov* 1907, no. 1 (February 2), p. 6.
119. When they did it was often handled awkwardly. In August 1905, for example, a worker wrote in *Pechatnyi vestnik* that "social classes, long existing in conditions of social chaos, are beginning to mobilize and take form. Class consciousness has appeared and as a result there have evolved conceptions of class contradictions." *Pechatnyi vestnik* 1905, no. 8 (August 21), p. 11. For other examples, ibid., p. 3; no. 15 (October 10), p. 11.
120. Ibid. 1905, no. 18 (November 27), p. 6; no. 4 (July 24), p. 5.
121. Ibid. 1905, no. 13 (September 25), p. 1; no. 16–17 (October 30), p. 1.

the legacy of *Naborshchik*'s moral vision and of the larger currents of social and ethical thought that it reflected[122] was plentifully visible. Workers' depiction of the opposition between good and evil was not simply drawing on a convenient metaphor for class conflict. Ethical judgments made class sensible to workers. Morality not only imbued conceptions of the class structure with emotional resonance but also brought with it specific values, principles, and views about the ends of class struggle. And virtually all of these had been heard before in the context of a quite different social argument.

At the heart of workers' language of protest, as in the protests of subordinate groups in many settings, was the notion of the human personality (*lichnost'*), its innate worth, and hence its natural rights. As before 1905, workers continually complained of offenses to their human worth. During the tariff negotiations in St. Petersburg in early 1905 workers chafed at their traditionally passive role as beneficiaries of employer grace. The "system of personal inquiry," as employers called their initial discussions with workers,[123] and the announced "mutual consideration" of the tariff on February 1, which turned out to be only an opportunity for workers to listen to employers announce their final proposal, were felt by many workers to have been insulting.[124] As labor protest accelerated during 1905 and continued into the years following, workers frequently and explicitly articulated the meaning of their struggles as responses to offended dignity. For too long, workers protested, they had been treated as "animals," "machines," and "slaves," verbally abused, physically beaten, and addressed as inferiors.[125] That such "arbitrary authority and compulsion" (*proizvol i nasilie*) should "reign over the human personality" in the "cultured environment" of printing seemed doubly degrading.[126] The time had come, it was repeatedly said, for employers and supervisors "to respect the humanity in each human being" (*chelovek v cheloveke*), to remember that "those who work for them are people, the same if not better than themselves."[127]

122. See Chapter 4.
123. Note from Roman Golike in TsGIA, f. 800, op. 1, d. 427, p. 51.
124. Resolution by workers' deputies in *Naborshchik i pechatnyi mir* 107 (March 10, 1905), pp. 113–14.
125. *Pechatnyi vestnik* 1905, no. 4 (July 24), p. 5; no. 5 (July 31), pp. 8–9; no. 11 (September 11), p. 7; no. 15 (October 10), pp. 5–6; *Naborshchik i pechatnyi mir* 105 (January 19, 1905), p. 4; 107 (March 10, 1905), pp. 103–05; *Vecherniaia pochta*, May 7, 1905, p. 2; *Pechatnik* 1906, no. 4 (May 21), pp. 7–8; no. 5 (May 28), pp. 5–7; no. 7 (July 9), p. 15; no. 8 (July 23), pp. 6–7.
126. *Pechatnyi vestnik* 1905, no. 4 (July 24), p. 5.
127. Ibid. 1905, no. 6 (August 7), pp. 3–4. See also no. 1 (May 15), p. 3; no. 2 (June 12), p. 15; no. 3 (June 23), pp. 21–23; no. 11 (September 11), p. 7.

The editors of *Pechatnyi vestnik* reported in 1905 that they had received many letters from workers complaining of "insult,"[128] and at
least one worker filed a defamation suit against a supervisor for calling him "a scoundrel [*merzavets*] and other things not suitable for
print."[129] Sometimes workers expressed their intolerance of humiliation more directly; for example, compositors at the Iablonskii press in
St. Petersburg dangled their foreman out of a third-story window until
he promised to stop beating apprentices.[130]

Even the most ordinary economic demands were often defined as assertions of human dignity. The very *act* of making economic demands
was said to demonstrate that workers "are people too." Demands such
as higher wages, shorter hours, paid vacations, cleaner lavatories, and
hot water for tea were themselves sometimes said to be "declarations of
our rights—the rights of man," the right to "live as human beings
ought to live."[131] Workers' resistance to employer suggestions that instead of Sunday rest they be given staggered weekly holidays reflected
this logic: "It is impossible to interpret the word rest only as a day free
to eat, drink, and sleep after a week of toil in the printing shop. Such
rest applies only to a pack of animals. A compositor is a human being.
He therefore requires more. Besides entertainment, he needs association
with members of his printing family."[132] Worker militants had nothing
but scorn for workers who reduced the meaning of class struggle to
mere material needs, to "kopeck interests" (*kopeechnye interesy*).[133]

The particular hostility often directed at supervisors and managers
highlights the moral definition of exploitation. Foremen and other supervisors, of course, had an immediate and direct relationship with
workers and thus were logical targets. But precisely because their relationship with workers was more direct than that of most employers, supervisors had more opportunity to be, as workers often said they were,

128. Ibid. 1905, no. 13 (September 25), p. 1.
129. Ibid. 1905, no. 5 (July 31), pp. 8–9.
130. *Kratkii istoricheskii obzor tipografii L.S.P.O.*, p. 15. It may be recalled that in
February 1905 workers at this press dangled a fellow worker out of a *fourth*-story window for supporting political demands at the Shidlovskii Commission. See Chapter 6.
131. *Pechatnyi vestnik* 1905, no. 9 (August 28), pp. 2–4; *Pechatnik* 1906, no. 3 (May
14), p. 13; no. 8 (July 23), pp. 6–7; *Vestnik pechatnikov* 1906, no. 8 (June 11), p. 3. Lenin, writing in 1899, concluded that this was the central emotional element in all strikes.
"O stachkakh," in *Polnoe sobranie sochinenii*, vol. 4, p. 292.
132. *Pechatnyi vestnik* 1905, no. 2 (June 12), p. 15.
133. Ibid. 1906, no. 1 (February 12), pp. 10–11; no. 2 (February 19), pp. 2–3. See
also *Istoriia leningradskogo soiuza*, pp. 247–49. In 1917 this complaint was still heard,
though inflation had increased its terms; now workers were said to view the class struggle
largely as a means of getting "big bucks" (*bol'shie rubli*). *Pechatnik* 1917, no. 2–3 (August 6), p. 6.

"rude," "cruel," and "despotic."[134] And since supervisors were usually former workers, it was felt to be doubly offensive that they should "comfortably enjoy themselves at the expense of the workers' blood, squeezing the last drops from their former comrades."[135] Thus, workers protested when supervisors beat workers or apprentices, when they fired a worker unjustly, when they made sexual advances toward women workers, and generally when they were "rude and insulting" in their language or behavior.[136]

The manner in which workers sought to redress these wrongs also suggests the moral logic that defined them. Although workers might simply insist that a supervisor be fired, their actions often included an element of moral punishment. Workers brought offending supervisors before union "courts of honor" (*sudy chesti*) or made them apologize before assemblies of workers.[137] Like the bindery master in 1906 who insulted unemployed workers by calling them "lazy," offending supervisors might be named in the press so that they would "not be taken by mistake for honest comrades."[138] Especially when printing workers other than compositors were involved, a supervisor might be treated to a "triumphal procession" out of the shop in a wheelbarrow or trash can,[139] or, as in 1906 when workers at the Office for the Manufacture of Government Paper decided to "thank" a guard for his public suggestion that troublesome workers ought to be shot, he might be shamed with "rough music": when the guard's shift ended, workers showered him with cucumbers, pirogi, buttered bread, and cutlets. Workers mockingly called this "dining with him."[140] As when directed at other workers, public apologies, judgment by a workers' court of honor, and shaming humor of this kind echoed village traditions of enforcing moral norms. However, although such acts of moral censure and punishment were sometimes, as in the peasant rituals they resembled, the prelude to reintegration, when directed at supervisors they

134. *Pechatnyi vestnik* 1905, no. 3 (June 23), p. 25; no. 5 (July 31), p. 8; no. 7 (August 14), pp. 9–10; no. 8 (August 21), pp. 9–10; no. 9 (August 28), pp. 3–5; no. 12 (September 18), p. 6; no. 15 (October 10), pp. 5–6.

135. Ibid. 1905, no. 5 (July 31), pp. 2–3.

136. In addition to examples from 1905 in the preceding notes, see *Pechatnik* 1906, no. 3 (May 14), p. 15; no. 7 (July 9), pp. 15–16; *Kur'er*, May 21 (June 3), 1906, p. 5; TsGAOR, f. 6864, d. 102, pp. 29, 40 (1913); Saf'ian and Marvits, *Ordenonosnyi "Pechatnyi dvor,"* pp. 13–14.

137. *Kur'er*, May 21 (June 3), 1906, p. 5.

138. *Vestnik pechatnikov* 1906, no. 1 (April 21), p. 8.

139. *Pechatnik* 1906, no. 3 (May 14), p. 16; TsGAOR, f. 6864, op. 1, d. 207, p. 123 (1906).

140. *Golos truda,* June 24 (July 7), 1906, p. 4.

were more often acts of permanent expulsion. When supervisors were carted out they were usually considered to have been fired by the workers (though employers often refused to recognize "such out-rageous compulsion").[141]

The ethical humanism that underlay these actions and words, the notions of offended dignity and violated natural rights, gave great emo-tional and moral force to workers' protests, as it has to the protests of subordinate groups in many settings. But this morality also reflected workers' ambiguous purposes. As in other movements of political or social rebellion, the argument that men are born equal and thus possess certain inalienable rights may express a challenge to the injustice of the status quo but also a demand for recognition and inclusion. The same moral logic that led workers to condemn social inequality—"the situ-ation that exists today," as the compositor Stepan Tsorn described it, "where one person has everything and another nothing, where one has bread and butter, a soft chair and an office, wine and women, while another has only that everlasting piece of stale bread"[142]—also led workers to seek "honor," "kindness," and "brotherhood."[143] That "hot water for tea" and Sunday rest could be seen as "rights of man" founded upon the human worth of the individual made even the most ordinary economic demands a radical challenge to inequality, but also suggested the plain and tangible terms in which workers' human rights might be realized.

Workers' vocabulary of protest in 1905 and 1906 was often the lan-guage of democratic revolution. Workers spoke of seeking "human rights" (*chelovechnye prava*), of the "inalienable rights of man and of the citizen" (*neot"emlemye prava cheloveka-grazhdanina*), and even of "liberty, equality, and fraternity."[144] When police threatened to break up a mass meeting of printing workers in Moscow in November unless they were allowed to attend as observers, it was decided after a long de-bate to let the police remain so that they might, in the words of one of the speakers, "become used to the speech of free Russian citizens."[145] A symbol of workers' civic subordination and humiliation—the required presence of police at meetings—had been made into its opposite, into a

141. TsGAOR, f. 6864, op. 1, d. 207, p. 123 (Bulletin of the Moscow employers' union, 1906).

142. *Pechatnyi vestnik* 1905, no. 5 (July 31), p. 3.

143. Ibid. 1905, no. 13 (September 25), p. 1.

144. For example, ibid. 1905, no. 9 (August 28), p. 8; no. 11 (September 11), pp. 3–4; no. 18 (November 27), p. 5; *Pechatnik* 1906, no. 8 (July 23), pp. 6–7; *Vestnik pechat-nikov* 1906, no. 3 (May 9), p. 4.

145. *Novaia zhizn'* 1905, no. 7 (November 7), p. 5.

symbol of workers' dignity and rights. This was to be, as it were, a civic and moral lesson for the police. Equally significant, mass meetings were often held in social spaces previously off-limits—the university, the conservatory, theaters—and thus themselves symbolized workers' challenge to their civic and social exclusion and subordination.

Like the language of democracy and citizenship generally, however, the language of rights in use in Russia in 1905 and after encouraged workers to think of themselves as part of a human rather than simply a class community. The ethical notion behind this rhetoric of rights, that all human beings possess a natural and equal worth, implied an identity that transcended class. Perhaps with this unifying message in mind, some employers and managers themselves sometimes embraced the ideal of workers' "human rights." At a gathering of owners and managers in St. Petersburg during the spring of 1905, in honor of the career anniversary of Ivan Galaktionov, a manager who had risen from the ranks, officials from the Compositors' Assistance Fund expressed their hope "that in the future the flames of unselfish love in defense of the human rights of printing workers will shine even more brightly among us."[146] As late as December, the leader of the Petersburg press-owners union, Roman Golike, expressed his sympathy for workers as they "fight for their rights."[147] Of course, in the view of most employers and managers, workers' rights had to be understood in the proper way. As Andrei Filippov and others associated with *Naborshchik* stated most clearly, the recognition of the "natural and inalienable rights of man and citizen," of the rights of liberty and equality, must be linked to the moral "fraternity" of employers and workers.[148]

As before 1905, the ambiguous logic of workers' claims to be treated as human beings may be seen in their struggles for culture. The problems of "drunkenness and other unseemly behavior," some workers felt, ought to be the most important concern of trade unions.[149] In their view, the main goal of labor organization ought to be to promote among workers "sobriety, industry [*trudoliubie*], thrift, and the thirst for knowledge."[150] But even activists who insisted on more militant

146. *Naborshchik i pechatnyi mir* 107 (March 10, 1905), p. 141.
147. LGIA, f. 1513, op. 1, d. 12, p. 8 (a printed message to his workers, dated December 10, 1905).
148. *Naborshchik i pechatnyi mir* 114 (October 10, 1905) (published after October 17), pp. 435–37.
149. *Pechatnyi vestnik* 1905, no. 12 (September 18), pp. 3–4.
150. Ibid. 1905, no. 9 (August 25), p. 7. Recall that in 1903 the underground Moscow printers' union had declared its motto to be "in unity—strength, in thrift—independence."

purpose still considered it essential to "aid the intellectual, professional, and moral development of printing workers," and planned to
this end to establish "libraries, reading rooms, public lectures, excursions, readings, courses, and talks."[151] Ivan Liubimtsev, the compositor
and Social Democrat who helped to organize the St. Petersburg printers' union, explained the importance of cultural activities: "It was
proven long ago that the more educated a person is, the more intellec-
tually developed he is, the more knowledge that he commands, the easier and more fruitful will be his struggle with the conditions around
him. . . . Therefore, the statement 'in knowledge is power' must have a
place among the main goals of the union."[152] But "knowledge" was
seen not only to have instrumental value in workers' class struggle.
Some activists saw the class struggle itself as necessary precisely to enable workers to buy books and attend lectures, join educational circles
and clubs, and send their children to school.[153]

Efforts to improve workers' "intellectual and moral" level remained
central to the definition of purpose among activist printing workers after 1905 as well. Trade unions invariably included cultural improvement in their programs and pursued it in practice by organizing lectures, libraries, reading rooms, classes, readings, and excursions.[154] In
the trade union press and at meetings workers repeatedly insisted on the
need for more "culture," "knowledge," and "personal development."[155]
Elected shop representatives were told by union leaders that they were

151. The programs of the St. Petersburg and Moscow unions were virtually identical
on these points. *Pechatnyi vestnik* 1905, no. 15 (October 10), p. 7; *Vecherniaia pochta*,
October 30, 1905, pp. 3–4. Similar statements were also made in the first draft of the St.
Petersburg charter and in the draft proposed by the Menshevik faction of the Social-
Democratic party. *Naborshchik i pechatnyi mir* 109 (May 10, 1905), p. 204; Strelskii
[Lavrov], *Samoorganizatsiia rabochogo klassa*, pp. 165, 169. In Moscow, the same concerns were expressed by the underground union in January and the legal union that the
Typographers' Fund tried to organize in June. Simonenko and Kostomarov, *Iz istorii
revoliutsii 1905 goda v Moskve*, pp. 142–44; *Vecherniaia pochta*, July 15, 1905, p. 3.
152. *Naborshchik i pechatnyi mir* 109 (May 10, 1905), p. 203. See also *Pechatnyi
vestnik* 1905, no. 1 (May 15), p. 1, and no. 4 (July 24), p. 1.
153. *Pechatnyi vestnik* 1905, no. 2 (June 12), p. 13.
154. For statements of purpose in charters: *Pechatnik* 1906, no. 4 (May 21), p. 8
(Moscow, 1906); LGIA, f. 287, op. 1, d. 43, pp. 36–37, 147, 157 (St. Petersburg, 1907
and 1910, though this point was ordered removed by the government registration board
before approval in 1910). For accounts of union activities: *Istoriia leningradskogo soiuza*,
pp. 251, 304, 376; *Vestnik pechatnikov* 1906, no. 1 (April 21), p. 7; TsGAOR, f. 518,
op. 1, d. 85a, p. 282 (Moscow union library, 1907); TsGIAgM, f. 2069, op. 1, d. 4, p. 14
(arrangements with People's University in Moscow).
155. *Pechatnyi vestnik* 1906, no. 2 (February 19), pp. 2–3; *Pechatnik* 1906, no. 8
(July 23), p. 16; TsGIAgM, f. 2069, op. 1, d. 4, p. 14 (protocol of delegates' meetings of
Moscow union, January 1907); *Protokoly pervoi vserossiiskoi konferentsii*, pp. 102,
108–10 (1907 conference).

responsible, as "conscious workers," not simply to collect union dues or even just to enforce autonomy regulations, but to bring less conscious workers "out of the mire of ignorance" by distributing among them "useful books, journals, and newspapers" and setting up lectures and excursions.[156]

Although these workers and union activists saw knowledge and culture as a means of strengthening the labor movement, this pursuit did not in itself represent a challenge to existing standards. When the Petersburg printers' union effectively took control of the older Typographers' Music and Drama Circle in 1907, by creating a workers' majority among members and then reelecting the officers, the new leaders of the circle made a point of sponsoring not "stupid vaudevilles" but plays by Ostrovskii, readings of Chekhov and Shakespeare (*Julius Caesar*), and lectures on writers such as Pushkin, Gogol, Griboedov, Nekrasov, and Belinskii.[157] Union leaders in Moscow in 1907 spoke of the importance of "dance evenings."[158] And union libraries stocked and workers checked out mainly belles lettres and a smaller number of books on history, economics, and socialism.[159]

Cultural improvement was closely connected to raising workers' "moral level." As a matter of principle, activist workers challenged the drunkenness, indiscipline, and crude manners that were widespread in workers' everyday lives. In efforts to extend workers' control at the workplace, especially as these were conceived by worker leaders, there was a virtual obsession with sobriety and self-discipline. Strict norms for workplace discipline were established, for example, in the supplementary "Guide" for deputies that the Moscow printers' union attached to its Statute on Factory Deputies in 1905. Deputies were to make certain that workers arrived at work on time, were sober, and generally did not "disturb the proper conduct of work." Violators were to be expelled from the shop, and if they refused to leave, a general meeting of all the workers was to decide whether the accused should be permanently dismissed.[160] Similarly, in St. Petersburg autonomy commissions assessed fines against workers found to be intoxicated or otherwise in violation of shop discipline.[161]

156. *Pechatnik* 1906, no. 8 (July 23), p. 14; *Protokoly pervoi vserossiiskoi konferentsii*, p. 11.
157. *Istoriia leningradskogo soiuza*, p. 376.
158. *Protokoly pervoi vserossiiskoi konferentsii*, p. 109.
159. TsGAOR, f. 518, op. 1, d. 85a, p. 282.
160. Sher, *Istoriia*, pp. 206–07.
161. *Vestnik pechatnikov* 1906, no. 1 (April 21), p. 8.

In the following years, as we have observed, workplace rules drafted by workers in individual shops or proposed by the unions in tariff negotiations almost always included prohibitions of coarse or "impolite" language, fighting, singing, playing games, and drinking during working hours, requirements that workers arrive and leave work at the designated time, and provisions allowing absence only with "good reason." Often, workers acted directly to punish workers guilty of drunkenness or moral indiscipline with public shaming, fines, or expulsions from the shop.[162] Such a guarantee of discipline was partly a practical concession to employers, but it was also part of the moral definition by "conscious" workers of what it meant to be a citizen and a human being.

In pursuit of this ideal, many of the everyday habits of workers' lives came under attack. Drunkenness remained the main target, but there were others. The frequently foul language that workers often used was challenged in a campaign that was especially widespread among printing workers in St. Petersburg in 1906 and 1907. As one essayist in the union paper complained in 1907,

> It is well known to us all that the atmosphere of the printing shop from morning until evening is filled with the most "exemplary" swearing. After holidays every comrade considers it his "moral" duty to relate to the others his "holiday adventures," calling things by their proper names without any embarrassment in the presence of women or apprentices. . . . There are songs (mainly of the same content). They think up various games. There are fights, etc.[163]

In the view of many worker activists, swearing and obscene language, like drunkenness, degraded workers' "dignity," corrupted their "morality," and encouraged their "base instincts."[164]

Following the same logic, male workers were challenged to alter the customary ways they treated women. Although the practical need for solidarity with the increasing number of women working in the industry was the main reason offered in appeals, which began to appear in 1906, to show more concern for the condition of female printers, there was also said to be a moral issue at stake. Using the familiar discourse of labor protest, men were told that women "are people too," whose own "honor and human dignity" must be recognized and defended. This meant, of course, that male workers should defend women work-

162. *Pechatnik* 1906, no. 3 (May 14), p. 14; no. 6 (June 4), p. 16; no. 7 (July 9), p. 15; *Knizhnyi vestnik* 1907, no. 41 (October 14), p. 1274; TsGAOR, f. 518, op. 1, d. 85a, pp. 142–43; *Istoriia leningradskogo soiuza*, p. 279.
163. *Zhizn' pechatnika* 1907, no. 8 (July 20), p. 12.
164. *Istoriia leningradskogo soiuza*, p. 279.

ers against employers and managers. But working men were also advised that they themselves must treat women with more respect. That male workers treated women workers coarsely—calling them "prostitutes" even in their presence—and treated their wives as "slaves" was not considered fitting for a conscious worker.[165]

Worker militants sought a cultural revolution in the everyday behavior of workers and tried to practice these standards themselves. Observers of a union meeting attended by approximately five thousand printing workers in Moscow in 1906 noted the remarkable "order" and "discipline" of the participants; when two drunken workers appeared, they were "quietly escorted" outside.[166] Likewise, a metalworker who attended meetings of printers in Moscow in 1906–07 observed that they "were pervaded with such seriousness and respectability [*polozhitel'-nost' i solidnost'*], that it seemed as if you were attending some sort of *zemstvo* assembly and not a workers' meeting."[167] On the other hand, there were complaints in St. Petersburg that "many" elected shop delegates would show up at delegate council meetings "in an unsober state," and in their own shops actively join in with their workmates in the usual "disgraces" (*bezobrazie*) of shop life.[168] The actual extent of moral order and discipline among printing workers likely remained small after 1905 as before. But these everyday practices of workers' lives had become increasingly offensive to "conscious" activists.

In these efforts to assert the human worth and rights of workers, the mixture of a class view of society and of notions of universal standards was complex. On the one hand, efforts to improve workers' culture and morality suggested conformity to the norms of the society around them. Sometimes workers even directly maintained the need to conform to what might be seen as bourgeois values. As one worker argued in 1907, capitalists are right to respond to "our heartfelt proletarian cry, 'Allow us to live like human beings,' [with] the malicious and laconic reply: 'Then spend less time contemplating the green signboard [of the state liquor monopoly].' "[169] If workers wished to be treated as human beings, these worker critics suggested, they must learn to act as such.

---

165. *Zhizn' pechatnika* 1907, no. 8 (July 20), p. 12; *Vestnik pechatnikov* 1906, no. 5 (May 20), p. 3; no. 6 (May 28), pp. 2–3; no. 12 (July 15), p. 3; *Pechatnik* 1906, no. 7 (July 9), p. 10; TsGIAgM, f. 2069, op. 1, d. 2, p. 26 (January 1907 general meeting of compositors in Moscow); *Istoriia leningradskogo soiuza*, p. 279.

166. *Pechatnik* 1906, no. 4 (May 21), p. 4.

167. Matveev, "Moskovskii soiuz rabochikh-metallistov v 1906–07 gg.," p. 251.

168. *Zhizn' pechatnika* 1907, no. 8 (July 20), p. 12.

169. *Pechatnoe delo* 15 (February 9, 1907), p. 7.

However, workers also often interpreted these moral standards from a particularistic class perspective. The corrupting influence of bourgeois society was blamed for the moral degradation of workers. Only "bourgeois morality" was said to tolerate the indignities suffered by women workers.[170] Swearing was said to have been "born out of lack of respect for the human personality, which only exists under the bourgeois order."[171] In general, "drunkenness, ignorance, and darkness" were viewed as the heritage of the oppressive political and social conditions.[172] And, of course, worker activists insisted that moral improvement facilitated their collective struggles.

Some labor leaders, especially socialist intellectuals, worried that workers were paying too much attention to cultural and moral improvement. Vasilii Sher, one of the leading party intellectuals active among Moscow printers, warned at the national printers' conference in 1907 that "one strike means twice as much for the development of class consciousness as a dozen dance parties."[173] But most activist workers saw no contradiction between, as it were, strikes and dances. In part, the perceived connection was utilitarian. Cultural and moral backwardness was seen to hinder the class struggle by making workers "passive," "apathetic," "undisciplined," "lacking in hope," and unable to "stand up for their interests." Drunkenness, in particular, was said to distract workers from the social and political movement, "obscure class consciousness," and generally "delight our enemies."[174] But culture and morality were also seen as having intrinsic worth. The purpose of collective struggle itself was said to be to provide workers with the time and money to afford a more cultured life.[175]

At issue was workers' right, as it was often said, to "live as human beings" (zhit' po-chelovecheski). But this remained an ambiguous claim. Workers' identity as human beings implied the common identity of all, the definition of self as rooted in a common humanity rather than in the variability of social place. At the same time, the very universalism of the notion of the dignity and rights of the human person paradoxically

170. Vestnik pechatnikov 1906, no. 8 (June 11), p. 3.
171. Istoriia leningradskogo soiuza, p. 279.
172. Pechatnoe delo 15 (February 9, 1907), p. 7. See also Pechatnik 1917, no. 2–3 (August 6), pp. 5–6.
173. Protokoly pervoi vserossiiskoi konferentsii, p. 110.
174. Pechatnik 1906, no. 1 (April 23), pp. 11–12; Pechatnoe delo 15 (February 9, 1907), p. 7; Protokoly pervoi vserossiiskoi konferentsii, pp. 80, 82, 109. For almost identical examples from 1917, see Pechatnoe delo 1917, no. 2 (June 4), p. 8; no. 3 (June 17), p. 7; Pechatnik 1917, no. 2–3 (August 6), pp. 5–7, 15; no. 6 (October 28), p. 8.
175. Pechatnyi vestnik 1906, no. 2 (February 19), pp. 2–3.

helped workers to identify their own particularistic identity as a class. Recognition of the worth of all people encouraged workers to identify themselves as an oppressed class, to become conscious of their common suffering, of their common humiliation and subordination. As in other movements of democratic political or social protest, the principle that people are born equal and thus possess certain inalienable rights implies simultaneously a subversive challenge to inequality and an appeal for civic and social inclusion into a larger human community.[176] Even the language of class struggle betrayed workers' ambivalent identity and purpose.

176. See the discussions of the dualistic logic of lower-class struggles for citizenship in Marshall, "Citizenship and Social Class" (1950), in his *Class, Citizenship, and Social Development,* esp. pp. 84–85; Bendix, *Nation-Building and Citizenship,* pp. 89–126. On the dualistic implications of the workers' democratic claims in Russia, see Bonnell, *Roots of Rebellion,* pp. 2–3, 190–91, 446–50; McDaniel, *Autocracy, Capitalism, and Revolution,* pp. 351–58; Surh, *1905 in St. Petersburg,* pp. 407–11; Zelnik, "Passivity and Protest in Germany and Russia," p. 497.

Conclusion

The challenge to the moral authority of capitalism had a long genealogy in Russia. Literary representations of the entrepreneur, from Ostrovskii to Chekhov, encouraged public distaste for the materialism and egoism of business. Even before Russian industrialization was fully under way, intellectuals of both left and right viewed with revulsion the greed and vulgarity of the European bourgeoisie and the amorality of an economy determined by individualistic competition in the marketplace. Even the economic and social policies of the Russian state were predicated to some extent on a desire to avoid the social and moral disorder of unbridled capitalism. That there should be, in Marx's words, "no other nexus between man and man than naked self-interest" was viewed by many Russians as both dangerous to the public order and an affront to morality. The fact that many entrepreneurs were from foreign backgrounds added to the perception that they represented something alien.

As producers of cultural commodities, printing employers were better situated than other entrepreneurs to assert their morality and worth, and more inclined to do so. Some employers vigorously defended their virtue with an alternative ethic that redefined social morality as devotion to one's calling, tireless labor, and individual success. More often, however, employers preferred to represent their authority as reflecting more familiar values. The most outspoken group of employers, which included most of the owners or directors of the largest printing enterprises, actually joined their critics in condemning "capitalists" and "exploiters" while insisting that they themselves were benevolent "fathers" to their workers. Distancing themselves from the image of the egoistic capitalist, they promoted a paternalistic and corporative model of social relations that envisioned workers and employers united by bonds of sympathy and by the acceptance of common values and rules.

This was a conservative ideal, though more imaginative than traditional, for there was no existing corporative tradition in Russian industry to preserve or restore. Like the patriarchal family on which it was modeled, the notion of a "family" of workers and employers was meant to strengthen, not undermine, hierarchy, dependence, and authority. Employers who evoked it sought not to efface differences in power and position in speaking of a moral community of masters and men but to reveal the necessity and legitimacy of these differences. They also sought to reassure *themselves* that their authority was held by moral right. Their logic was seamless: nakedly exploitative class relations were wrong because they were hazardous, and hazardous because they were wrong. They, therefore, practiced charity, made genuine efforts to improve workplace conditions, and constructed a network of trade institutions to unite workers and employers. And since their ideal assumed a consensus of norms and rules, their efforts were necessarily verbal and demonstrative as much as constructive. This entailed risks, however, for proclaimed notions of community and morality were flexible enough to be contestable. It was not difficult for workers to put to their own uses employers' critique of egoistic profiteering or to appropriate their professed ideals of social morality.

Workers resisted employers' authority in numerous routine and everyday ways, even when the surface of social relations remained calm. In the free and stolen moments during the workday and in the few waking hours each day when workers' time was their own, printing workers, especially compositors and other skilled craftsmen, created the rudiments of a separate community among themselves. Frequent and often ritualized drinking, fitful work rhythms, mobility between jobs, and an often playful coarseness and profanity in their speech and manner brought workers together in informal ways but also defied employers' efforts to define and control workers' behavior. In ways as tenacious as they were ordinary, workers challenged their own domination.

A different challenge to authority was offered by workers who in varying degrees stood apart from this ordinary working-class culture, who sought a more "cultured" and "conscious" way of life. Paradoxically, before 1905, many of these workers shared employers' dream of a community in which masters and men were united in mutual assistance and in the common pursuit of shared values. But this proved to be a fragile consensus. Although many workers joined employers in admiring benevolent authority and disparaging greed, and believed in the possibility of a shared community of values, they understood and applied these common ideas in different ways. Where employers saw a means to enhance their personal and social honor before society and their moral authority at the workplace, workers saw a way to improve their material conditions and assert their worth as individuals. Where employers emphasized their own role as benevolent but powerful fathers, workers envisioned a more fraternal relationship. While employers organized charity and collaborative rituals, workers tended to seek morality in more practical things, such as good wages and shorter hours. Most important, whereas employers viewed the benevolence of authority as the expression of virtuous will, workers were much more likely to treat it as a moral obligation, deriving from a recognition of the natural dignity and equality of every person.

This worker critique remained ambivalent, however. It was directed as much against other workers as against employers. Although some workers simply withdrew into a kind of internal exile to spend their leisure time in "useful" and uplifting ways rather than in the "boozing and scandals" that they said preoccupied most of their fellow workers, many others constantly preached the virtues of moral discipline and cultural self-improvement and disparaged workers who ignored or resisted their standards. For this moral vanguard, violations of the workers' dignity represented a personal failing of the workers themselves as much as an effect of their oppression.

Moreover, although they acknowledged the existence of exploitation, avarice, and cruelty, and recognized these as contradicting the ideal of the moral community, they viewed these as the sins of individuals rather than the structurally determined practices of an entire social class. These worker critics exposed greed and oppression in order to awaken employers to their moral responsibilities not to overturn the social order.

By the end of 1905, however, even in St. Petersburg where the practices and rhetoric of moral community were most deeply rooted and persistent, the structure and psychology of social relations in the printing industry had undergone a dramatic transformation. The pursuit of class interest and power, previously only implied in the differing ways workers and employers defined morality and community, became more direct and aggressive. Henceforth, class identity and interests would explicitly shape the structure of social relations in the industry, as workers and employers parted into their separate organizations and confronted each other with growing suspicion and hostility.

Like other idioms, however, class acquired different meanings as individuals and groups adapted it to their needs and desires, producing often eclectic and ambiguous results. Just as notions of community had been malleable enough to allow workers and employers to use them to promote their own interests and even to challenge one another, so was the language of class flexible enough to encompass values of social community and morality. The leaders of the class organizations of printing workers and employers in 1905 through 1907, a number of whom had previously been active in organizations of trade community, continued to voice familiar ideals of regulation, normalization, and common purpose and to pursue these aims in practice, even as they defended their material interests and authority.

Most important, ideas and actions continued to be represented in ethical terms. Many employers continued to describe their authority as sentimental and moral, to insist that material interest and gain were not their only goals, and to define their own interests as inseparable from "just and humane" relations with workers. And as before there was no simple separation in employers' motives between calculated masking of domination and inequality—what radical workers described as employers "dressing up in sheep's clothing"—and their own personal need to feel themselves to be just and honorable men.

Even workers who considered themselves class-conscious socialists imbued their views of both class and politics with a moral sensibility and logic. Reflecting a faith in the righteousness of their cause, such workers spoke of their struggles as "sacred" and "just," as a battle of "honor" against "evil." Although many workers formally embraced Marxism, the most rationalistic and scientistic of socialist ideologies, the politics and social vision of most activist printing workers in these years remained essentially moral and even utopian. Like the socialist workers in nineteenth-century France and England about whom Friedrich Engels had complained, these Russian printers viewed socialism as "the expression of absolute truth, reason and justice, [which] has only to be discovered to conquer all the world by virtue of its own power."[1] Mobilized workers expressed this moral faith in their insis-

1. See Engels, "Socialism: Utopian and Scientific," in *The Marx-Engels Reader,* p. 693.

tence on a solidarity that was often coercive, expressed by the beating of strikebreakers, the ostracism of workers who violated collective norms, and the pressure for unanimity in voting. Beyond the practical necessity for class unity, the idea of a united class was conceived by many as a type of moral community.

Workers' emerging class culture also contained specific ethical principles and values. As in past years, printing workers voiced their outrage at being treated like "animals," "machines," and "slaves" and insisted on their "honor" and "dignity" and their "rights" to live "as human beings." This discovery of self, of a nature made for more than labor and poverty, was encouraged by the distinctiveness of printing workers, especially of type compositors. Everyday labor amidst letters and words did not make every compositor a philosopher, but it encouraged printers to think of themselves as distinguished by their cultured labor and thus to feel more offended by the real conditions of their lives. Like others at the margins, printers stood more closely to the boundaries that divided people into classes and thus felt their exclusion more sharply. Both class militance and dreams of community reflected this perception.

But the uniqueness of printers should not be overstated. Even many compositors remained, as their more "conscious" fellows saw them, in intellectual and moral darkness. And many workers besides printers spoke of human worth and natural rights. One observer of working-class life in Russia, Lev Kleinbort, described workers' constant insistence on their dignity, honor, and rights as a "cult of the human personality" (*kul't lichnosti* or *kul't cheloveka*).[2] Its sources were varied. Becoming skilled, we know from many studies, often led workers to feel a sense of personal and group pride that made everyday hardships offensive and encouraged thoughts about human nature and worth. As has been said of privileged radicals of an earlier time, workers "generalized from a sense of their own dignity to the ideal of the dignity of all men."[3] Workers also discovered their offended dignity in experiences outside of daily work—in witnessing social inequality and meanness, but also in reflecting on the ideas and images produced by literate

2. Kleinbort, "Ocherki rabochei demokratii," part 1 (March 1913), pp. 24–25, and part 5 (November 1913), pp. 178–85 (esp. pp. 182, 185). The notion of a modern "cult of the personality" was an important idea in the work of Emile Durkheim, though Kleinbort does not mention him directly. See Durkheim's 1898 essay, "L'Individualisme et les intellectuels," pp. 19–30, esp. p. 24; and *Emile Durkheim: Selected Writings*, ed. Giddens, p. 23.

3. Malia, *Alexander Herzen and the Birth of Russian Socialism*, p. 421.

society. Workers' humanism often echoed the discourse of the educated—the propaganda of populists and socialists, religious teachings,
essays in the legal press, novels, stories, and verse. Of course, we expect
to find workers like compositors reading books and journals; but weav-
ers, machinists, bakers, and others also read and were read to.

The humanistic class consciousness these workers articulated remained an ambiguous ethic. Recognition of the natural worth of each
person led workers, in Russia as elsewhere, to define their own identity
as a separate class but also as part of universal humanity. The simple
awareness that "workers are people too" encouraged workers to per-
ceive more sharply their own shared suffering and oppression, their
common fate as excluded and insulted members of a human community. Workers generalized in reverse, as it were, from the dignity of all
men to their own particular humiliation. At the same time, notions of
the intrinsic and equal worth of the human personality implied a view
of self that transcended class.

The intersection of universal and particularistic sources of value and
identity colored the behavior and mutual relations of both workers and
employers with a persistent ambiguity. Employers continued to speak of
love and justice for workers while defending their own power and profits. Workers articulated a socially embracing ideal of human worth and
rights side by side with exclusionary assertions of class identity and interest. Employers and workers both fought to extend their own authority and control at the workplace while seeking to normalize workplace
conflicts through conciliation, bargaining, and collective contract.

These were not conflicting choices, nor stages of consciousness, nor
mere "ethical embellishments" of social egoism,[4] but a mixture of considerations of both morality and power, of humanism and class struggle, that would not easily be untangled. In the minds of some workers,
certainly, Marxism had resolved the contradiction by defining the
unique historical mission of the working class as the achievement
through class struggle of the end of class divisions in society and hence
the achievement of universal emancipation. But this dialectical and historical solution could not erase the practical contradiction of fighting
as a class in the name of a "really human morality which stands above
class antagonisms."[5] This ambiguity would remain even in the midst of
social revolution. In the middle of 1917, Lenin explained the readiness
of Russian workers to demolish capitalism as an expression mainly of

4. Michels, *Political Parties*, pp. 52–60.
5. Engels, *Anti-Dühring* (1878), p. 88.

"instinct, emotion, and attraction."[6] It may also have been at this essential level that workers saw no contradiction between seeking to live in a more comradely and moral society and fighting bitterly against the social classes and individuals responsible for their exclusion and humiliation.

6. Lenin, "O tverdoi revoliutsionnoi vlasti" (May 6, 1917), *Polnoe sobranie sochinenii,* vol. 32, p. 32.

Appendix: Employer Activists, 1880–1904

St. Petersburg, 1880–1904

	Assistance Funds	Printing School	First Congress	Printing Society	Enterprise Paternalism
Arngold, Ernest [Arngol'd E. E.] 31 workers Baltic-born		X	X	X	
Böhnke, Alexander [Benke, A. E.] 86 Prussian-born	X	X	X	X	
Caspary, Alvin [Kaspari, A. A.] 116 German-speaking	X	X	X	X	
Demakov, V. F. 28		X		X	
Dobrodeev, S. E. [250]	X	X			
Dressen, V. F. [80]	X	X	X	X	
Erlikh, Iu. N. 46			X	X	
Evdokimov, E. A. 160 Noble		X	X	X	

Gavrilov, A. V. / Synod press / 186 / Noble		X		X
Goldberg, Isidor / [Gol'dberg, I. A.] / [150] / Prussian-born		X	X	
Golenishchev, S. P. / E. Tile press / 120		X		
Golike, Roman R. / 176 / Father Baltic-born	X	X	X	
Golitsyn, B. B. / Office for the Manufacture / of Government Paper / 3600 (1700 printers) / Prince			X	
Hartmann, Teodor / [Gartmann, F. A.] / Lehmann typefoundry / 268 / German-born	X	X		
Hoppe, Eduard / [Goppe, E. D.] / [170] / Prussian subject		X		
Il'in, A. A. / 144 / Noble		X		X

Continued on next page

St. Petersburg, 1880–1904—*Continued*

	Assistance Funds	Printing School	First Congress	Printing Society	Enterprise Paternalism
Kirshbaum, V. F. 222 Noble	X	X		X	X
Komarov, Vissarion 78 Noble		X	X		
Lehmann, Josef [Leman, I. I.] 268 (typefoundry) Grandfather Prussian	X	X	X	X	
Mark, Franz 12 (typefoundry)	X	X			
Markevich, V. I. State press 500 Noble				X	X
Marx, Adolf [Marks, A. F.] 617 Prussian-born		X		X	
Mikhailov, P. A. Lehmann typefoundry 268	X	X	X	X	

	Col 1	Col 2	Col 3	Col 4	Col 5
Nedel'kovich, S. I. Naval press 100 Noble	X	X	X	X	
Propper, S. M. 134		X		X	
Austrian subject Schröder, Heinrich [Shreder, G. F.] [100] Prussian subject	X	X		X	
Shcherbakov, N. I.	X			X	
Suvorin, A. S. (typefoundry) 440	X		X	X	X
Father noble Trenke, A. G. 95 Probably Swiss		X		X	
Vishniakov, V. I. Obshchestvennaia pol'za 138	X	X	X		
Wilborg, Artur [Vil'borg, A. I.] 95	X	X	X	X	

Continued on next page

Moscow, 1880–1903—*Continued*

	Assistance Funds	Graphic Circle	First Congress	Printing Society	Enterprise Paternalism
Borovik, V. F. Kushnerev press 540	X			X	
Chuksin, I. G. 51	X			X	
Grosman, N. I. Owner, 1900+ 40	X		X	X	
Herbeck, Otto [Gerbek, O. O.] 29 Bavarian-born, Prussian subject	X	X		X	
Iakovlev, S. P. 342 Noble	X		X		
Jürgensohn, Peter and son Boris [Iurgenson] 93 Peter from Baltic		X	X	X	
Kushnerev, I. N. (d. 1896) 500 Father noble	X	X			X

Name		1	2	3	4	5
Levenson, A. A. 497 Noble		X	X	X		
Mamontov, M. A. 208		X	X			X
Romahn, Julius [Roman, Iu. I.]					X	X
Sytin, I. D. 741 (at 2 plants)		X	X	X	X	X
Vasil'ev, A. V. Owner, 1898+ 201			X		X	X

SOURCES Card file on employer activists compiled largely from publications by associations and individual enterprises, reports in the professional press, and government lists of enterprises published at the turn of the century. Major sources include Grents and Galaktionov, *Obzor*, pp. 3–25; *Otchet dvadtsatipiatiletnei VKN*, pp. 9–41; *Piatidesiatiletie sushchestvovaniia Vspomogatel'noi kassy dlia tipografov; Sbornik svedenii VKT; Obzor graficheskikh iskusstv* 1881, no. 3 (February 1), p. 23; *Pervaia russkaia shkola*, 1884–1894, p. 22; *Trudy pervogo s"ezda*, pp. 1–3; *Otchet soveta RODPD; RODPD-MO, Kratkii otchet o deiatel'nosti za 1902–3 god*, addendum; *Spisok zavedenii pechati* (1887 and 1900); Ginlein, *Adresnaia kniga*, pp. 80–91; *Spisok fabrik i zavodov*, pp. 150–55, 162–67; Pogozhev, *Adresnaia kniga*, pp. 104–08, 113–15.

NOTES This Appendix includes owners and directing managers (*direktora* or *upravliaiushchie*) of private and state-owned printing enterprises who were involved in at least *two* of the listed activities. These activities, and the definition of involvement, are as follows:

Assistance Funds: officer of or financial contributor to the Buchdrucker-Hilfskasse, the Compositors' Assistance Fund, or the Burial Society in St. Petersburg, or the Typographers' Assistance Fund in Moscow.

Printing Society: founder or officer of the Russian Printing Society or of its Moscow branch.

First Congress: served on a committee, read a report, or commented on a report at the 1895 Congress of Printing.

Graphic Circle (Moscow): member of Otto Herbeck's organization of the early 1880s.

Printing School (St. Petersburg): founder, administrator (trustee), or financial supporter of the Petersburg Printing School.

Enterprise Paternalism: undertook within their own firms organized efforts to raise the "material and moral" level of workers through subsidized assistance funds, schools, choirs, libraries, etc.

Workforce figures in brackets are estimates based on the number of printing presses.

Bibliography

ABBREVIATIONS OF ORGANIZATIONAL NAMES

MOT-L	Moskovskoe obshchestvo tipo-litografov
RODPD	Russkoe obshchestvo deiatelei pechatnogo dela
RODPD-MO	Russkoe obshchestvo deiatelei pechatnogo dela, Moskovskoe otdelenie
VKN	Vspomogatel'naia kassa naborshchikov v S.-Peterburge
VKT	Vspomogatel'naia kassa tipografov v Moskve

ARCHIVES (institutional names as of the mid-1980s)

MOSCOW

Central State Archive of the October Revolution (TsGAOR)
    Fond 58, Gendarmes
    Fond 63, Moscow Okhrana
    Fond 102, Department of Police
    Fond 518, Union of Unions
    Fond 6864, Historical Archive of the Central Committee of the Union of Printers
    Fond 6935, Historical Archive of the Central Council of Trade Unions
Central State Historical Archive of the City of Moscow (TsGIAgM)
    Fond 16, Governor General
    Fond 2069, Moscow printers' union (1906–1908)
    Fond 2316, Sytin press

LENINGRAD (ST. PETERSBURG)

Central State Historical Archive (TsGIA)
  Fond 20, Department of Trade and Manufacture, Ministry of Finance
  Fond 23, Ministry of Trade and Industry
  Fond 150, Society of Factory and Mill Owners
  Fond 800, Synod press
  Fond 1284, Ministry of Internal Affairs
Leningrad State Historical Archive (LGIA)
  Fond 1216, Kirkhner bindery
  Fond 1229, St. Petersburg Factory Inspectorate
  Fond 1391, Iakovlev press
  Fond 1458, Office for the Manufacture of Government Paper
  Fond 1510, State press
  Fond 1513, Golike and Wilborg press

PRINTING TRADE PERIODICALS

EMPLOYERS' AND TRADE JOURNALS

Biulleten' Russkogo obshchestva deiatelei pechatnogo dela (RODPD). St. Petersburg, February 1901–September 1903 (supplement to *Pechatnoe iskusstvo*).
Graficheskie iskusstva i bumazhnaia promyshlennost'. St. Petersburg, 1886–1889, 1895–1900.
Knigovedenie. Moscow, 1894–1897.
Knizhnik. Moscow, 1865.
Knizhnyi mir. St. Petersburg, 1902–1911.
Knizhnyi vestnik. St. Petersburg, 1860–1867, 1884–1916.
Obzor graficheskikh iskusstv. St. Petersburg, 1878–1885.
Obzor pervoi vserossiiskoi vystavki pechatnogo dela. St. Petersburg, February–June 1895.
Pechatnoe iskusstvo. St. Petersburg, October 1901–September 1903.
Posrednik pechatnogo dela. St. Petersburg, September 1891–July 1892.
Tipografskii zhurnal. St. Petersburg, 1867–1869.
Vestnik graficheskogo dela. St. Petersburg, 1897–1898.
Vestnik pechatnogo dela i izvestiia Obshchestva vladel'tsev pechatnykh zavedenii v S.-Peterburge. December 1908–December 1910.

WORKERS' JOURNALS

Balda: iumoristicheskii, satiricheskii, i karikaturnyi zhurnal rabochikh pechatno-perepletnogo dela. St. Petersburg, January 1907.
Biulleten' S.R.P.D. St. Petersburg, 1907.
Golos pechatnika. St. Petersburg, August 1906–January 1907.
Naborshchik. St. Petersburg, October 1902–December 1904.
Naborshchik i pechatnyi mir. St. Petersburg, January 1905–December 1916.

Pechatnik. Moscow, April–July 1906.
Pechatnoe delo. Moscow, September 1906–June 1907.
Pechatnoe slovo. Moscow, November 1906–June 1907.
Pechatnyi vestnik. St. Petersburg, May 1905–March 1906.
Topor: iumoristicheskii, satiricheskii, i karikaturnyi zhurnal rabochikh pechatno-perepletnogo dela. St. Petersburg, February 1907.
Trud pechatnika. St. Petersburg, October 1907.
Vestnik pechatnikov. St. Petersburg, April 1906–March 1907.
Vestnik soiuza tipografskikh rabochikh. Moscow, [September?] 1903–August 1905.
Zhizn' pechatnika. St. Petersburg, May–October 1907.

BOOKS AND ARTICLES

Adariukov, V. Ia. *Ocherk po istorii litografii v Rossii.* St. Petersburg, 1911.
Admiral'skii, A. M., and S. V. Belov. *Rytsar' knigi: ocherki zhizni i deiatel'nosti P. P. Soikina.* Leningrad, 1970.
Ainzaft, S. S. *Pervyi etap professional'nogo dvizheniia v Rossii, 1905–1907 gg.* Moscow, 1924.
Aktsionernoe delo v Rossii. St. Petersburg, 1899.
Aktsionernoe obshchestvo O. I. Leman v S.-Peterburge i Moskve. St. Petersburg, 1900.
Alfavitnyi spisok tipografiiam i t. p. zavedeniiam podlezhashchim nadzoru inspektsii po delam pechati v Moskve. Moscow, 1883.
Ambler, Effie. *Russian Journalism and Politics: The Career of Aleksei S. Suvorin, 1861–1881.* Detroit, 1972.
Aminzade, Ronald. "Capitalist Industrialization and Patterns of Industrial Protest: A Comparative Urban Study of Nineteenth-Century France." *American Sociological Review* 49 (August 1984): 437–53.
Arenin, E. M., and M. S. Vaniukov. *Imeni pervopechatnika.* Moscow, 1967.
Ascher, Abraham. *The Revolution of 1905: Russia in Disarray.* Stanford, 1988.
Bailes, Kendall. *Technology and Society under Lenin and Stalin.* Princeton, 1978.
Bakhtiarov, A. A. *Slugi pechati: ocherki knigopechatnogo dela.* St. Petersburg, 1893.
Balabanov, M. *Ocherki po istorii rabochego klassa v Rossii.* Moscow, 1926.
Balmuth, Daniel. *Censorship in Russia, 1865–1905.* Washington, D.C., 1979.
Barenbaum, I. E., and T. E. Davydova. *Istoriia knigi.* Moscow, 1971.
Bater, James H. *St. Petersburg: Industrialization and Change.* London, 1976.
Beier, Gerhard. *Schwarze Kunst und Klassenkampf.* Frankfurt, 1966.
Belov, S. V., and A. P. Tolstiakov. *Russkie izdateli kontsa XIX–nachala XX veka.* Leningrad, 1976.
Bender, I. "K stachechnomu dvizheniiu na iuge Rossii v 1903 g." *Arkhiv istorii truda v Rossii* 6–7 (1923): 183–87.
———. "K stachechnomu dvizheniiu na Kavkaze v 1903 g." *Arkhiv istorii truda v Rossii* 5 (1922): 23–27.

Bendix, Reinhard. *Max Weber: An Intellectual Portrait*. Berkeley, 1977.
——— . *Nation-Building and Citizenship*. Berkeley, 1977.
——— . *Work and Authority in Industry: Ideologies of Management in the Course of Industrialization*. Revised edition, Berkeley, 1974; 1st edition, 1956.
Bennett, John W., and Iwao Ishino. *Paternalism in the Japanese Economy*. Minneapolis, 1963.
Berlin, P. A. *Russkaia burzhuaziia v staroe i novoe vremia*. 2d edition. Leningrad and Moscow, 1925.
Bernshtein-Kogan, S. V. *Chislennost', sostav i polozhenie peterburgskikh rabochikh*. St. Petersburg, 1910.
Bezucha, Robert J. *The Lyon Uprising of 1834*. Cambridge, Mass., 1974.
Bill, Valentine. *The Forgotten Class: The Russian Bourgeoisie from the Earliest Beginnings to 1900*. New York, 1959.
Boiko, V. P. "K voprosu o sotsial'noi psikhologii krupnoi rossiiskoi burzhuazii vo vtoroi polovine XIX v. (po memuarnym istochnikam)." In G. Kh. Rabinovich, ed., *Iz istorii burzhuazii v Rossii*. Tomsk, 1982.
Bonnell, Victoria E. *Roots of Rebellion: Workers' Politics and Organizations in St. Petersburg and Moscow, 1900–1914*. Berkeley, 1983.
Bonnell, Victoria E., ed. *The Russian Worker*. Berkeley, 1983.
Bourdieu, Pierre. *Outline of a Theory of Practice*. Trans. Richard Nice. Cambridge, U.K., 1977.
Bradley, Joseph. *Muzhik and Muscovite: Urbanization in Late Imperial Russia*. Berkeley, 1985.
Brenton, James J., ed. *Voices from the Press: A Collection of Sketches, Essays, and Poems: By Practical Printers*. New York, 1850.
Brooks, Jeffrey. "The Kopeck Novels of Early Twentieth Century Russia." *Journal of Popular Culture* 13:1 (Summer 1979): 85–97.
——— . "Readers and Reading at the End of the Tsarist Era." In William Mills Todd III, ed., *Literature and Society in Imperial Russia, 1800–1914*. Stanford, 1978.
——— . *When Russia Learned to Read: Literacy and Popular Literature, 1861–1917*. Princeton, 1985.
Brower, Daniel. "Labor Violence in Russia in the Late Nineteenth Century." *Slavic Review* 41:3 (Fall 1982): 417–31.
Buiko, A. M. *Put' rabochego: vospominaniia putilovtsa*. Leningrad, 1964 (1st edition, 1934).
Buryshkin, Pavel A. *Moskva kupecheskaia*. New York, 1954.
Certeau, Michel de. *The Practice of Everyday Life*. Trans. Steven Rendall. Berkeley, 1984.
400 let russkogo knigopechataniia, 1564–1964. Vol. 1: *Russkoe knigopechatanie do 1917 goda*. Moscow, 1964.
Chartier, Roger. *Cultural History: Between Practices and Representations*. Trans. Lydia G. Cochrane. Cambridge, U.K., 1988.
Child, John. *Industrial Relations in the British Printing Industry*. London, 1967.
Chislennost' i sostav rabochikh v Rossii. St. Petersburg, 1906.

Chistov, N. "Moskovskie pechatniki v revoliutsii 1905 goda." *Katorga i ssylka* 73 (1931): 132–44.

Claes, Valère. *L'Organisation professionelle et le contrat collectif de travail des imprimeurs allemands.* Paris and Louvain, 1908.

"Le Compositeur typographe." Paris, ca. 1832. [Extract from a damaged volume, title and author unknown, in the graphic arts collection of Columbia University.]

Crossick, G. *An Artisan Elite in Victorian Society.* London, 1978.

Davis, Natalie Zemon. *Society and Culture in Early Modern France.* Stanford, 1975.

——— . "A Trade Union in Sixteenth-Century France." *Economic History Review,* 2d ser., 19:1 (April 1966): 48–69.

Davydov, K. V. *Otchet za 1885 g. fabrichnogo inspektora S.-Peterburgskogo okruga.* St. Petersburg, 1886.

Dawley, Alan. *Class and Community: The Industrial Revolution in Lynn.* Cambridge, Mass., 1976.

Degot', V. "Odesskie pechatniki v revoliutsionnom dvizhenii (iz lichnykh vospominaniia." In *Materialy po istorii professional'nogo dvizheniia v Rossii.* Vol. 3. Moscow, 1925.

Dement'ev, A. G., A. V. Zapadov, and M. S. Cherepakhov, eds. *Russkaia periodicheskaia pechat' (1702–1894).* Moscow, 1959.

Dinershtein, E. A. "Izdatel'skaia deiatel'nost' A. S. Suvorina." *Kniga: issledovaniia i materialy* 48 (1984): 82–118.

——— . *I. D. Sytin.* Moscow, 1983.

Dmitriev-Mamonov, B. A. *Ukazatel' deistvuiushchikh v Imperii aktsionernykh predpriiatii i torgovykh domov.* 2 vols. St. Petersburg, 1905.

Dore, Ronald. *British Factory, Japanese Factory.* Berkeley, 1973.

Durkheim, Emile. "L'Individualisme et les intellectuels" (1898). Trans. Steven Lukes. *Political Studies* 17:1 (March 1969): 19–30.

——— . *Emile Durkheim: Selected Writings.* Ed. Anthony Giddens. Cambridge, U.K., 1972.

Dvadtsatipiatiletie kartograficheskogo zavedeniia A. Il'ina, 1859–1884. St. Petersburg, 1884.

Dvadtsatipiatiletie skoropechatni tovarishchestva A. A. Levenson, Moskva 1881–1906. Moscow, 1907.

Dvadtsatipiatiletie tipografii vysochaishe utverzhdennogo Tovarshchestva I. N. Kushnerev i Ko., 1869–1894. Moscow, 1894.

Dvadtsatipiatiletie tipografsko-izdatel'skoi deiatel'nosti Petra Petrovicha Soikina, 1885–1910. St. Petersburg, 1910.

Dvukhklassnaia tserkovno-prikhodskaia shkola pri Moskovskoi sinodal'noi tipografii. Moscow, 1906.

Eisenstein, Elizabeth L. "The Early Printer as 'Renaissance Man.'" *Printing History* 3:1 (1981): 6–16.

——— . *The Printing Press as an Agent of Change.* Cambridge, U.K., 1979.

E[izen], I. M. *Ocherk istorii perepletnogo dela: K dvadtsatipiatiletiiu Perepletnoi fabriki O. F. Kirkhnera v S.-Peterburge.* St. Petersburg, 1896.

Engels, Friedrich. *Anti-Dühring.* In Karl Marx and Frederick Engels, *Collected Works.* Vol. 25. New York and Moscow, 1987.

Engelstein, Laura. *Moscow, 1905: Working-Class Organization and Political Conflict.* Stanford, 1982.

Entsiklopedicheskii slovar'. Ed. F. A. Brokgauz [Brockhaus] and I. A. Efron. 43 vols. St. Petersburg, 1890–1907.

Esin, B. I. *N. V. Shelgunov.* Moscow, 1977.

———. "Russkaia legal'naia pressa kontsa XIX–nachala XX veka." In *Iz istorii russkoi zhurnalistiki.* Moscow, 1973.

Fabrichno-zavodskie predpriiatiia rossiiskoi imperii. Petrograd, 1914.

Fabrika knigi "Krasnyi proletarii." Moscow, 1932.

Filippov, A. A. "Avtonomiia pechatnikov v 1905 godu." [Unpublished essay in TsGAOR, f. 6864, op. 1, d. 75.]

———. "Pechatnoe delo." *Zhenskoe delo* 1:5 (May 1899): 93–99.

Filippov, N. G. *Nauchno-tekhnicheskie obshchestva Rossii (1866–1917 gg.).* Moscow, 1976.

Flynn, Charles P. *Insult and Society: Patterns of Comparative Interaction.* Port Washington, N.Y., 1977.

Frank, Stephen P. "Popular Justice, Community, and Culture among the Russian Peasantry, 1870–1900." *Russian Review* 46: 3 (July 1987): 239–66.

Galaktionov, I. D. *Besedy naborshchika.* Petrograd, 1922.

———. *Bol'nichnye kassy.* St. Petersburg, 1913.

———. [Shponik]. *Lebedinaia pesn'.* Moscow, 1904.

———. *Obshchestvo sluzhashchikh v pechatnykh zavedeniiakh.* St. Petersburg, 1914.

———. *Pervaia shkola pechatnogo dela.* St. Petersburg, 1914.

———. *Petrovskaia koloniia dlia truzhenikov pechatnogo dela v Sestroretske.* St. Petersburg, 1913.

———. *Zhurnaly pechatnogo dela s 1867 g. po 1914 g.* St. Petersburg, 1914.

Garvi, P. A. *Revoliutsionnye siluety.* New York, 1962.

Gavrilov, A. S. *Ocherk istorii Sankt-Peterburgskoi sinodal'noi tipografii.* St. Petersburg, 1911.

Geertz, Clifford. *The Interpretation of Cultures.* New York, 1973.

Gellershtein, S. G., and A. G. Ittin. *Psikhologicheskii analiz professii naborshchika.* Moscow, 1924.

Gerasimova, Iu. I. *Iz istorii russkoi pechati v period revoliutsionnoi situatsii kontsa 1850-kh–nachala 1860-kh gg.* Moscow, 1974.

Gerschenkron, Alexander. *Economic Backwardness in Historical Perspective.* Cambridge, Mass., 1966.

Giddens, Anthony. *Capitalism and Modern Social Theory.* Cambridge, U.K., 1971.

———. *Central Problems in Social Theory.* Berkeley, 1979.

Giliarovskii, V. *Moskva i moskvichi.* Moscow, 1983.

Gindin, I. F. "Russkaia burzhuaziia v period kapitalizma: ee razvitie i osobennosti." *Istoriia SSSR* 1963, no. 2 (March–April): 57–78, and no. 3 (May–June): 37–60.

Ginlein, R. E., ed. *Adresnaia kniga knigoprodavtsev, izdatelei, torgovtsev notami, redaktsii gazet i zhurnalov, bibliotek dlia chteniia i zavedenii pechati v Rossii, 1900–1901.* St. Petersburg, 1900.

Glickman, Rose L. *Russian Factory Women: Workplace and Society, 1880–1914.* Berkeley, 1984.

Gordon, Maks. *Ocherk ekonomicheskoi bor'by rabochikh Rossii.* Leningrad, 1925.

Gorkii, M. "O pisateliakh-samouchkakh." In *Sobranie sochinenii* 24. Moscow, 1953.

Gorshkov, Iu. A. "Russkii lubok: ot manufaktury k fabrike." *Kniga: issledovaniia i materialy* 47 (1983): 103–16.

Govorov, A. A. *Istoriia knizhnoi torgovli.* Moscow, 1966.

Gray, R. Q. *The Labour Aristocracy in Victorian Edinburgh.* Oxford, 1976.

Grents, G. L., and I. D. Galaktionov. *Obzor sorokaletnei deiatelnosti vspomogatel'noi kassy naborshchikov v S.-Peterburge.* St. Petersburg, 1906.

Grier, Philip. *Marxist Ethical Theory in the Soviet Union.* Dordrecht, Netherlands, 1978.

Grinevich, V. P. [M. G. Kogan]. *Professional'noe dvizhenie rabochikh v Rossii.* St. Petersburg, 1908.

Guroff, Gregory, and Fred V. Carstensen, eds. *Entrepreneurship in Imperial Russia and the Soviet Union.* Princeton, 1983.

Gutman, Herbert G. "Work, Culture, and Society in Industrializing America, 1815–1919." *American Historical Review* 78:3 (June 1973): 531–88.

Haimson, Leopold H. "The Problem of Social Identities in Early Twentieth Century Russia." *Slavic Review* 47:1 (Spring 1988): 1–20.

———. "The Problem of Social Stability in Urban Russia, 1905–1917." *Slavic Review* 23:4 (December 1964): 619–42 and 24:1 (March 1965): 1–22.

Hamburg, Gary M. *Politics of the Russian Nobility.* Rutgers, 1984.

Hamilton, Alice, and Charles H. Verrill. *Hygiene of the Printing Trades.* Washington, D.C., 1917.

Hanagan, Michael P. *The Logic of Solidarity: Artisans and Industrial Workers in Three French Towns, 1871–1914.* Urbana, Ill., 1980.

Harbison, Frederick, and Charles A. Myers. *Management in the Industrial World.* New York, 1959.

Hobsbawm, Eric. *Labouring Men: Studies in the History of Labour.* London, 1968; 1st edition, 1964.

———. *Workers: Worlds of Labor.* New York, 1984.

Hobsbawm, Eric, and Terence Ranger, eds. *The Invention of Tradition.* Cambridge, U.K., 1983.

Howe, Ellic, ed. *The London Compositor.* London, 1947.

———. *Passages from the Literature of the Printing Craft, 1550–1935.* London, 1943.

Hunt, Lynn, ed. *The New Cultural History.* Berkeley, 1989.

Istoricheskie svedeniia o tsenzure v Rossii. St. Petersburg, 1862.

Istoriia knizhnoi torgovli v S.S.S.R. Moscow, 1976.

Istoriia leningradskogo soiuza rabochikh poligraficheskogo proizvodstva. Leningrad, 1925.

Iuferovyi, D. V., and G. N. Sokolovskii, eds. *Akademicheskaia tipografiia, 1728–1928.* 2d ed., Leningrad, 1929.

Ivan Dmitrievich Galaktionov, 12/II/1915. Petrograd, 1915.

Ivan Dmitrievich Galaktionov, 1880–25/II-1925. Leningrad, 1925.

Ivanov, L. M. "O soslovno-klassovoi strukture gorodov kapitalisticheskoi Rossii." In *Problemy sotsial'no-ekonomicheskoi istorii Rossii: Sbornik.* Moscow, 1971.

Ivanov, L. M., et. al., eds. *Rossiiskii proletariat: oblik, bor'ba, gegemoniia.* Moscow, 1970.

Ivanova, S. "S. G. Khrenkova." *Katorga i ssylka* 8 (1924).

Johnson, Robert. *Peasant and Proletarian: The Working Class of Moscow in the Late Nineteenth Century.* New Brunswick, N.J., 1979.

Jones, Gareth Stedman. *Languages of Class: Studies in English Working Class History, 1832–1982.* Cambridge, U.K., 1983.

Joyce, Patrick. *Work, Society and Politics.* New Brunswick, N.J., 1980.

Kaiser, Daniel H., ed. *The Workers' Revolution in Russia, 1917: The View from Below.* Cambridge, U.K., 1987.

Karelin, Aleksei E. "Deviatoe ianvaria i Gapon: vospominaniia." *Krasnaia letopis'* 1 (1922): 106–16.

———. "Soiuz litografskikh rabochikh." In *Pechatnyi vestnik: iubileinyi vypusk.* Leningrad, 1930.

———. "Vospominaniia o rabochikh kruzhkakh Brusnevskoi organizatsii." In *V nachale puti.* Leningrad, 1975.

Kaser, M. C. "Russian Entrepreneurship." In *Cambridge Economic History of Europe,* vol. 6, part 2. Cambridge, U.K., 1978.

Katalog russkogo otdela. Mezhdunarodnaia vystavka pechatnogo dela i grafika v Leiptsige, 1914. St. Petersburg, 1914.

Katznelson, Ira, and Aristide R. Zolberg, eds. *Working-Class Formation: Nineteenth-Century Patterns in Western Europe and the United States.* Princeton, 1986.

Kilby, Peter L., ed. *Entrepreneurship and Economic Development.* New York, 1971.

King, Victoria Palmer. "The Emergence of the St. Petersburg Industrialist Community, 1870 to 1905." Ph.D. diss., University of California, Berkeley, 1982.

Kir'ianov, Iu. I. *Perekhod k massovoi politicheskoi bor'be: rabochii klass nakanune pervoi rossiiskoi revoliutsii.* Moscow, 1987.

———. *Zhiznennyi uroven' rabochikh Rossii.* Moscow, 1979.

Kiselevich, M. L. "Soiuz rabochikh pechatnogo dela." In *Istoriia soveta rabochikh deputatov v g. S.-Peterburga.* St. Petersburg, 1906.

Kleinbort, L. M. "Ocherki rabochei demokratii." *Sovremennyi mir* (March 1913): 22–45; (May 1913): 151–72; (August 1913): 175–98; (October 1913): 150–76; (November 1913): 168–90; (December 1913): 148–68; (January 1914): 212–35; (April 1914): 28–52.

———. *Ocherki rabochei intelligentsii.* Petrograd, 1923.

Knigovedenie: Entsiklopedicheskii slovar'. Moscow, 1981.

Koenker, Diane. *Moscow Workers and the 1917 Revolution*. Princeton, 1981.

Kolokol'nikov, P., and S. Rapoport, eds. *1905–1907 gg. v professional'nom dvizhenii: I i II Vserossiiskie konferentsii professional'nykh soiuzov*. Moscow, 1925.

Kolomnin, Petr. *Kratkie svedeniia po tipografskomu delu*. St. Petersburg, 1899.

Korelin, A. P. *Dvorianstvo v poreformennoi Rossii, 1861–1904 gg*. Moscow, 1979.

Koz'min, B. P. *Rabochee dvizhenie v Rossii do revoliutsii 1905 goda*. Moscow, 1925.

Kratkii istoricheskii obzor tipografii L.S.P.O., 1884–1924 gg. Leningrad, 1924.

Kratkii ocherk istorii i sovremennogo sostoianiia S.-Peterburgskoi Sinodal'noi tipografii. St. Petersburg, 1895.

Kratkii ocherk izdatel'skoi deiatel'nosti A. S. Suvorina i razvitiia prinadlezhashchei emu tipografii "Novogo vremeni." St. Petersburg, 1900.

Kratkii ocherk o polozhenii vspomogatel'noi kassy naborshchikov v S.-Peterburge. St. Petersburg, 1895.

Kratkii ocherk razvitiia i deiatel'nosti tipografii P. P. Soikina za desiat' let ee sushchestvovaniia (1885–1895). St. Petersburg, 1895.

Kratkii ocherk razvitiia masterskikh vysochaishe utverzhdennogo Tovarishchestva I. N. Kushnerev i Ko. v Moskve. Moscow, 1895.

Kufaev, M. N. *Istoriia russkoi knigi v XIX veke*. Leningrad, 1927.

Kushnerev, I. N. *Sochineniia*. 3 vols., Moscow, 1895.

———. *Zemliakam*. Moscow, 1892.

Laurie, Bruce. " 'Nothing on Compulsion': Life Styles of Philadelphia Artisans, 1820–1850." *Labor History* 15:3 (Summer 1974): 337–66.

Laverychev, V. Ia. *Krupnaia burzhuaziia v poreformennoi Rossii, 1861–1900*. Moscow, 1974.

———. *Tsarizm i rabochii vopros v Rossii, 1861–1917*. Moscow, 1972.

Lavrov, P. L. *Istoricheskie pis'ma* [1868–69]. St. Petersburg, 1906.

Lebedev, V. "K istorii kulachnykh boev na Rusi." *Russkaia starina* 155 (July 1913): 103–23, and (August 1913): 323–40.

Lemke, M. K. *Dumy zhurnalista*. St. Petersburg, 1903.

———. *Epokha tsenzurnykh reform, 1859–1865 godov*. St. Petersburg, 1904.

———. "Tret'e otdelenie i tsenzura, 1826–1855 gg." *Russkoe bogatstvo*, 1905, no. 9 (September): 190–221, no. 10 (October): 47–86, and no. 11 (November): 30–55.

Lenin, V. I. *Polnoe sobranie sochinenii*. 5th ed. 55 vols. Moscow, 1958–1965.

Leninskii zakaz. Moscow, 1969.

Levenson, A. A., Tovarishchestvo. *Istoricheskii ocherk i opisanie masterskikh, 1881–1903*. Moscow, 1903.

Librovich, S. F. *Na knizhnom postu*. Petrograd and Moscow, 1916.

Lidtke, Vernon L. *The Alternative Culture: Socialist Labor in Imperial Germany*. New York, 1985.

Lindenmeyr, Adele. "Charity and the Problem of Unemployment: Industrial Homes in Late Imperial Russia." *Russian Review* 45:1 (January 1986): 1–22.

——— . "A Russian Experiment in Voluntarism: The Municipal Guardianships of the Poor, 1894–1914." *Jahrbücher für Geschichte Osteuropas* 30 (1982): 429–51.

Lipset, Seymour Martin, Martin Trow, and James Coleman. *Union Democracy: The Internal Politics of the International Typographic Union*. New York, 1956.

Lisovskii, N. M. *Kratkii ocherk stoletnei deiatel'nosti tipografii Glazunovykh*. St. Petersburg, 1903.

——— . "Periodicheskaia pechat' v Rossii, 1703–1903 gg." *Sbornik statei po istorii i statistike russkoi periodicheskoi pechati, 1703–1903*. St. Petersburg, 1903.

——— . *Russkaia periodicheskaia pechat', 1703–1900*. Petrograd, 1915.

——— . *Sobiranie i razrabotka statisticheskikh svedenii o knigoizdatel'stve i periodicheskoi pechati v Rossii*. St. Petersburg, 1896.

Liubimtsev, I. M. *Ob osnovnykh printsipakh organizatsii Soiuza rabochikh pechatnogo dela*. St. Petersburg, 1905.

Livesey, Harold C. "Entrepreneurial History." In *Encyclopedia of Entrepreneurship*. Englewood Cliffs, N.J., 1982.

Lowry, Martin. *The World of Aldus Manutius: Business and Scholarship in Renaissance Venice*. Oxford, 1979.

Luedtke, Alf. "Cash, Coffee Breaks, Horseplay: *Eigensinn* and Politics among Factory Workers in Germany circa 1900." In Michael Hanagan and Charles Stephenson, eds., *Confrontation, Class Consciousness, and the Labor Process: Studies in Proletarian Class Formation*. New York and Westport, 1986.

Luppov, S. P. *Kniga v Rossii v pervoi chetverti XVIII veka*. Leningrad, 1973.

——— . *Kniga v Rossii v XVII veke*. Leningrad, 1970.

McDaniel, Tim. *Autocracy, Capitalism, and Revolution in Russia*. Berkeley, 1988.

McKay, John P. *Pioneers for Profit: Foreign Entrepreneurship and Russian Industrialization, 1885–1913*. Chicago, 1970.

McLaurin, Melton Alonza. *Paternalism and Protest: Southern Cotton Mill Workers and Organized Protest, 1875–1905*. Westport, Conn., 1971.

Madsen, Richard. *Morality and Power in a Chinese Village*. Berkeley, 1984.

Malia, Martin. *Alexander Herzen and the Birth of Russian Socialism*. New York, 1961.

Marker, Gary. *Publishing, Printing, and the Origins of Intellectual Life in Russia, 1700–1800*. Princeton, 1985.

——— . "Russia and the 'Printing Revolution': Notes and Observations." *Slavic Review* 41:2 (Summer 1982): 266–83.

Markson, A. E., ed. *Tipografskii karmannyi kalendar' na 1914 god*. St. Petersburg, 1914.

Marshall, T. H. *Class, Citizenship, and Social Development*. New York, 1964.

Marx, Karl, and Friedrich Engels. "The Communist Manifesto." In *The Marx-Engels Reader*. Ed. Robert C. Tucker. New York, 1978.

Materialy po istorii professional'nogo dvizheniia rabochikh poligraficheskogo proizvodstva (pechatnogo dela) v Rossii. Moscow, 1925.

Materialy po istorii revoliutsii 1905–1907 gg. Moscow, 1967.

Matveev, G. "Moskovskii soiuz rabochikh-metallistov v 1906–07 gg." In *Materialy po istorii professional'nogo dvizheniia v Rossii.* Vol. 2. Moscow, 1924.

Medvedev, A. V. "Pervaia zabastovka i organizatsiia moskovskikh pechatnikov." In *Moskovskie pechatniki v 1905 godu.* Moscow, 1925.

Michels, Robert. *Political Parties.* New York, 1962.

Mikhailovskii, Ia. T. *Otchet za 1885 god glavno gofabrichnogo inspektora.* St. Petersburg, 1886.

Mikhailovskii, V. I. *Ekspeditsiia zagotovleniia gosudarstvennykh bumag.* St. Petersburg, 1900.

———. *Obzor i plany nekotorykh masterskikh i obshchiia svedeniia ob Ekspeditsii zagotovleniia gosudarstvennykh bumag.* St. Petersburg, 1901.

Mill, John Stuart. *Principles of Political Economy.* Boston, 1848.

Milonov, Iu. K. *Kak voznikli professional'nye soiuzy v Rossii.* Moscow, 1929.

Miretskii, N. I. "Ot Sytina k Pervoi obraztsovoi," *Bor'ba klassov* 1932, no. 5: 74–90.

———. *Pervaia obraztsovaia tipografiia.* Moscow, 1933.

Monas, Sidney. *The Third Section: Police and Society under Nicholas I.* Cambridge, Mass., 1961.

Montgomery, David. "The Working Classes of the Preindustrial American City, 1780–1830." *Labor History* 9 (1968): 3–22.

Moore, Barrington, Jr. *Injustice: The Social Bases of Obedience and Revolt.* White Plains, 1978.

Moskovskie pechatniki v 1905 godu. Moscow, 1925.

Moskovskoe obshchestvo tipo-litografov. *Ustav i pravila.* Moscow, 1908.

Nachalo pervoi russkoi revoliutsii. Moscow, 1955.

Na pamiat' o desiatiletii "Novogo vremeni," 1876–1886 gg. St. Petersburg, 1886.

Nekrasov, A. I. "Knigopechataniia v Rossii v XVI i XVII vekakh." In V. Ia. Adariukov and A. A. Sidorov, eds., *Kniga v Rossii.* Vol. 1. Moscow, 1924.

Nemirovskii, E. L. "Zhizn' i deiatel'nost' pervopechatnika Ivana Fedorova v svete noveishchikh issledovanii." *Kniga: issledovaniia i materialy* 47 (1983): 79–85.

Netesin, Iu. N. "K voprosu o sotsial'no-ekonomicheskikh korniakh i osobennostiakh 'rabochei aristokratii' v Rossii." In *Bol'shevistskaia pechat' i rabochii klass Rossii.* Moscow, 1965.

Newby, Howard. "Paternalism and Capitalism." In Richard Scase, ed., *Industrial Society: Class, Cleavage and Control.* New York, 1977.

Novoe vremia (1876–1916): istoricheskii ocherk. Petrograd, 1916.

Novyi entsiklopedicheskii slovar'. St. Petersburg, 1911–1916.

Obshcheprofessional'nye organy 1905–1907 gg. Moscow, 1926.

Obshchestvo pooshchreniia trudoliubiia v Moskve: letopis' pervogo dvadtsatipiatiletiia. Moscow, 1888.

Obzor deiatel'nosti vspomogatel'noi kassy "Obshchestva Tipografshchikov v S.-Peterburge." St. Petersburg, 1865.

Ocherk izdatel'skoi deiatel'nosti t-va I. D. Sytina v Moskve. Moscow, 1900.

Ocherk razvitiia i opisanie masterskikh Slovolitni O. I. Leman v S.-Peterburge. St. Petersburg, 1896.

Ocherki po istorii russkoi zhurnalistiki i kritiki. 2 vols. Leningrad, 1965.

Ol'khin, P. M. *Rukovodstvo k pechatnomu delu.* St. Petersburg, 1903.

Orlov, B. P. *Poligraficheskaia promyshlennost' Moskvy: ocherk razvitiia do 1917 goda.* Moscow, 1953.

Os'makov, N. V. *Russkaia proletarskaia poeziia, 1890–1917.* Moscow, 1968.

Otchet dvadtsatipiatiletnei deiatel'nosti vspomogatel'noi kassy naborshchikov v S.-Peterburge, 1866–1891 gg. St. Petersburg, 1891.

Otchet po pervoi shkole pechatnogo dela Imperatorskogo Russkogo Tekhnicheskogo Obshchestva za 1885–6 uchebnyi god. St. Petersburg, 1886.

Otchet po shkole pechatnogo dela Imperatorskogo Russkogo tekhnicheskogo obshchestva. St. Petersburg, 1907–1910.

Otchet pravleniia Obshchestva vzaimopomoshchi sluzhashchikh i rabotaiushchikh v Senatskoi tipografii. St. Petersburg, 1910–1912.

Otchet soveta Russkogo Obshchestva deiatelei pechatnogo dela. St. Petersburg, 1900–1904.

Owen, Thomas C. "Entrepreneurship and the Structure of Enterprise in Russia, 1800–1880," in Gregory Guroff and Fred V. Carstensen, eds., *Entrepreneurship in Imperial Russia and the Soviet Union.* Princeton, 1983.

——— . *Capitalism and Politics in Russia: A Social History of the Moscow Merchants, 1855–1905.* Cambridge, U.K., 1981.

——— . *RUSCORP: A Database of Corporations in the Russian Empire, 1700–1914.* Distributed by Inter-University Consortium for Political and Social Research, 1980.

Pamiatnaia knizhka S.-Peterburgskoi gubernii na 1863–1864 gg. St. Petersburg, 1863–1864.

Pankratova, A. M. *Fabzavkomy Rossii v bor'be za sotsialisticheskuiu fabriku.* Moscow, 1923.

Pavlov, I. N. *Zhizn' russkogo gravera.* 3d ed., Moscow, 1963.

Pazhitnov, K. A. *Polozhenie rabochego klassa v Rossii.* St. Petersburg, 1906.

Pechatnia R. R. Golike. St. Petersburg, 1902.

"Pechatnoe delo v Peterburge v 1802–1811," *Russkaia starina* 41 (January–March 1884): 458–59.

Pechatnyi vestnik: iubileinyi vypusk. Leningrad, 1930.

Perepis' Moskvy 1882 goda. Vypusk 2. Moscow, 1885.

Perepis' Moskvy 1902 goda. Part 1, vypusk 2. Moscow, 1906.

Perrot, Michelle. *Workers on Strike: France 1871–1890.* New Haven, 1987.

Persits, M. M. *Ateizm russkogo rabochego (1870–1905 gg.).* Moscow, 1965.

Pervaia russkaia shkola pechatnogo dela Imperatorskogo Russkogo Tekhnicheskogo Obshchestva [IRTO], 1884–1894. St. Petersburg, 1895.

Pervaia shkola pechatnogo dela Imperatorskogo Russkogo Tekhnicheskogo Obshchestva, 1884–1914. Petrograd, 1914.

Pervoe desiatiletie russkogo obshchestva knigoprodavtsev i izdatelei i zhurnala "Knizhnyi vestnik," 1883–1893. St. Petersburg, 1894.

Piatidesiatiletie sushchestvovaniia Vspomogatel'noi kassy dlia tipografov, slovolitchikov, litografov, ksilografov i fotografov v S.-Peterburge. St. Petersburg, 1890.

Piatidesiatiletnii iubilei tipografii Ivana Grigor'evicha Chuksina. Moscow, 1902.

Pipes, Richard. *Social Democracy and the St. Petersburg Labor Movement, 1885–1897.* Cambridge, Mass., 1963.

Pogozhev, A. V., ed. *Adresnaia kniga fabrichno-zavodskoi i remeslennoi promyshlennosti vsei Rossii.* St. Petersburg, 1905.

Poliak, A. "Na zare rabochego dvizheniia v Zapadnoi Rossii (iz vospominaniia)." *Katorga i ssylka* 48 (1928): 7–17.

Polveka dlia kniga, 1866–1916: Literaturno-khudozhestvennyi sbornik, posviashchennyi piatidesiatiletiiu izdatel'skoi deiatel'nosti I. D. Sytina. Moscow, 1916.

Popov, M. A. "Sof'ia Germanovna Khrenkova." In *Moskovskie pechatniki v 1905 godu.* Moscow, 1925.

Po povodu tridtsatiletiia vspomogatel'noi kassy tipografov v Moskve: vospominaniia naborshchika. Moscow, 1901.

Portal, Roger. "Aux origines d'une bourgeoisie industrielle en Russie." *Revue d'histoire moderne et contemporaine* 8 (January–March 1961): 35–60.

Prodolzhitel'nost' rabochego dnia i zarabotnaia plata rabochikh. St. Petersburg, 1896.

"Proekt normal'nogo tarifa dlia pechatnykh zavedenii goroda S.-Peterburga." Part 1: "Tarif dlia gg. naborshchikov." St. Petersburg, 1905 [special supplement to *Naborshchik i pechatnyi mir,* issued February 1].

Proekt ustava Obshchestvennoi biblioteki pri RODPD v S.-Peterburge. St. Petersburg, 1903.

Proekt ustava Russkogo Obshchestva deiatelei pechatnogo dela. St. Petersburg, n.d. [1897?].

"Programma rossiiskoi sotsial-demokraticheskoi rabochei partii" (1903). In *KPSS v rezoliutsiakh i resheniiakh.* Vol. 1: *1898–1905.* Moscow, 1953.

Prokopovich, S. N. *K rabochemu voprosu v Rossii.* St. Petersburg, 1905.

"Proletarskaia poeziia." In *Istoriia russkoi literatury.* Vol. 14. Leningrad, 1983.

Protokoly pervoi vserossiiskoi konferentsii soiuzov rabochikh pechatnogo dela. St. Petersburg, 1907.

Rabinovich, G. Kh., ed. *Iz istorii burzhuazii v Rossii.* Tomsk, 1982.

Rabinow, Paul, and William M. Sullivan. "The Interpretive Turn." In Paul Rabinow and William M. Sullivan, *Interpretive Social Science: A Second Look.* Berkeley, 1987.

Rabochee dvizhenie v Rossii v 1901–1904 gg: sbornik dokumentov. Leningrad, 1975.

Rancière, Jacques. "The Myth of the Artisan: Critical Reflections on a Category of Social History." *International Labor and Working Class History* 24 (Fall 1983).

———. *The Nights of Labor: The Workers' Dream in Nineteenth-Century France.* Trans. John Drury. Philadelphia, 1989.

Rashin, A. G. *Formirovanie rabochego klassa Rossii.* Moscow, 1958.

Reichman, Henry. *Railwaymen and Revolution: Russia, 1905.* Berkeley, 1987.

Reid, Alastair. "Intelligent Artisans and Aristocrats of Labor." In Jay Winter, ed., *The Working Class in Modern British History.* Cambridge, U.K., 1983.

Reid, Donald. "Industrial Paternalism: Discourse and Practice in Nineteenth-Century French Mining and Metallurgy." *Comparative Studies in Society and History* 27:4 (October 1985): 579–607.

Reshetov, S. I. "Stachka tret'ego goda." In *Moskovskie pechatniki v 1905 godu.* Moscow, 1925.

Revoliutsiia 1905–1907 gg. v Rossii: dokumenty i materialy. Moscow, 1955–1963.

Riabushinskii, Vladimir. "Kupechestvo moskovskoe." *Den' russkogo rebenka* 18 (April 1951): 168–89.

Rieber, Alfred J. *Merchants and Entrepreneurs in Imperial Russia.* Chapel Hill, 1982.

Roberts, David. *Paternalism in Early Victorian England.* New Brunswick, N.J., 1979.

Roberts, James S. "Drink and Industrial Work Discipline in Nineteenth Century Germany." *Journal of Social History* 15:1 (Fall 1981): 25–38.

Rock, Howard B. *Artisans of the New Republic: The Tradesmen of New York City in the Age of Jefferson.* New York, 1979.

Rosovsky, Henry. "The Serf Entrepreneur in Russia." *Explorations in Entrepreneurial History* 6:4 (May 1954): 207–33.

Rossiiskaia sotsial-demokraticheskaia rabochaia partiia, Moskovskii komitet. *Pis'mo k moskovskim naborshchikam.* Geneva, 1899.

Rubakin, N. A. "Knizhnyi potok." *Russkaia mysl'* 1903, no. 3 (March): part 2, 1–8.

Ruckman, Jo Ann. *The Moscow Business Elite: A Social and Cultural Portrait of Two Generations, 1840–1905.* De Kalb, Ill., 1984.

The Russian Imperial State Paper Manufactory. St. Petersburg, 1893.

Russkoe obshchestvo deiatelei pechatnogo dela, Moskovskoe otdelenie. *Kratkii otchet o deiatel'nosti za 1902–3 god.* Moscow, 1903.

Ruud, Charles A. *Fighting Words: Imperial Censorship and the Russian Press, 1804–1906.* Toronto, 1982.

———. *Russian Entrepreneur: Publisher Ivan Sytin of Moscow, 1851–1934.* Montreal, 1990.

S., N. "Ocherk knigopechatnogo dela v Rossii." *Russkaia bibliografiia: 1878 g.* Vypusk 2, otdel' 3. (St. Petersburg, 1879).

S.-Peterburg po perepisi 15 dekabria 1881 goda. Vol. 1, part 2. St. Petersburg, 1884.

S.-Peterburg po perepisi 15 dekabria 1900 goda. Vypusk 2. St. Petersburg, 1903.

S.-Peterburgskaia Sinodal'naia tipografiia. St. Petersburg, 1914.

Sablinsky, Walter. *The Road to Bloody Sunday.* Princeton, 1977.

Saf'ian, B. I., and Z. B. Marvits. *Ordenonosnyi "Pechatnyi dvor."* Moscow, 1969.

Sales, Hubert. *Les Relations industrielles dans l'imprimerie française.* Paris, 1967.

Savinov, I. *Ukazatel' goroda Moskvy.* Moscow, 1866.

Sbornik svedenii o deiatel'nosti vspomogatel'noi kassy tipografov v Moskve za 30 let. Moscow, 1901.

Schneiderman, Jeremiah. *Sergei Zubatov and Revolutionary Marxism.* Ithaca, 1976.

Scott, James C. *Domination and the Arts of Resistance: Hidden Transcripts.* New Haven, 1990.

———. *Weapons of the Weak: Everyday Forms of Peasant Resistance.* New Haven, 1985.

Scott, Joan Wallach. *Gender and the Politics of History.* New York, 1988.

Semanov, S. N. *Peterburgskie rabochie nakanune pervoi russkoi revoliutsii.* Moscow, 1966.

Senatskaia tipografiia. St. Petersburg, 1903.

Sennett, Richard, and Jonathan Cobb. *The Hidden Injuries of Class.* New York, 1972.

Severianin, Petr. "Soiuz rabochikh pechatnogo dela." *Bez zaglaviia* 14 (April 23, 1906): 52–62.

Sewell, William H., Jr. *Work and Revolution in France: The Language of Labor from the Old Regime to 1848.* Cambridge, U.K., 1980.

Shalyt, Z. S. "Revoliutsionnoe gnezdo." In *Pechatnyi vestnik: iubileinyi vypusk.* Leningrad, 1930.

Shchelgunov, M. I. *Iskusstvo knigopechataniia v ego istoricheskom razvitii.* Moscow, 1923.

Sher, V. V. *Istoriia professional'nogo dvizheniia rabochikh pechatnogo dela v Moskve.* Moscow, 1911.

———. "Moskovskie pechatniki v revoliutsii 1905 g." In *Moskovskie pechatniki v 1905 godu.* Moscow, 1925.

Shishkin, V. F. *Tak skladyvalas' revolutsionnaia moral': istoricheskii ocherk.* Moscow, 1967.

Shkola pri tipografii gazety "Novoe vremia" (A. S. Suvorina), 1884–1911. St. Petersburg, 1911.

Shorter, Edward, and Charles Tilly. *Strikes in France, 1830–1968.* New York, 1974.

"Shponik." See Galaktionov, I. D.

Shuster, U. A. *Petersburgskie rabochie v 1905–1907 gg.* Leningrad, 1976.

Sider, Gerald M. *Culture and Class in Anthropology and History: A Newfoundland Illustration.* Cambridge, U.K., 1986.

Sidorov, A. A. *Istoriia oformleniia russkoi knigi.* Moscow and Leningrad, 1946.

Simonenko, V. V., and G. D. Kostomarov, eds. *Iz istorii revoliutsii 1905 goda v Moskve i Moskovskoi gubernii: materialy i dokumenty.* Moscow, 1931.

Skabichevskii, A. M. *Ocherki istorii russkoi tsenzury, 1700–1863 gg.* St. Petersburg, 1892.

Slabkin, A. S. *Mirovozrenie N. V. Shelgunova.* Kharkov, 1960.

Slovolitnia Ottona O. Gerbeka. Moscow, n.d.

Smith, S. A. *Red Petrograd: Revolution in the Factories, 1917–1918.* Cambridge, U.K., 1983.

Société d'édition J. D. Sytin à Moscou. Moscow, 1900.

Sokolov, Y. M. *Russian Folklore*. Trans. Catherine Ruth Smith. Hatsboro, Penna., 1966.

Solov'ev, A. N. *Gosudar'ev pechatnyi dvor i Sinodal'noi tipografii v Moskve*. Moscow, 1903.

Somov, S. I. "Iz istorii sotsialdemokraticheskogo dvizheniia v Peterburge v 1905 gody." *Byloe* 1907, no. 4 (April): 22–55; no. 5 (May): 152–78.

Sostav sluzhashchikh v promyshlennykh zavedeniiakh. St. Petersburg, 1904.

Spisok fabrik i zavodov evropeiskoi Rossii. St. Petersburg, 1903.

Spisok zavedenii pechati nakhodiashchikhsia v vedenie inspektorskogo nadzora v S.-Peterburge. St. Petersburg, 1875–1900.

Statisticheskii atlas goroda Moskvy. Moscow, 1911.

Stearns, Peter N. *Be a Man: Males in Modern Society*. New York, 1979.

Steinberg, Mark D. "Culture and Class in a Russian Industry: The Printers of St. Petersburg, 1860–1905." *Journal of Social History* 23:3 (Spring 1990): 513–33.

————. "Conciousness and Conflict in a Russian Industry: The Printers of St. Petersburg and Moscow, 1855–1905." Ph.D. diss., University of California, Berkeley, 1987.

Steinberg, S. H. *Five Hundred Years of Printing*. Harmondsworth, 1974.

Strelskii, P. [V. S. Lavrov]. *Samoorganizatsiia rabochego klassa*. St. Petersburg, 1905.

Surh, Gerald D. *1905 in St. Petersburg: Labor, Society, and Revolution*. Stanford, 1989.

————. "Petersburg Workers in 1905." Ph.D. diss., University of California, Berkeley, 1979.

Svavitskii, A., and V. Sher. *Ocherk polozheniia rabochikh pechatnogo dela v Moskve*. St. Petersburg, 1909.

Sviatlovskii, V. V. "Iz istorii kass i obshchestv vzaimopomoshchi rabochikh." *Arkhiv istorii truda v Rossii* 4 (1922): 32–46.

————. *Truzheniki pechatnogo dela: professiia naborshchikov s tochki zreniia gigienicheskoi nauki*. Poltava, 1893.

Sytin, I. D. *Zhizn' dlia knigi*. Ed. A. Z. Okorokova. Moscow, 1960.

"Tarifnoe dvizhenie v Petrograde za 1917–1918 gg." In *Materialy po statistike truda*. Vypusk 6. Petrograd, 1919.

Tens, A. *Russkii rabochii zagranitsei: putevye zametki naborshchika*. St. Petersburg, 1903.

Thompson, E. P. *The Making of the English Working Class*. London, 1980; 1st edition, 1963.

————. "The Moral Economy of the English Crowd in the Eighteenth Century." *Past and Present* 50 (February 1971): 76–136.

————. *The Poverty of Theory and Other Essays*. New York, 1978.

————. "Time, Work-Discipline, and Industrial Capitalism." *Past and Present* 38 (December 1967): 59–97.

Thompson, Lawrence S. *Folklore of the Chapel*. Chicago, 1950.

Tiger, Lionel. *Men in Groups*. New York, 1969.

Tikhomirov, M. N. "Nachalo knigopechataniia v Rossii." In *U istokov russkogo knigopechataniia*. Moscow, 1959.

Tipografiia Lenizdata: K 175-letiiu so dnia osnovaniia tipografii imeni Volodar-skogo Lenizdata. Leningrad, 1970.

Tipografiia "Novogo vremeni" (A. S. Suvorina) v S.-Peterburge. St. Petersburg, 1895.

Torgovo-promyshlennye zavedeniia goroda Moskvy v 1885–1890 gg. Moscow, 1893.

Tridtsatipiatiletie vysochaishe utverzhdennogo tovarshchistva "Obshchestven-naia pol'za," 1860–1895. St. Petersburg, 1895.

Trotskii, I. "Ekonomicheskie i sanitarnye usloviia truda v peterburgskikh tipografiiakh." *Promyshlennost' i zdorov'e* 7 (April 1903): 72–86; 8 (May–August 1903): 87–106.

Trotsky, Leon. *1905.* Harmondsworth, 1971.

Trudy pervogo s"ezda russkikh deiatelei po pechatnomy delu v S.-Peterburge (5–12 aprelia 1895 goda). St. Petersburg, 1896.

Tucker, Robert C., ed. *The Marx-Engels Reader.* 2d ed., New York, 1978.

Ustav Moskovskogo obshchestva tipo-litografov. Moscow, 1907.

Ustav Russkogo Obshchestva deiatelei pechatnogo dela. St. Petersburg, 1899.

Ustav tekhnicheskoi shkoly pri Ekspeditsii zagotovleniia gosudarstvennykh bumag. St. Petersburg, 1903.

Ustav vspomogatel'noi kassy naborshchikov v S.-Peterburge. St. Petersburg, 1891.

Varzar, V. E. *Statisticheskie svedeniia o fabrikakh i zavodakh po proizvod-stvam neoblozhennykh aktsizom za 1900 god.* St. Petersburg, 1903.

——— . *Statisticheskie svedeniia o stachkakh rabochikh na fabrikakh i za-vodakh za desiatiletie 1895–1904 gg.* St. Petersburg, 1905.

Vasil'ev-Severianin, P. V. "Tarifnaia bor'ba soiuza rabochikh pechatnogo dela v 1905–7 godakh." In *Materialy po istorii professional'nogo dvizheniia v Peterburge za 1905–1907 gg: Sbornik.* Leningrad, 1926.

Vechtomova, E. A. *Zdes' pechatalas' "Pravda": ocherk istorii tipografii No. 4.* Leningrad, 1969.

Ves' Peterburg na 1901 god. St. Petersburg, 1901.

Virenius, A. S. "Gigiena naborshchika." *Meditsinskaia beseda* 5:16 (August 1891): 421–26; 5:17 (September 1891): 453–61.

Vol'f, M. O. *K dvadtsatipiatiletiiu izdatel'skoi deiatel'nosti M. O. Vol'fa, 1853–1878.* St. Petersburg, 1878.

Von Laue, T. H., ed. "A Secret Memorandum of Sergei Witte on the Industri-alization of Russia." *Journal of Modern History* 26:1 (March 1954).

Vorob'ev, N. *Kratkii ocherk deiatel'nosti vspomogatel'noi kassy naborshchikov v S.-Peterburge s 1866–1881 gg.* St. Petersburg, 1882.

Vospominaniia rabochikh 16-i tipo-litografii Mospoligraf (b. Levenson). Moscow, 1925.

Voznesenskii, S. V. *Sto let Ekspeditsiia zagotovleniia gosudarstvennykh bumag, 1818–1918.* Petrograd, 1918.

——— . *Sto let Ekspeditsii zagotovleniia gosudarstvennykh bumag v sviazi s is-toriei bumazhno-denezhnogo obrashcheniia v Rossii.* Vol. 1: *1818–1861 gg.* Petrograd, 1918.

Vserossiiskaia politicheskaia stachka v Oktiabre 1905 goda. Moscow, 1955.

Vysshii pod"em revoliutsii 1905–1907 gg. Moscow, 1955.

Wilentz, Sean. *Chants Democratic: New York City and the Rise of the American Working Class, 1788–1850.* New York, 1984.

Wilentz, Sean, ed. *Rites of Power: Symbolism, Ritual, and Politics since the Middle Ages.* Philadelphia, 1985.

Wilken, Paul H. *Entrepreneurship: A Comparative and Historical Study.* Norwood, N.J., 1979.

Wuthnow, Robert, James Davison Hunter, Albert Bergesen, and Edith Kurzweil. *Cultural Analysis: The Work of Peter L. Berger, Mary Douglas, Michel Foucault, and Jürgen Habermas.* London, 1984.

Zaitsev, A. A. "Knigopechataniia v Rossii na rubezhe XVIII i XIX vv." In A. A. Sidorov and S. P. Luppov, eds., *Kniga v Rossii do serediny XIX veka.* Leningrad, 1978.

Zakharov, V. V. "Svedeniia o nekotorykh peterburgskikh tipografiiakh (1810–1830-e gody)." *Kniga: issledovaniia i materialy* 26 (1973): 65–79.

Zapadov, A. V., ed. *Istoriia russkoi zhurnalistiki XVIII–XIX veka.* 3d edition. Moscow, 1973.

Zelnik, Reginald E. *Labor and Society in Tsarist Russia.* Stanford, 1971.

——— . "Passivity and Protest in Germany and Russia: Barrington Moore's Conception of Working-Class Responses to Injustice." *Journal of Social History* 15:3 (Spring 1982): 485–512.

——— . "Russian Bebels." *Russian Review* 35:3 (July 1976): 249–89; 36:4 (October 1976): 417–47.

——— . " 'To the Unaccustomed Eye': Religion and Irreligion in the Experience of St. Petersburg Workers in the 1870s." *Russian History* 16:2–4 (1989): 297–326.

Zelnik, Reginald E., ed. *A Radical Worker in Tsarist Russia: The Autobiography of Semen Ivanovich Kanatchikov.* Stanford, 1986.

Zinov'ev, P. P. *Na rubezhe dvukh epokh.* Moscow, 1932.

GENERAL AND POLITICAL PRESS (dates indicate materials used)

Biulleten' muzeiia sodeistviia trudu. Moscow. 1905.
Bor'ba. Moscow. 1905.
Dvadtsatyi vek. St. Petersburg. 1906.
Ekho. St. Petersburg. 1883–1884.
Golos truda. St. Petersburg. 1906.
Iskra. Geneva. 1900–1905.
Kur'er. St. Petersburg. 1906.
Moskovskaia gazeta. Moscow. 1905.
Nasha zhizn'. St. Petersburg. 1905.
Nevskaia gazeta. St. Petersburg. 1906.
Novaia zhizn'. St. Petersburg. 1905.
Novoe vremia. St. Petersburg. 1895, 1905, 1907.
Peterburgskaia gazeta. St. Petersburg. 1894.
Peterburgskii listok. St. Petersburg. 1868.
Pravitel'stvennyi vestnik. St. Petersburg. 1869, 1883, 1894, 1895.

Pravo. Moscow. 1905.

Professional'nyi soiuz. St. Petersburg. 1905–1906.

Russkie vedomosti. Moscow. 1905.

Russkii kur'er. Moscow. 1883.

Russkii listok. Moscow. 1905.

Russkoe slovo. Moscow. 1905.

Slovo. St. Petersburg. 1904, 1906.

Torgovo-promyshlennaia gazeta. St. Petersburg. 1905–1907.

Vecherniaia pochta. Moscow. 1905.

Index

WIDENER UNIVERSITY
WOLFGRAM
LIBRARY
CHESTER, PA

TE DUE